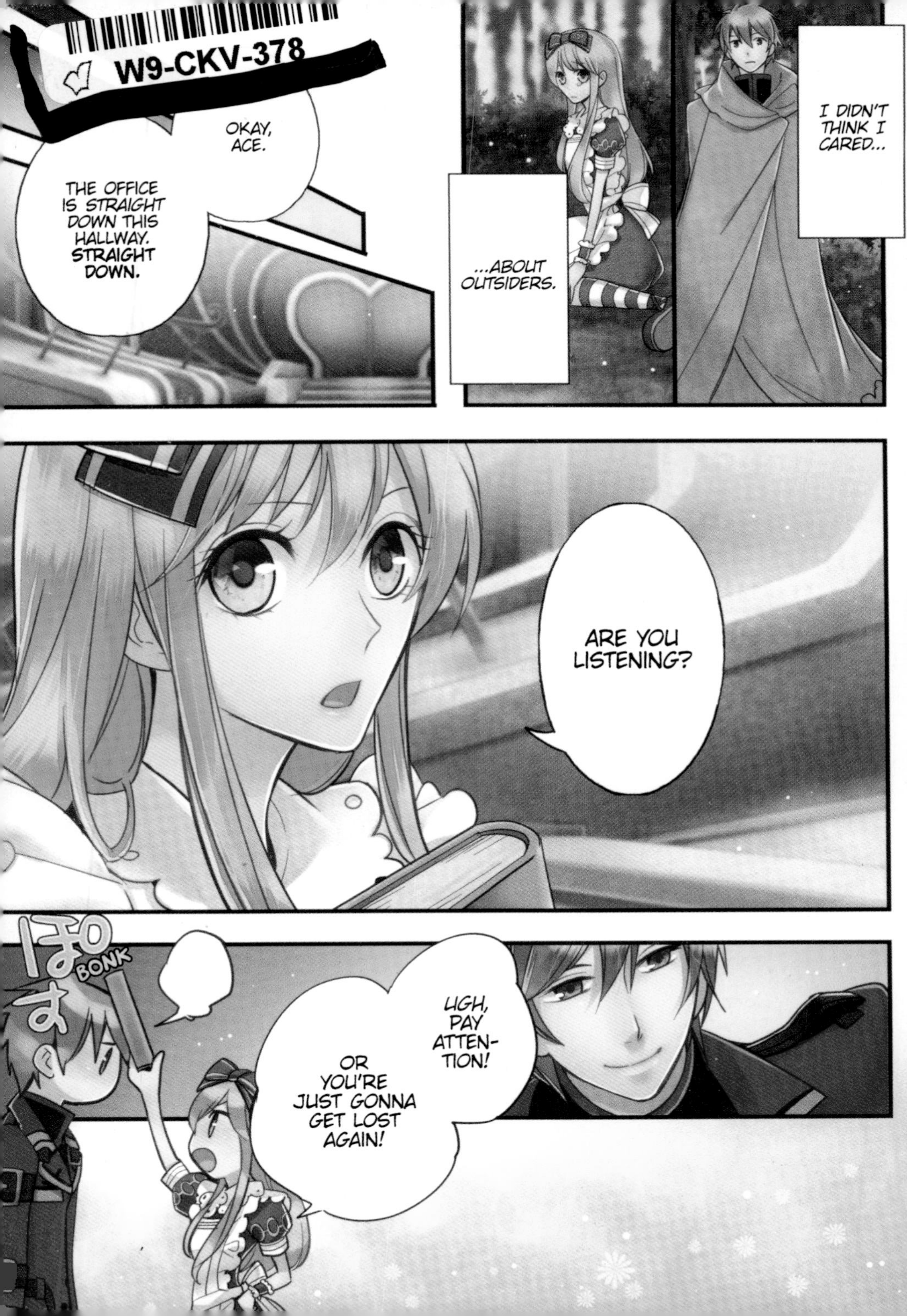
I DIDN'T THINK I CARED...
...ABOUT OUTSIDERS.
OKAY, ACE.
THE OFFICE IS STRAIGHT DOWN THIS HALLWAY. STRAIGHT DOWN.
ARE YOU LISTENING?
UGH, PAY ATTEN-TION!
OR YOU'RE JUST GONNA GET LOST AGAIN!
BONK

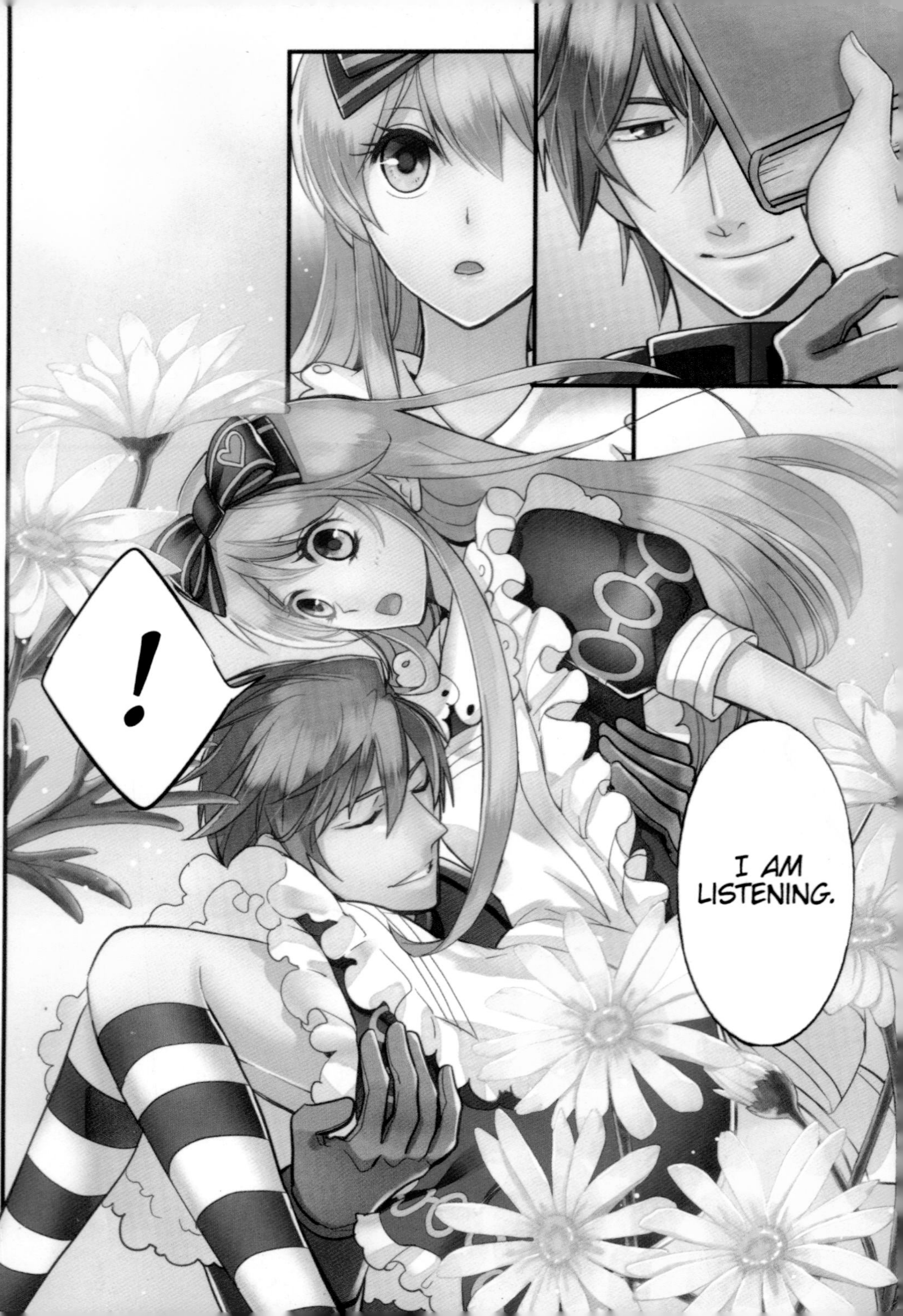
I AM LISTENING.
!

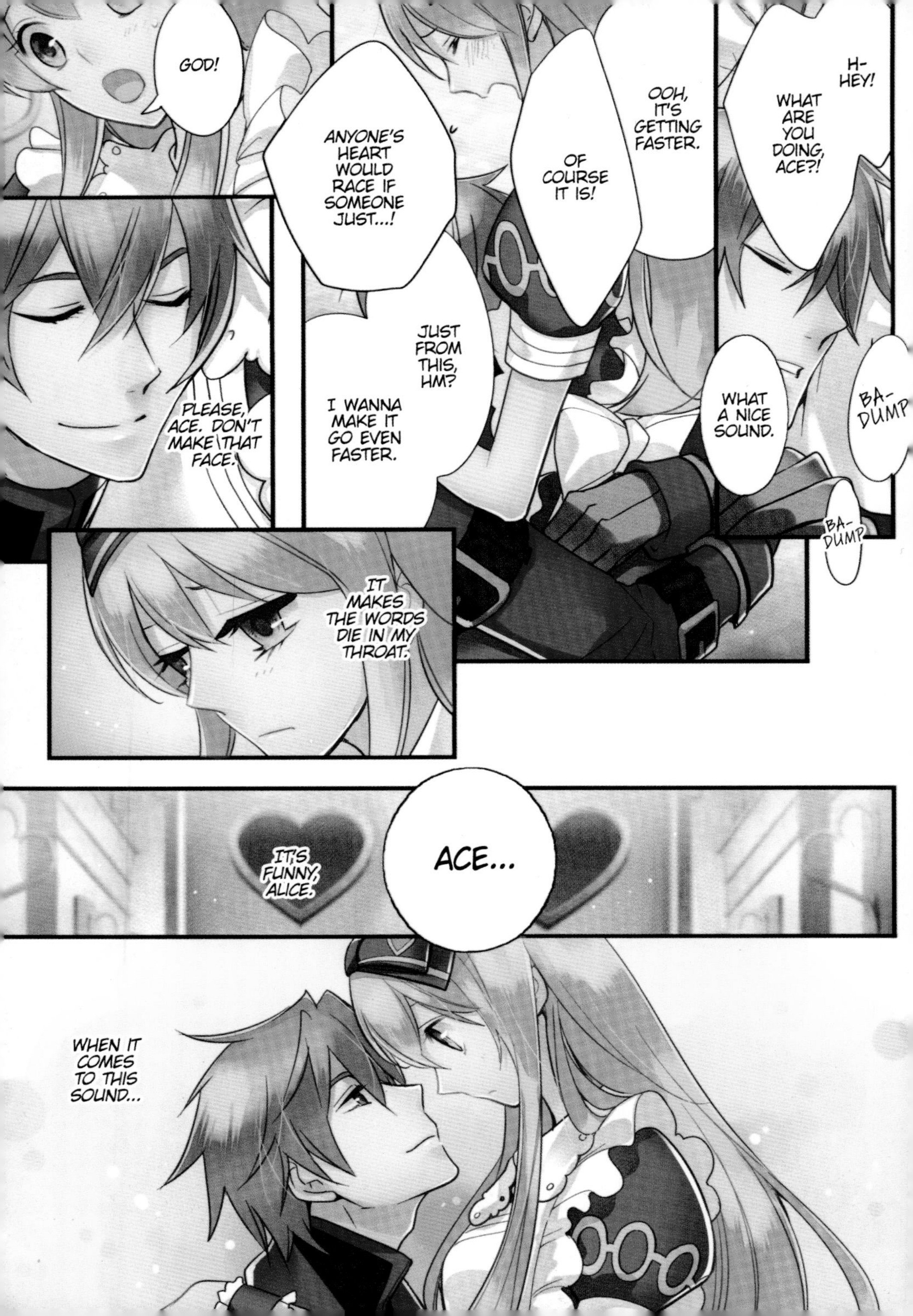
H-HEY! WHAT ARE YOU DOING, ACE?!
OOH, IT'S GETTING FASTER.
OF COURSE IT IS!
ANYONE'S HEART WOULD RACE IF SOMEONE JUST...!
GOD!
BA-DUMP
WHAT A NICE SOUND.
BA-DUMP
JUST FROM THIS, HM?
I WANNA MAKE IT GO EVEN FASTER.
PLEASE, ACE. DON'T MAKE THAT FACE.
IT MAKES THE WORDS DIE IN MY THROAT.
ACE...
IT'S FUNNY, ALICE.
WHEN IT COMES TO THIS SOUND...

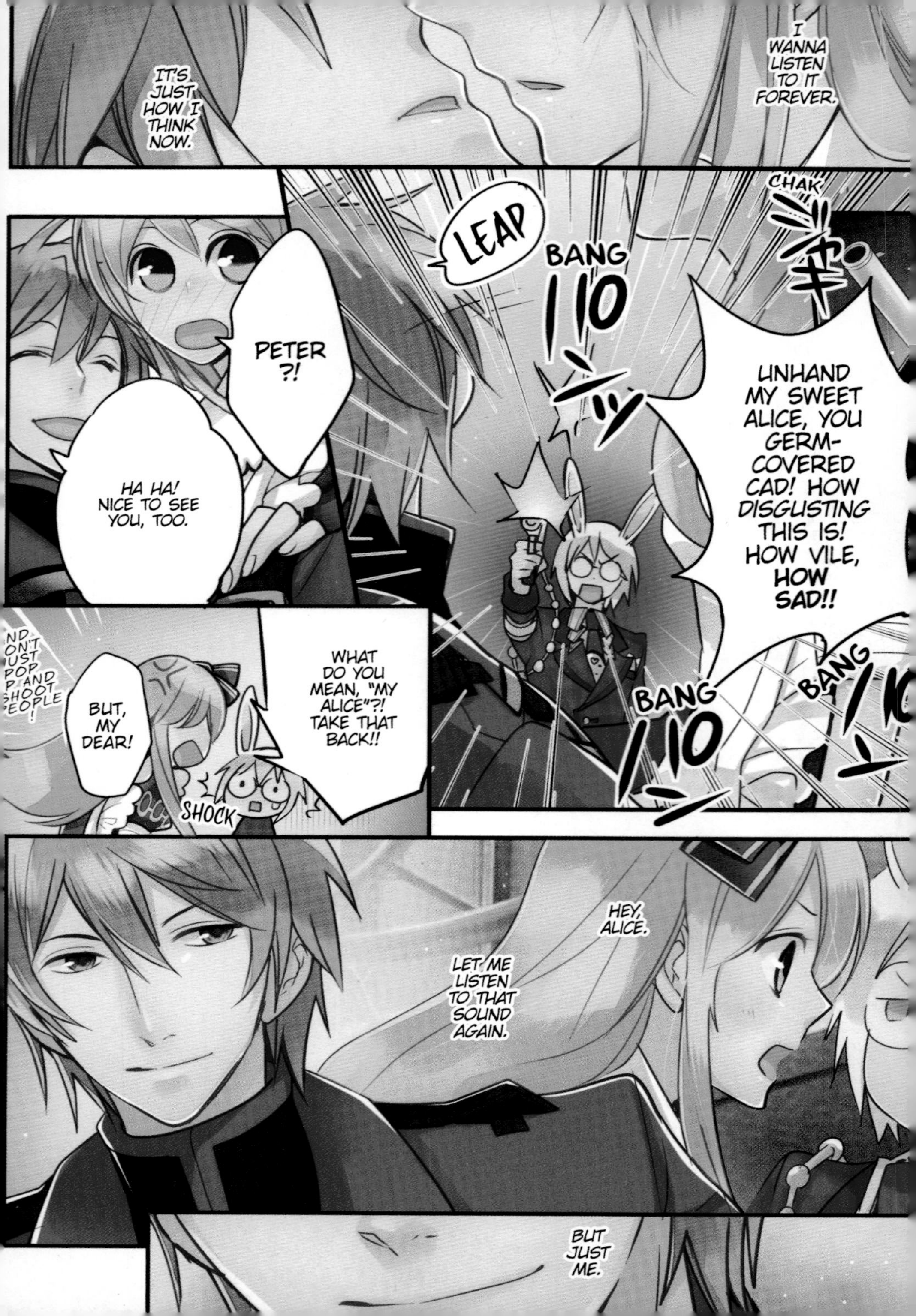
I WANNA LISTEN TO IT FOREVER.
IT'S JUST HOW I THINK NOW.
CHAK
LEAP
BANG
UNHAND MY SWEET ALICE, YOU GERM-COVERED CAD! HOW DISGUSTING THIS IS! HOW VILE, HOW SAD!!
BANG
BANG
PETER?!
HA HA! NICE TO SEE YOU, TOO.
WHAT DO YOU MEAN, "MY ALICE"?! TAKE THAT BACK!!
BUT, MY DEAR!
SHOCK
ND ON'T UST POP P AND SHOOT EOPLE!
HEY, ALICE.
LET ME LISTEN TO THAT SOUND AGAIN.
BUT JUST ME.

# ALICE IN THE COUNTRY OF CLOVER 3
## ~Knight's Knowledge~

SAI ASAI

浅井 西

# SEVEN SEAS ENTERTAINMENT PRESENTS

# Alice IN THE COUNTRY OF Clover

## KNIGHT'S KNOWLEDGE VOL.3

### art by SAI ASAI / story by QUINROSE

TRANSLATION
**Angela Liu**

ADAPTATION
**Lianne Sentar**

LETTERING AND LAYOUT
**Laura Scoville**

LOGO DESIGN
**Courtney Williams**

COVER DESIGN
**Nicky Lim**

PROOFREADER
**Rebecca Scoble**
**Lee Otter**

MANAGING EDITOR
**Adam Arnold**

PUBLISHER
**Jason DeAngelis**

FOLLOW US ONLINE: **www.gomanga.com**

# READING DIRECTIONS

This book reads from *right to left*, Japanese style. If this is your first time reading manga, you start reading from the top right panel on each page and take it from there. If you get lost, just follow the numbered diagram here. It may seem backwards at first, but you☐ll get the hang of it! Have fun!!

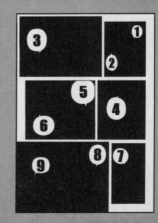

Alice in the Country of Clover

クローバーの国の

アリス

~Wonderful Wonder World~

---

# - STORY -

---

In *Alice in the Country of Clover*, the game starts with Alice having not fallen in love, but still deciding to stay in Wonderland.

She's acquainted with all the characters from the previous game, *Alice in the Country of Hearts*.

Since love would now start from a place of friendship rather than passion with a new stranger, she can experience a different type of romance from that in the previous game. Her dynamic with the characters is different because of this friendship—characters can't always be forceful with her, and in many ways it's more comfortable to grow intimate. The relationships *between* the Ones With Duties have also become more of a factor.

In this game, the story focuses on Heart Castle. Alice attends the suited meetings (forcefully) and gets involved in various gunfights (forcefully), among other things.

Land fluctuations, sea creatures in the forest, and whispering doors—it's a game more fantastic and more eerie than the first.

Will our everywoman Alice be able to have a romantic relationship in a world devoid of common sense?

# Alice in the Country of Clover
## Character Information

### Elliot March
VA: Tsuguo Mogami

Blood's right-hand man has a criminal past... and a temperamental present. But he's not as bad as he used to be, so that's something. Joining Blood has been good(?) for him.

### Blood Dupre
VA: Katsuyuki Konishi

The head of the mafia Hatter Family, Blood is a cunning yet moody puppet-master. Alice now has the pleasure of having him for a landlord.

### Alice Liddell
VA: Rie Kugimiya

A normal girl with a bit of a chip on her shoulder. Deciding to stay in the Wonderland she was carried to, she's adapted to her strange new lifestyle.

### Vivaldi
VA: Yuuko Kaida

The beautiful Queen of Hearts has an unrivaled temper—which is really saying something in Wonderland. Although a picture-perfect Mad Queen, she cares for Alice as if Alice were her little sister...or a very interesting plaything.

### Tweedle Dum
VA: Jun Fukuyama

The second "Bloody Twin" is equally cute and equally scary. In *Clover*, Dum can also turn into an adult.

### Tweedle Dee
VA: Jun Fukuyama

One of the "Bloody Twin" gatekeepers of the Hatter territory, Dee can be cute when he's not being terrifying. In *Clover*, he sometimes turns into an adult.

### Boris Airay
VA: Noriaki Sugiyama

This riddle-loving cat has a signature smirk—and in *Clover*, a new toy. One of his favorite pastimes is giving the Sleepy Mouse a hard time.

### Ace
VA: Daisuke Hirakawa

The unlucky knight of Hearts was a former subordinate of Vivaldi and is perpetually lost. Even though he's depressed to be separated from his friend and boss Julius, he stays positive and tries to overcome it with a smile. He seems like a classic nice guy... or is he?

### Peter White
VA: Kouki Miyata

The Prime Minister of Heart Castle—who has rabbit ears growing out of his head—invited (kidnapped) Alice to Wonderland. He loves Alice and hates everything else. His cruel, irrational actions are disturbing, but he acts like a completely different person (rabbit?) when in the throes of his love for Alice.

### Gray Ringmarc
VA: Kazuya Nakai

Nightmare's subordinate in *Clover*. He used to have strong social ambition and considered assassinating Nightmare... but since Nightmare was such a useless boss, Gray couldn't help but feel sorry for him and ended up a dedicated assistant. He's a sound thinker with a strong work ethic. He's also highly skilled with his blades, rivaling even Ace.

### Nightmare Gottschalk
VA: Tomokazu Sugita

A sickly nightmare who hates the hospital and needles. He has the power to read people's thoughts and enter dreams. Even though he likes to shut himself away in dreams, Gray drags him out to sulk from time to time. He technically holds a high position and has many subordinates, but since he can't even take care of his own health, he leaves most things to Gray.

### Pierce Villiers
VA: Souichirou Hoshi

New to *Clover*, Pierce is an insomniac mouse who drinks too much coffee. He loves Nightmare (who can help him sleep) and hates Boris (who terrifies him). He dislikes Blood and Vivaldi for discarding coffee in favor of tea. He likes Elliot and Peter well enough, since rabbits aren't natural predators of mice.

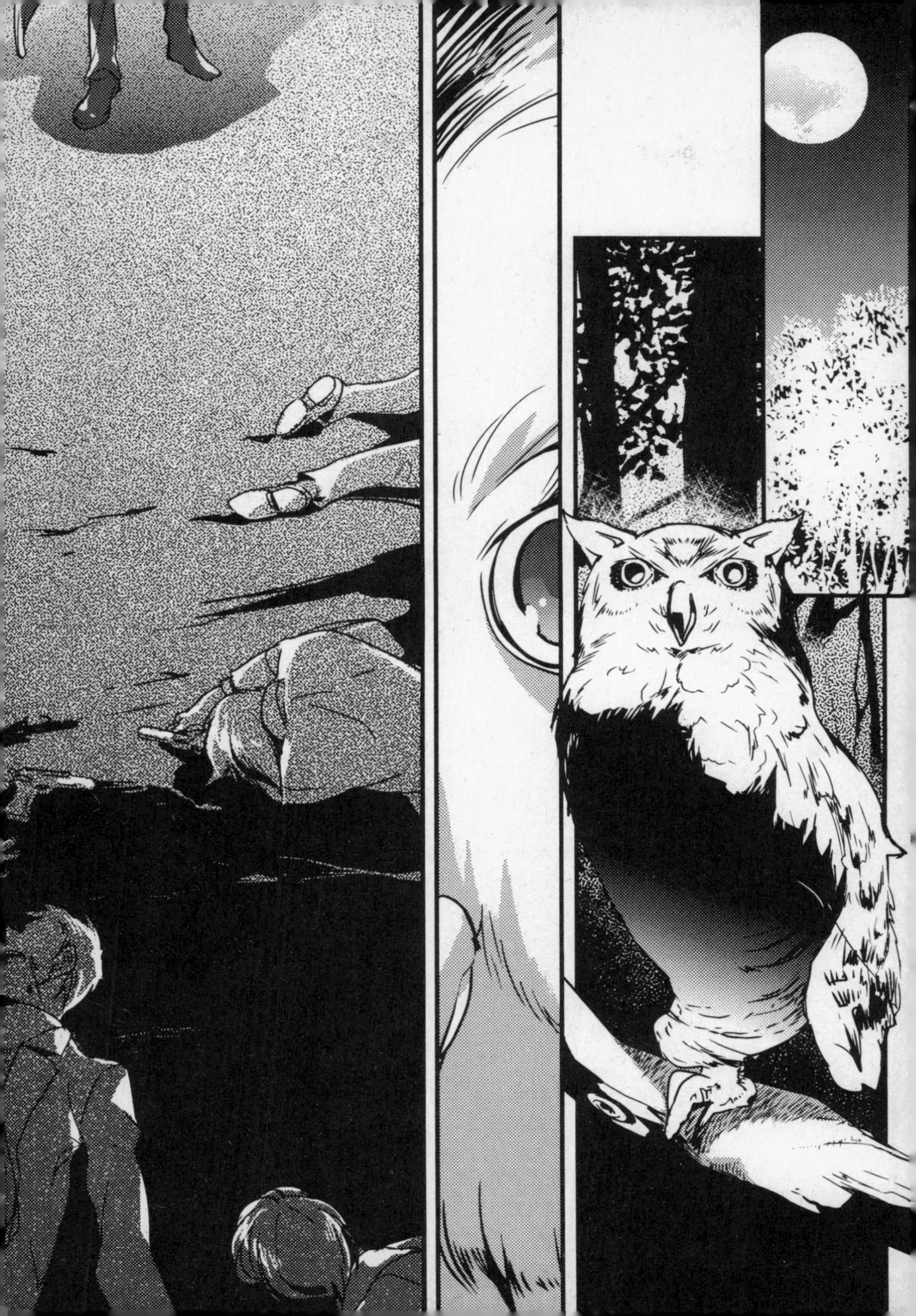

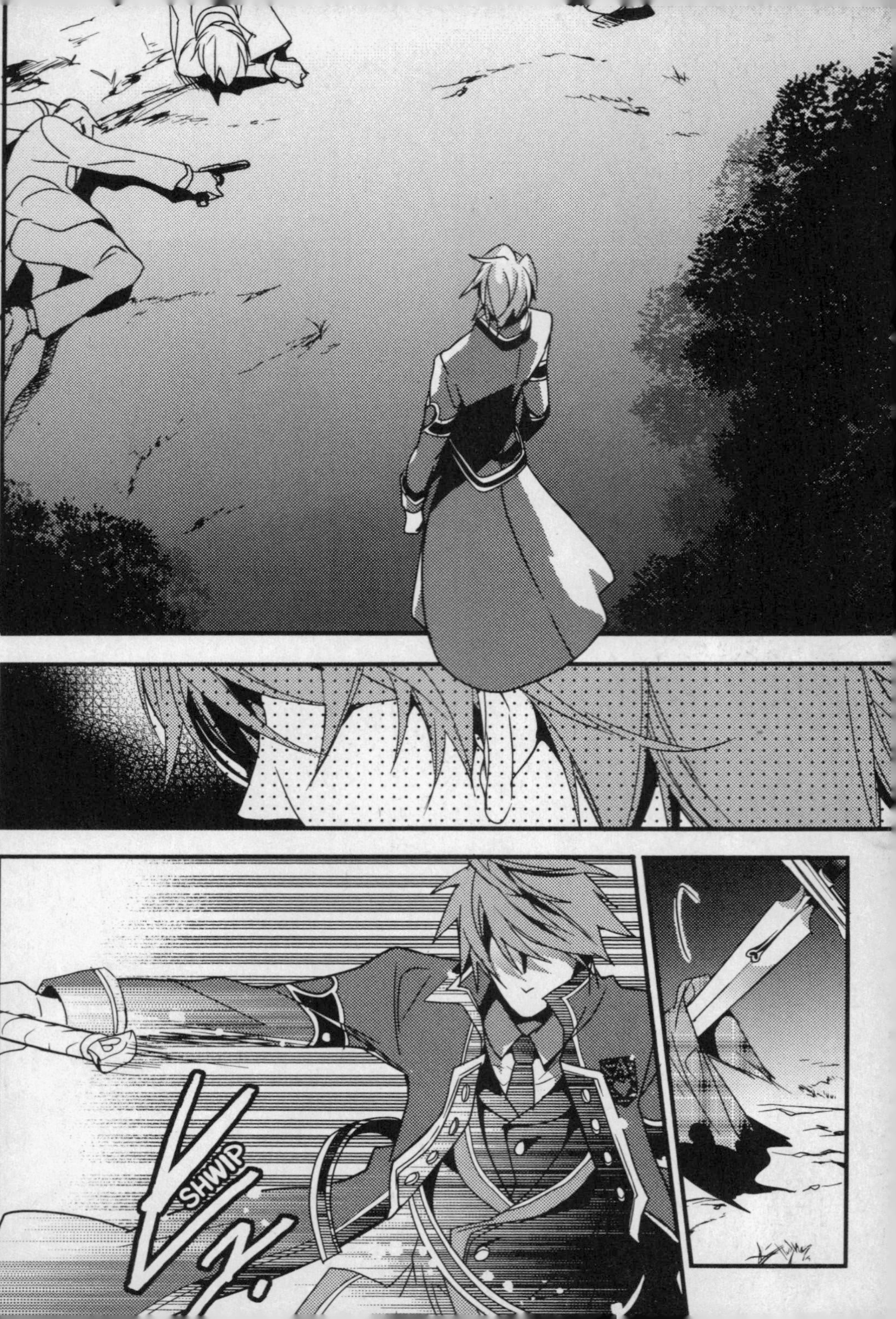
SHWIP

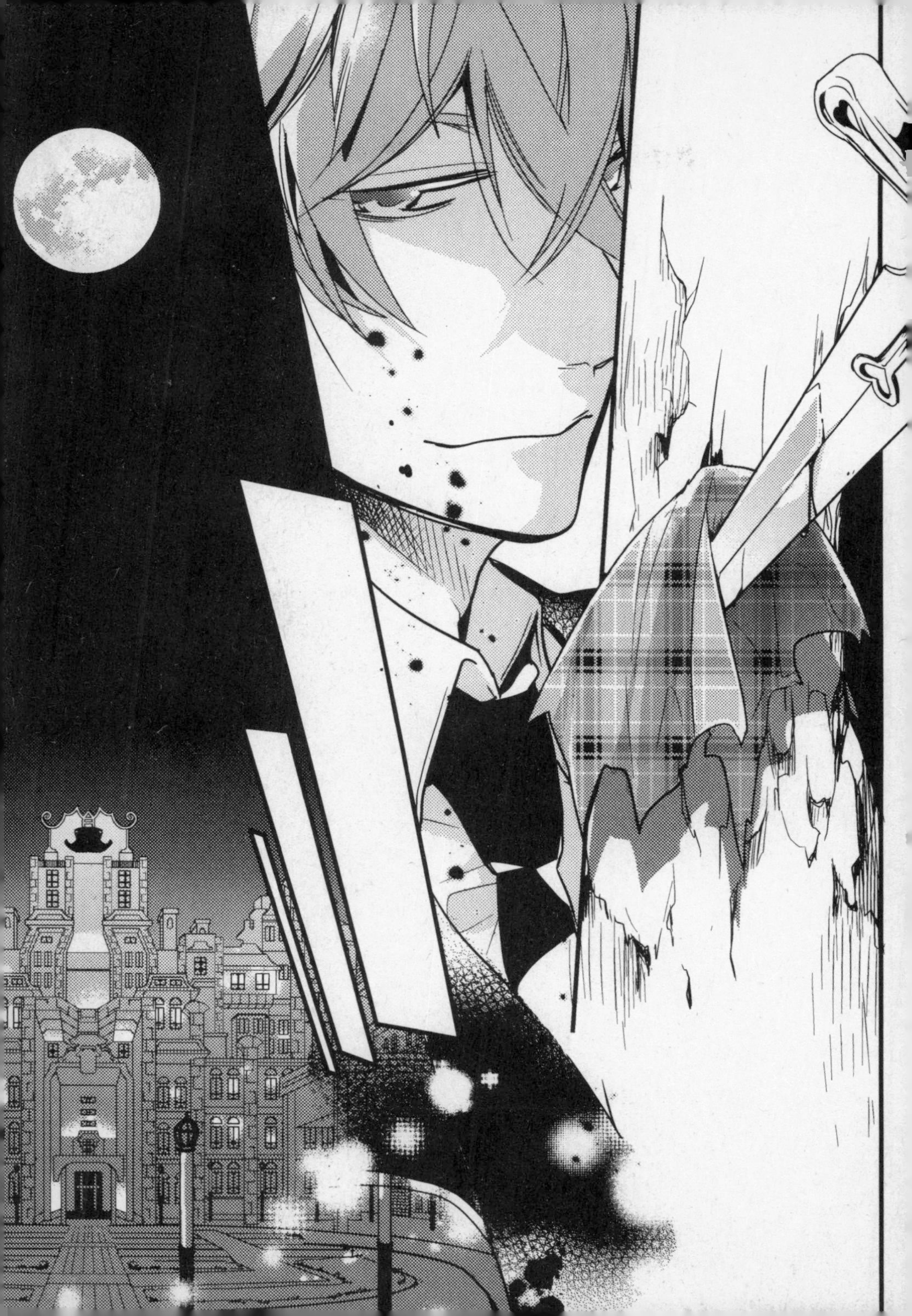

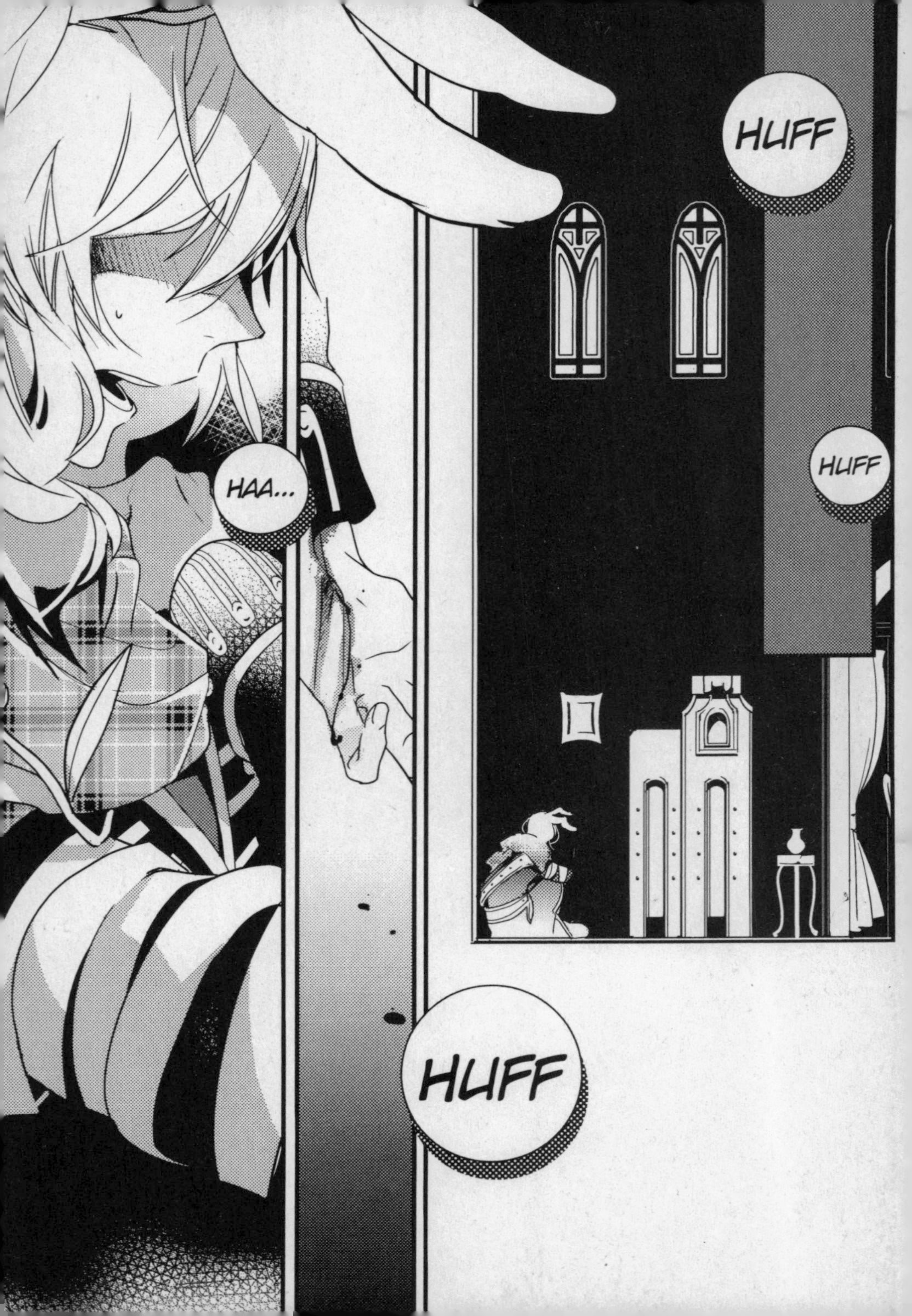
HUFF
HUFF
HUFF
HAA...

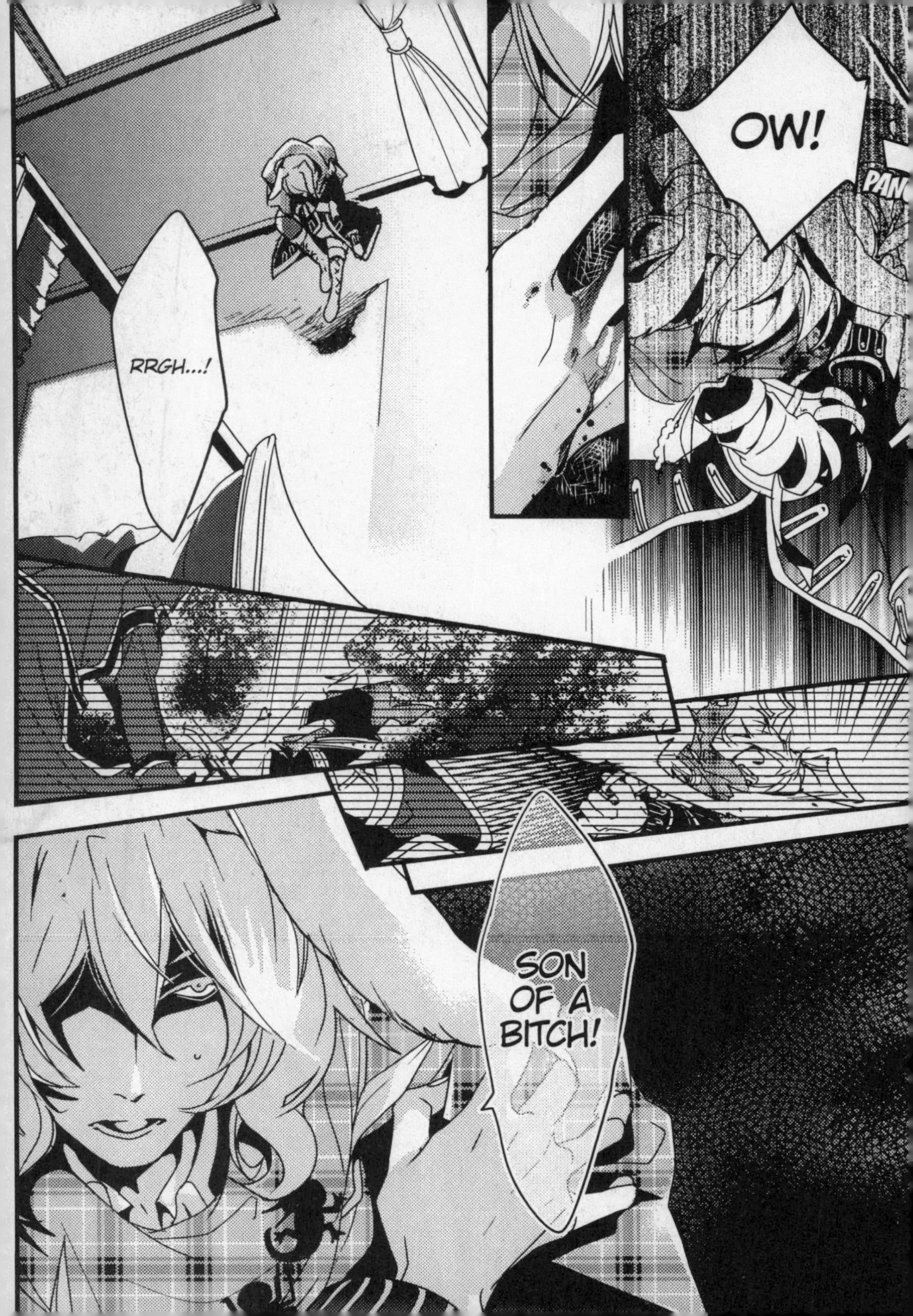
OW!
PAN
RRGH...!
SON OF A BITCH!

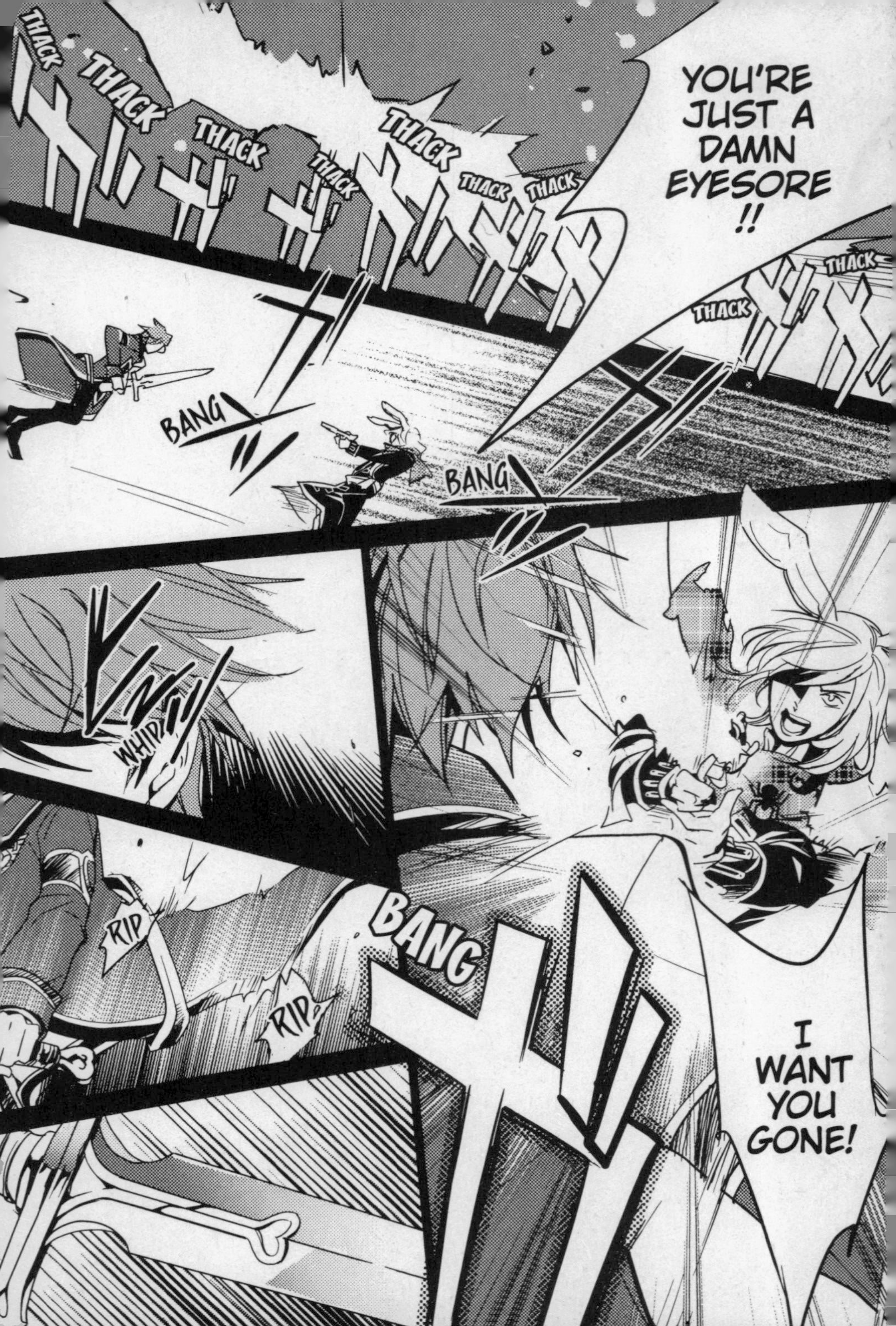
YOU'RE JUST A DAMN EYESORE!!
THACK THACK
THACK THACK
THACK
THACK
THACK
THACK
THACK
THACK
BANG
BANG
I WANT YOU GONE!
WHIP
BANG
RIP
RIP

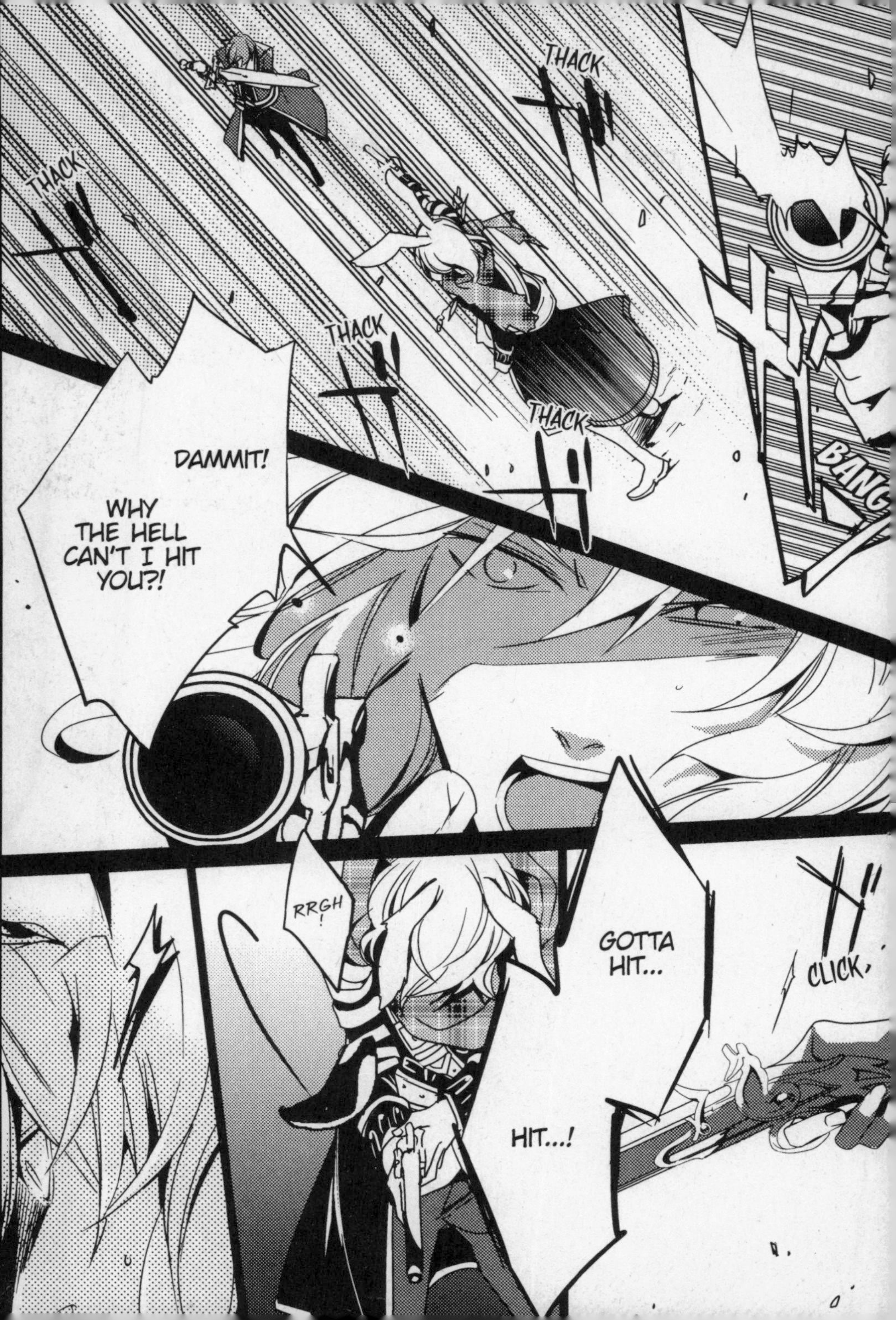
THACK
THACK
THACK
THACK
BANG
DAMMIT!
WHY THE HELL CAN'T I HIT YOU?!
CLICK
GOTTA HIT...
HIT...!
RRGH!

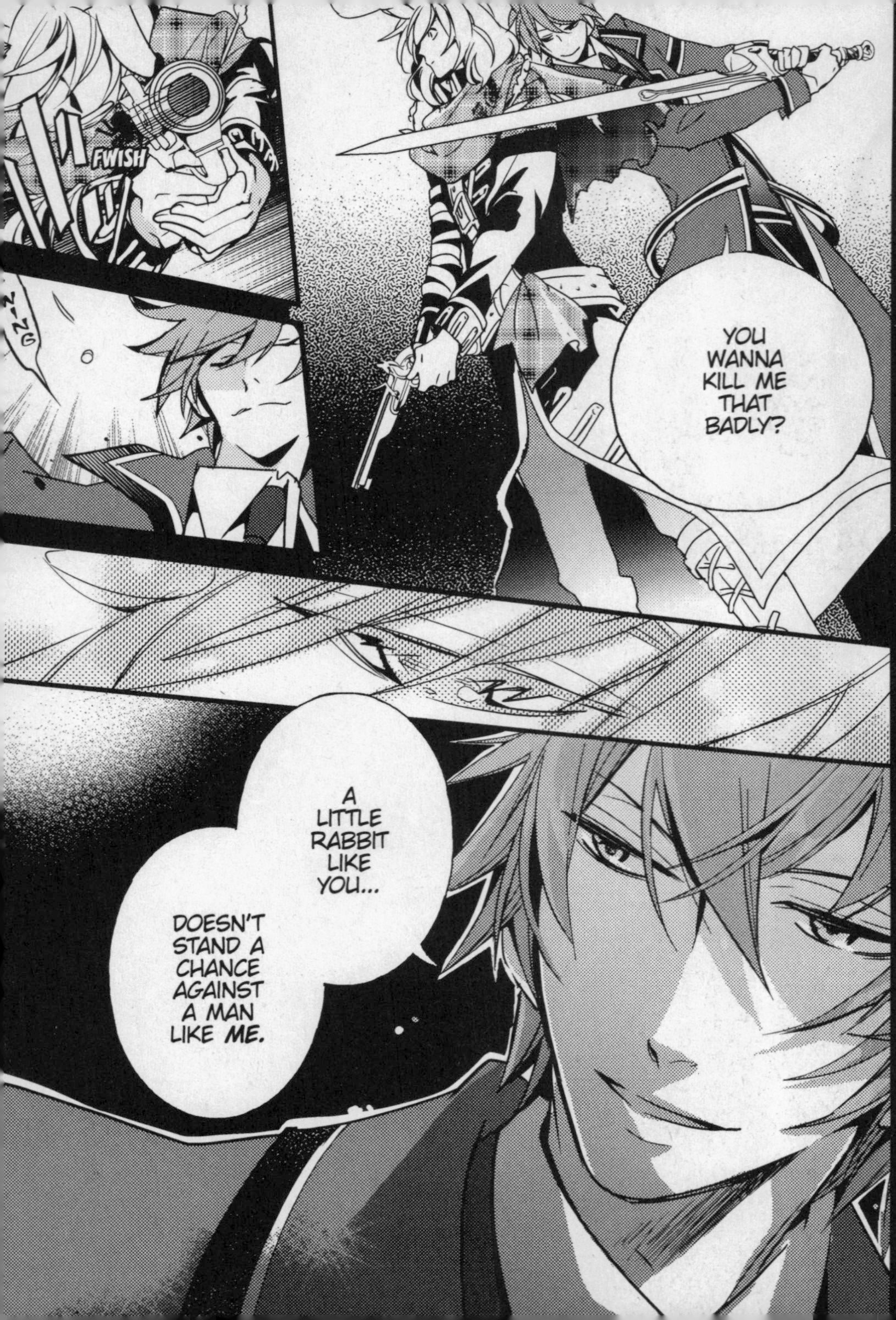
YOU WANNA KILL ME THAT BADLY?
FWISH
N-NG
A LITTLE RABBIT LIKE YOU...
DOESN'T STAND A CHANCE AGAINST A MAN LIKE *ME*.

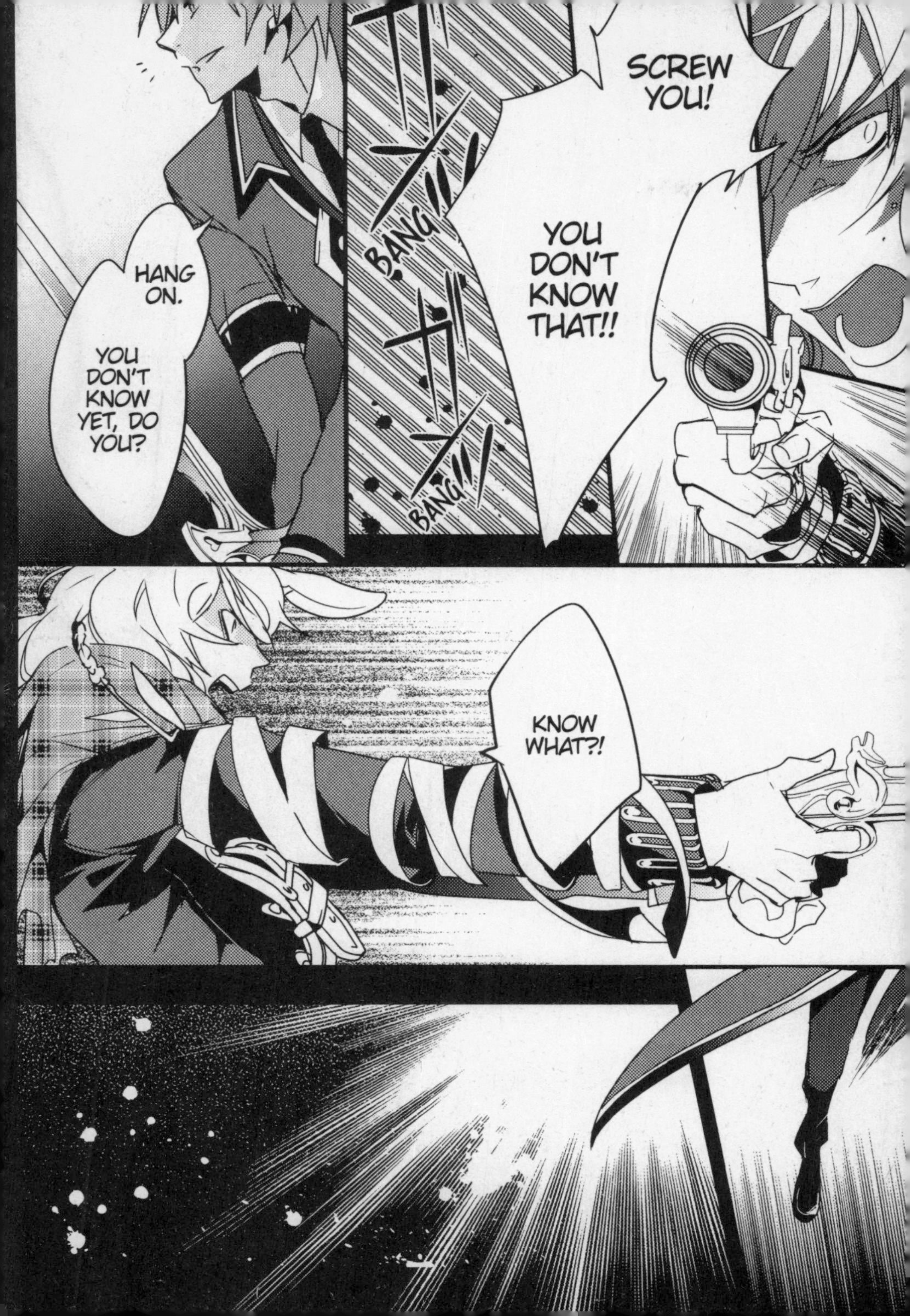
SCREW YOU!
YOU DON'T KNOW THAT!!
BANG BANG
HANG ON.
YOU DON'T KNOW YET, DO YOU?
KNOW WHAT?!

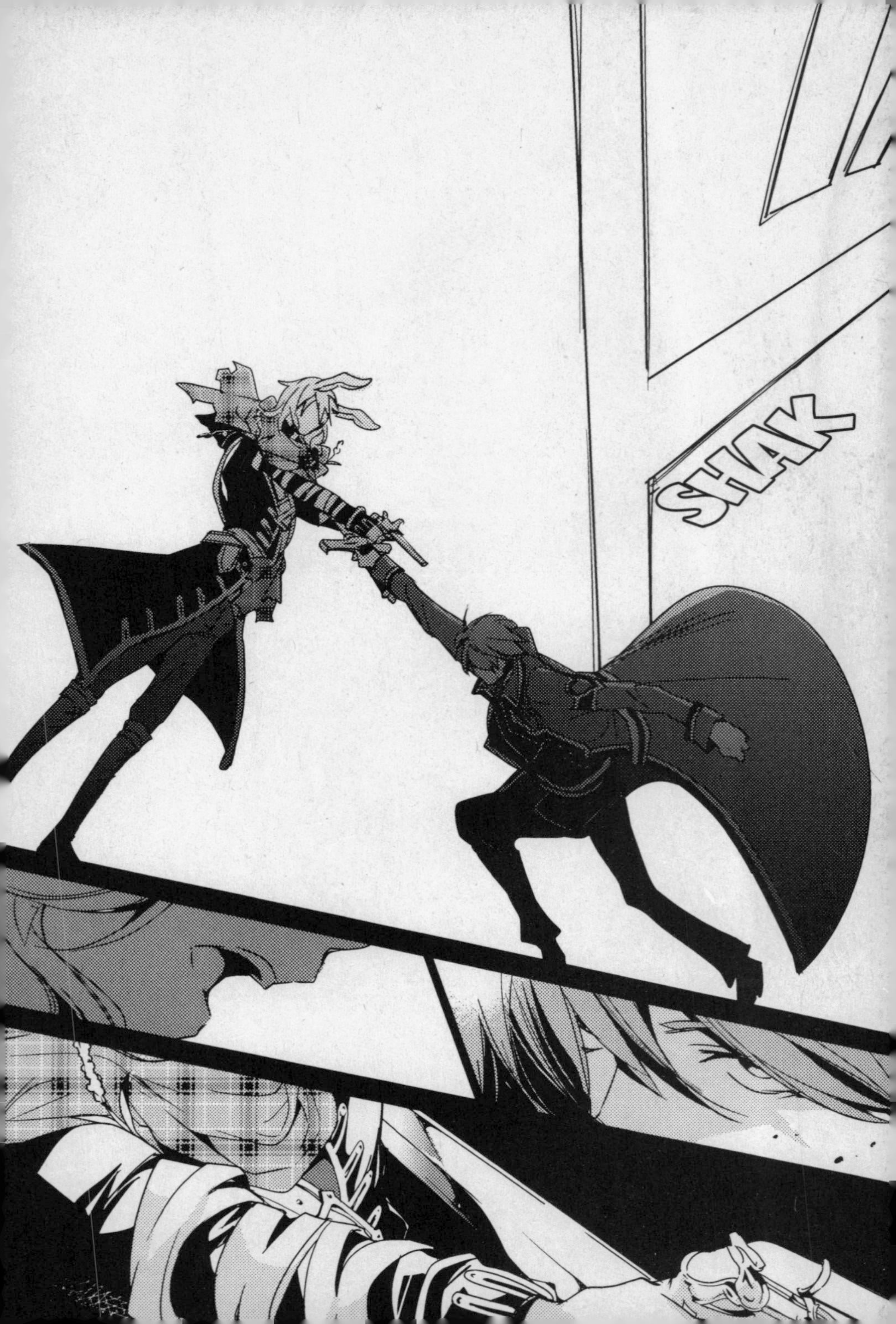
SHAK

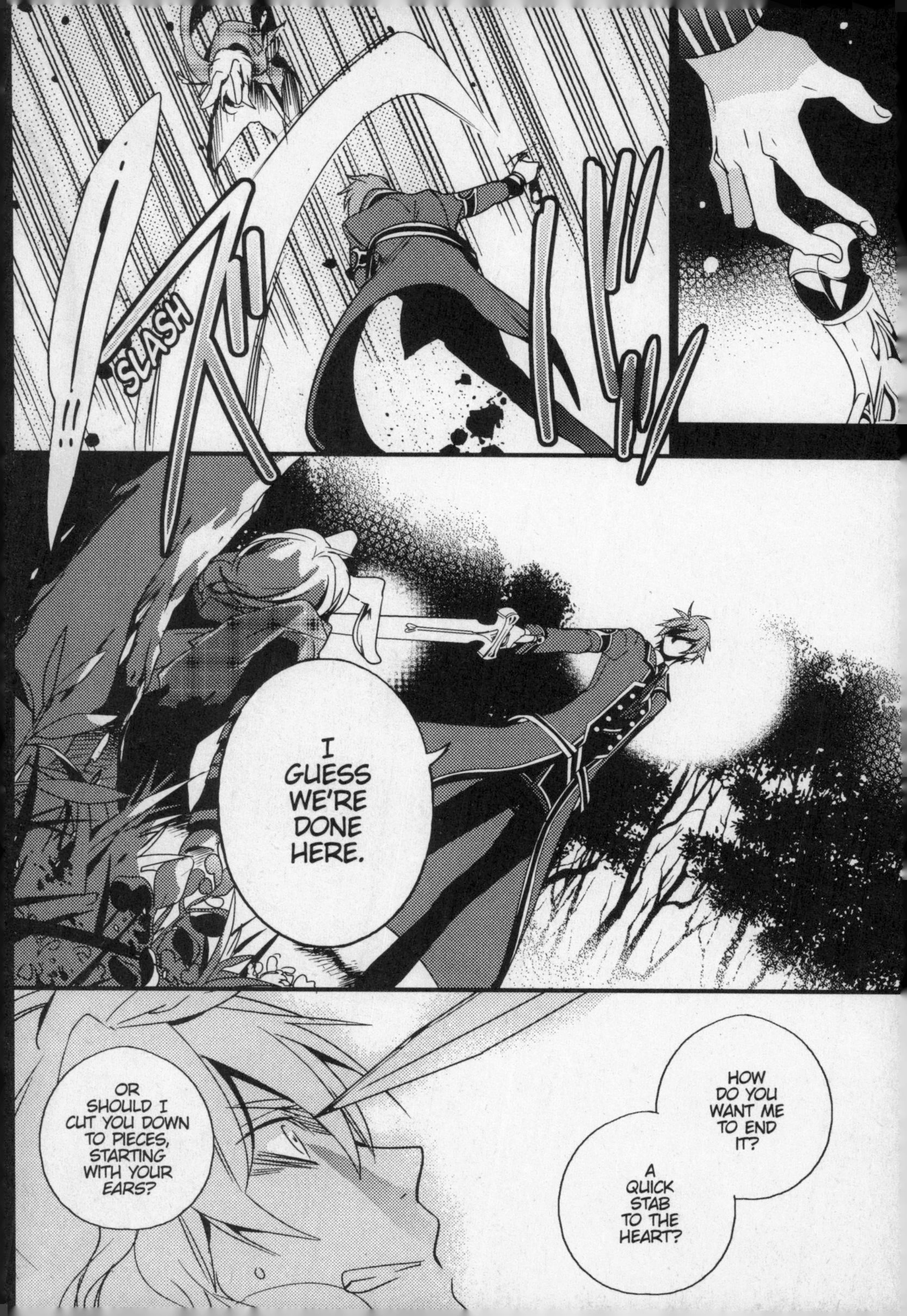
SLASH
I GUESS WE'RE DONE HERE.
HOW DO YOU WANT ME TO END IT?
A QUICK STAB TO THE HEART?
OR SHOULD I CUT YOU DOWN TO PIECES, STARTING WITH YOUR EARS?

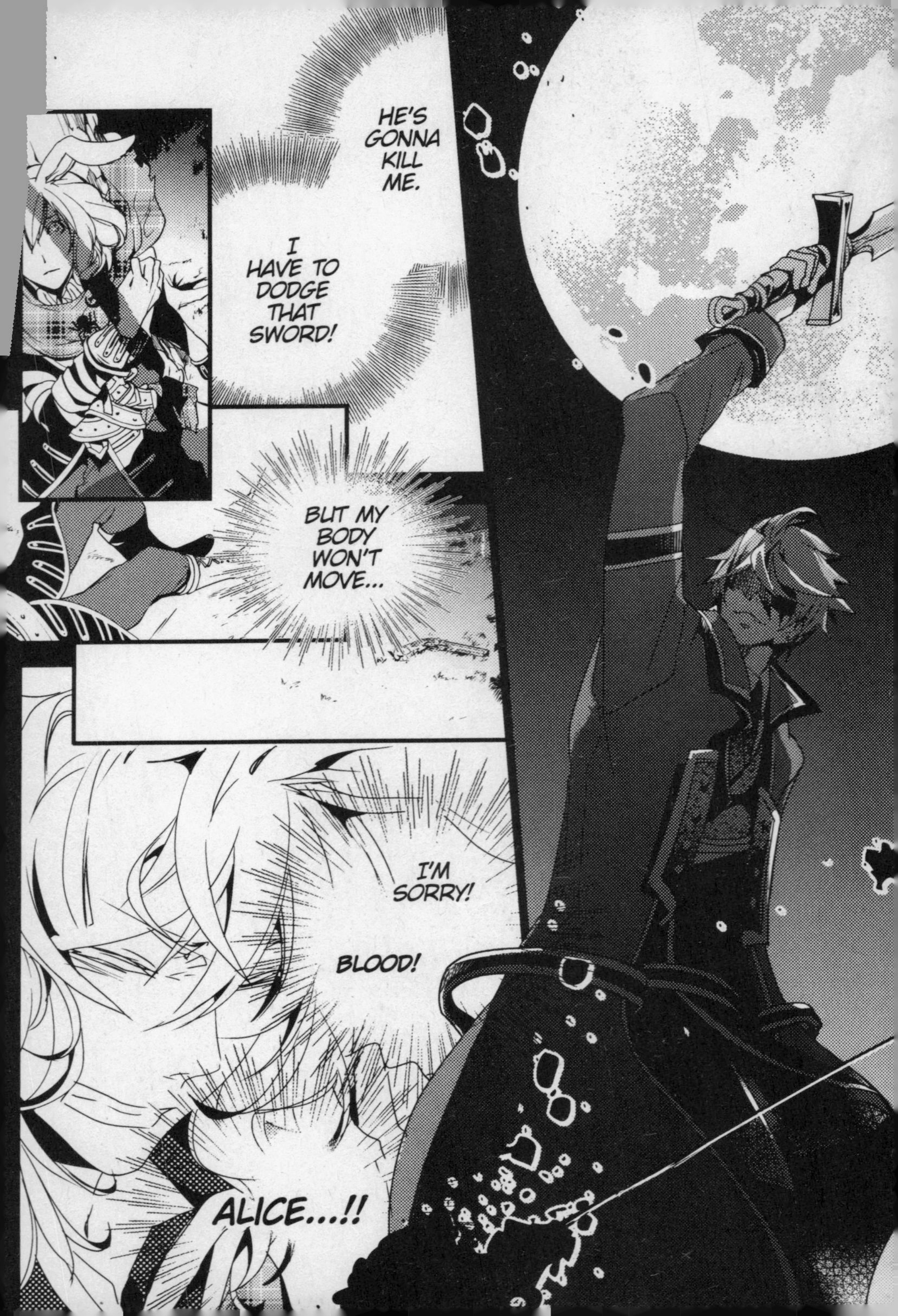
HE'S GONNA KILL ME.
I HAVE TO DODGE THAT SWORD!
BUT MY BODY WON'T MOVE...
I'M SORRY!
BLOOD!
ALICE...!!

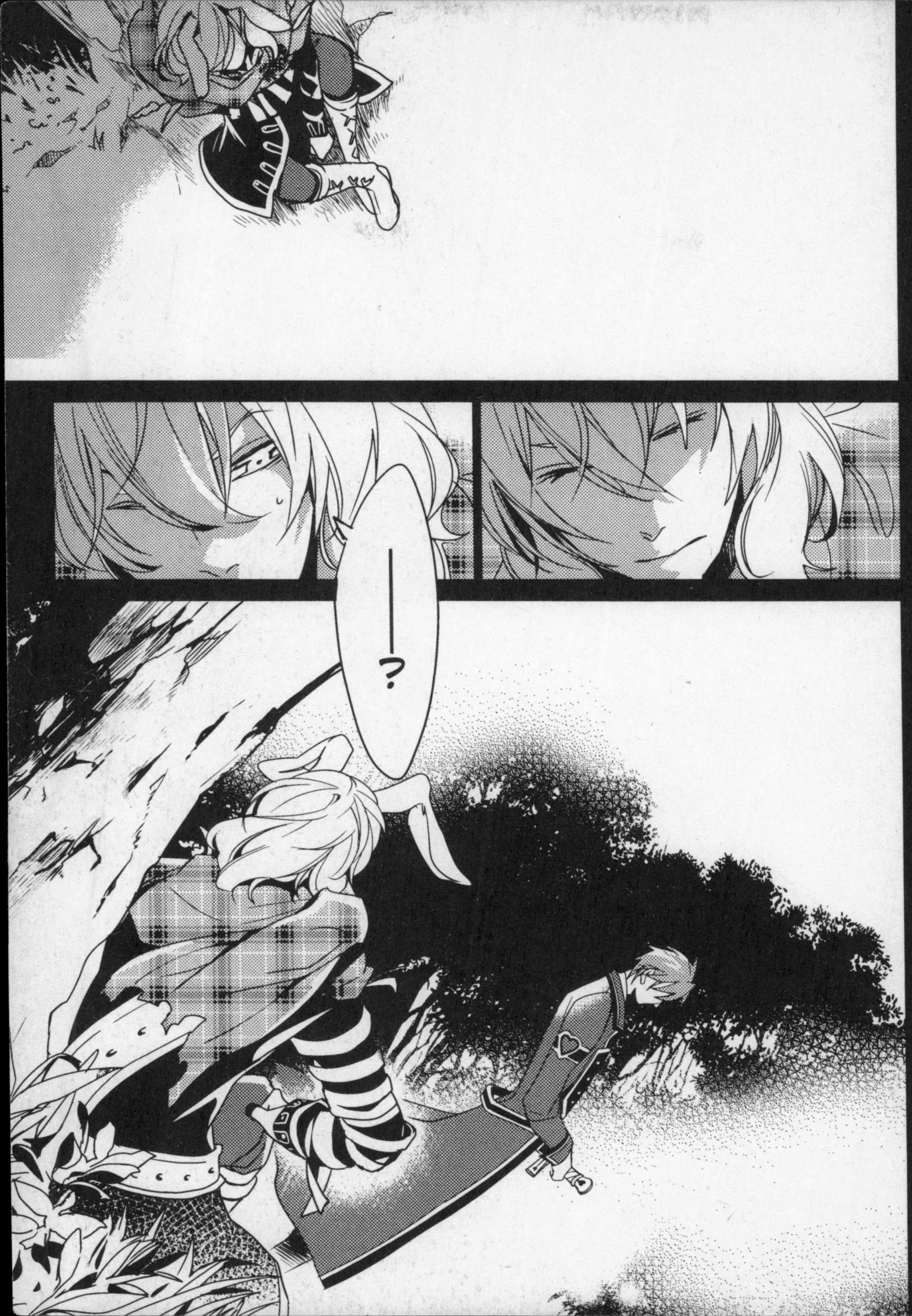
――?

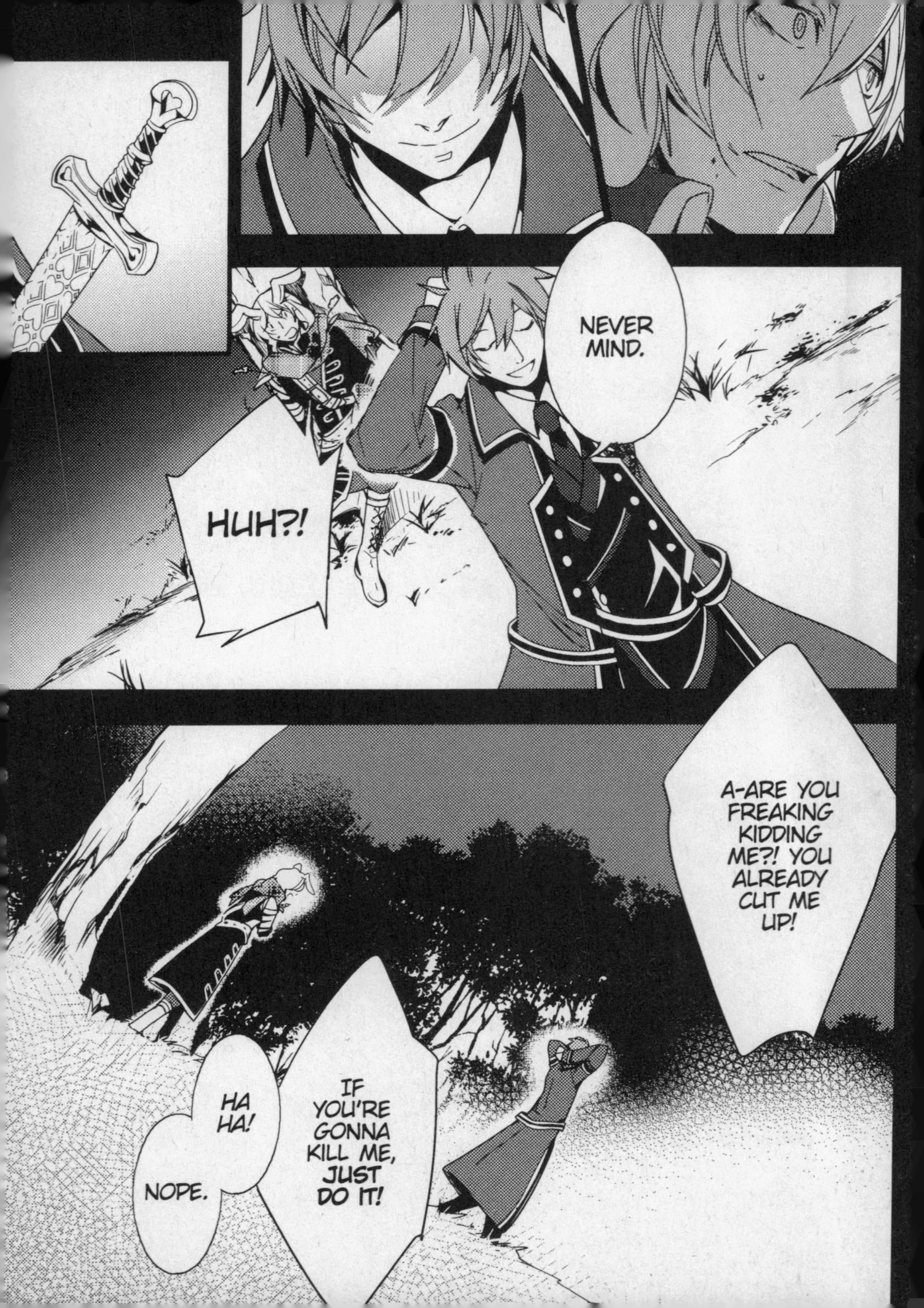
NEVER MIND.
HUH?!
A-ARE YOU FREAKING KIDDING ME?! YOU ALREADY CUT ME UP!
IF YOU'RE GONNA KILL ME, JUST DO IT!
HA HA!
NOPE.

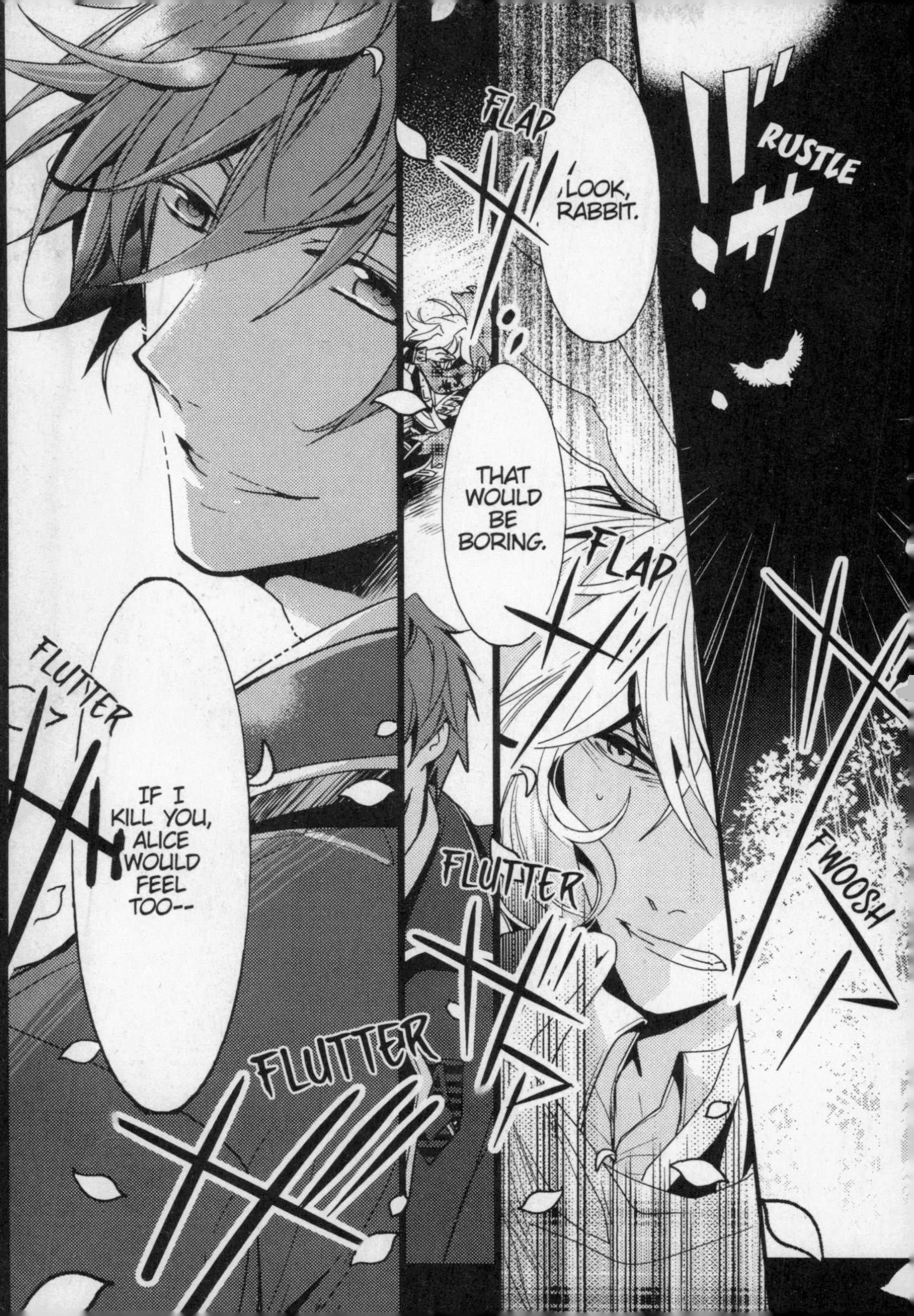
RUSTLE
FLAP
LOOK, RABBIT.
THAT WOULD BE BORING.
FLAP
FWOOSH
FLUTTER
FLUTTER
IF I KILL YOU, ALICE WOULD FEEL TOO--
FLUTTER

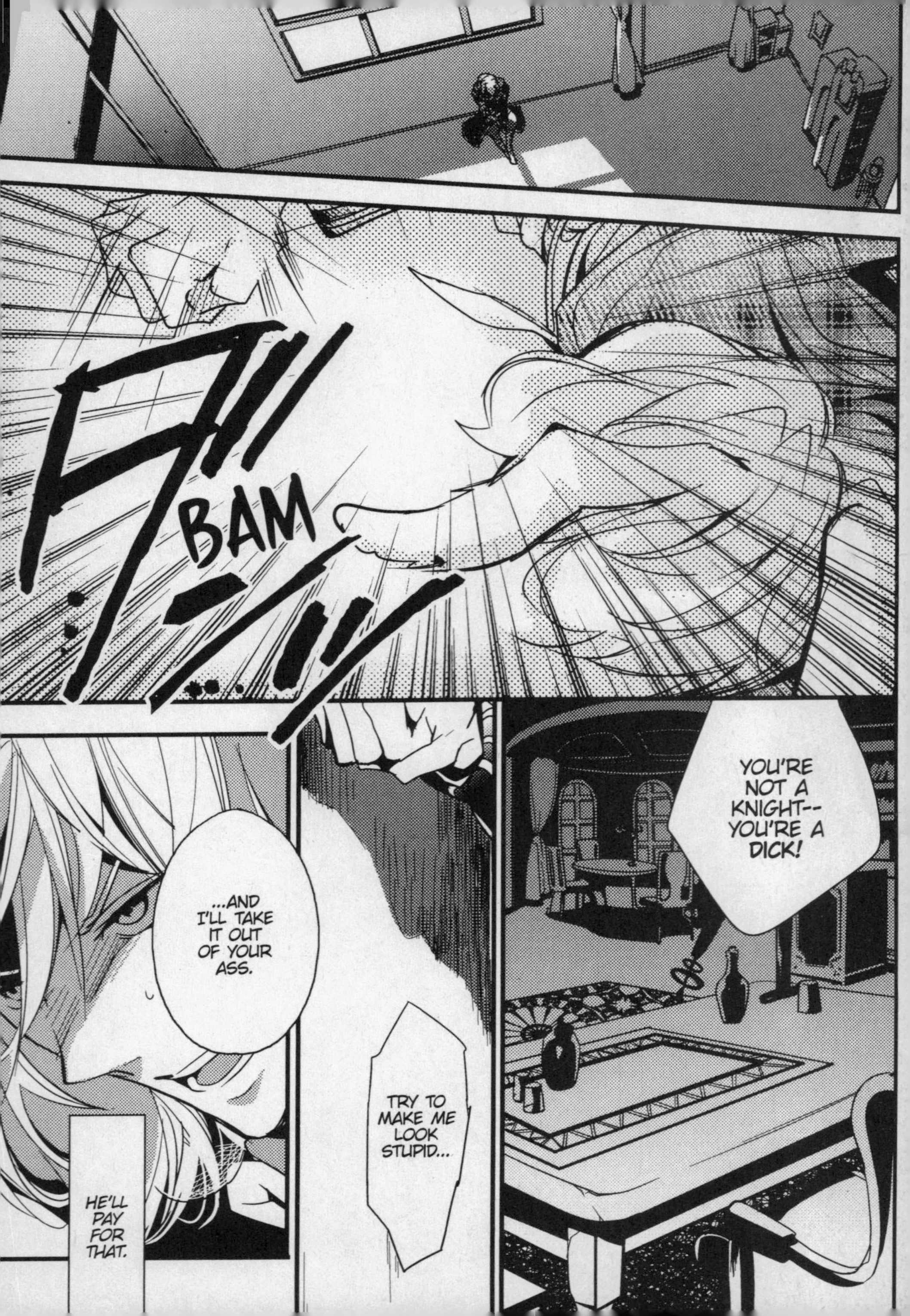
BAM
YOU'RE NOT A KNIGHT-- YOU'RE A DICK!
TRY TO MAKE ME LOOK STUPID...
...AND I'LL TAKE IT OUT OF YOUR ASS.
HE'LL PAY FOR THAT.

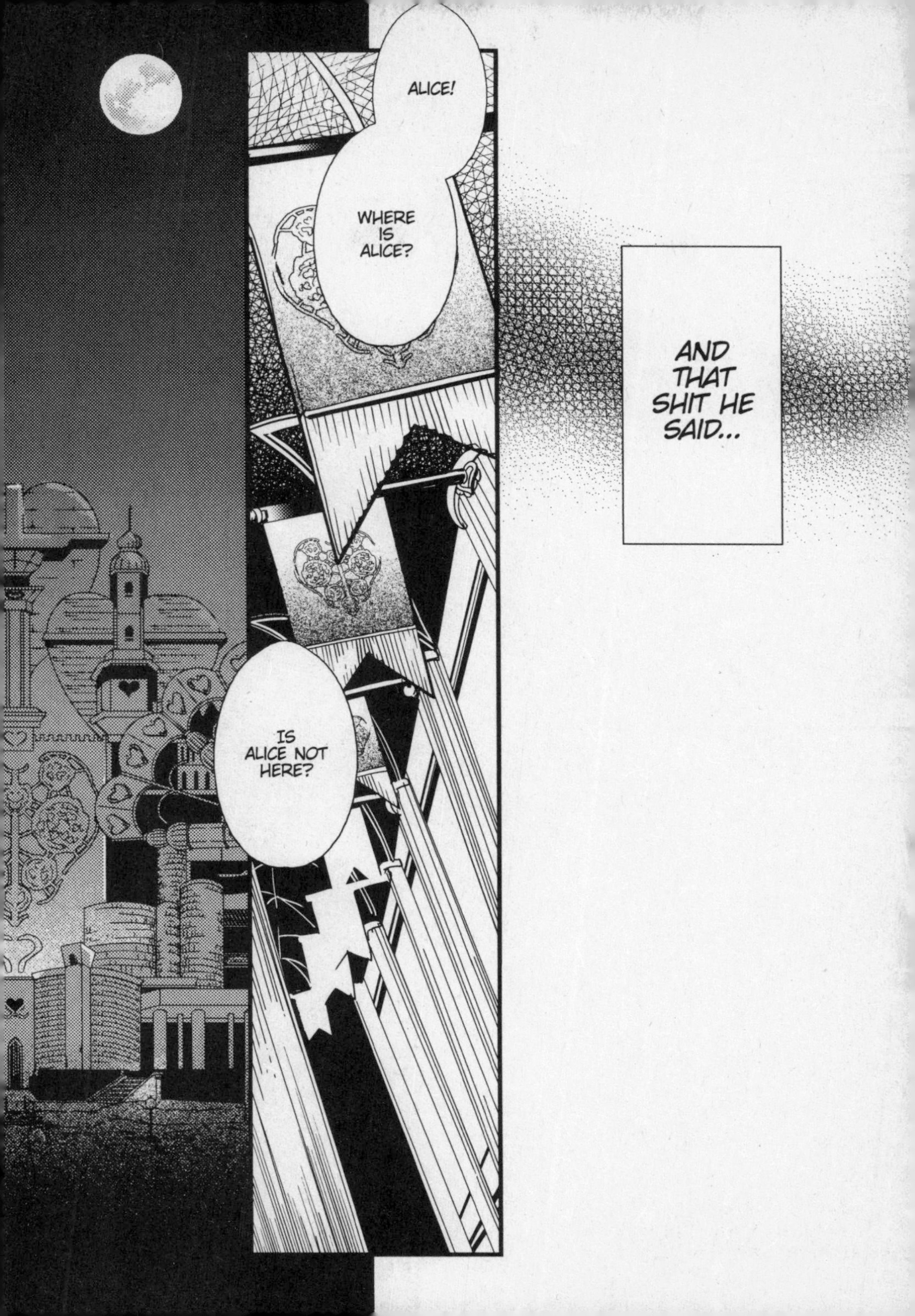
AND THAT SHIT HE SAID...
ALICE!
WHERE IS ALICE?
IS ALICE NOT HERE?

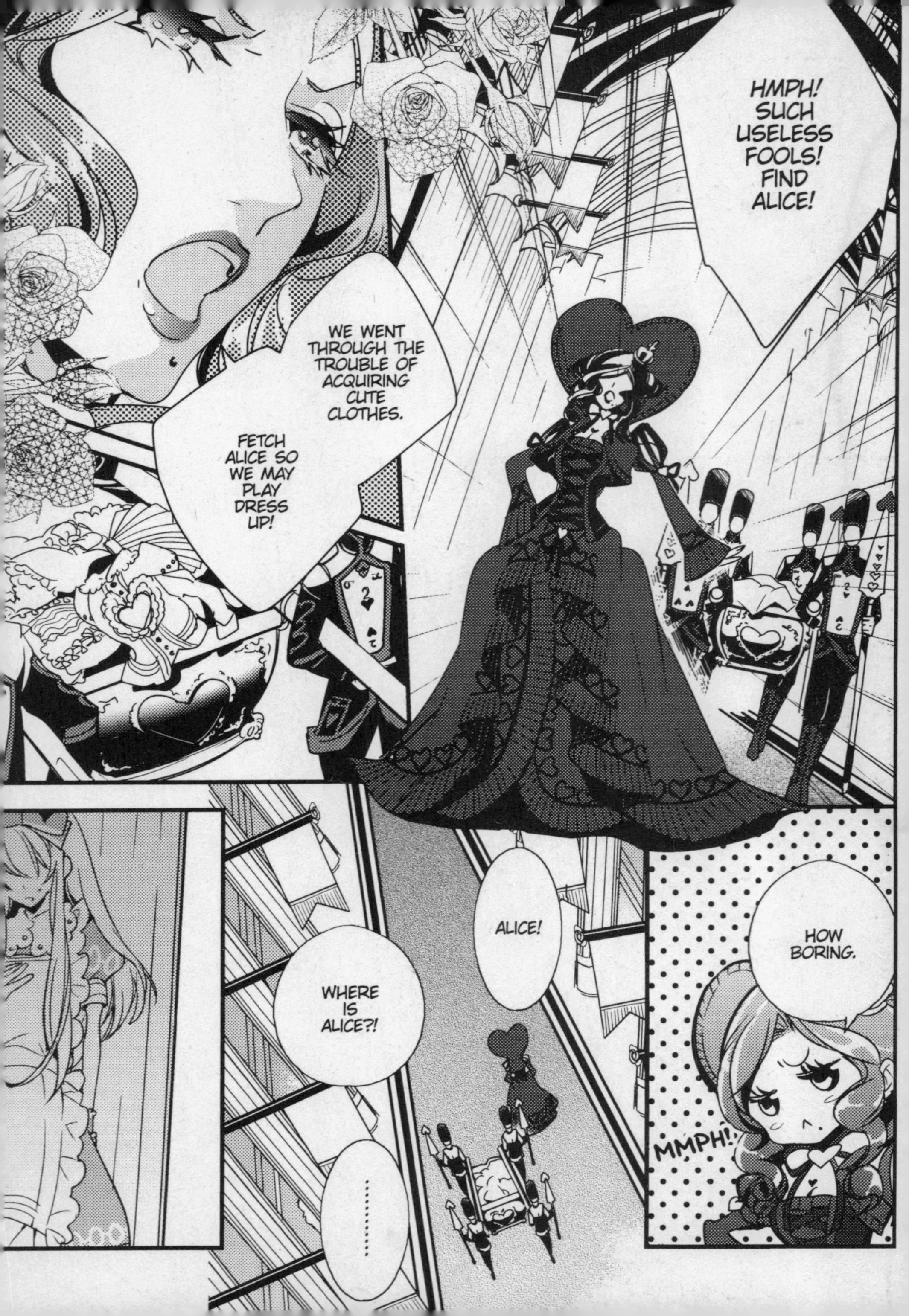
HMPH! SUCH USELESS FOOLS! FIND ALICE!
WE WENT THROUGH THE TROUBLE OF ACQUIRING CUTE CLOTHES.
FETCH ALICE SO WE MAY PLAY DRESS UP!
HOW BORING.
MMPH!
ALICE!
WHERE IS ALICE?!
......

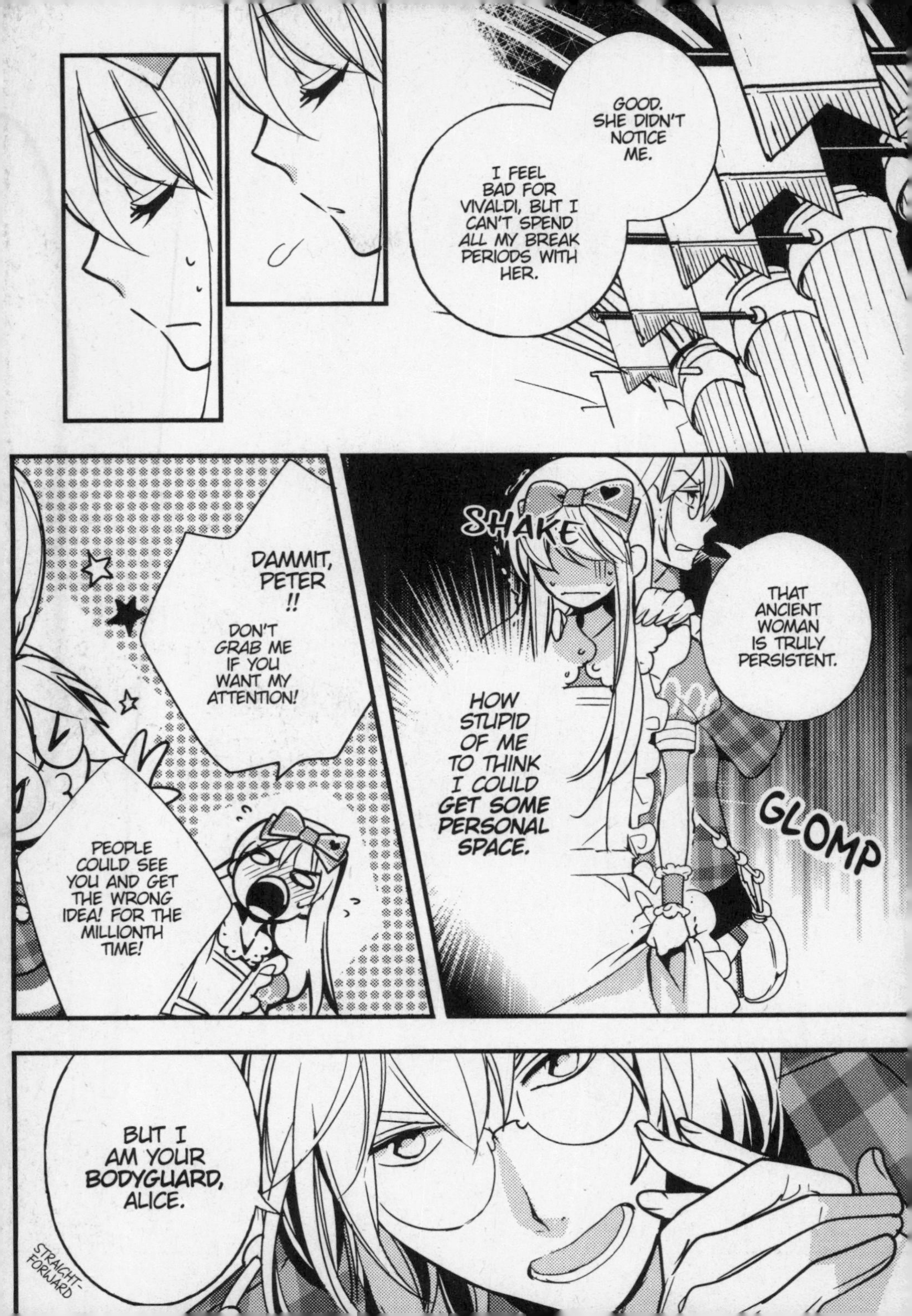
GOOD. SHE DIDN'T NOTICE ME.
I FEEL BAD FOR VIVALDI, BUT I CAN'T SPEND ALL MY BREAK PERIODS WITH HER.
SHAKE
THAT ANCIENT WOMAN IS TRULY PERSISTENT.
HOW STUPID OF ME TO THINK I COULD GET SOME PERSONAL SPACE.
GLOMP
DAMMIT, PETER !!
DON'T GRAB ME IF YOU WANT MY ATTENTION!
PEOPLE COULD SEE YOU AND GET THE WRONG IDEA! FOR THE MILLIONTH TIME!
BUT I AM YOUR BODYGUARD, ALICE.
STRAIGHT-FORWARD

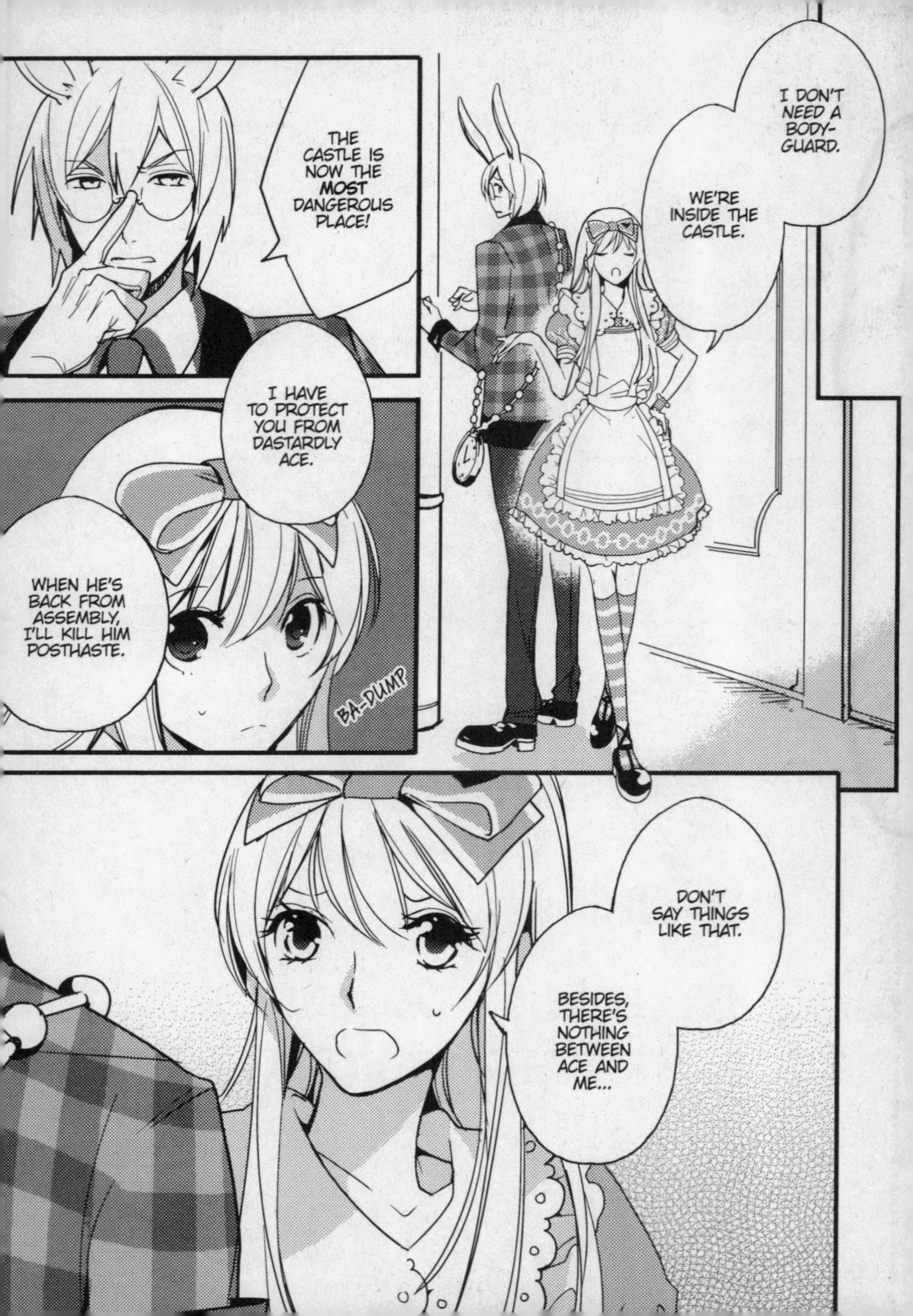
I DON'T NEED A BODY-GUARD.
WE'RE INSIDE THE CASTLE.
THE CASTLE IS NOW THE MOST DANGEROUS PLACE!
I HAVE TO PROTECT YOU FROM DASTARDLY ACE.
WHEN HE'S BACK FROM ASSEMBLY, I'LL KILL HIM POSTHASTE.
BA-DUMP
DON'T SAY THINGS LIKE THAT.
BESIDES, THERE'S NOTHING BETWEEN ACE AND ME...

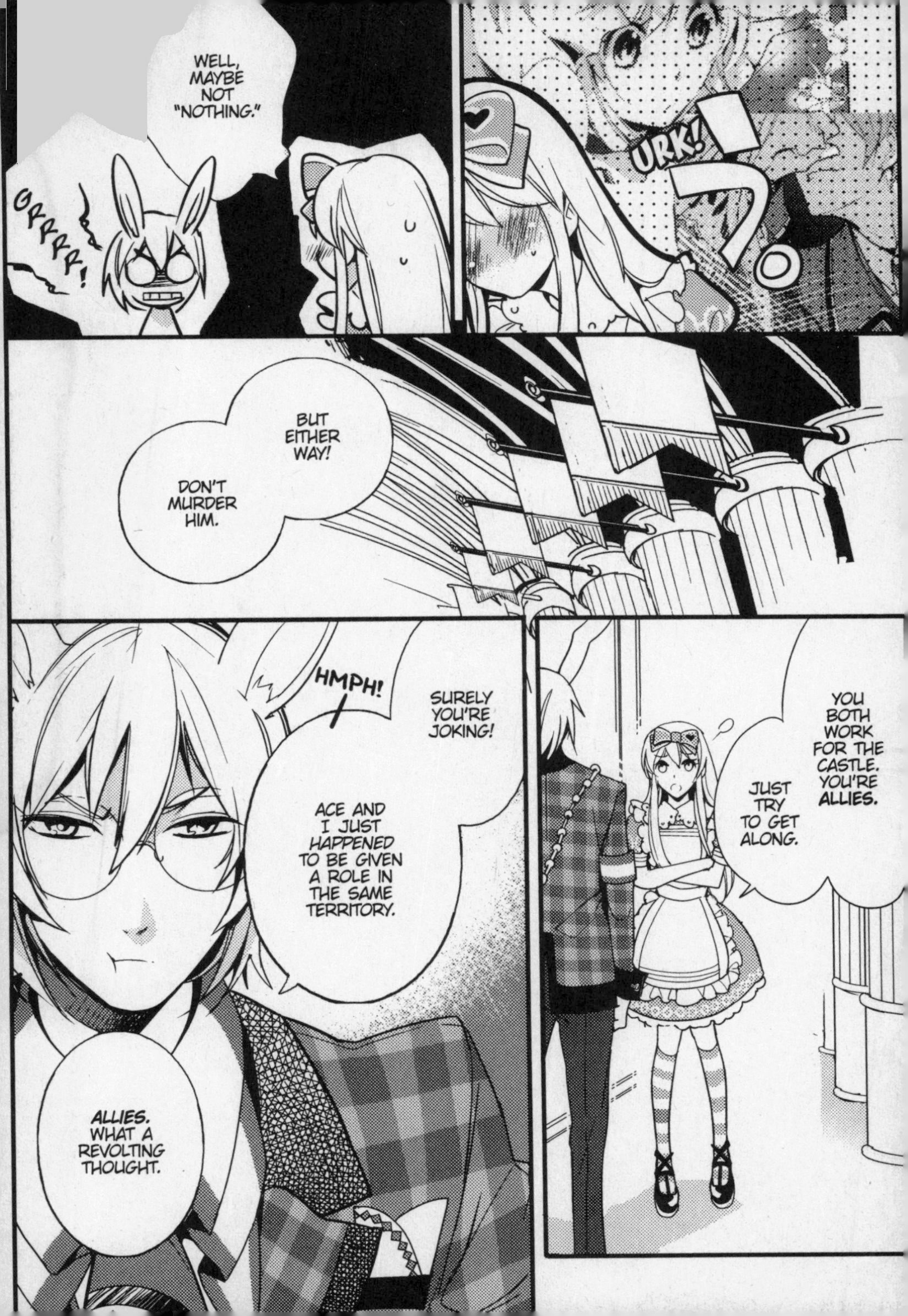
URK!
WELL, MAYBE NOT "NOTHING."
GRRRR!
BUT EITHER WAY!
DON'T MURDER HIM.
YOU BOTH WORK FOR THE CASTLE. YOU'RE ALLIES.
JUST TRY TO GET ALONG.
HMPH!
SURELY YOU'RE JOKING!
ACE AND I JUST HAPPENED TO BE GIVEN A ROLE IN THE SAME TERRITORY.
ALLIES. WHAT A REVOLTING THOUGHT.

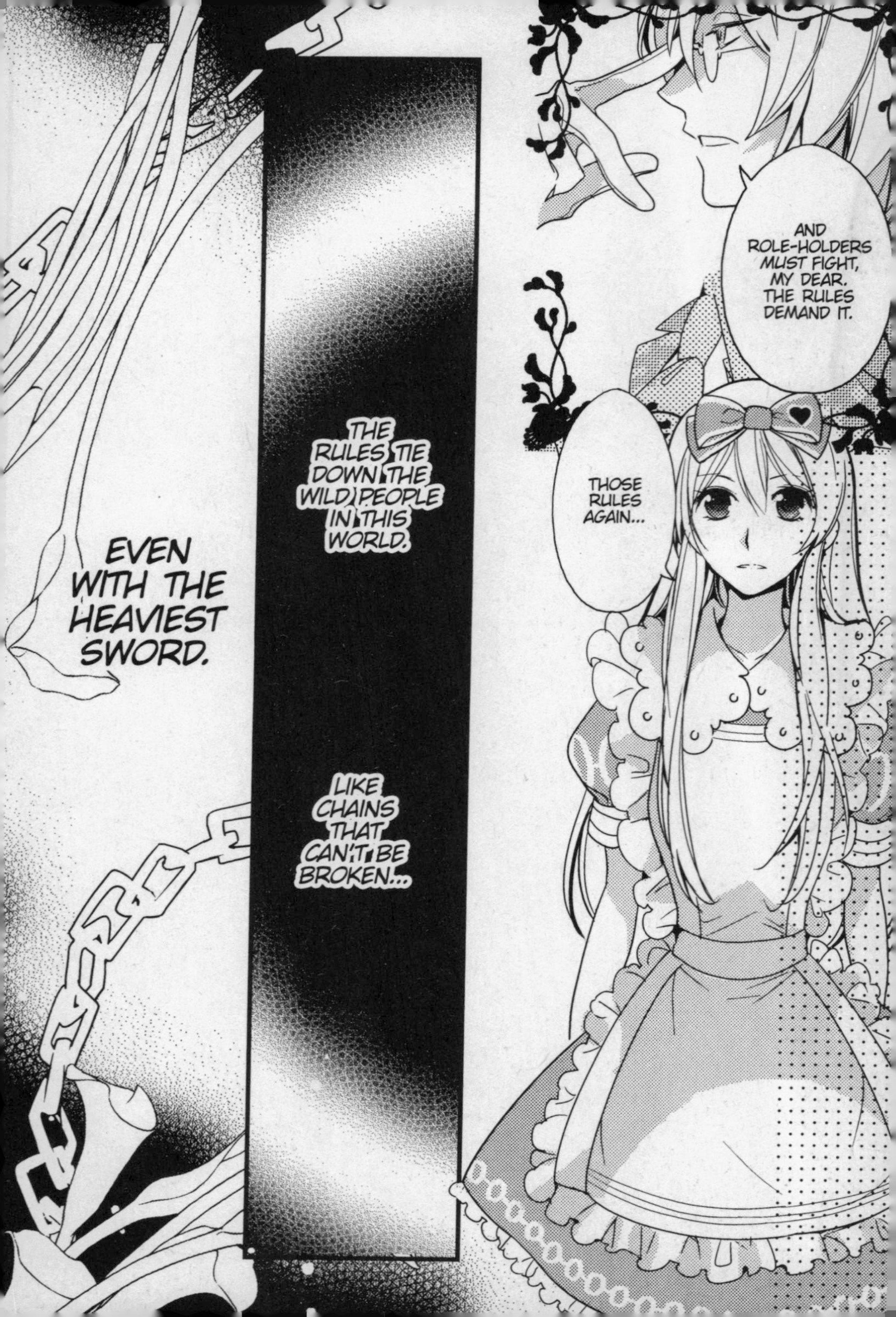
AND ROLE-HOLDERS MUST FIGHT, MY DEAR. THE RULES DEMAND IT.
THOSE RULES AGAIN...
THE RULES TIE DOWN THE WILD PEOPLE IN THIS WORLD.
LIKE CHAINS THAT CAN'T BE BROKEN...
EVEN WITH THE HEAVIEST SWORD.

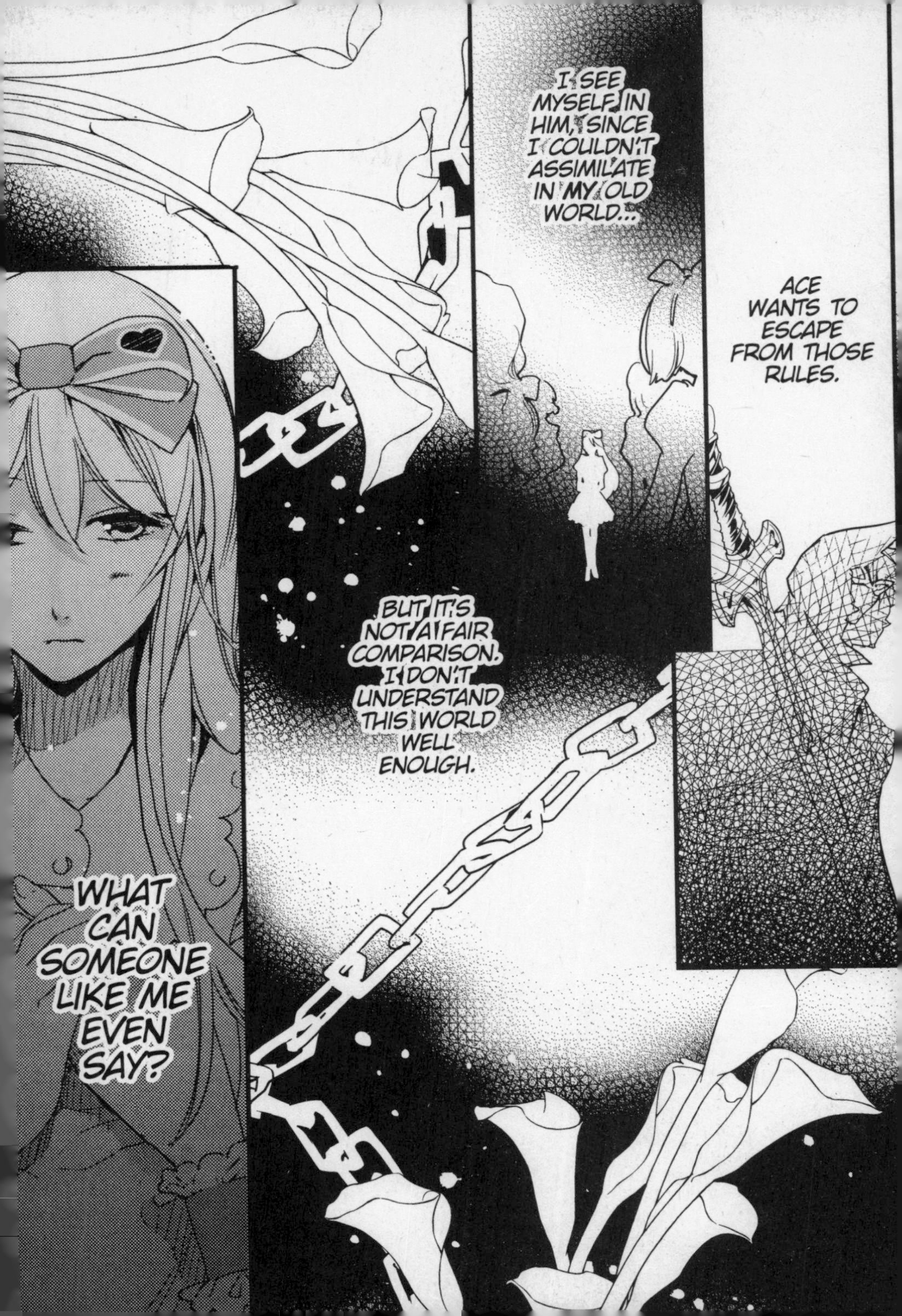
ACE WANTS TO ESCAPE FROM THOSE RULES.
I SEE MYSELF IN HIM, SINCE I COULDN'T ASSIMILATE IN MY OLD WORLD...
BUT IT'S NOT A FAIR COMPARISON. I DON'T UNDERSTAND THIS WORLD WELL ENOUGH.
WHAT CAN SOMEONE LIKE ME EVEN SAY?

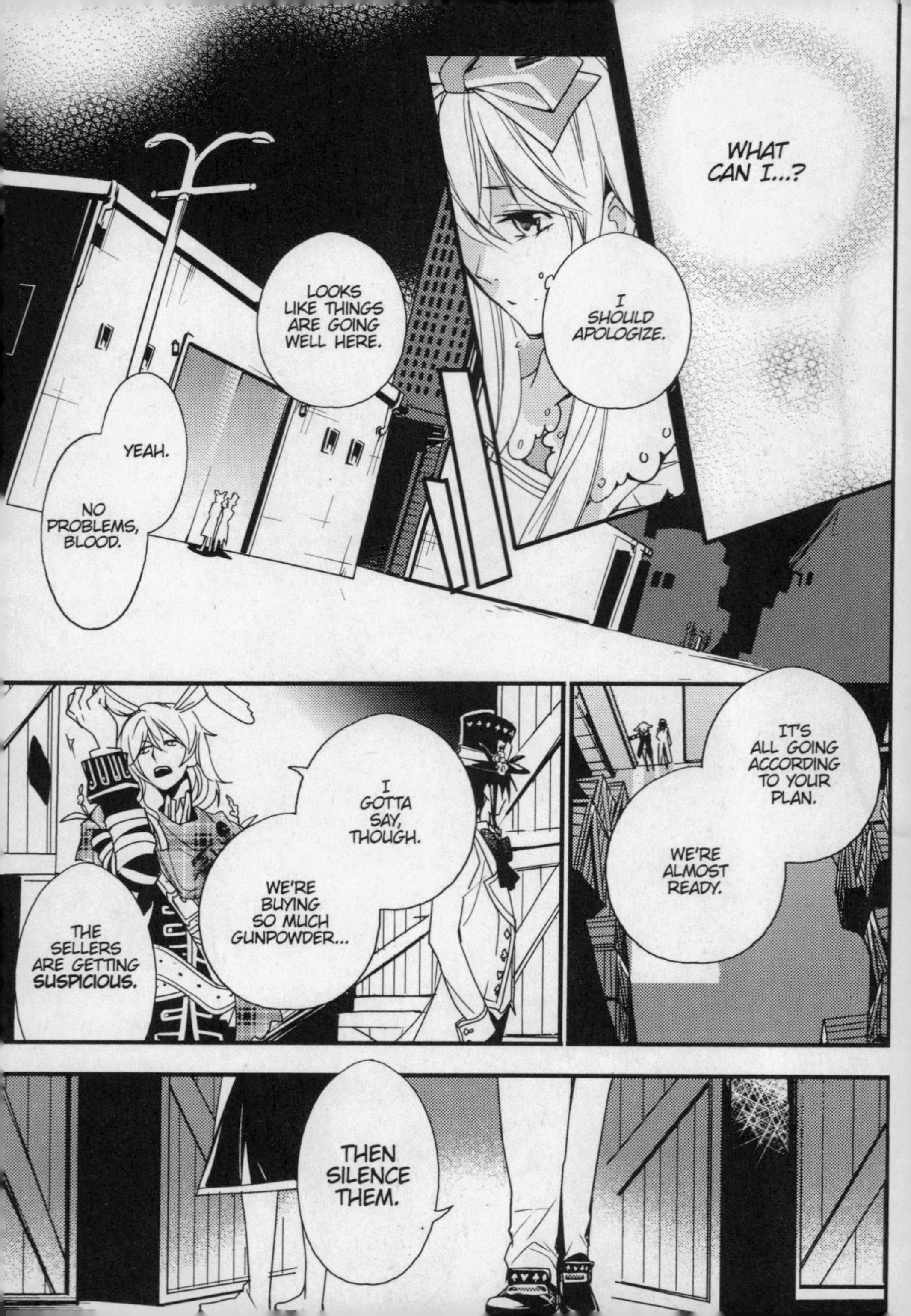
WHAT CAN I...?
I SHOULD APOLOGIZE.
LOOKS LIKE THINGS ARE GOING WELL HERE.
YEAH.
NO PROBLEMS, BLOOD.
IT'S ALL GOING ACCORDING TO YOUR PLAN.
WE'RE ALMOST READY.
I GOTTA SAY, THOUGH.
WE'RE BUYING SO MUCH GUNPOWDER...
THE SELLERS ARE GETTING SUSPICIOUS.
THEN SILENCE THEM.

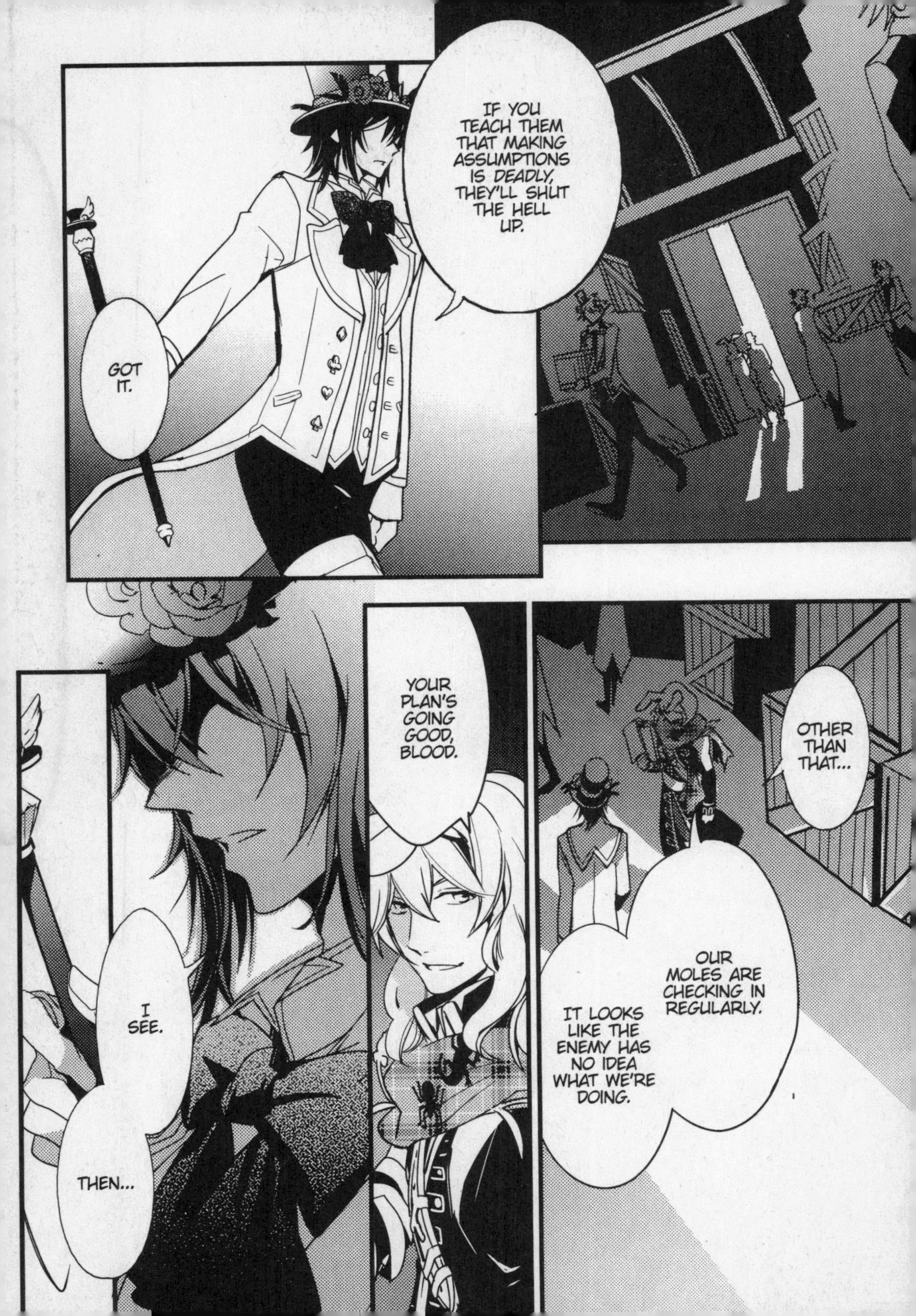
IF YOU TEACH THEM THAT MAKING ASSUMPTIONS IS *DEADLY*, THEY'LL SHUT THE HELL UP.
GOT IT.
OTHER THAN THAT...
OUR MOLES ARE CHECKING IN REGULARLY.
IT LOOKS LIKE THE ENEMY HAS NO IDEA WHAT WE'RE DOING.
YOUR PLAN'S GOING GOOD, BLOOD.
I SEE.
THEN...

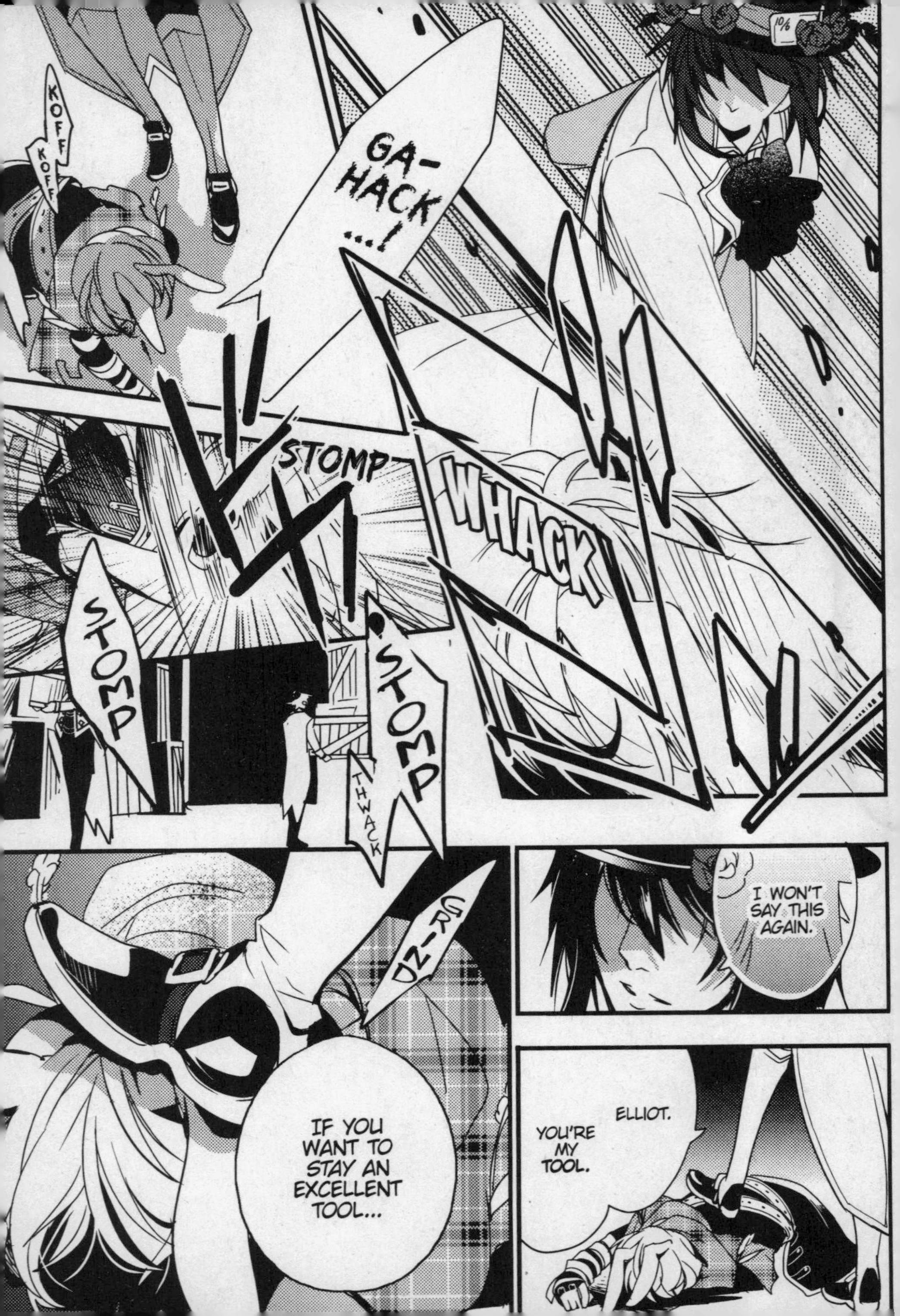
WHACK
GA-HACK ...!
KOFF KOFF
STOMP
STOMP
STOMP
THWACK
I WON'T SAY THIS AGAIN.
ELLIOT.
YOU'RE MY TOOL.
GRIND
IF YOU WANT TO STAY AN EXCELLENT TOOL...

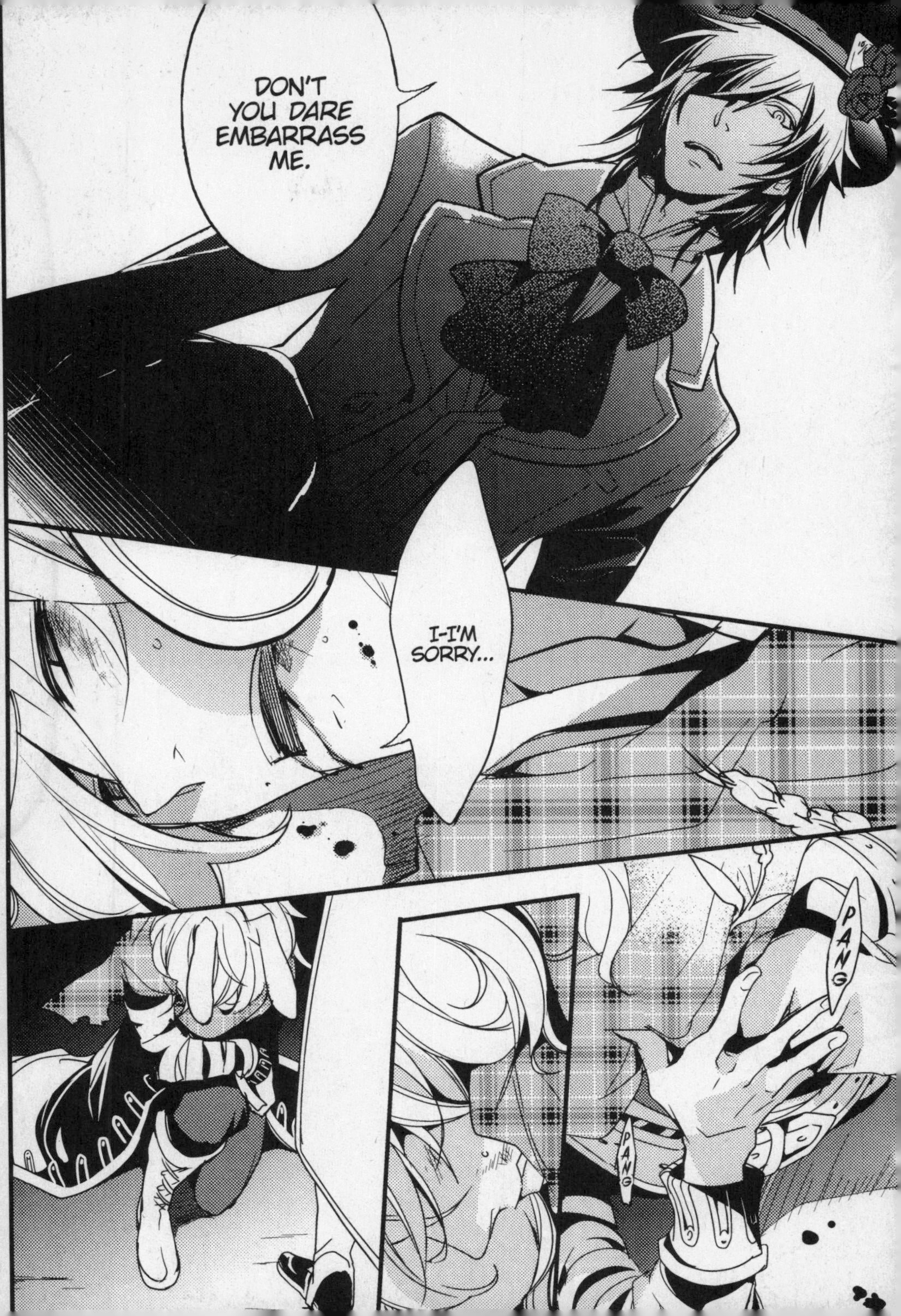
DON'T YOU DARE EMBARRASS ME.
I-I'M SORRY...
PANG
PANG

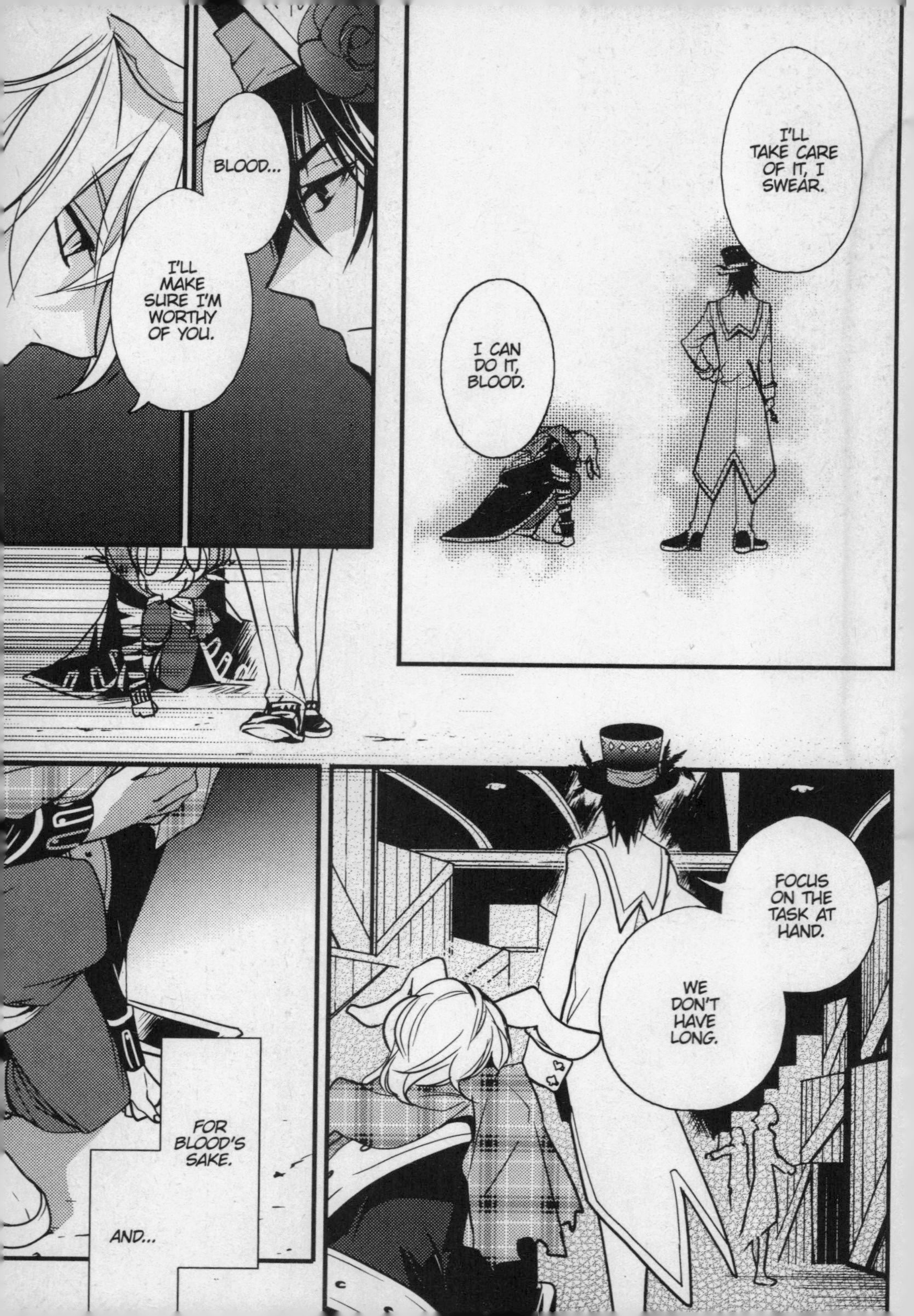
I'LL TAKE CARE OF IT, I SWEAR.
I CAN DO IT, BLOOD.
BLOOD...
I'LL MAKE SURE I'M WORTHY OF YOU.
FOCUS ON THE TASK AT HAND.
WE DON'T HAVE LONG.
FOR BLOOD'S SAKE.
AND...

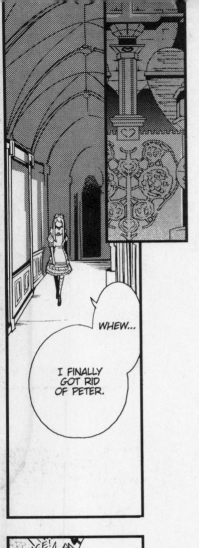

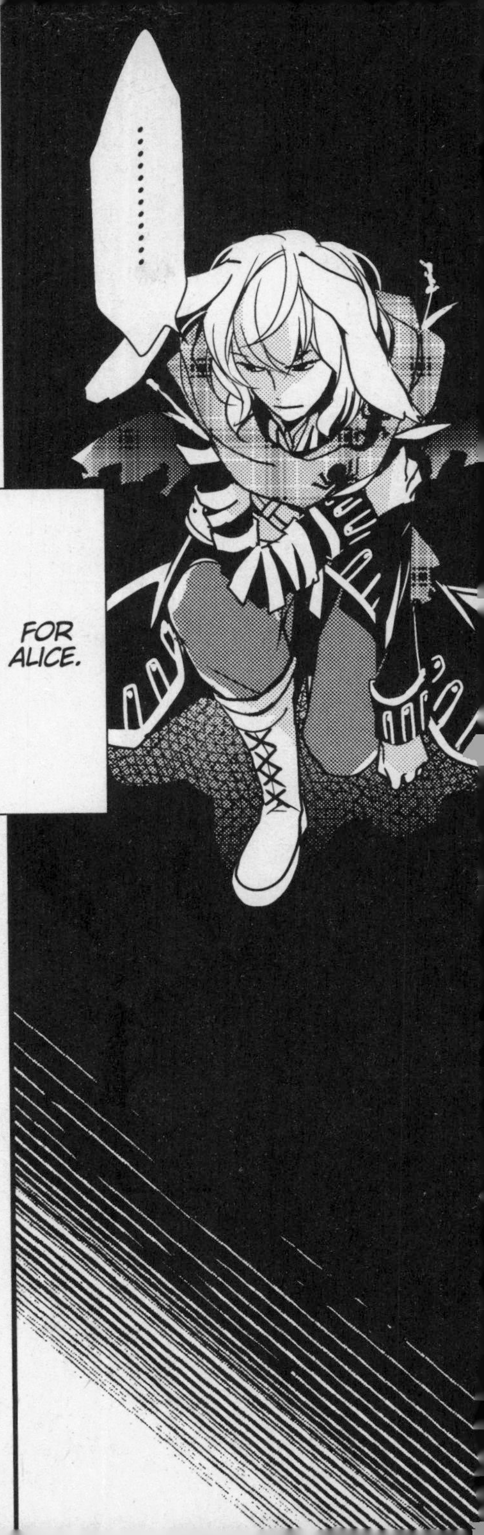
......
FOR ALICE.
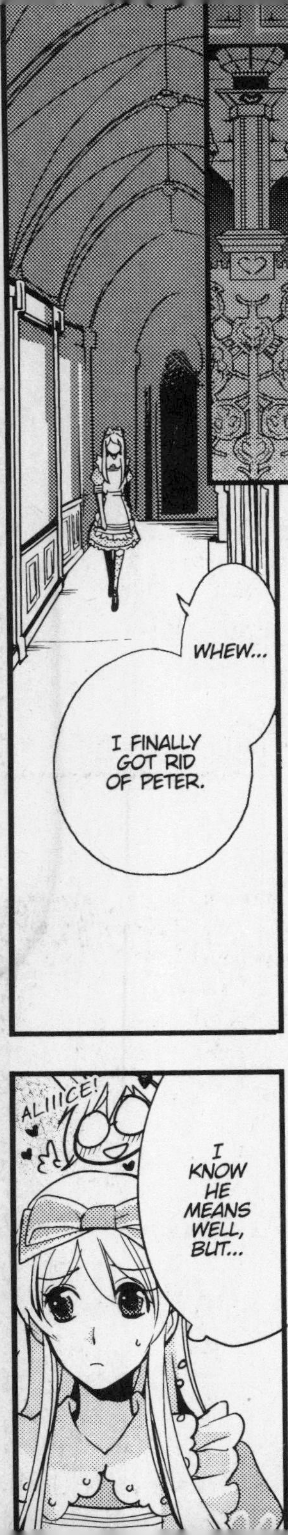
WHEW...
I FINALLY GOT RID OF PETER.
ALIIICE!
I KNOW HE MEANS WELL, BUT...

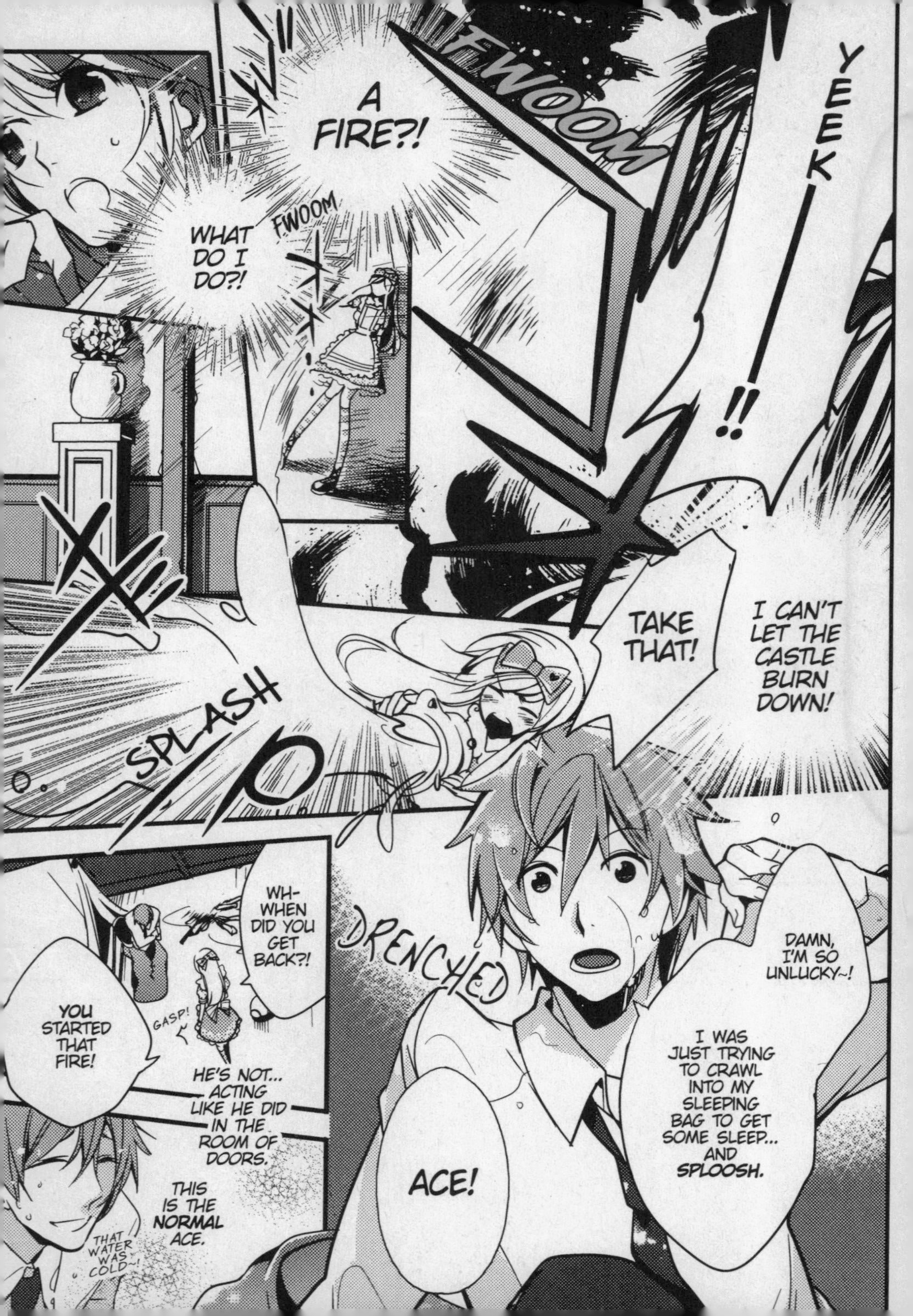
YEEK!!
FWOOM
A FIRE?!
FWOOM
WHAT DO I DO?!
I CAN'T LET THE CASTLE BURN DOWN!
TAKE THAT!
SPLASH
DAMN, I'M SO UNLUCKY~!
I WAS JUST TRYING TO CRAWL INTO MY SLEEPING BAG TO GET SOME SLEEP... AND SPLOOSH.
DRENCHED
ACE!
WH-WHEN DID YOU GET BACK?!
GASP!
YOU STARTED THAT FIRE!
HE'S NOT... ACTING LIKE HE DID IN THE ROOM OF DOORS.
THIS IS THE NORMAL ACE.
THAT WATER WAS COLD~!

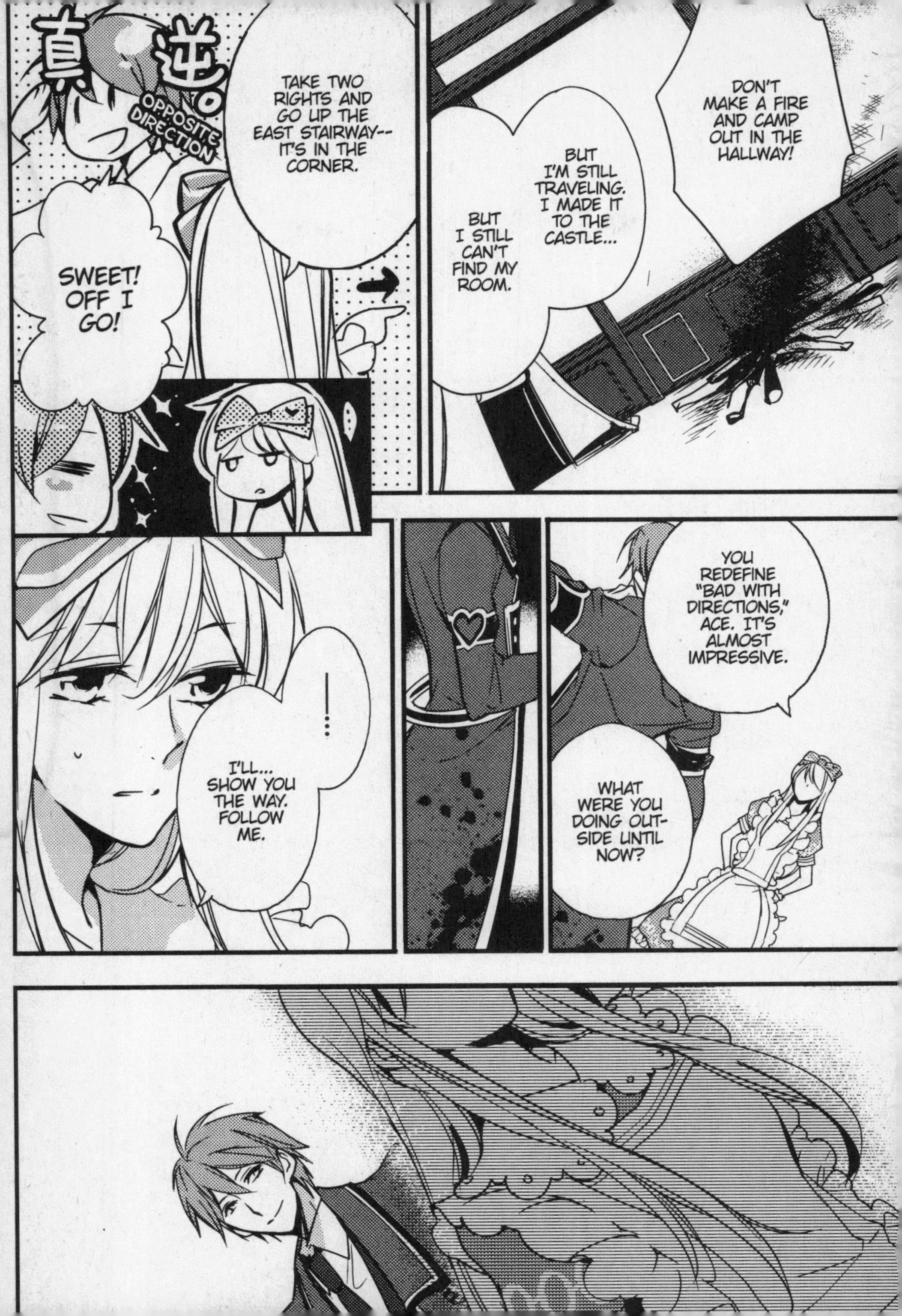
DON'T MAKE A FIRE AND CAMP OUT IN THE HALLWAY!
BUT I'M STILL TRAVELING. I MADE IT TO THE CASTLE...
BUT I STILL CAN'T FIND MY ROOM.
TAKE TWO RIGHTS AND GO UP THE EAST STAIRWAY-- IT'S IN THE CORNER.
真逆
OPPOSITE DIRECTION
SWEET! OFF I GO!
...
YOU REDEFINE "BAD WITH DIRECTIONS," ACE. IT'S ALMOST IMPRESSIVE.
WHAT WERE YOU DOING OUT-SIDE UNTIL NOW?
—....
I'LL... SHOW YOU THE WAY. FOLLOW ME.

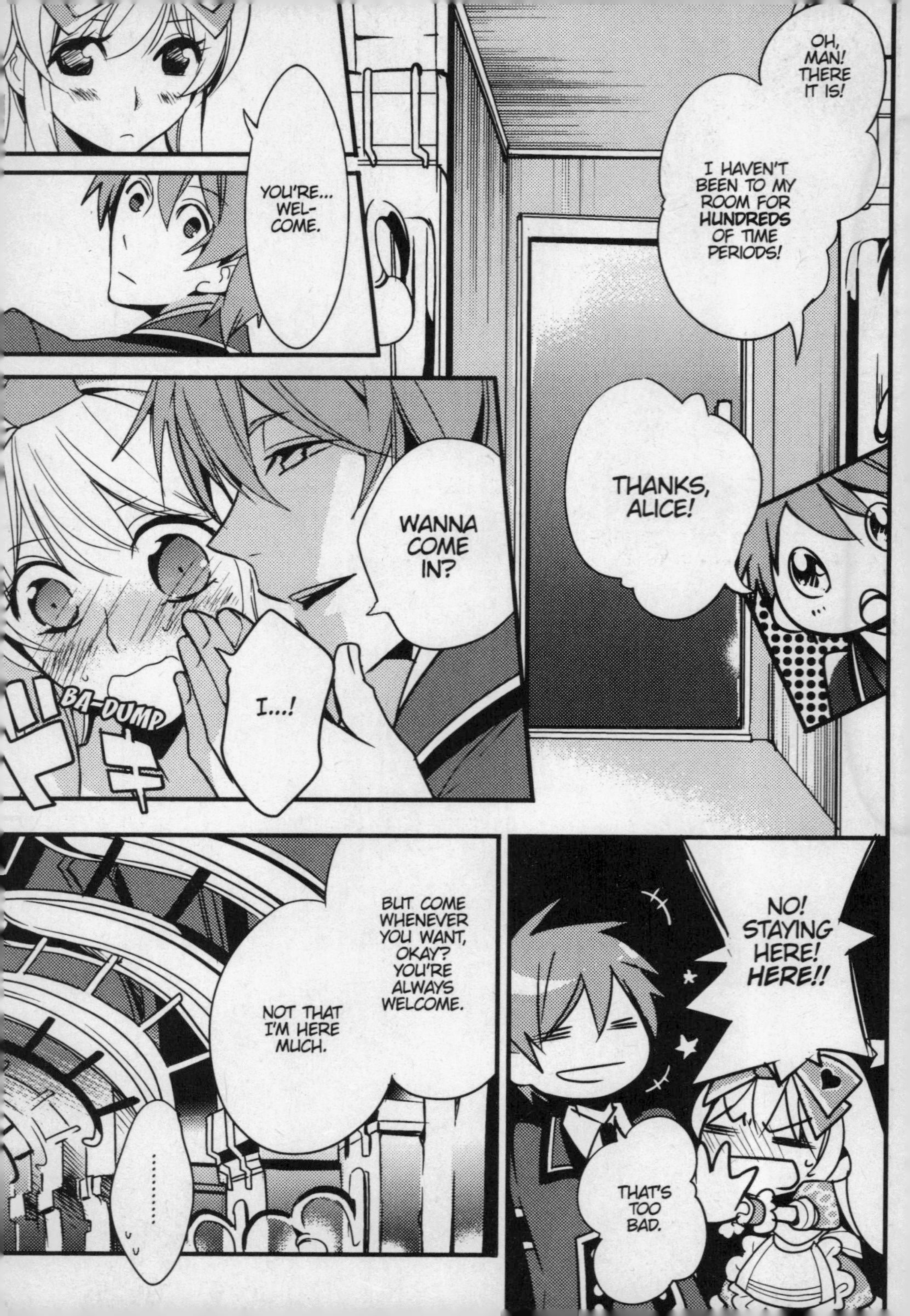
OH, MAN! THERE IT IS!
I HAVEN'T BEEN TO MY ROOM FOR HUNDREDS OF TIME PERIODS!
THANKS, ALICE!
YOU'RE... WEL-COME.
WANNA COME IN?
I...!
BA-DUMP
NO! STAYING HERE! HERE!!
THAT'S TOO BAD.
BUT COME WHENEVER YOU WANT, OKAY? YOU'RE ALWAYS WELCOME.
NOT THAT I'M HERE MUCH.
......

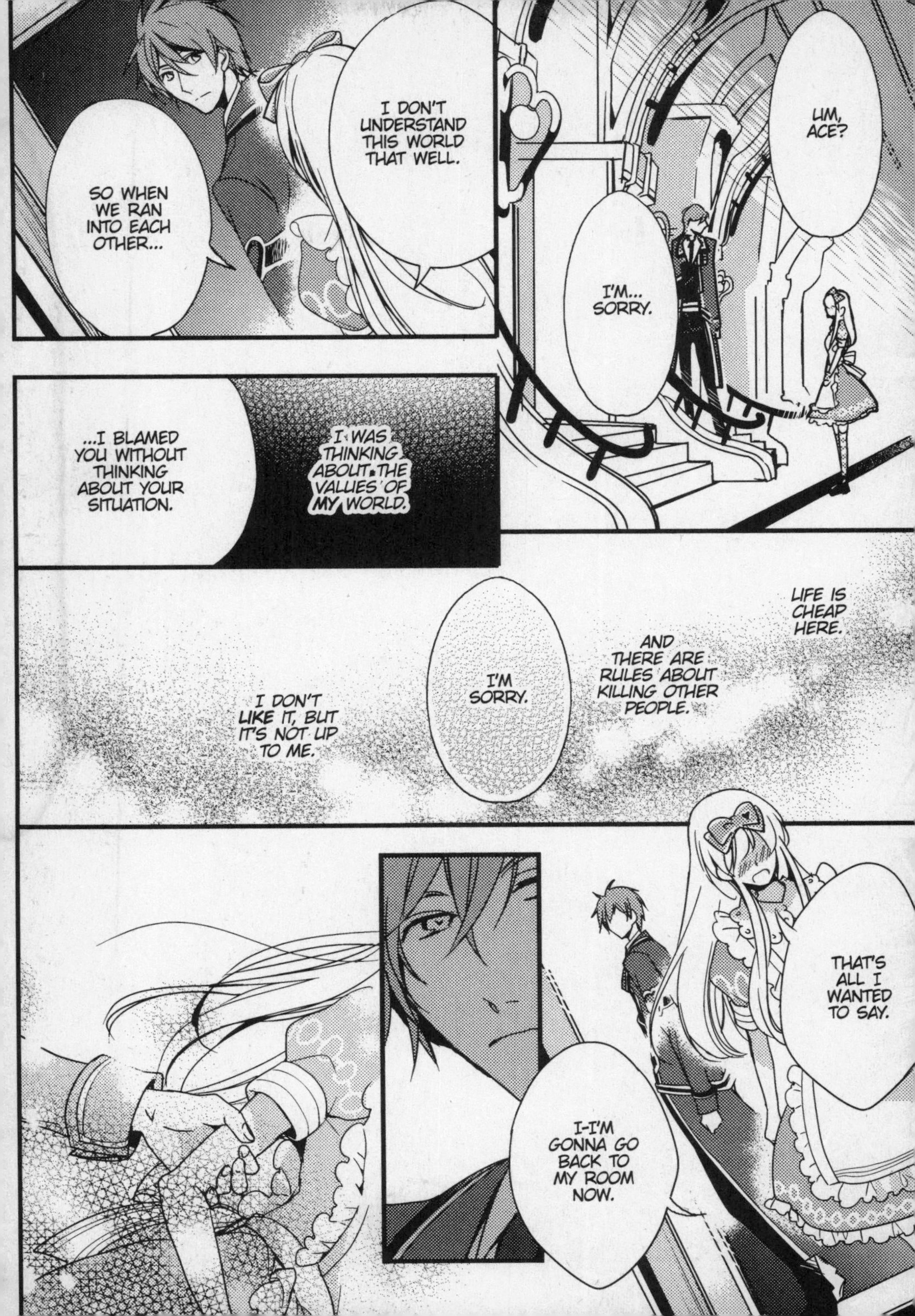
UM, ACE?
I'M... SORRY.
I DON'T UNDERSTAND THIS WORLD THAT WELL.
SO WHEN WE RAN INTO EACH OTHER...
I WAS THINKING ABOUT THE VALUES OF MY WORLD.
...I BLAMED YOU WITHOUT THINKING ABOUT YOUR SITUATION.
LIFE IS CHEAP HERE.
AND THERE ARE RULES ABOUT KILLING OTHER PEOPLE.
I'M SORRY.
I DON'T LIKE IT, BUT IT'S NOT UP TO ME.
THAT'S ALL I WANTED TO SAY.
I-I'M GONNA GO BACK TO MY ROOM NOW.

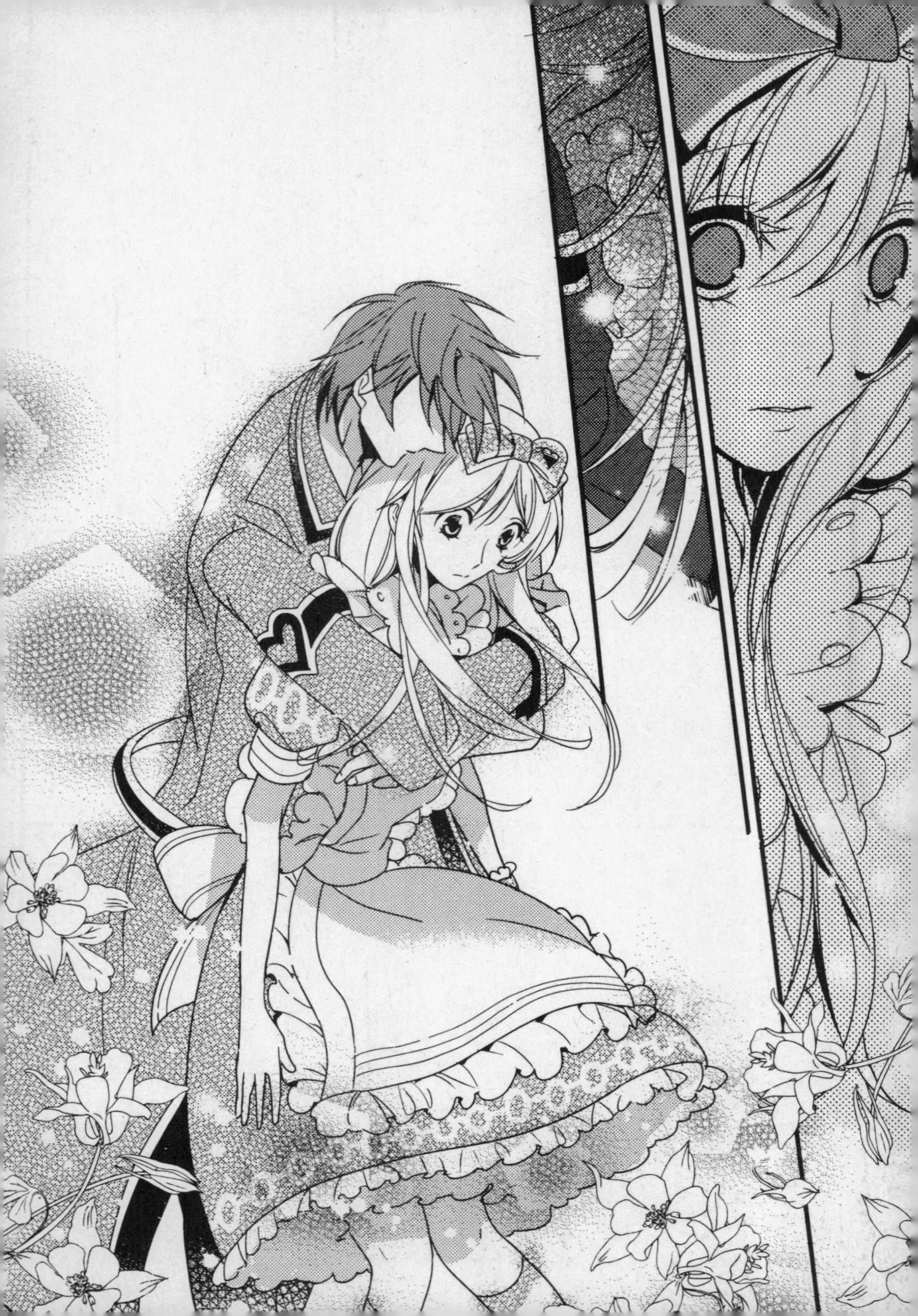

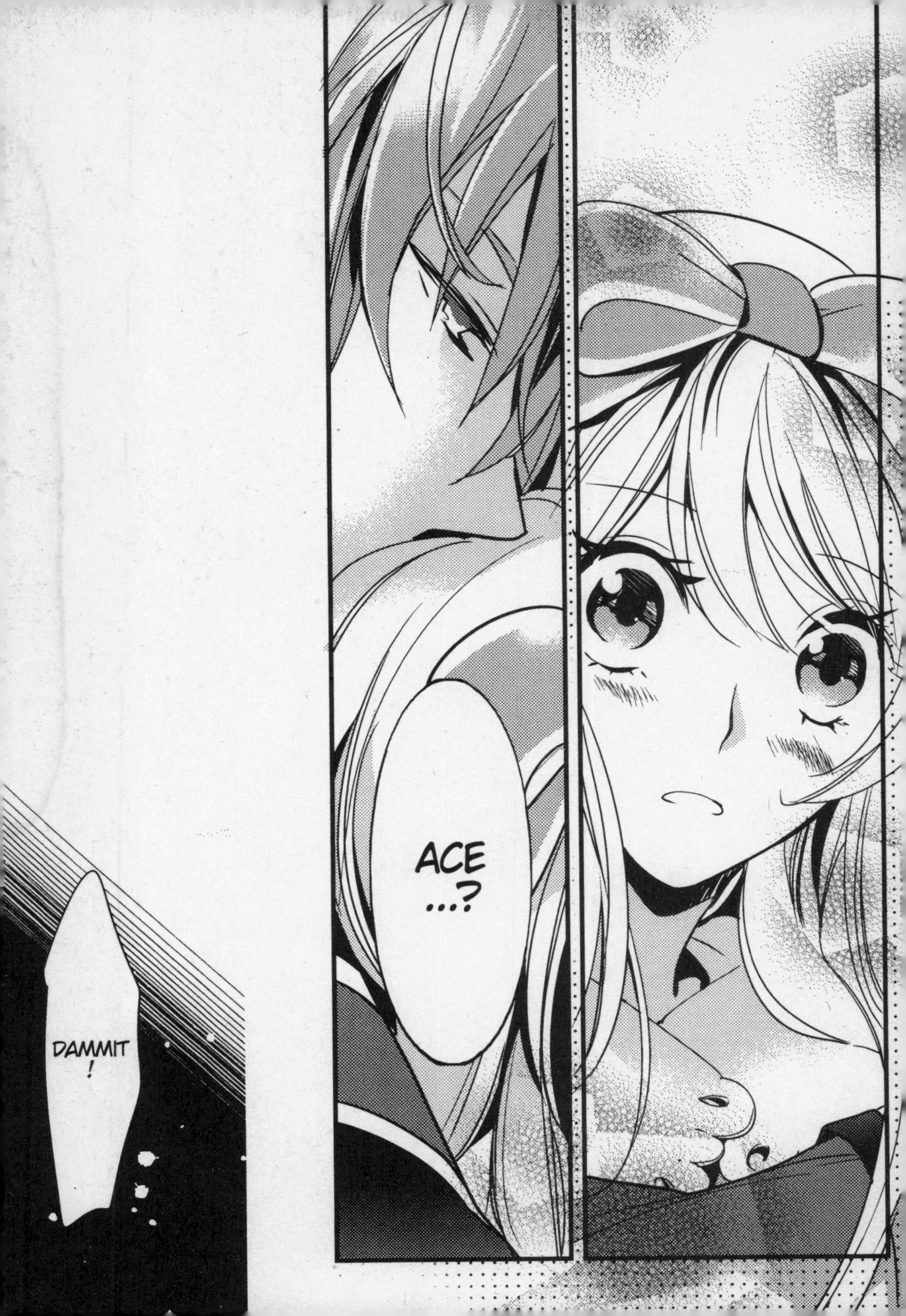
ACE ...?
DAMMIT!

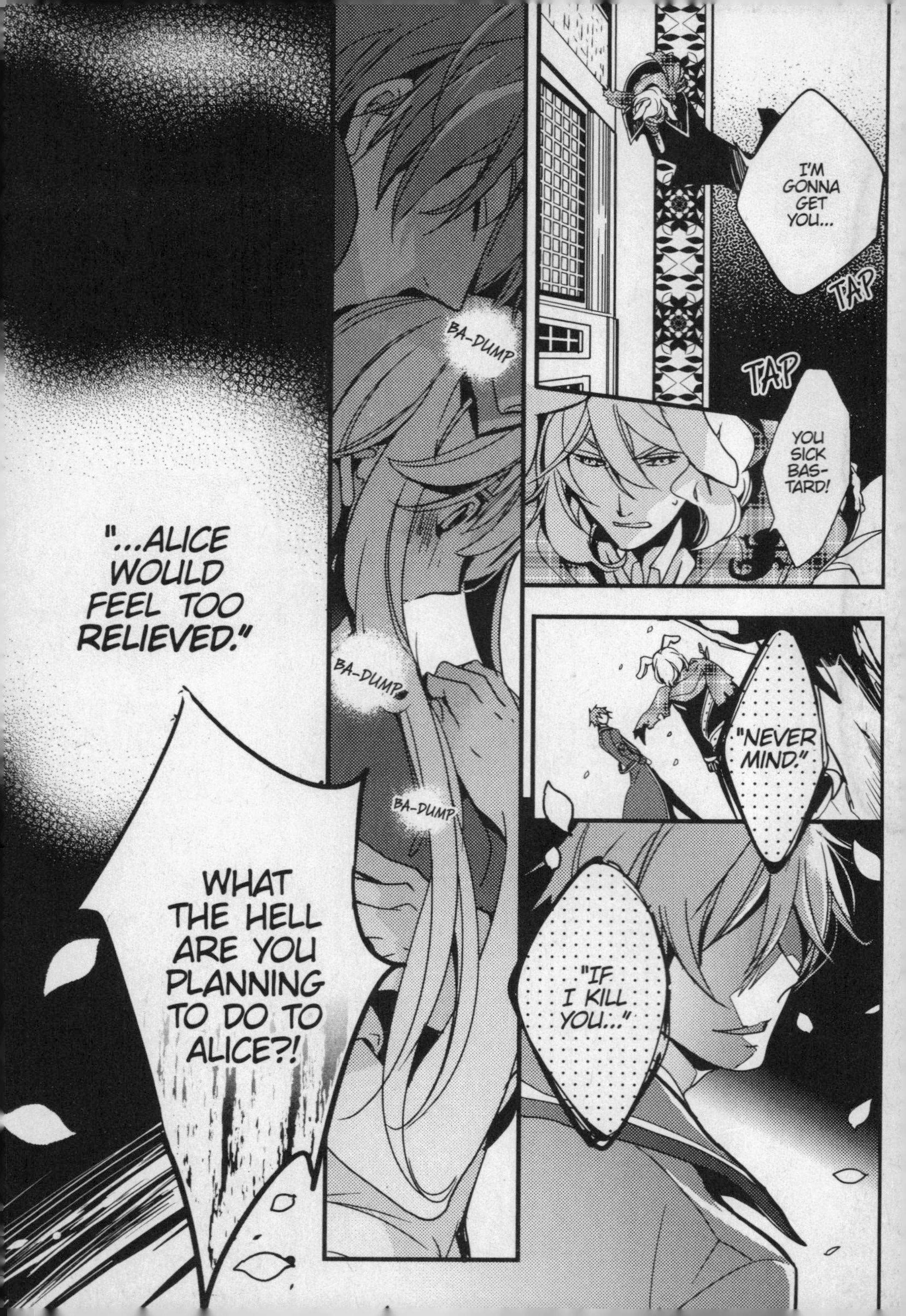
I'M GONNA GET YOU...
TAP
TAP
YOU SICK BAS-TARD!
"NEVER MIND."
"IF I KILL YOU..."
BA-DUMP
BA-DUMP
BA-DUMP
"...ALICE WOULD FEEL TOO RELIEVED."
WHAT THE HELL ARE YOU PLANNING TO DO TO ALICE?!

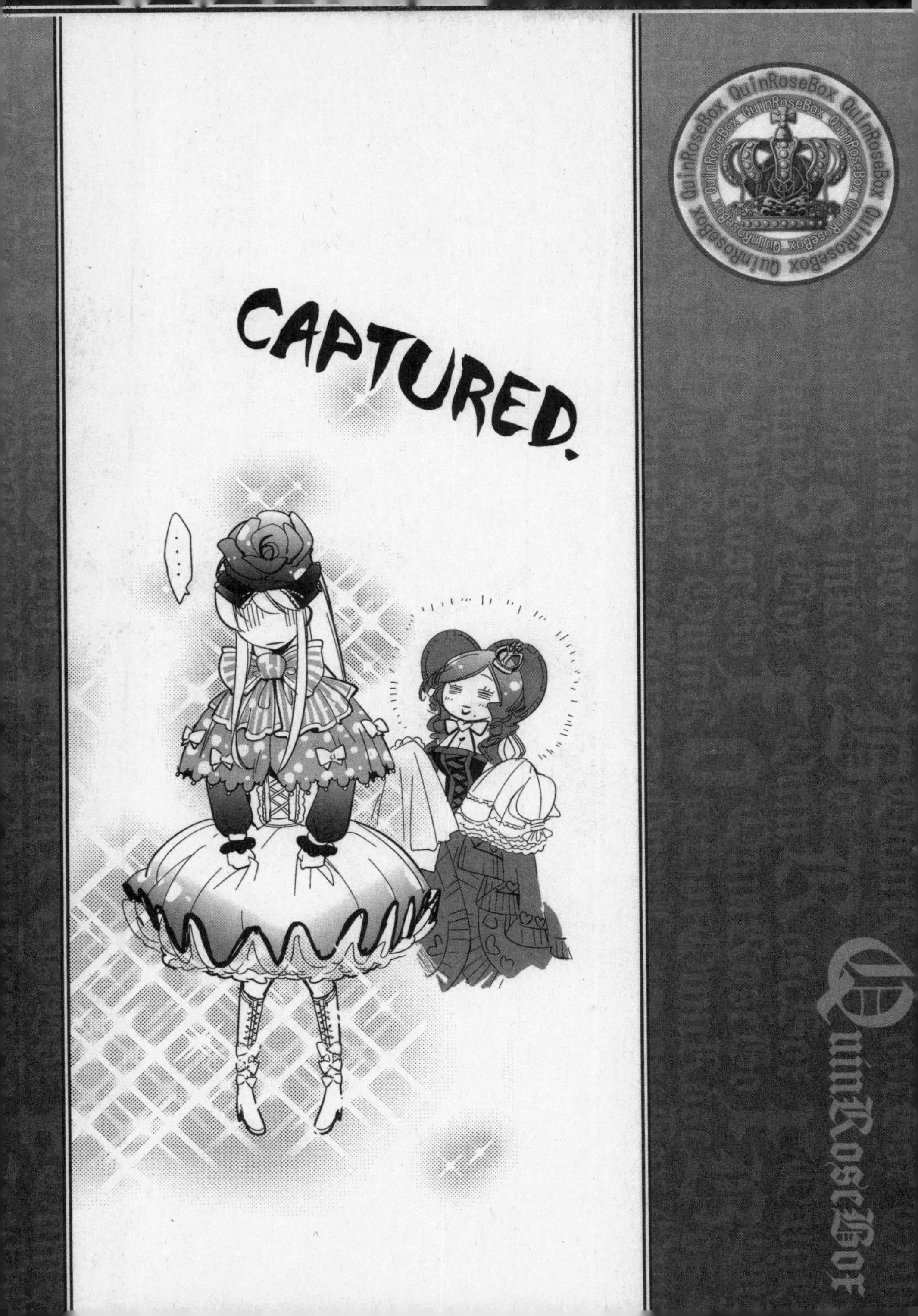
CAPTURED.

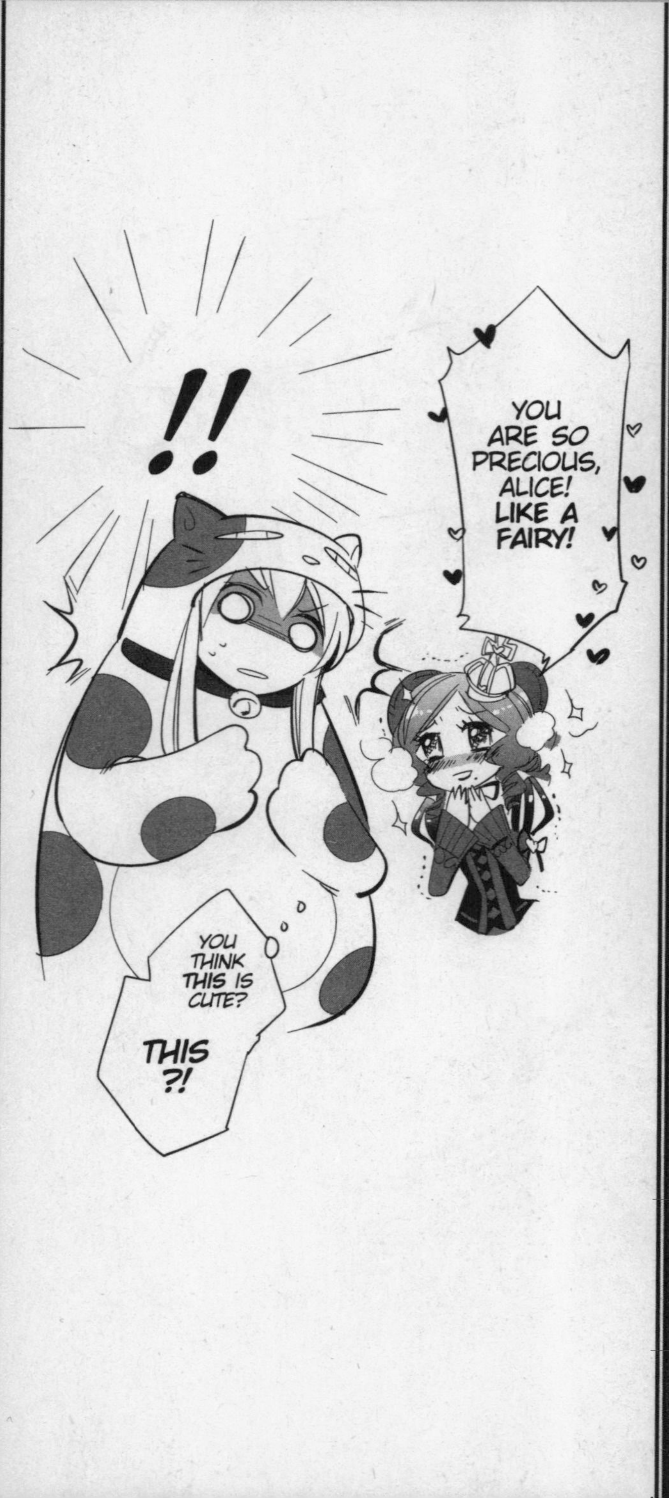
YOU ARE SO PRECIOUS, ALICE! LIKE A FAIRY!
!!
YOU THINK THIS IS CUTE?
THIS ?!

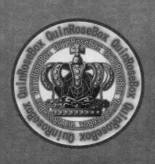

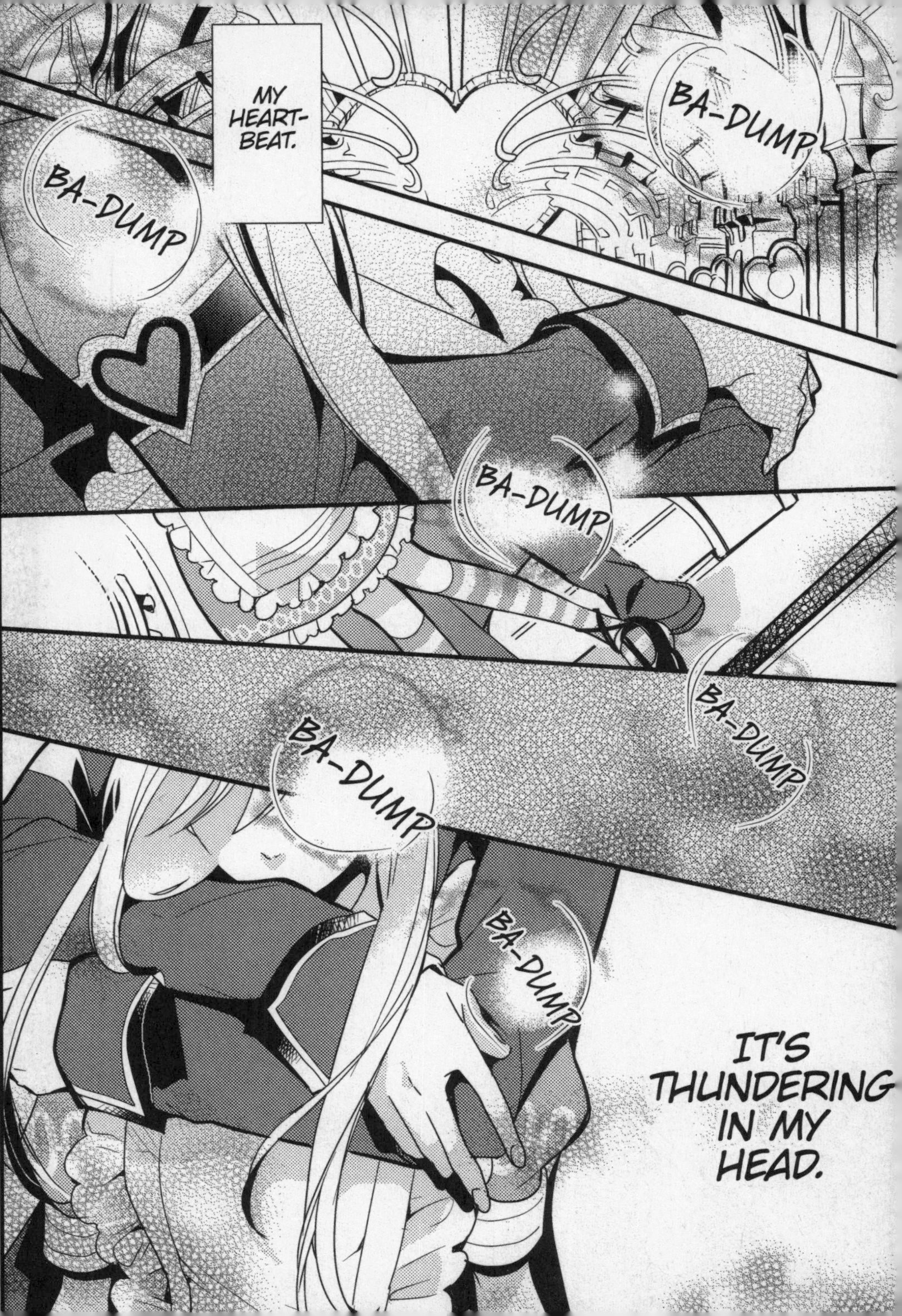
BA-DUMP
MY HEART-BEAT.
BA-DUMP
BA-DUMP
BA-DUMP
BA-DUMP
BA-DUMP
IT'S THUNDERING IN MY HEAD.

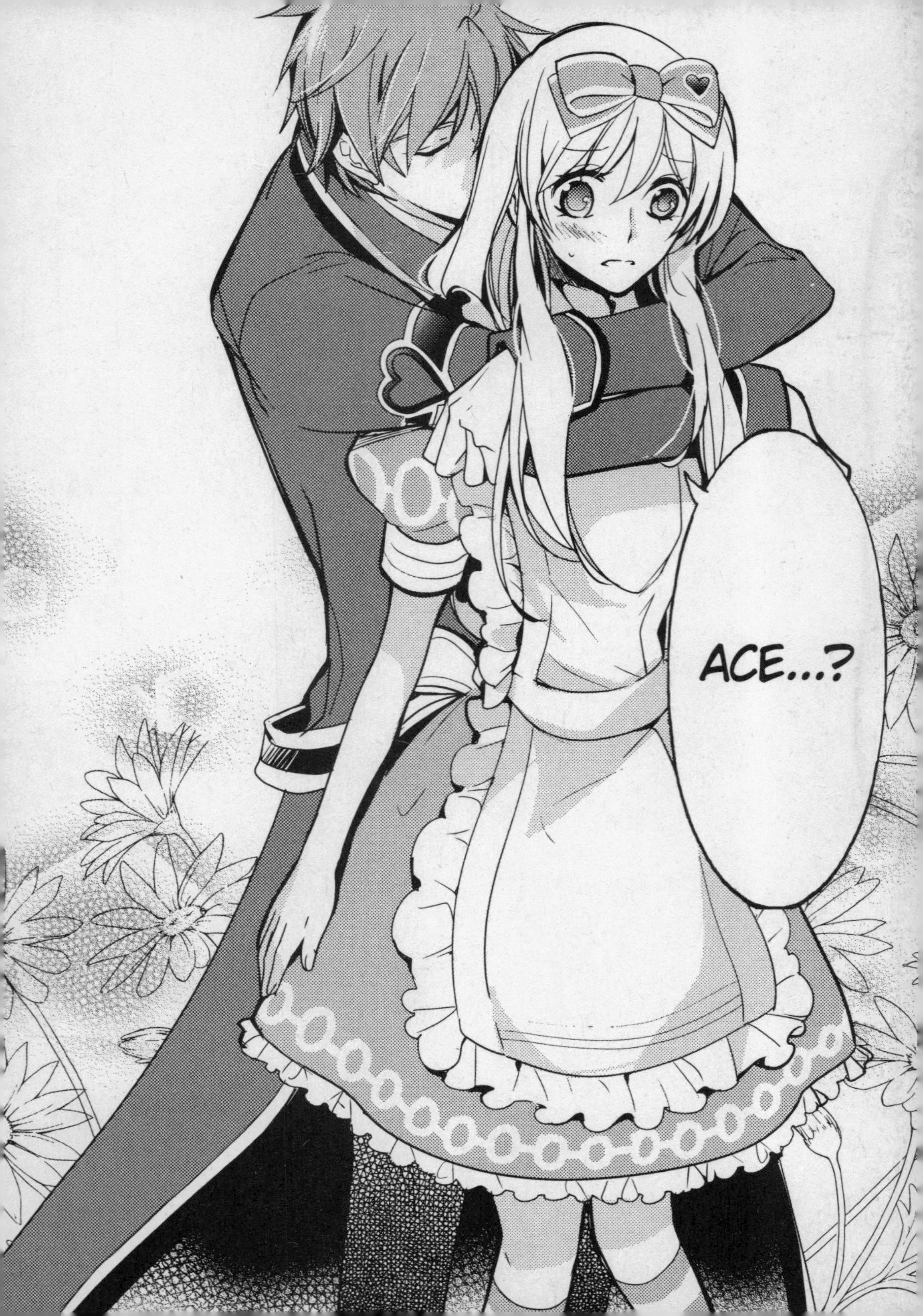
ACE...?

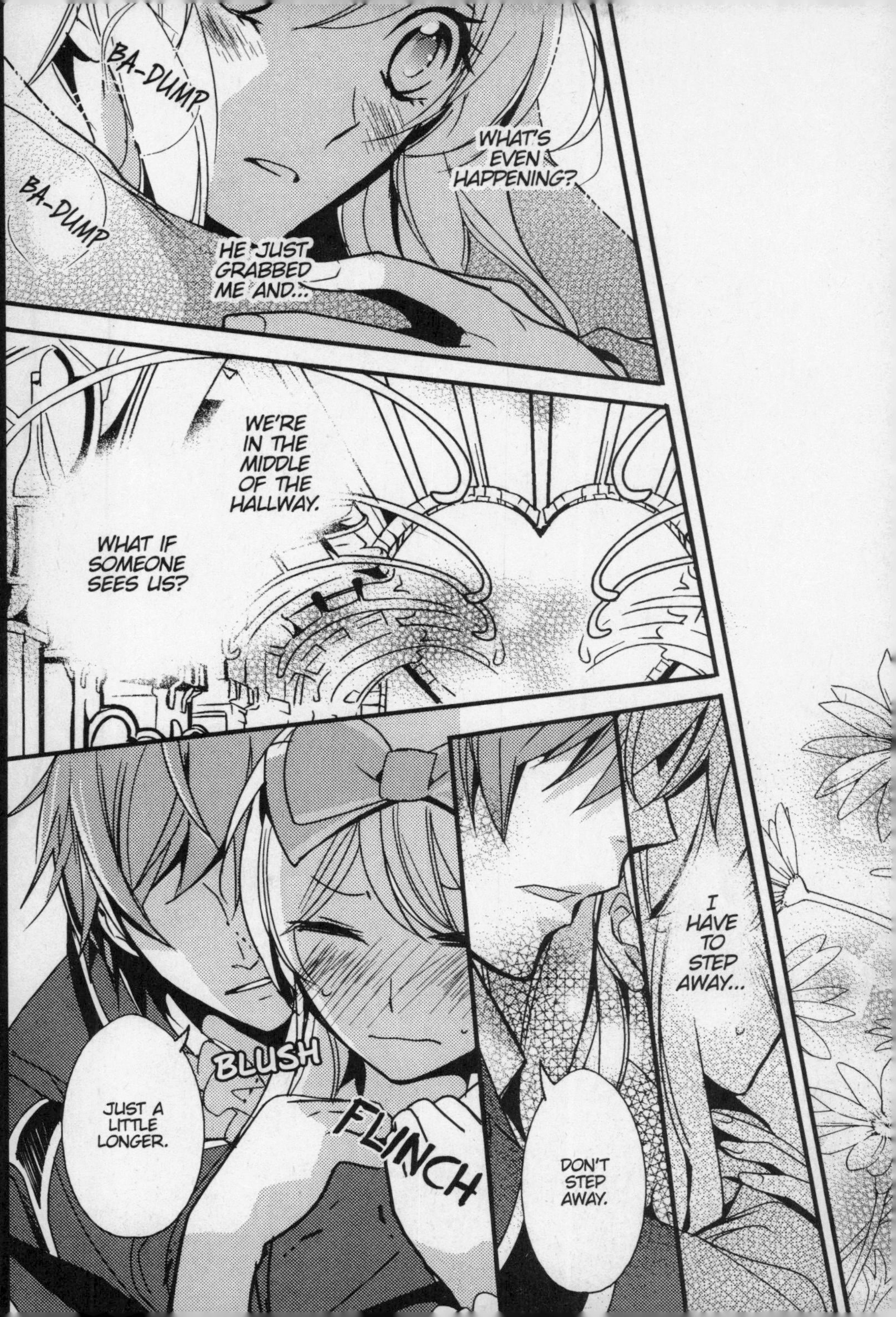
WHAT'S EVEN HAPPENING?
BA-DUMP
HE JUST GRABBED ME AND...
BA-DUMP
WE'RE IN THE MIDDLE OF THE HALLWAY.
WHAT IF SOMEONE SEES US?
I HAVE TO STEP AWAY...
DON'T STEP AWAY.
FLINCH
BLUSH
JUST A LITTLE LONGER.

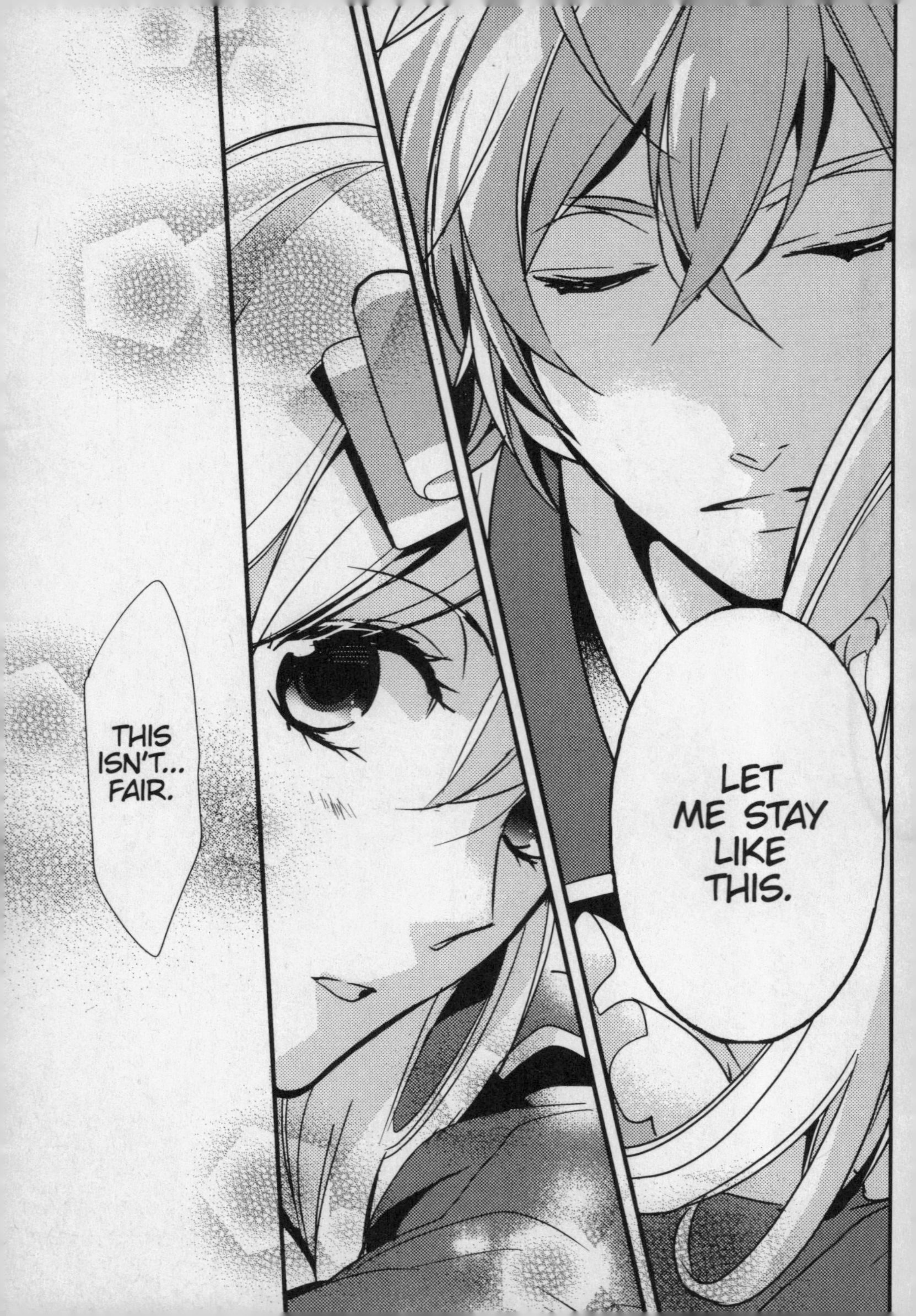
LET ME STAY LIKE THIS.
THIS ISN'T... FAIR.

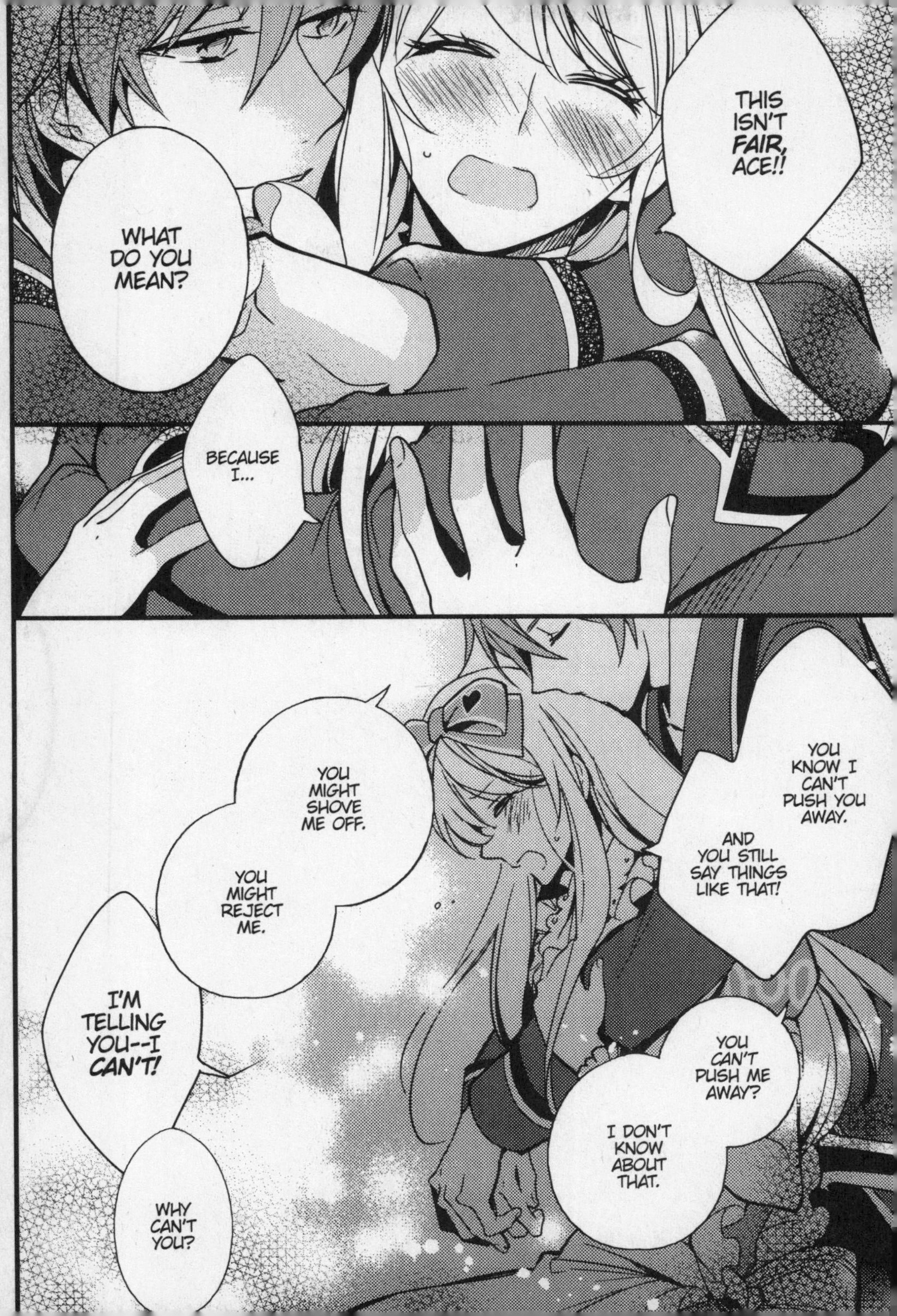
THIS ISN'T FAIR, ACE!!
WHAT DO YOU MEAN?
BECAUSE I...
YOU KNOW I CAN'T PUSH YOU AWAY.
AND YOU STILL SAY THINGS LIKE THAT!
YOU MIGHT SHOVE ME OFF.
YOU MIGHT REJECT ME.
I'M TELLING YOU--I CAN'T!
YOU CAN'T PUSH ME AWAY?
I DON'T KNOW ABOUT THAT.
WHY CAN'T YOU?

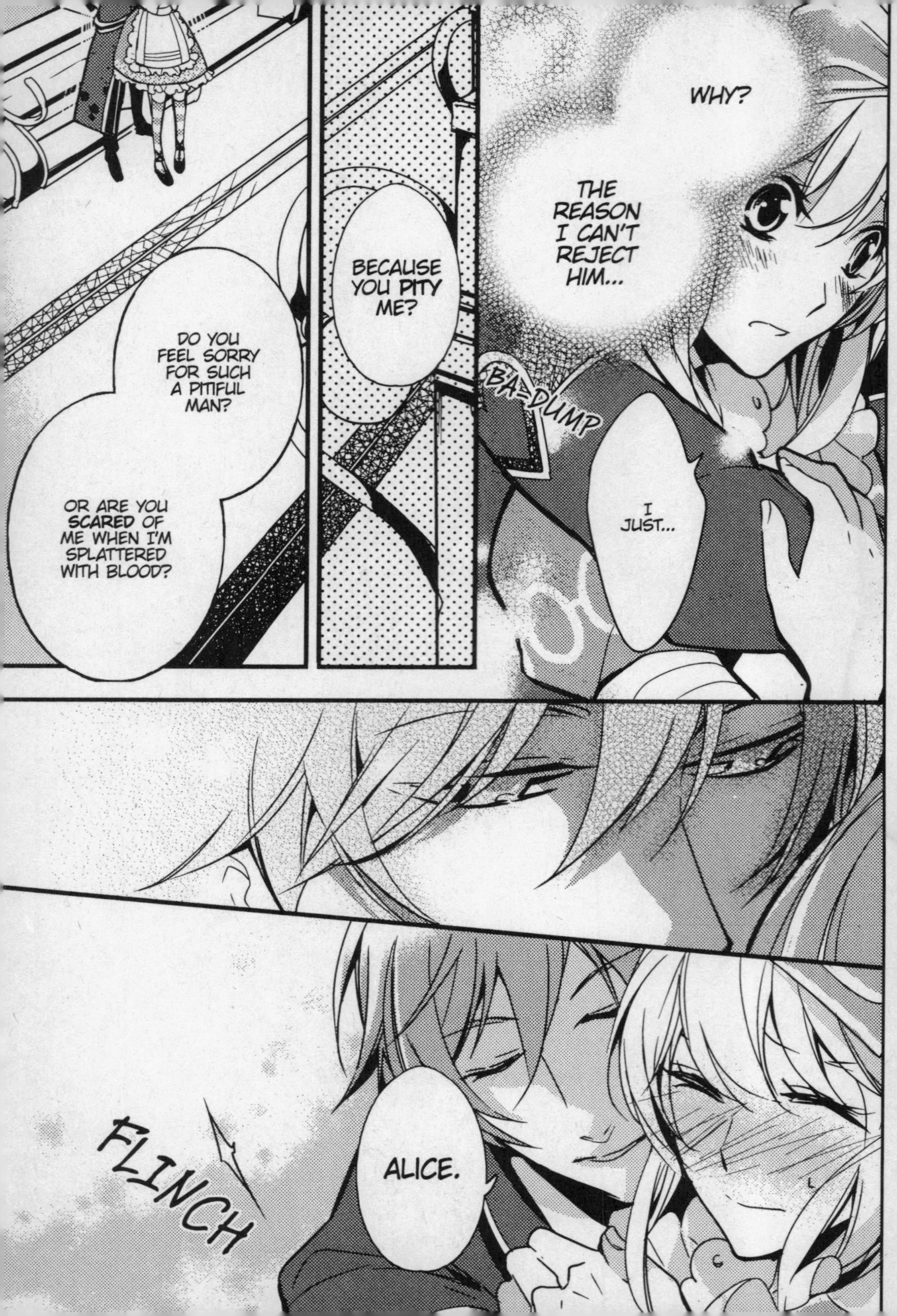
WHY?
THE REASON I CAN'T REJECT HIM...
BA-DUMP
I JUST...
BECAUSE YOU PITY ME?
DO YOU FEEL SORRY FOR SUCH A PITIFUL MAN?
OR ARE YOU SCARED OF ME WHEN I'M SPLATTERED WITH BLOOD?
ALICE.
FLINCH

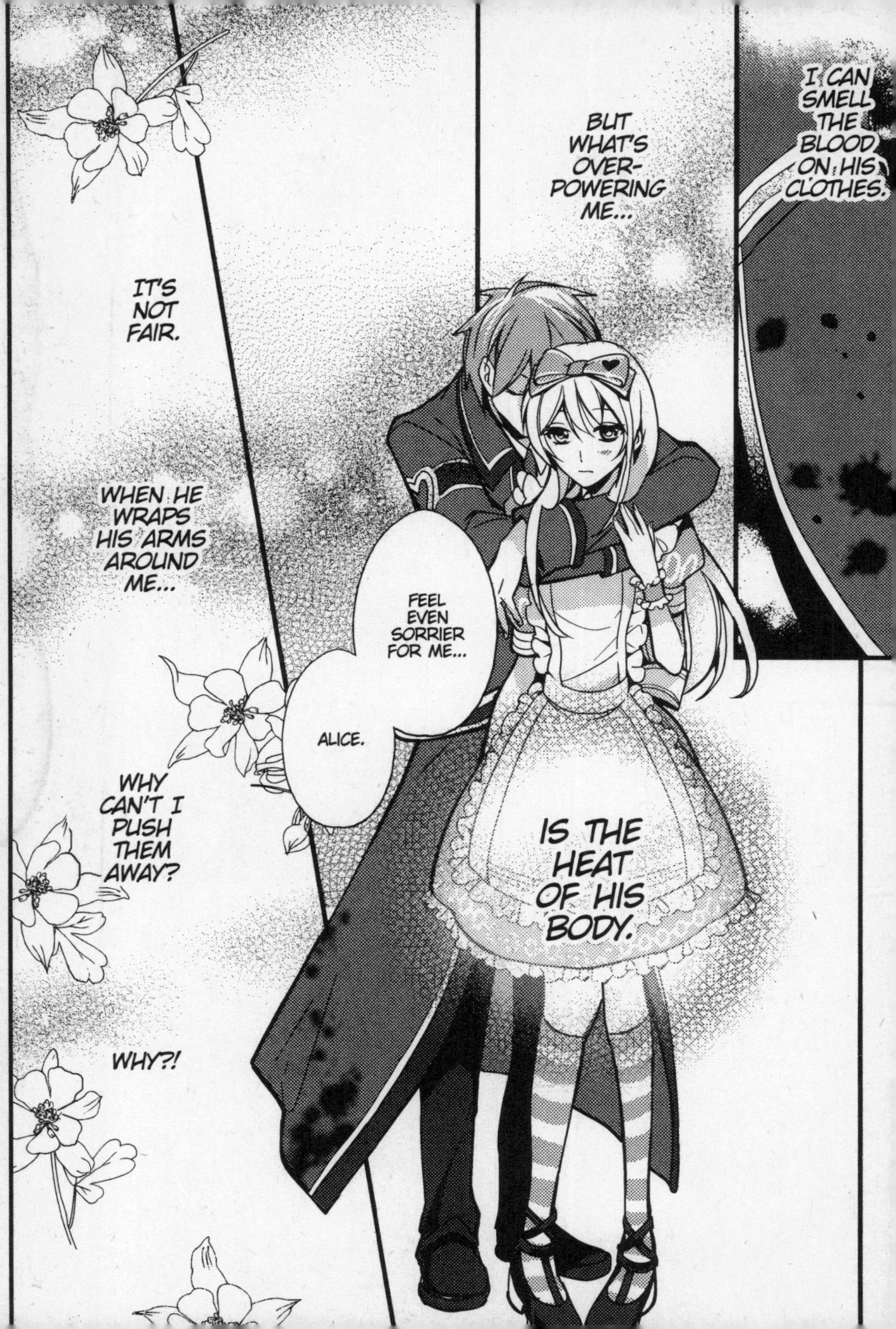
I CAN SMELL THE BLOOD ON HIS CLOTHES.
BUT WHAT'S OVER-POWERING ME...
IS THE HEAT OF HIS BODY.
FEEL EVEN SORRIER FOR ME...
ALICE.
IT'S NOT FAIR.
WHEN HE WRAPS HIS ARMS AROUND ME...
WHY CAN'T I PUSH THEM AWAY?
WHY?!

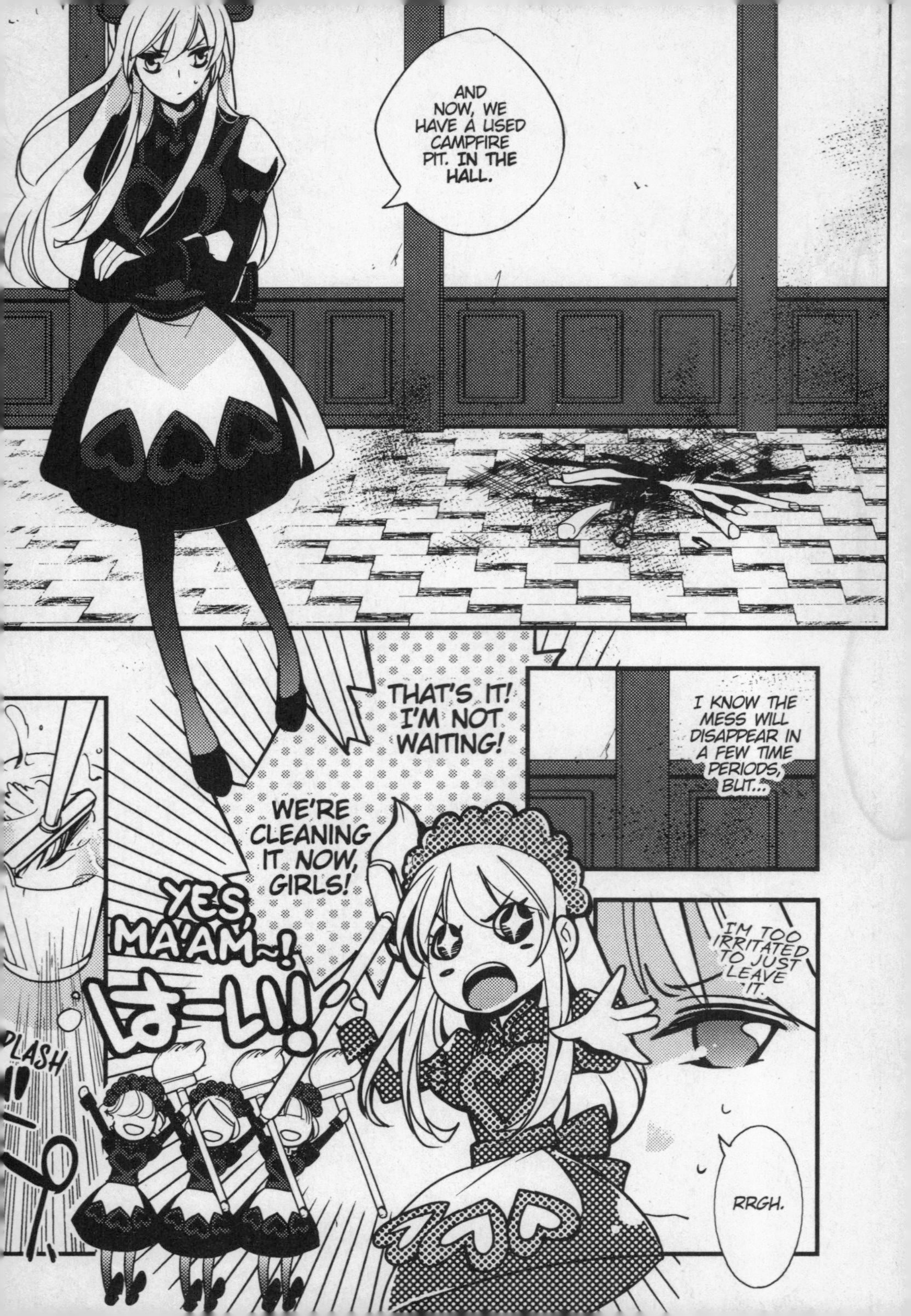
AND NOW, WE HAVE A USED CAMPFIRE PIT. IN THE HALL.
I KNOW THE MESS WILL DISAPPEAR IN A FEW TIME PERIODS, BUT...
I'M TOO IRRITATED TO JUST LEAVE IT.
RRGH.
THAT'S IT! I'M NOT WAITING!
WE'RE CLEANING IT NOW, GIRLS!
YES MA'AM~!
はーい!!
PLASH

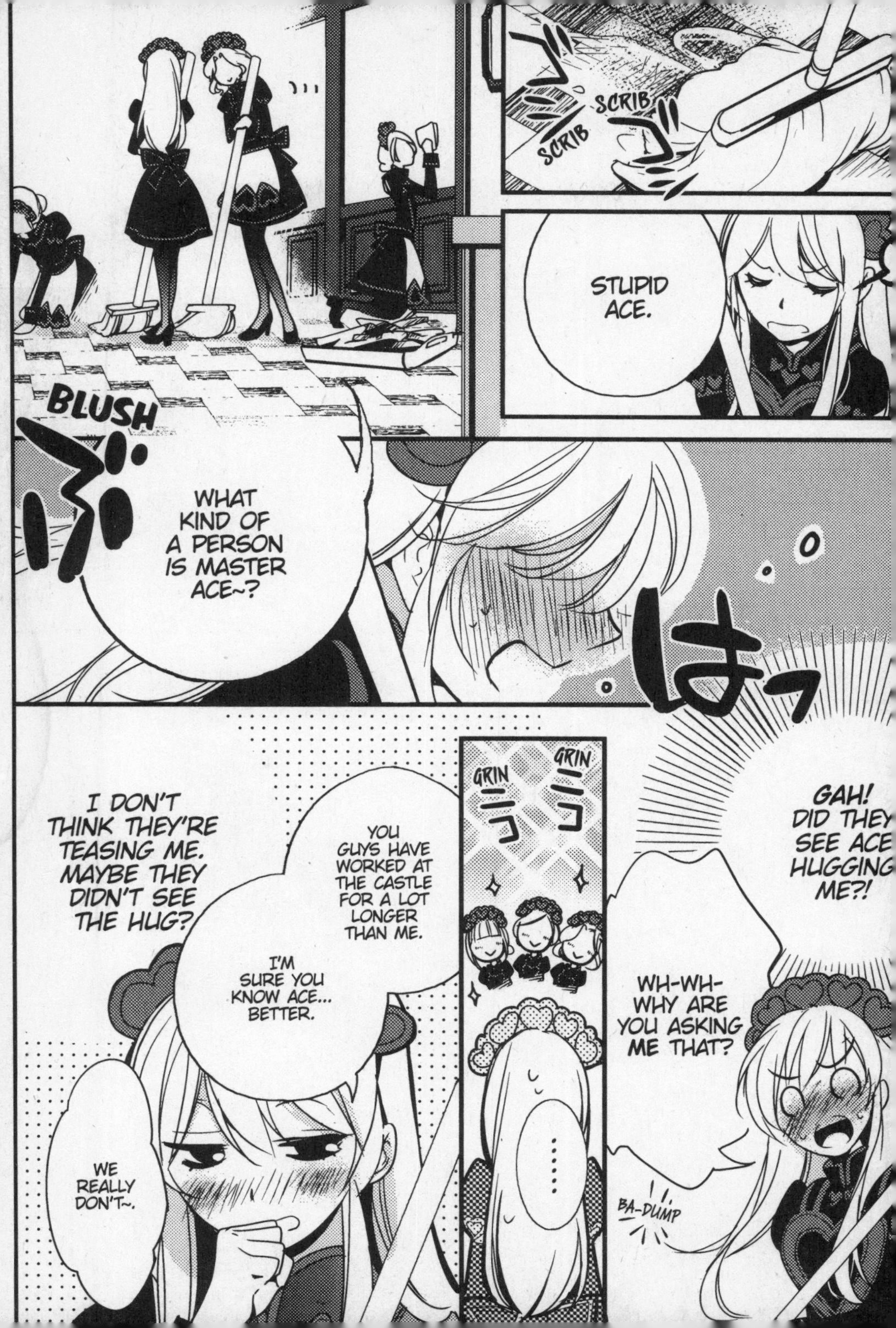
SCRIB
SCRIB
STUPID ACE.
...
はっ
WHAT KIND OF A PERSON IS MASTER ACE~?
BLUSH
GAH! DID THEY SEE ACE HUGGING ME?!
WH-WH-WHY ARE YOU ASKING ME THAT?
BA-DUMP
GRIN
GRIN
......
YOU GUYS HAVE WORKED AT THE CASTLE FOR A LOT LONGER THAN ME.
I'M SURE YOU KNOW ACE... BETTER.
I DON'T THINK THEY'RE TEASING ME. MAYBE THEY DIDN'T SEE THE HUG?
WE REALLY DON'T~.

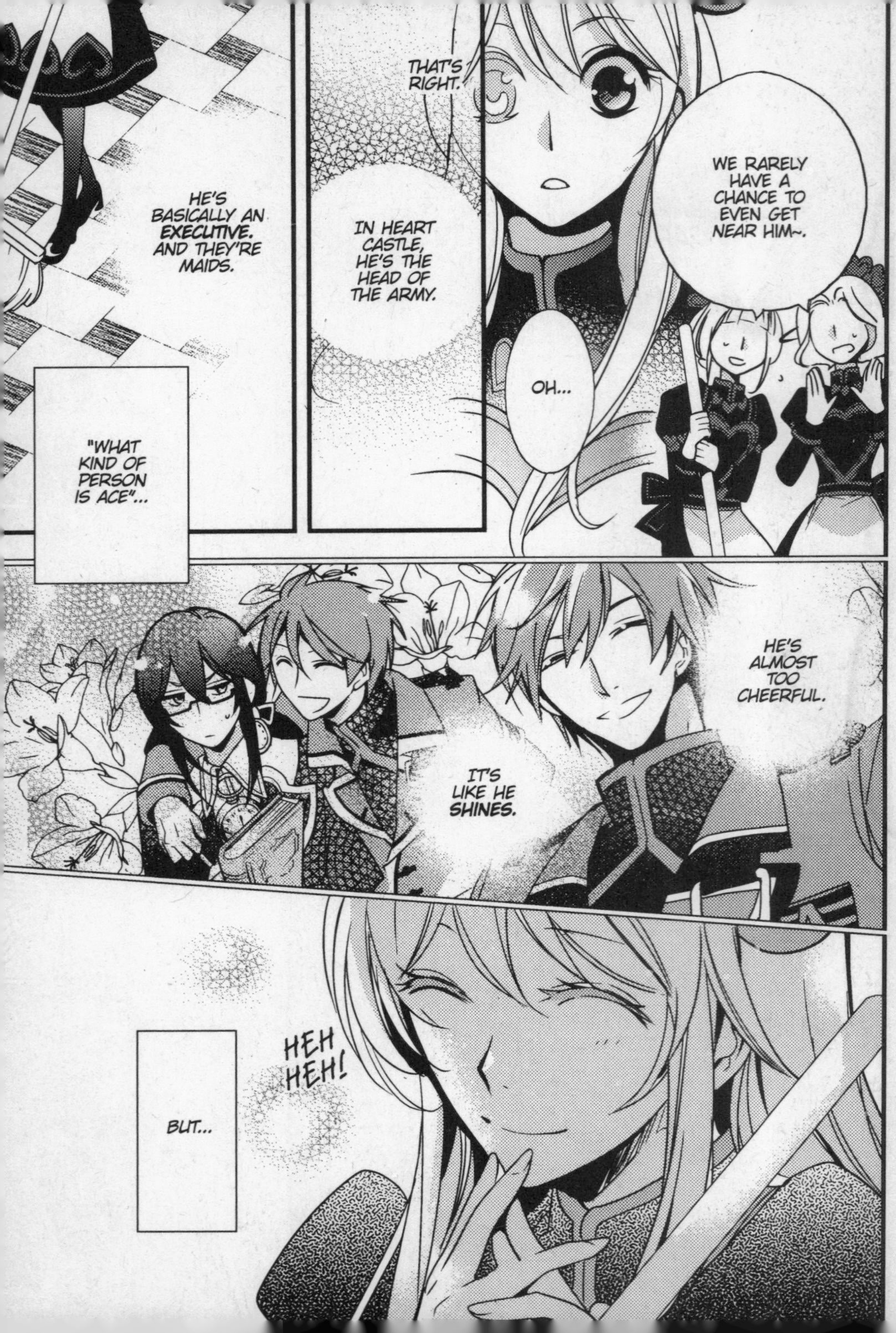

WE RARELY HAVE A CHANCE TO EVEN GET NEAR HIM~.
OH...
THAT'S RIGHT.
IN HEART CASTLE, HE'S THE HEAD OF THE ARMY.
HE'S BASICALLY AN **EXECUTIVE.** AND THEY'RE MAIDS.
"WHAT KIND OF PERSON IS ACE"...
HE'S ALMOST TOO CHEERFUL.
IT'S LIKE HE **SHINES.**
HEH HEH!
BUT...

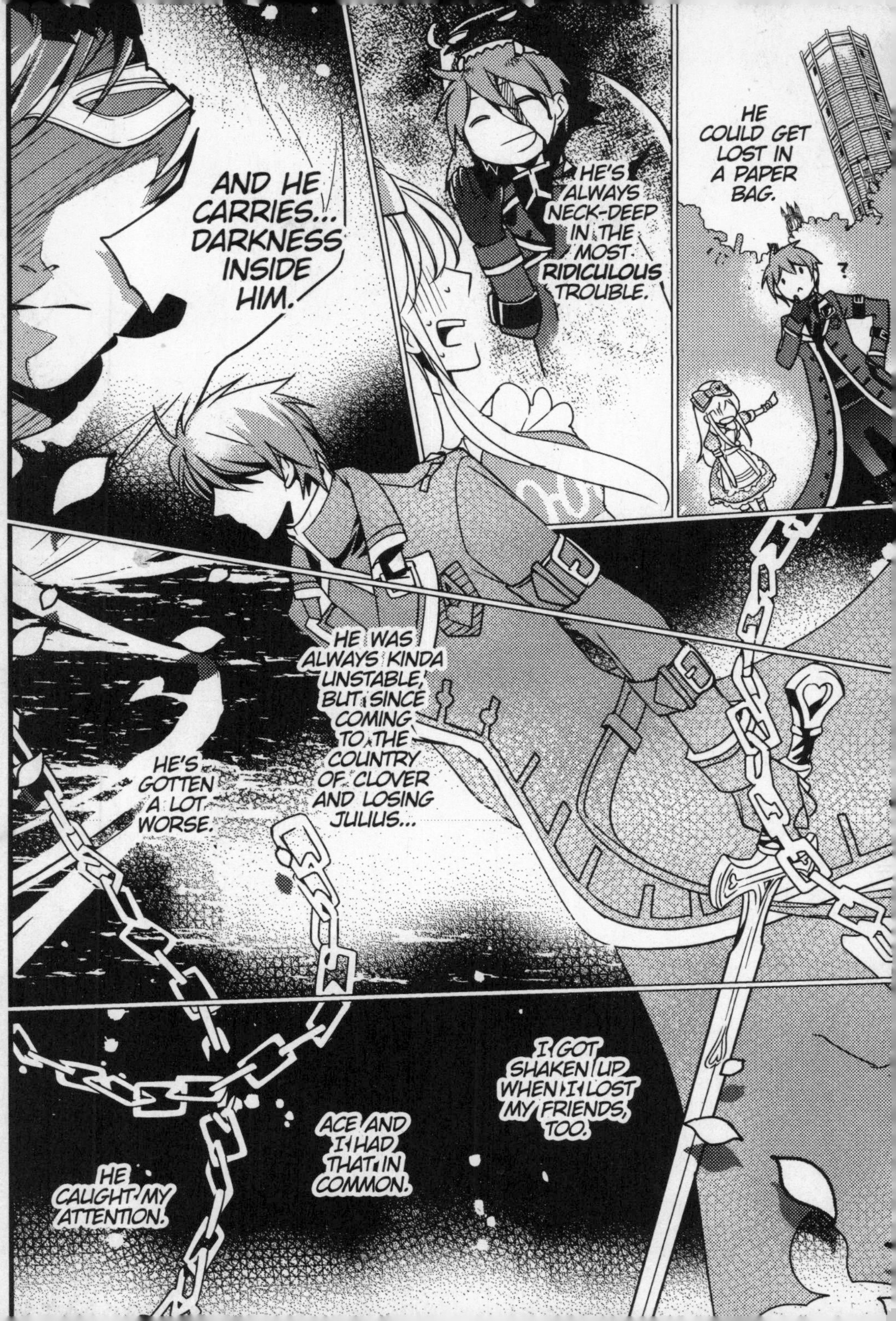
HE COULD GET LOST IN A PAPER BAG.
HE'S ALWAYS NECK-DEEP IN THE MOST RIDICULOUS TROUBLE.
AND HE CARRIES... DARKNESS INSIDE HIM.
HE WAS ALWAYS KINDA UNSTABLE, BUT SINCE COMING TO THE COUNTRY OF CLOVER AND LOSING JULIUS...
HE'S GOTTEN A LOT WORSE.
I GOT SHAKEN UP WHEN I LOST MY FRIENDS, TOO.
ACE AND I HAD THAT IN COMMON.
HE CAUGHT MY ATTENTION.

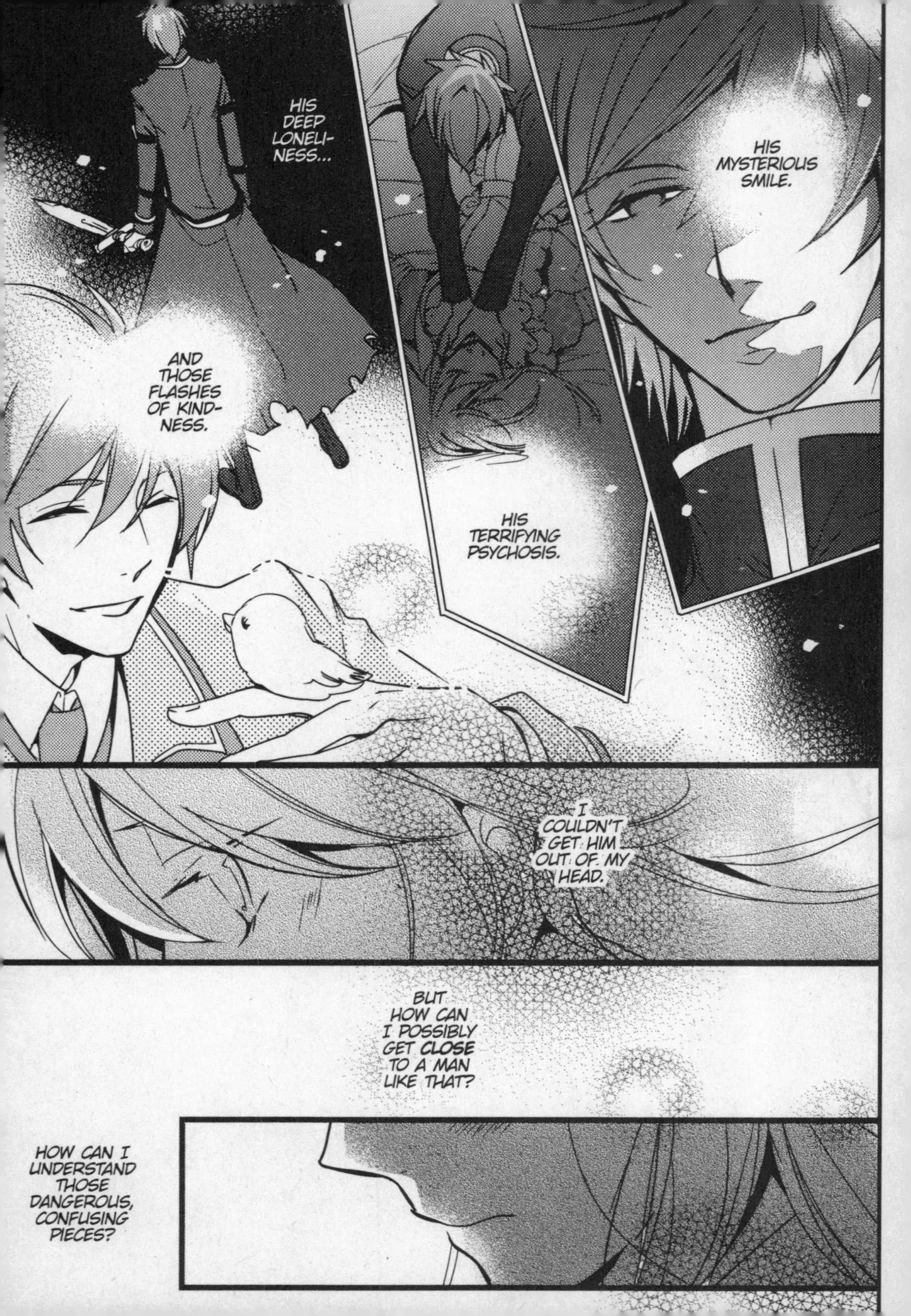
HIS MYSTERIOUS SMILE.
HIS TERRIFYING PSYCHOSIS.
HIS DEEP LONELI-NESS...
AND THOSE FLASHES OF KIND-NESS.
I COULDN'T GET HIM OUT OF MY HEAD.
BUT HOW CAN I POSSIBLY GET CLOSE TO A MAN LIKE THAT?
HOW CAN I UNDERSTAND THOSE DANGEROUS, CONFUSING PIECES?

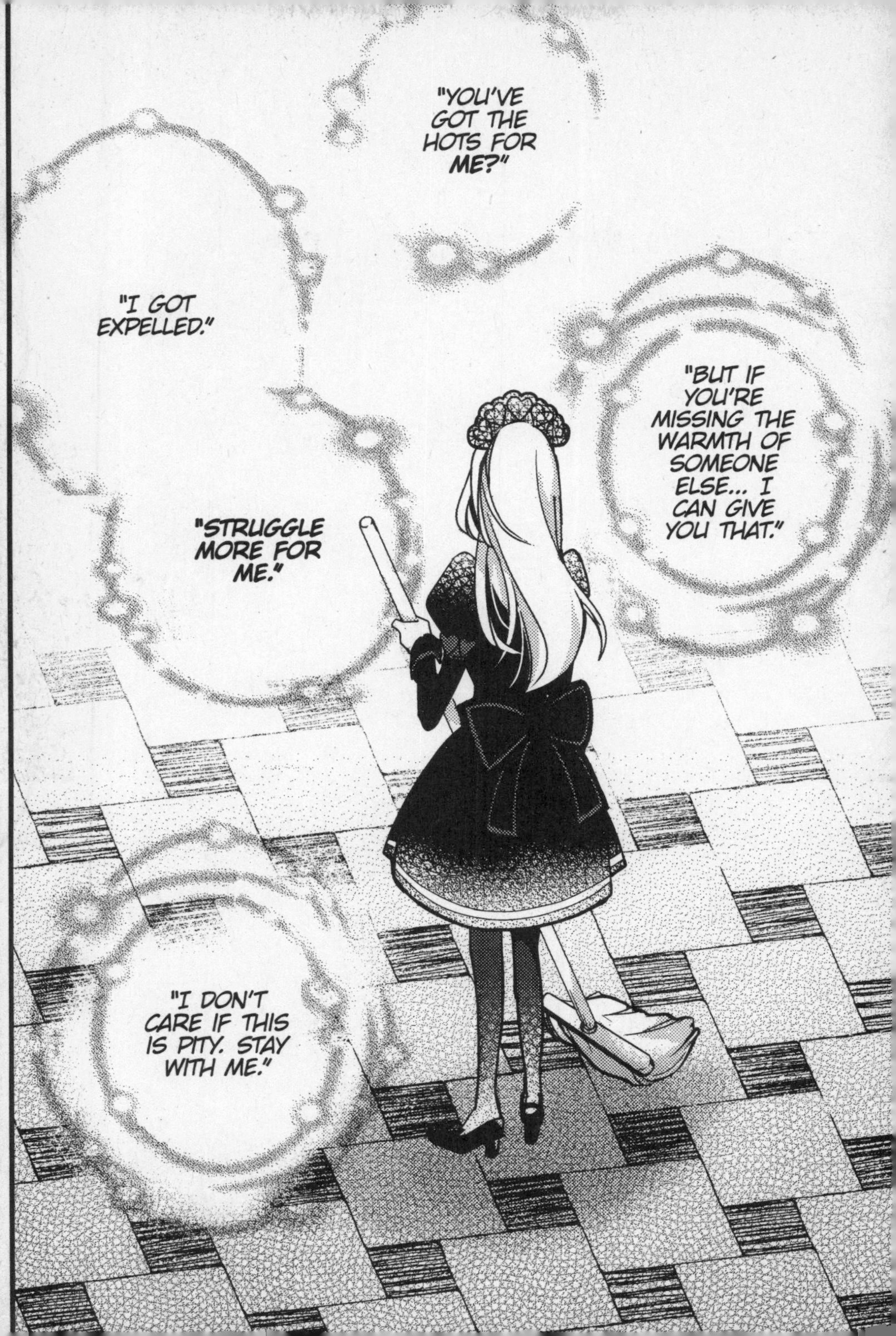
"YOU'VE GOT THE HOTS FOR ME?"
"BUT IF YOU'RE MISSING THE WARMTH OF SOMEONE ELSE... I CAN GIVE YOU THAT."
"I GOT EXPELLED."
"STRUGGLE MORE FOR ME."
"I DON'T CARE IF THIS IS PITY. STAY WITH ME."

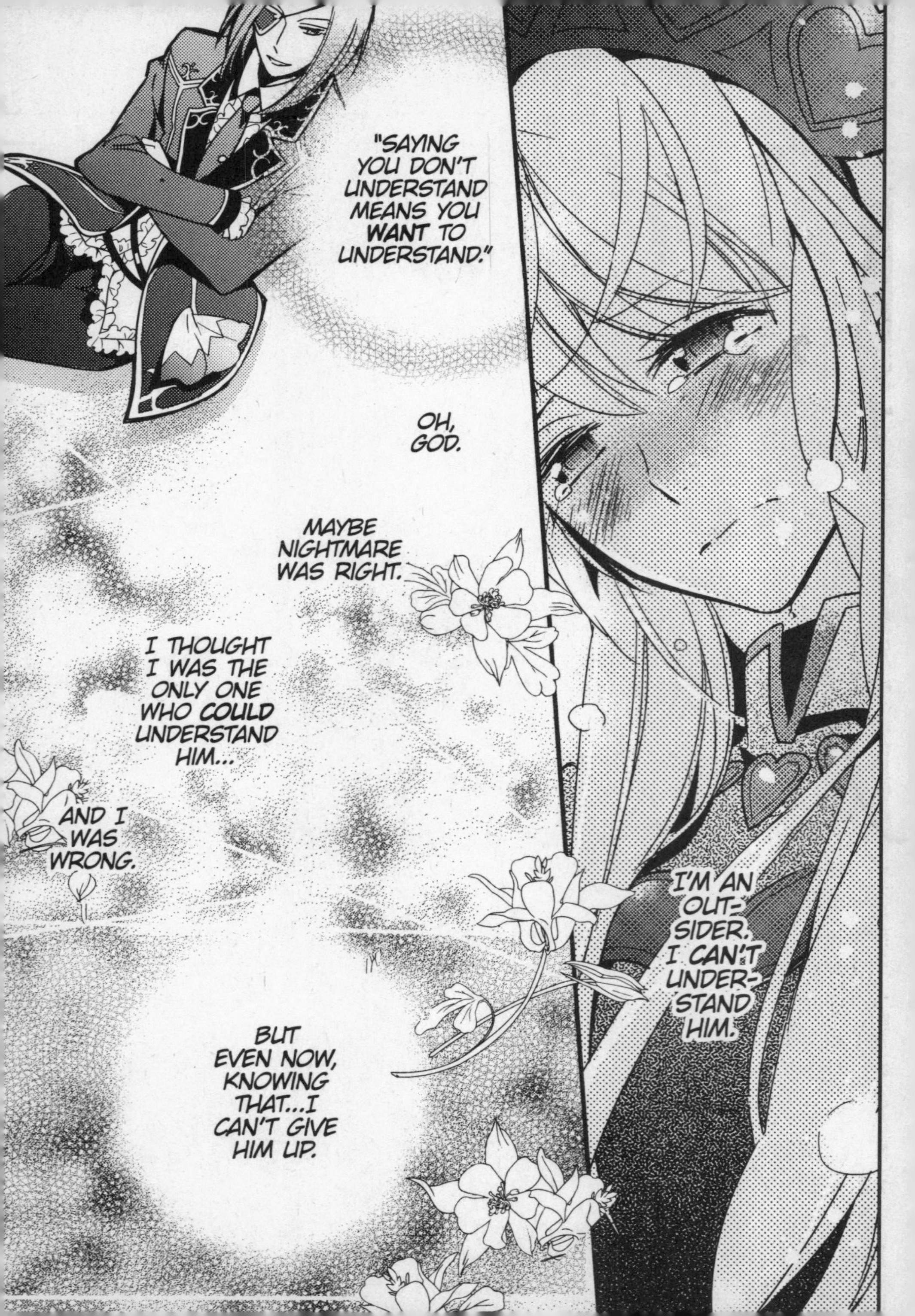
"SAYING YOU DON'T UNDERSTAND MEANS YOU WANT TO UNDERSTAND."
OH, GOD.
MAYBE NIGHTMARE WAS RIGHT.
I THOUGHT I WAS THE ONLY ONE WHO COULD UNDERSTAND HIM...
AND I WAS WRONG.
I'M AN OUTSIDER. I CAN'T UNDERSTAND HIM.
BUT EVEN NOW, KNOWING THAT...I CAN'T GIVE HIM UP.

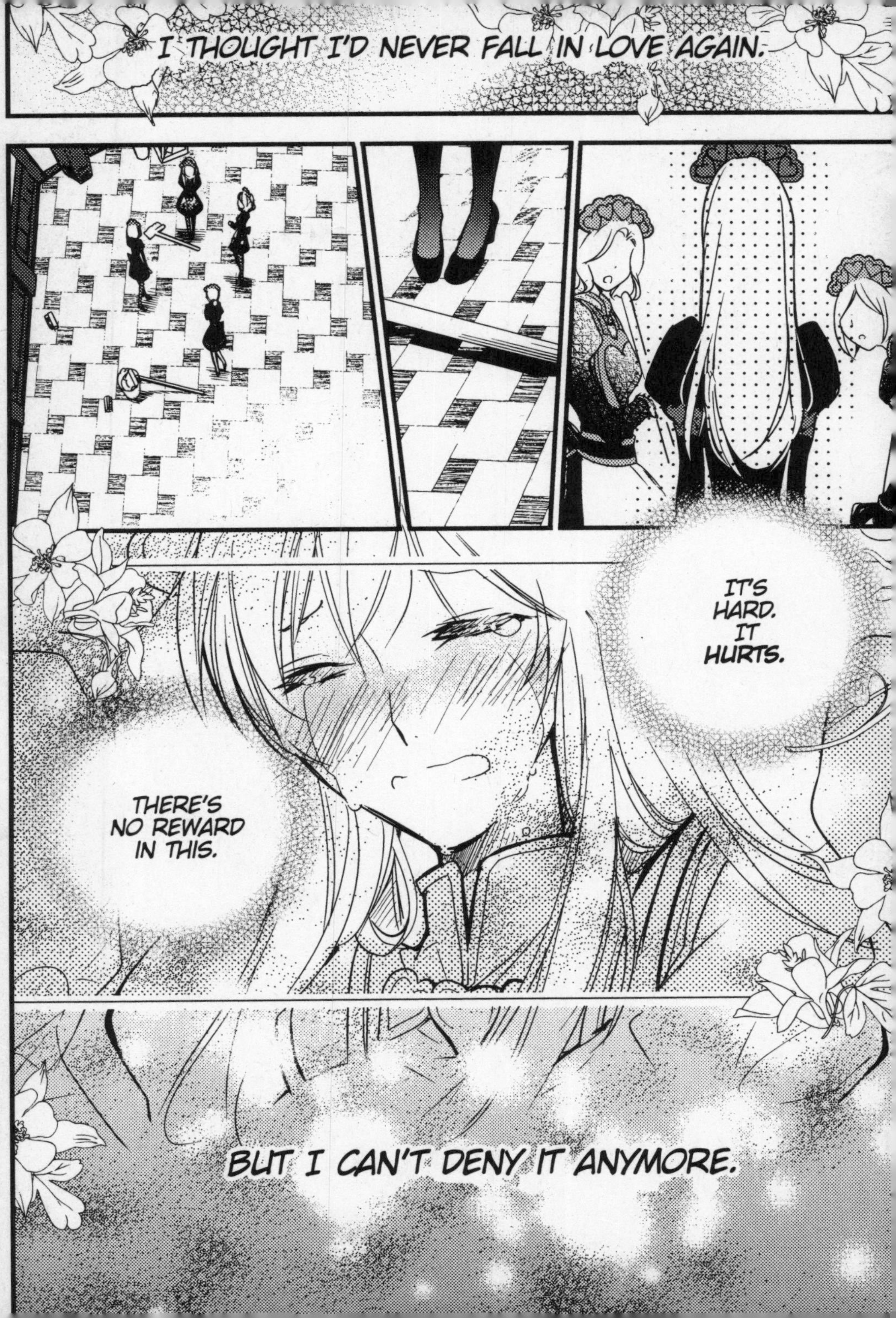
I THOUGHT I'D NEVER FALL IN LOVE AGAIN.
IT'S HARD. IT HURTS.
THERE'S NO REWARD IN THIS.
BUT I CAN'T DENY IT ANYMORE.

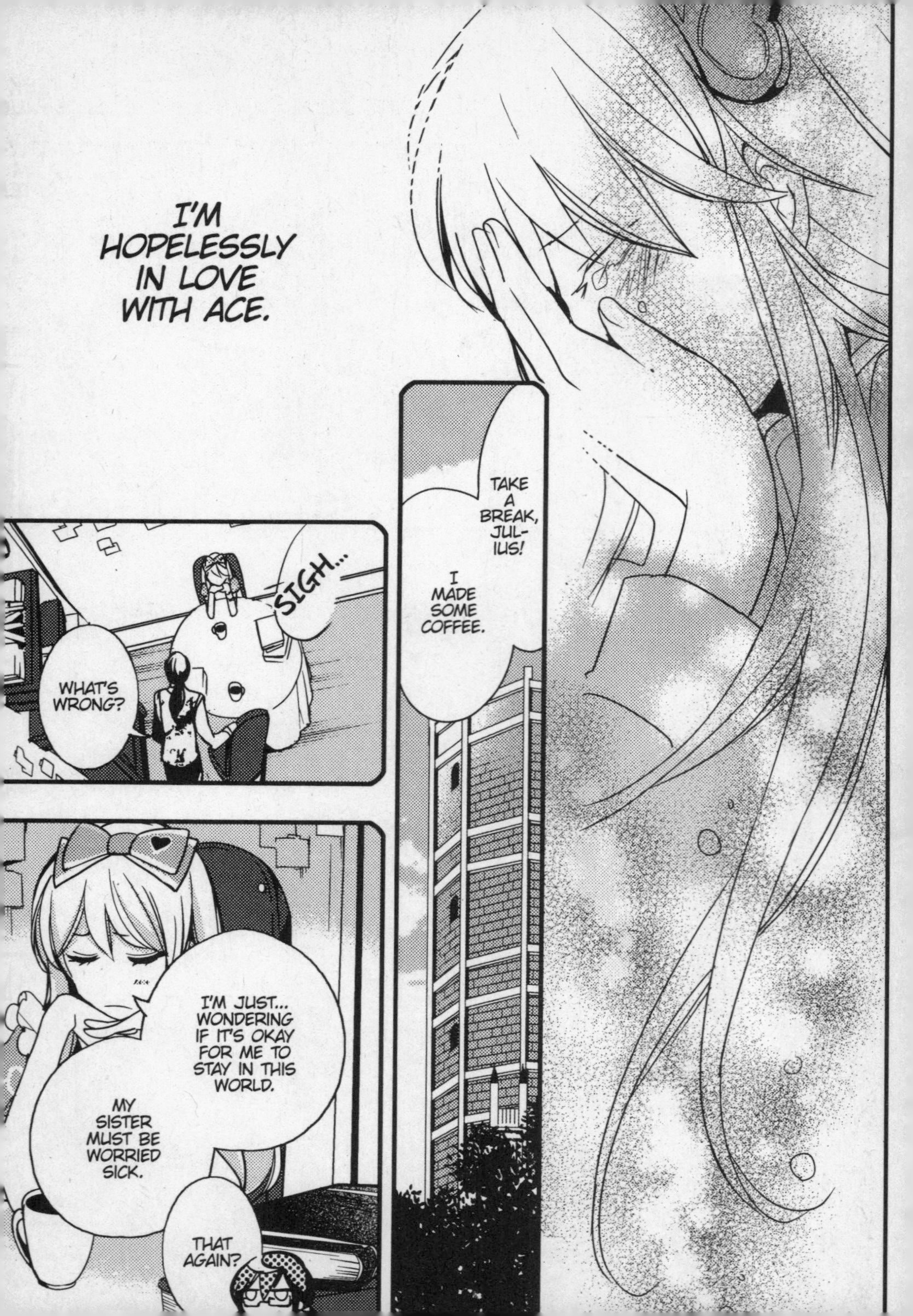
I'M HOPELESSLY IN LOVE WITH ACE.
TAKE A BREAK, JULIUS!
I MADE SOME COFFEE.
SIGH...
WHAT'S WRONG?
I'M JUST... WONDERING IF IT'S OKAY FOR ME TO STAY IN THIS WORLD.
MY SISTER MUST BE WORRIED SICK.
THAT AGAIN?

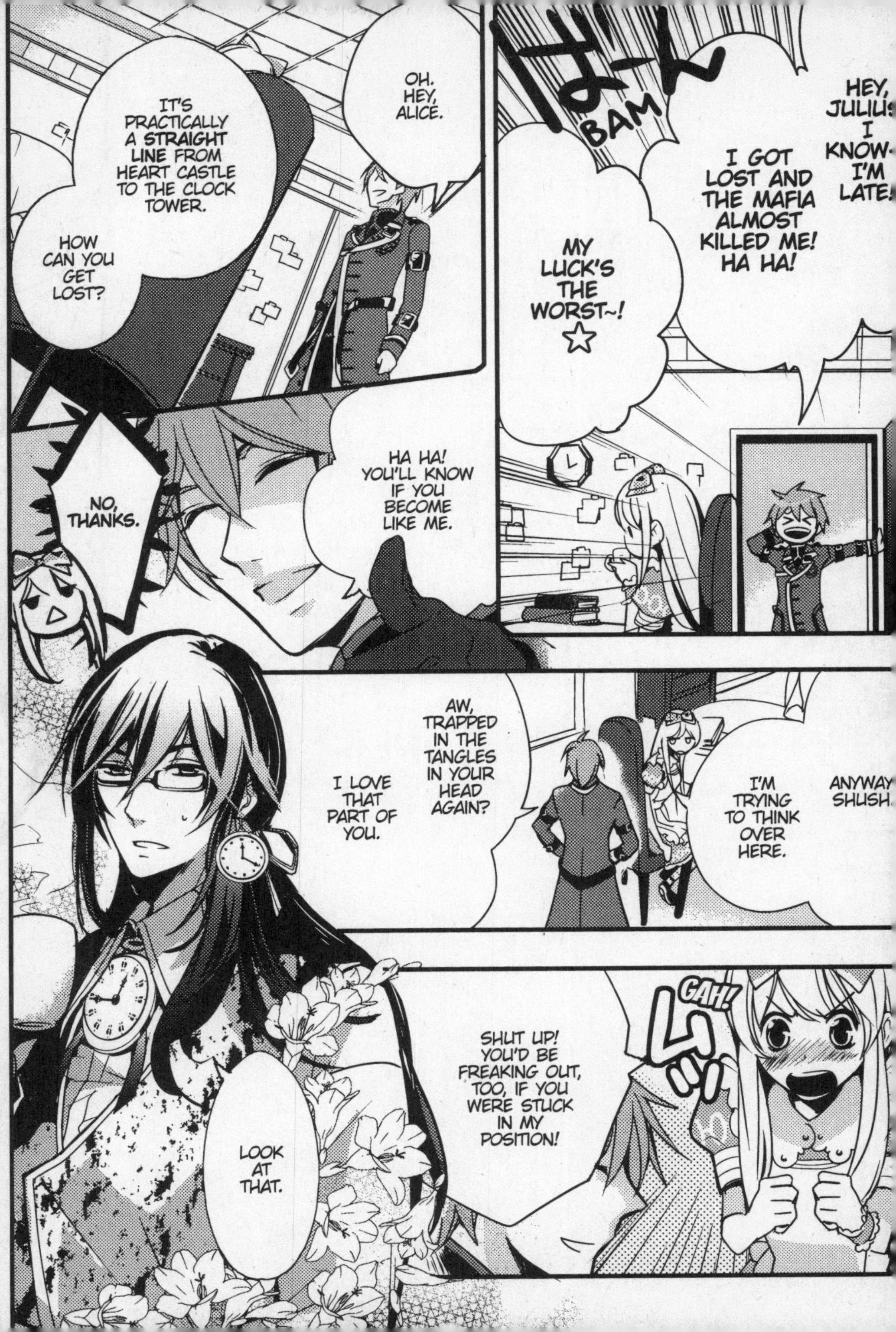
BAM
HEY, JULIUS I KNOW- I'M LATE!
I GOT LOST AND THE MAFIA ALMOST KILLED ME! HA HA!
MY LUCK'S THE WORST~! ☆
OH. HEY, ALICE.
IT'S PRACTICALLY A STRAIGHT LINE FROM HEART CASTLE TO THE CLOCK TOWER.
HOW CAN YOU GET LOST?
HA HA! YOU'LL KNOW IF YOU BECOME LIKE ME.
NO, THANKS.
ANYWAY SHUSH.
I'M TRYING TO THINK OVER HERE.
AW, TRAPPED IN THE TANGLES IN YOUR HEAD AGAIN?
I LOVE THAT PART OF YOU.
GAH!
SHUT UP! YOU'D BE FREAKING OUT, TOO, IF YOU WERE STUCK IN MY POSITION!
LOOK AT THAT.

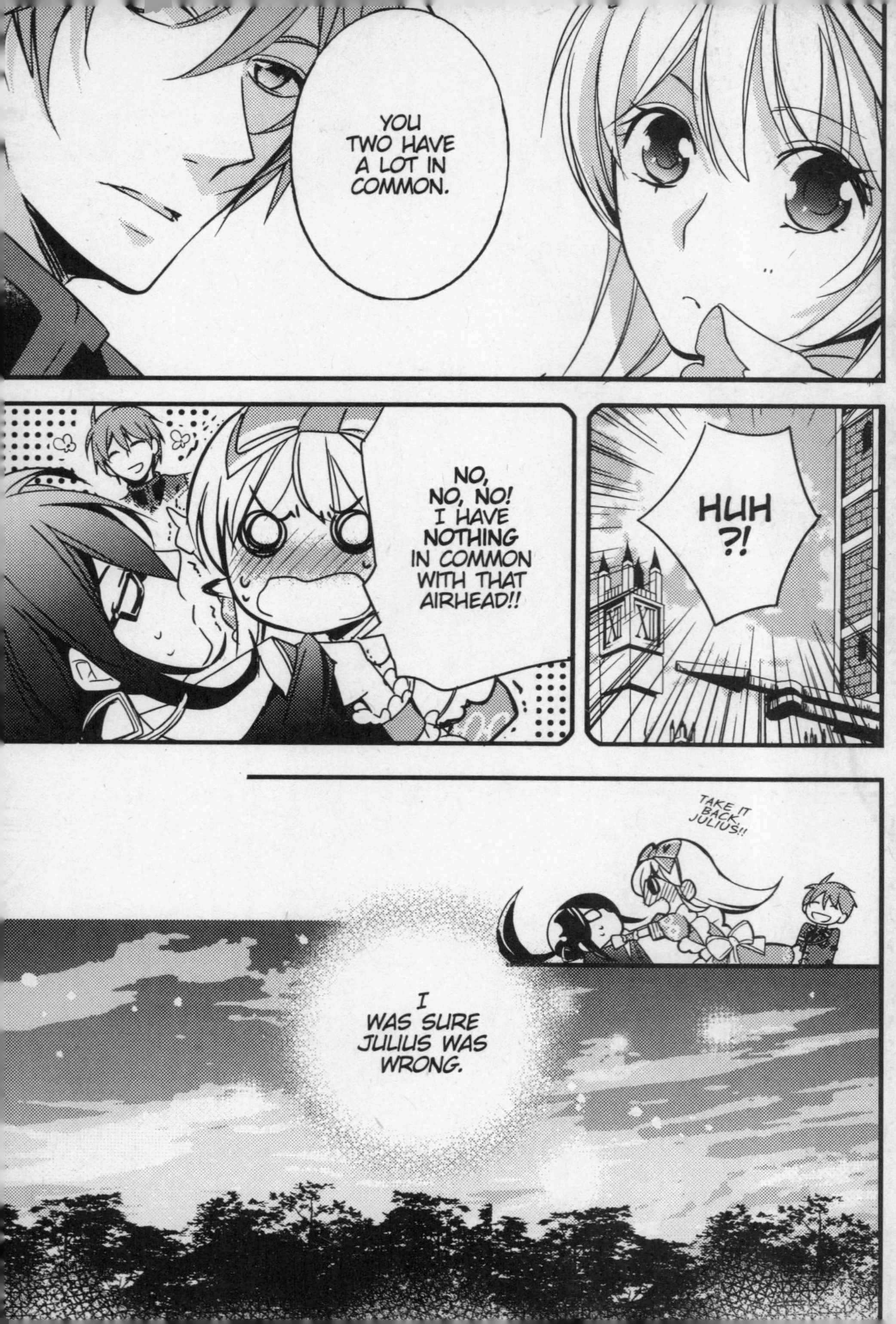
YOU TWO HAVE A LOT IN COMMON.
HUH ?!
NO, NO, NO! I HAVE NOTHING IN COMMON WITH THAT AIRHEAD!!
TAKE IT BACK, JULIUS!!
I WAS SURE JULIUS WAS WRONG.

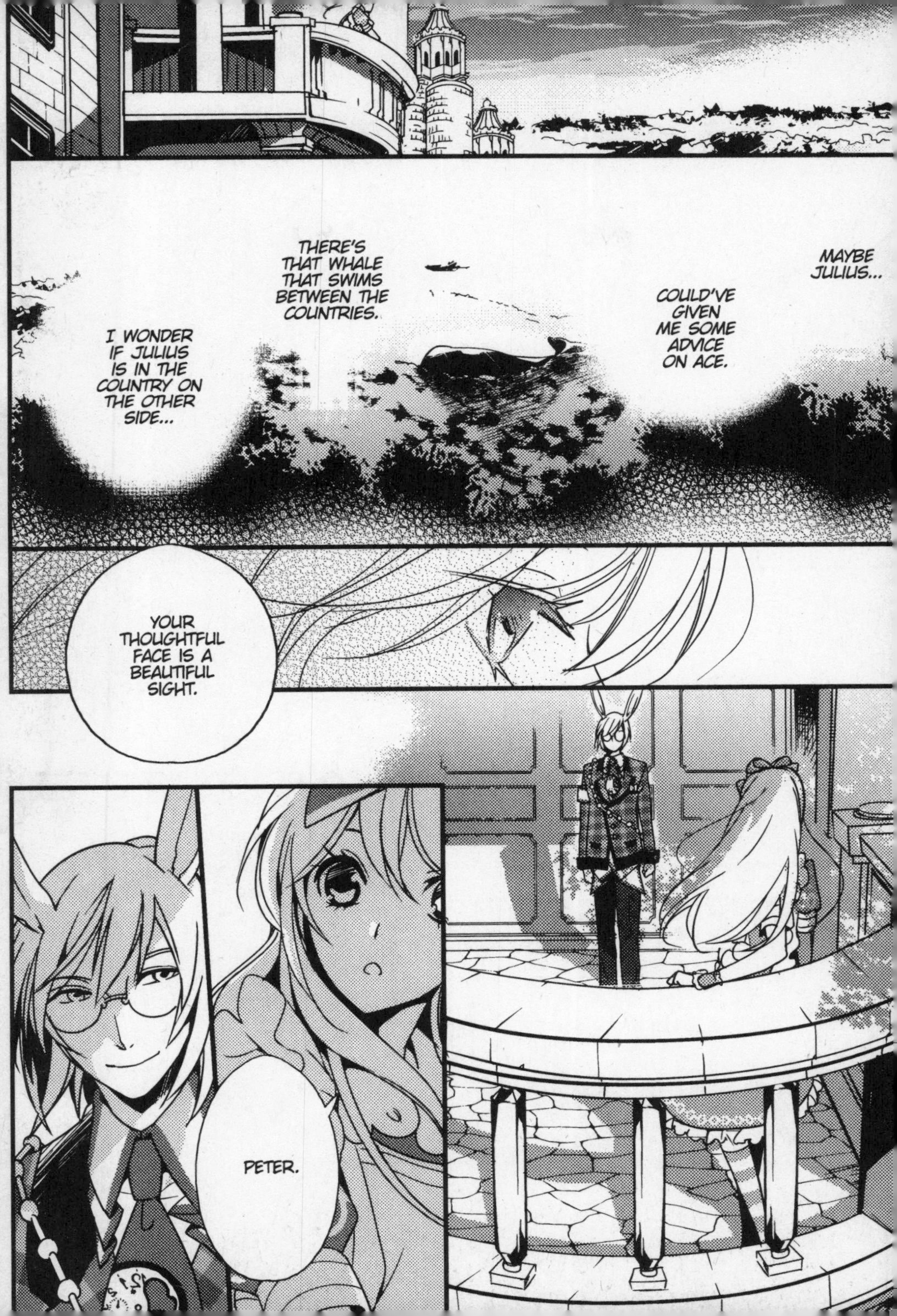
MAYBE JULIUS...
COULD'VE GIVEN ME SOME ADVICE ON ACE.
THERE'S THAT WHALE THAT SWIMS BETWEEN THE COUNTRIES.
I WONDER IF JULIUS IS IN THE COUNTRY ON THE OTHER SIDE...
YOUR THOUGHTFUL FACE IS A BEAUTIFUL SIGHT.
PETER.

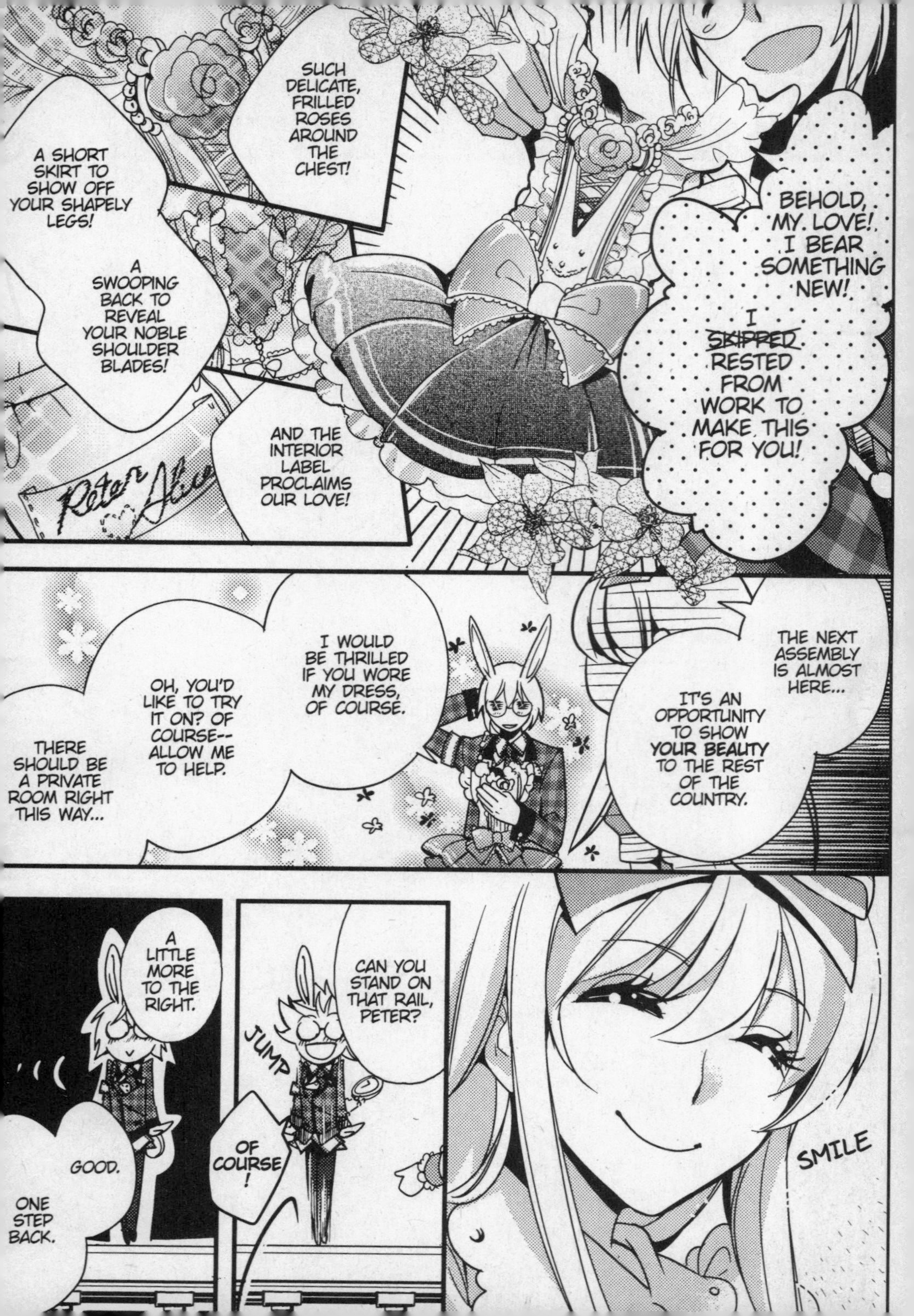
BEHOLD, MY LOVE! I BEAR SOMETHING NEW!
I ~~SKIPPED~~ RESTED FROM WORK TO MAKE THIS FOR YOU!
SUCH DELICATE, FRILLED ROSES AROUND THE CHEST!
A SHORT SKIRT TO SHOW OFF YOUR SHAPELY LEGS!
A SWOOPING BACK TO REVEAL YOUR NOBLE SHOULDER BLADES!
AND THE INTERIOR LABEL PROCLAIMS OUR LOVE!
THE NEXT ASSEMBLY IS ALMOST HERE...
IT'S AN OPPORTUNITY TO SHOW **YOUR BEAUTY** TO THE REST OF THE COUNTRY.
I WOULD BE THRILLED IF YOU WORE MY DRESS, OF COURSE.
OH, YOU'D LIKE TO TRY IT ON? OF COURSE-- ALLOW ME TO HELP.
THERE SHOULD BE A PRIVATE ROOM RIGHT THIS WAY...
SMILE
CAN YOU STAND ON THAT RAIL, PETER?
JUMP
OF COURSE!
A LITTLE MORE TO THE RIGHT.
GOOD.
ONE STEP BACK.

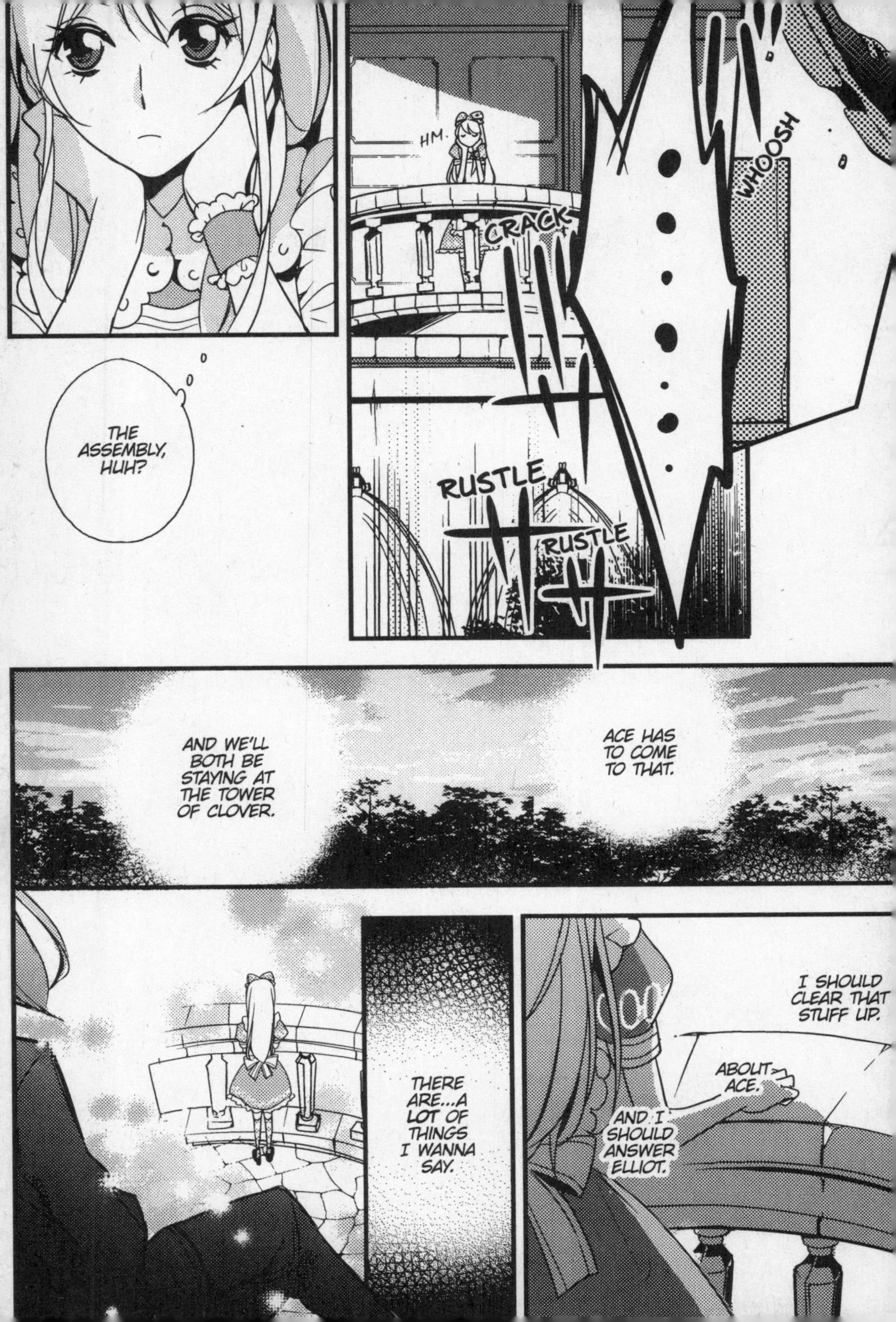
WHOOSH
HM.
CRACK
RUSTLE
RUSTLE
THE ASSEMBLY, HUH?
ACE HAS TO COME TO THAT.
AND WE'LL BOTH BE STAYING AT THE TOWER OF CLOVER.
I SHOULD CLEAR THAT STUFF UP.
ABOUT ACE.
AND I SHOULD ANSWER ELLIOT.
THERE ARE...A LOT OF THINGS I WANNA SAY.

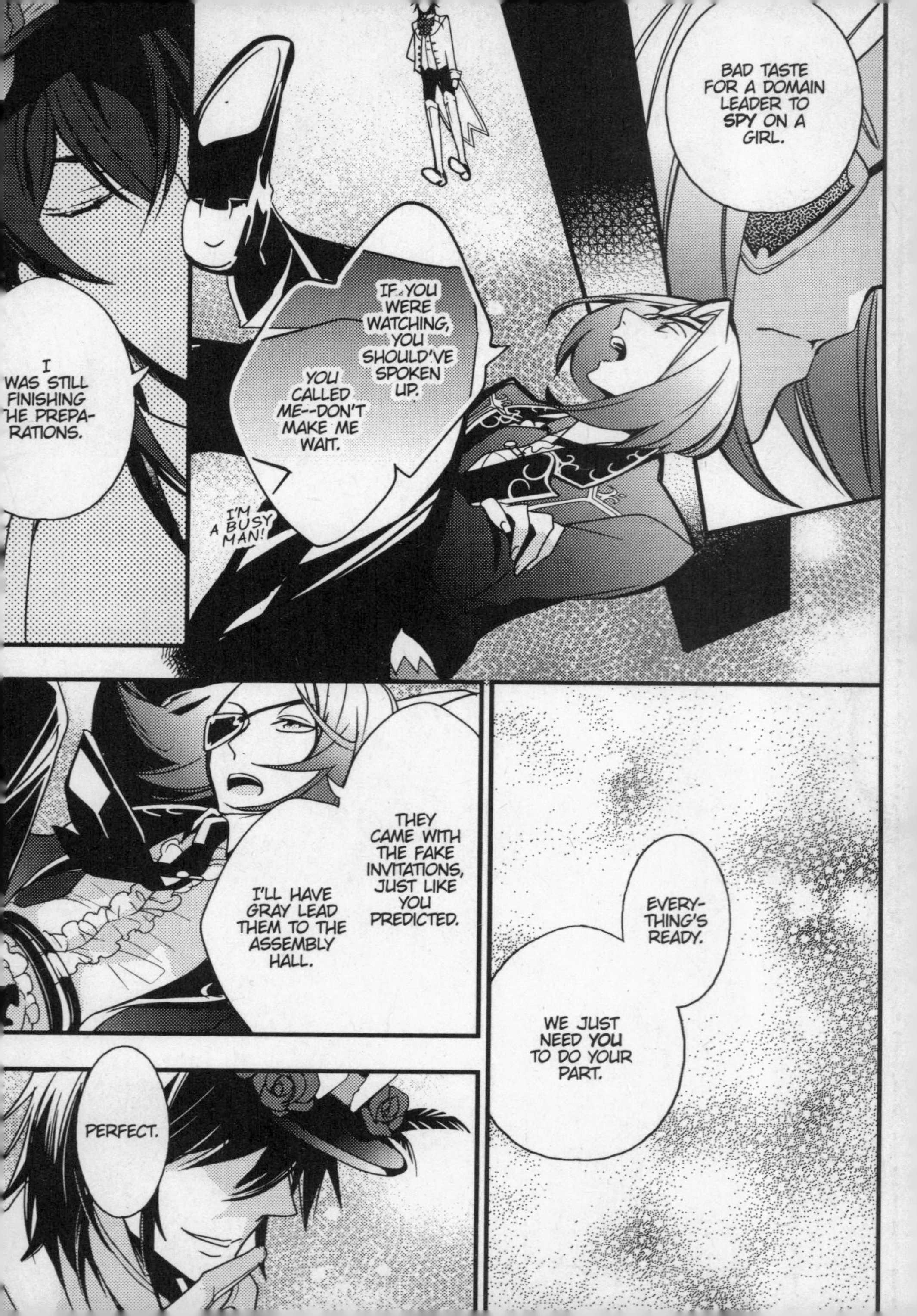
BAD TASTE FOR A DOMAIN LEADER TO SPY ON A GIRL.
IF YOU WERE WATCHING, YOU SHOULD'VE SPOKEN UP.
YOU CALLED ME--DON'T MAKE ME WAIT.
I'M A BUSY MAN!
I WAS STILL FINISHING HE PREPA-RATIONS.
EVERY-THING'S READY.
WE JUST NEED YOU TO DO YOUR PART.
THEY CAME WITH THE FAKE INVITATIONS, JUST LIKE YOU PREDICTED.
I'LL HAVE GRAY LEAD THEM TO THE ASSEMBLY HALL.
PERFECT.

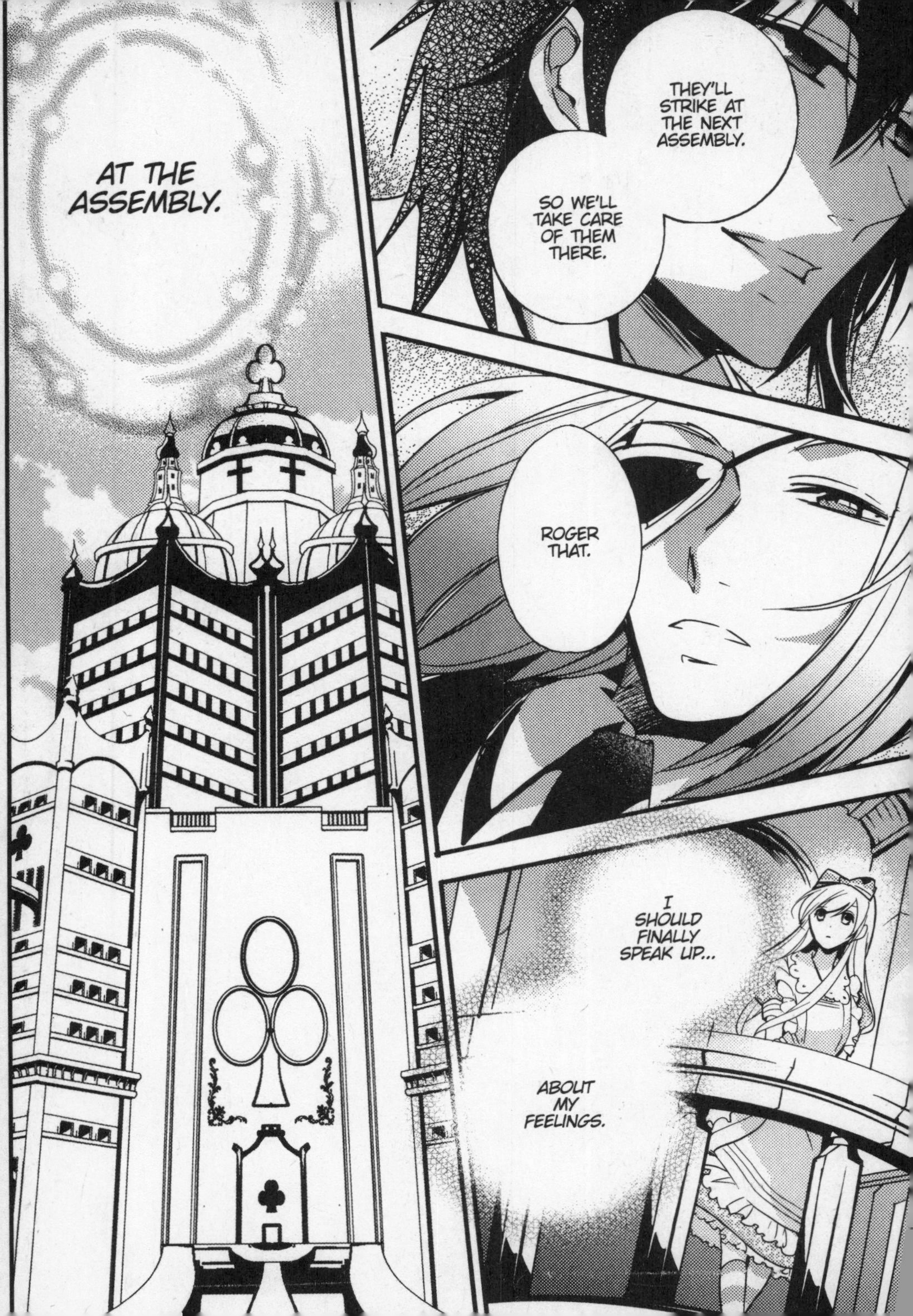
THEY'LL STRIKE AT THE NEXT ASSEMBLY.
SO WE'LL TAKE CARE OF THEM THERE.
ROGER THAT.
I SHOULD FINALLY SPEAK UP...
ABOUT MY FEELINGS.
AT THE ASSEMBLY.

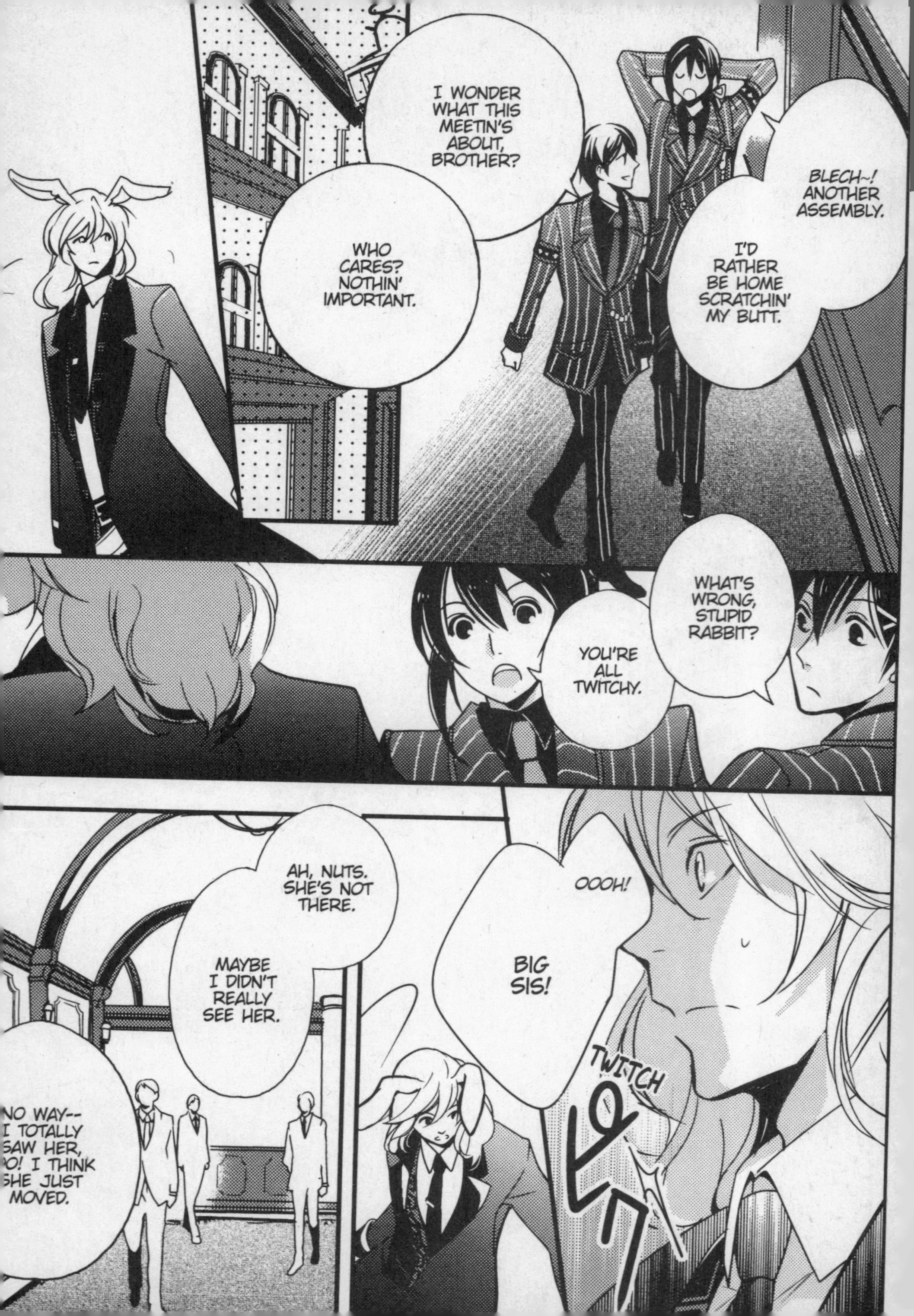
BLECH~! ANOTHER ASSEMBLY.
I'D RATHER BE HOME SCRATCHIN' MY BUTT.
I WONDER WHAT THIS MEETIN'S ABOUT, BROTHER?
WHO CARES? NOTHIN' IMPORTANT.
WHAT'S WRONG, STUPID RABBIT?
YOU'RE ALL TWITCHY.
OOOH!
BIG SIS!
TWITCH
AH, NUTS. SHE'S NOT THERE.
MAYBE I DIDN'T REALLY SEE HER.
NO WAY-- I TOTALLY SAW HER, TOO! I THINK SHE JUST MOVED.

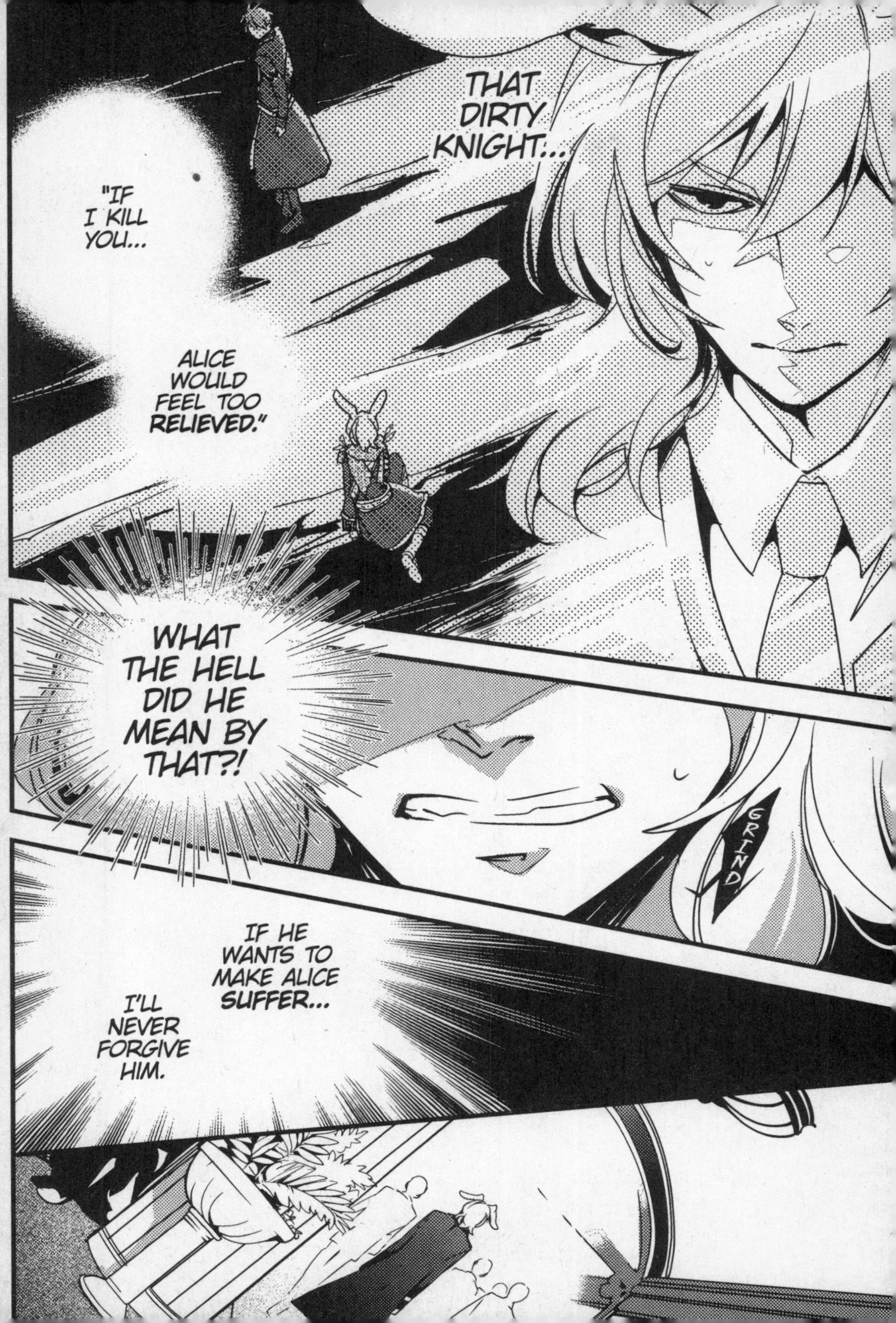
THAT DIRTY KNIGHT...
"IF I KILL YOU...
ALICE WOULD FEEL TOO RELIEVED."
WHAT THE HELL DID HE MEAN BY THAT?!
GRIND
IF HE WANTS TO MAKE ALICE SUFFER...
I'LL NEVER FORGIVE HIM.

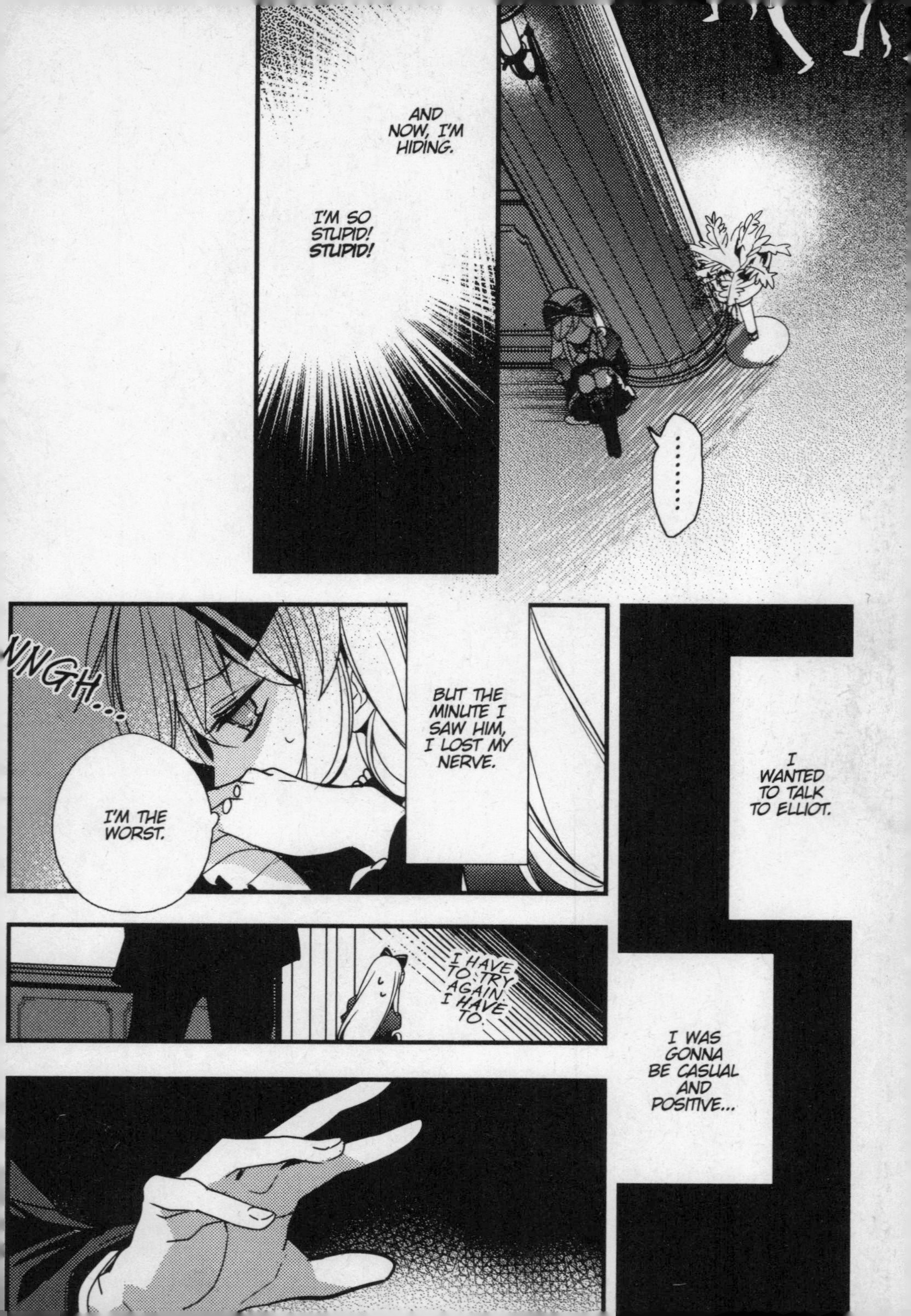
......
AND NOW, I'M HIDING.
I'M SO STUPID! STUPID!
I WANTED TO TALK TO ELLIOT.
I WAS GONNA BE CASUAL AND POSITIVE...
BUT THE MINUTE I SAW HIM, I LOST MY NERVE.
NNGH...
I'M THE WORST.
I HAVE TO TRY AGAIN. I HAVE TO.

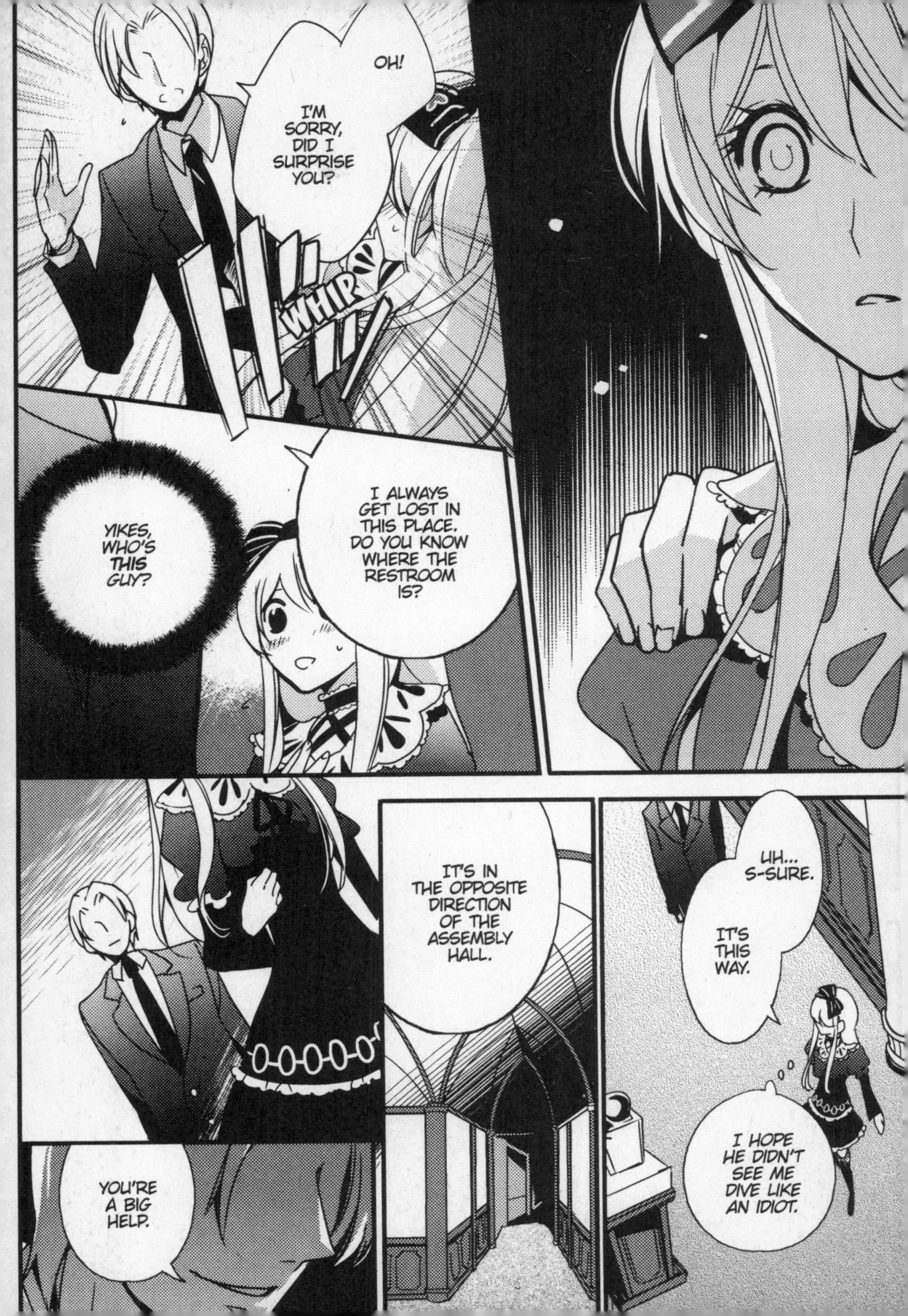
OH!
I'M SORRY, DID I SURPRISE YOU?
WHIP
I ALWAYS GET LOST IN THIS PLACE. DO YOU KNOW WHERE THE RESTROOM IS?
YIKES, WHO'S THIS GUY?
UH... S-SURE.
IT'S THIS WAY.
I HOPE HE DIDN'T SEE ME DIVE LIKE AN IDIOT.
IT'S IN THE OPPOSITE DIRECTION OF THE ASSEMBLY HALL.
YOU'RE A BIG HELP.

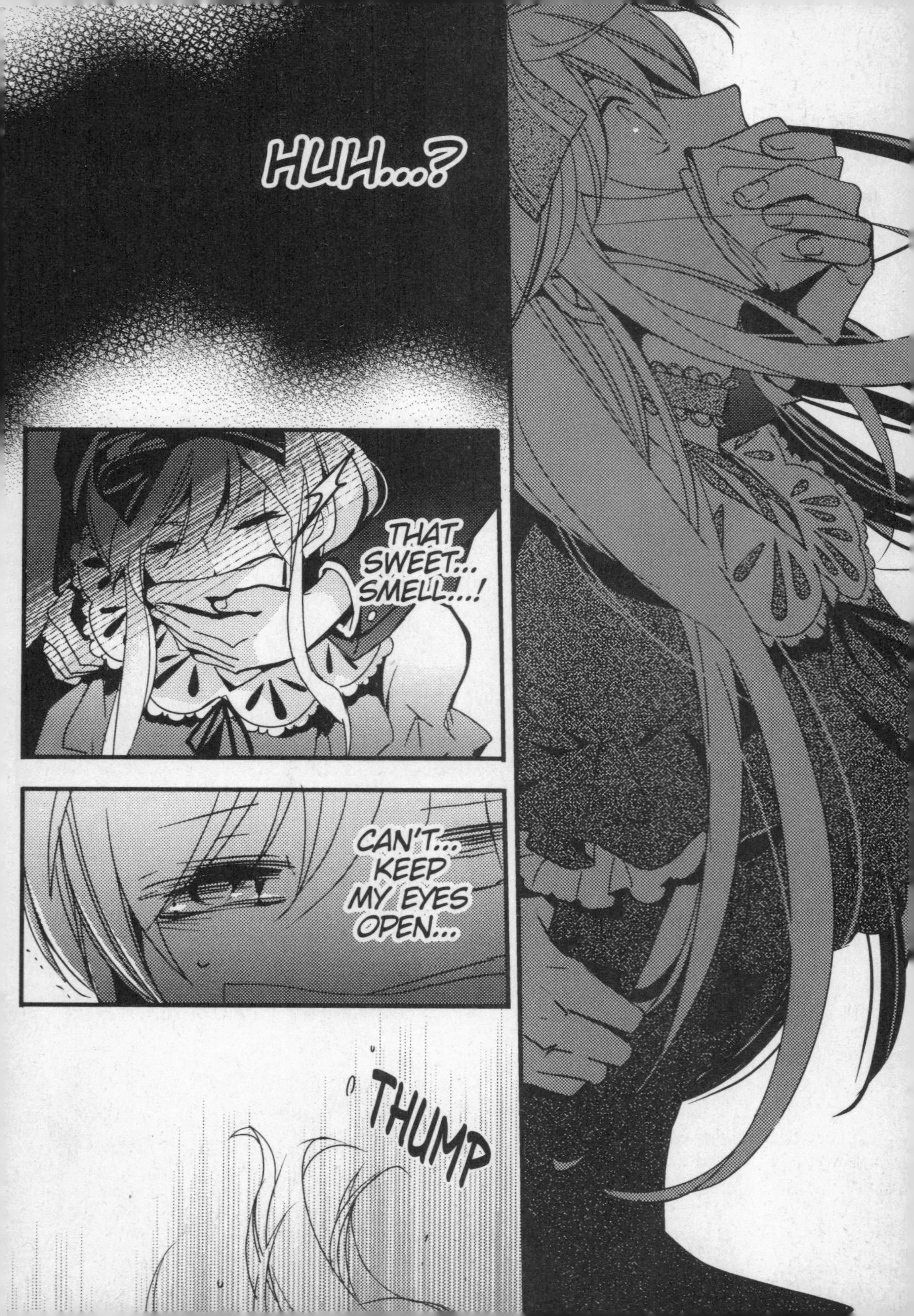
HUH...?
THAT SWEET... SMELL...!
CAN'T... KEEP MY EYES OPEN...
THUMP

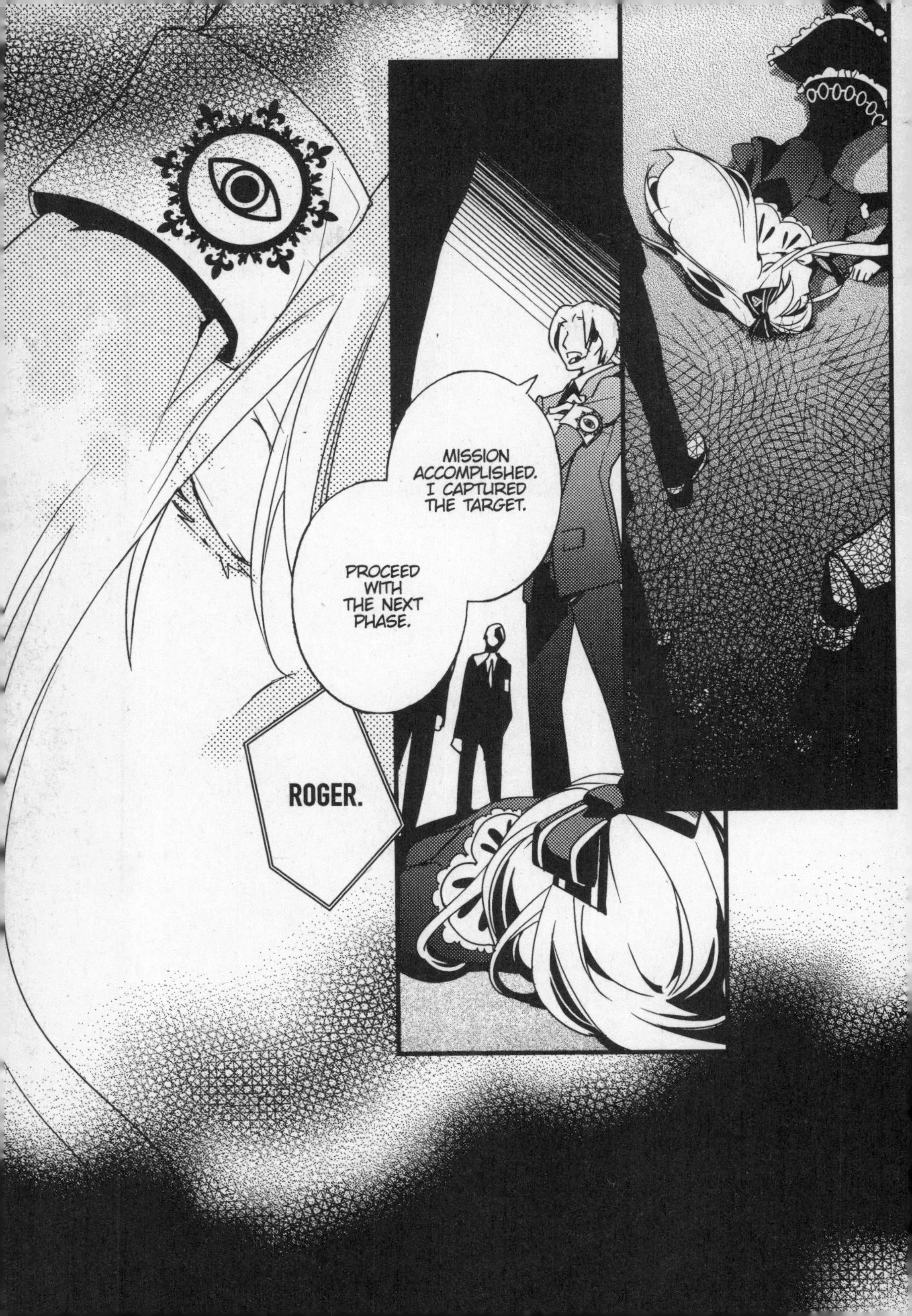
MISSION ACCOMPLISHED. I CAPTURED THE TARGET.
PROCEED WITH THE NEXT PHASE.
ROGER.

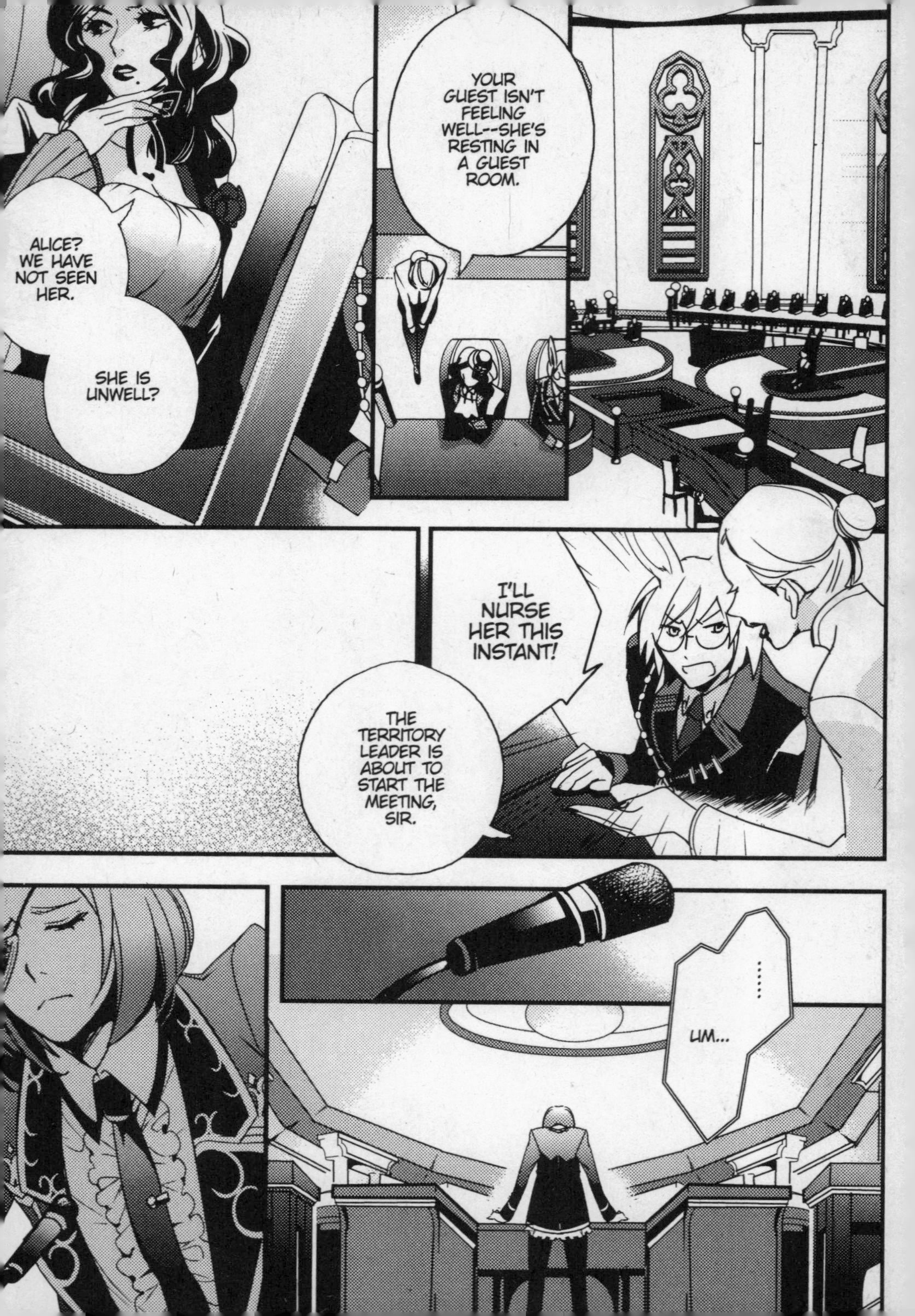
YOUR GUEST ISN'T FEELING WELL--SHE'S RESTING IN A GUEST ROOM.
ALICE? WE HAVE NOT SEEN HER.
SHE IS UNWELL?
I'LL NURSE HER THIS INSTANT!
THE TERRITORY LEADER IS ABOUT TO START THE MEETING, SIR.
......
UM...

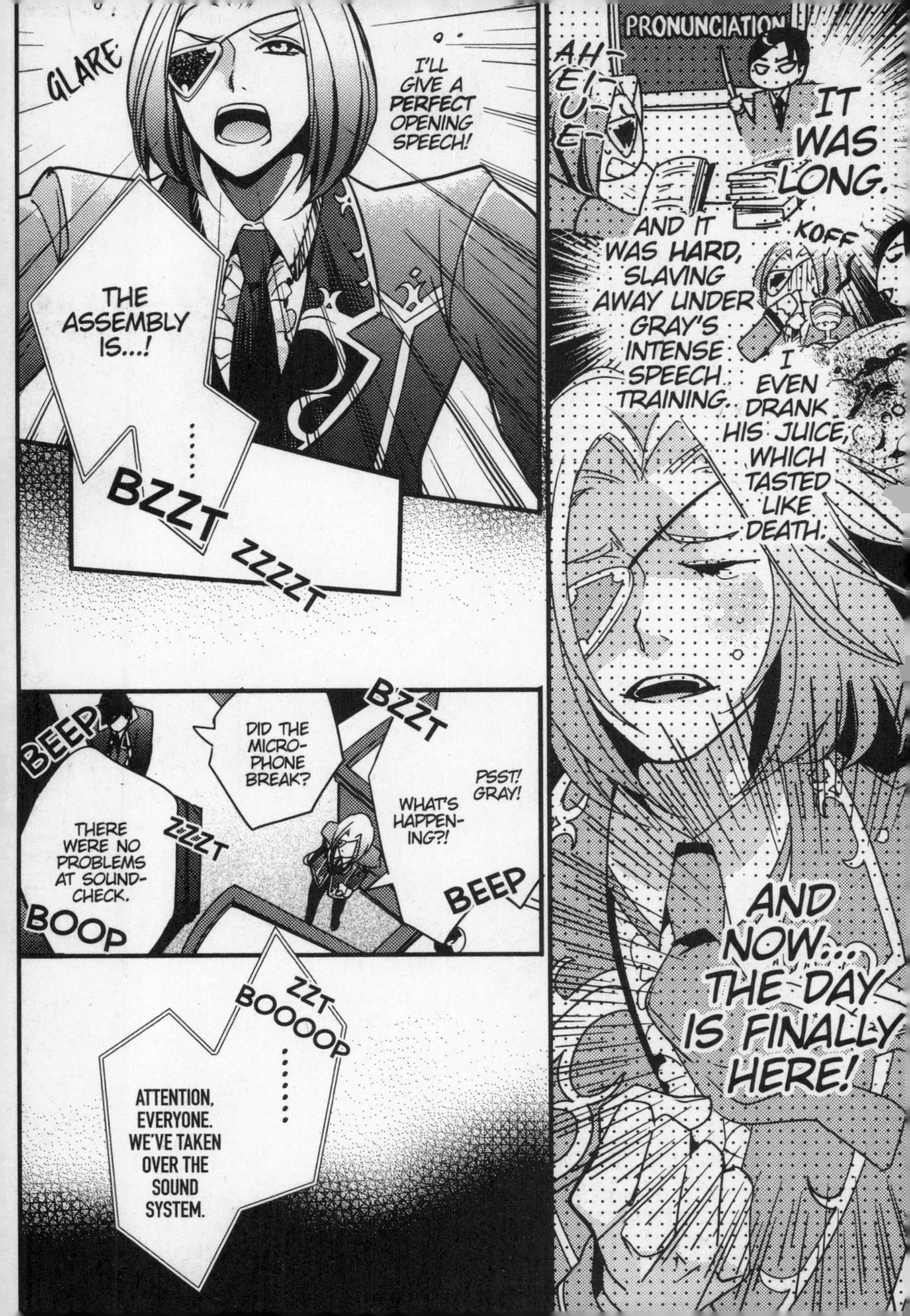
PRONUNCIATION
AH- E- I- U- E-
IT WAS LONG.
AND IT WAS HARD, SLAVING AWAY UNDER GRAY'S INTENSE SPEECH TRAINING.
KOFF
I EVEN DRANK HIS JUICE, WHICH TASTED LIKE DEATH.
AND NOW... THE DAY IS FINALLY HERE!
GLARE
I'LL GIVE A PERFECT OPENING SPEECH!
THE ASSEMBLY IS...!
......
BZZZT
ZZZZZT
BZZZT
DID THE MICRO-PHONE BREAK?
PSST! GRAY!
WHAT'S HAPPEN-ING?!
BEEP
BEEP
THERE WERE NO PROBLEMS AT SOUND-CHECK.
ZZZT
BOOP
ZZT
BOOOOP
......
ATTENTION, EVERYONE. WE'VE TAKEN OVER THE SOUND SYSTEM.

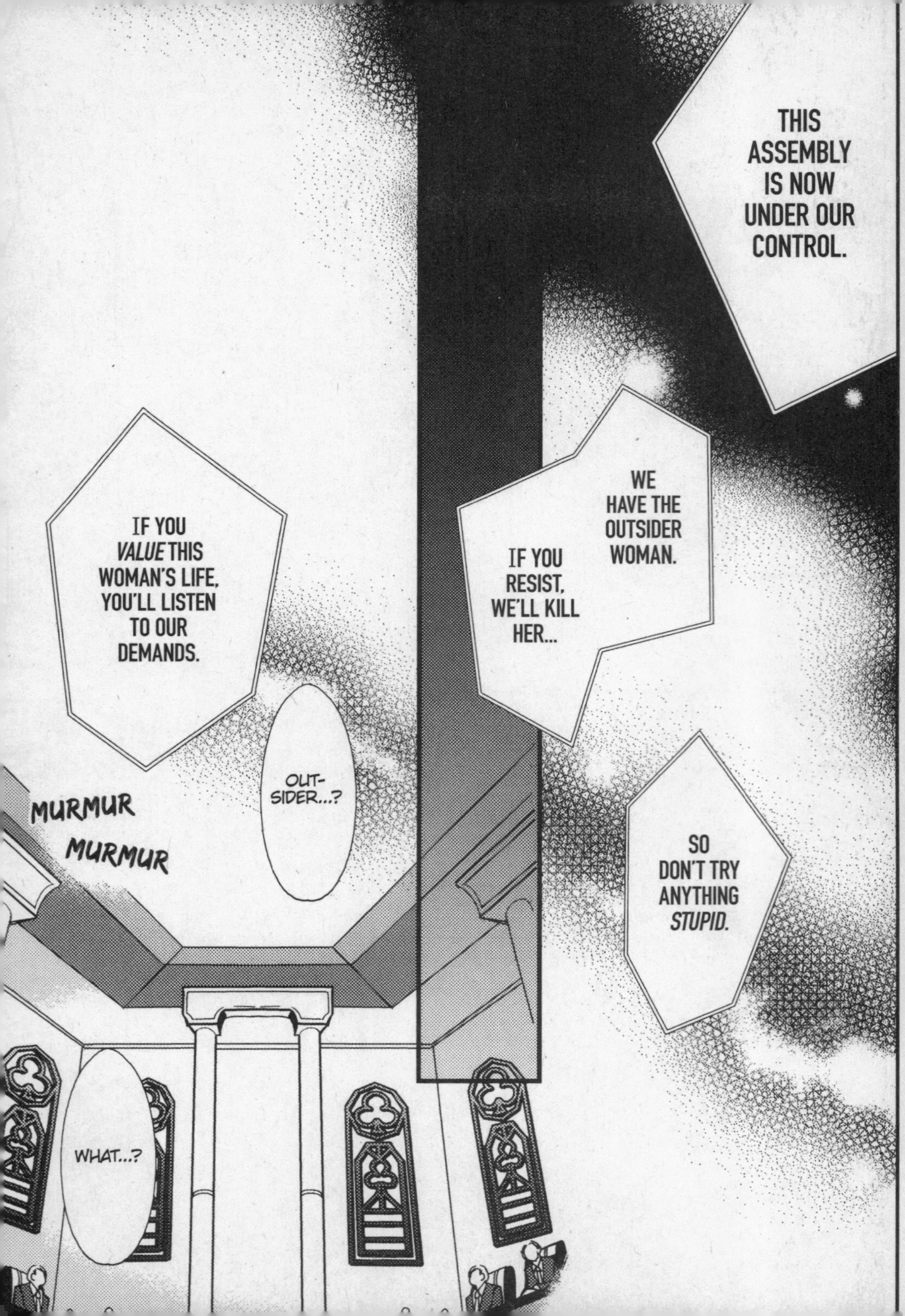
THIS ASSEMBLY IS NOW UNDER OUR CONTROL.
WE HAVE THE OUTSIDER WOMAN.
IF YOU RESIST, WE'LL KILL HER...
SO DON'T TRY ANYTHING *STUPID.*
IF YOU *VALUE* THIS WOMAN'S LIFE, YOU'LL LISTEN TO OUR DEMANDS.
OUT-SIDER...?
MURMUR
MURMUR
WHAT...?

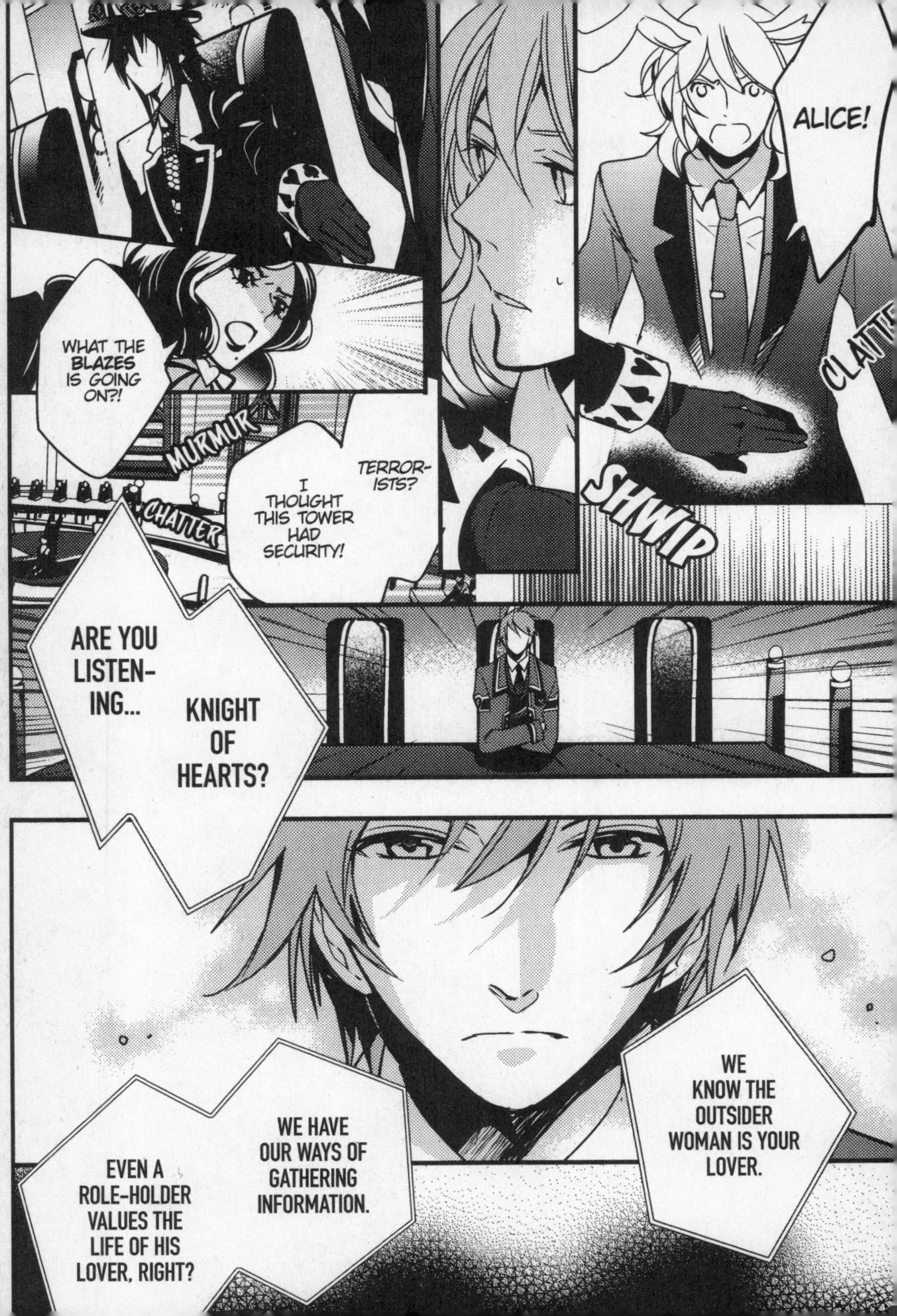
ALICE!
CLATTE
SHWIP
WHAT THE BLAZES IS GOING ON?!
MURMUR
CHATTER
TERROR-ISTS?
I THOUGHT THIS TOWER HAD SECURITY!
ARE YOU LISTEN-ING...
KNIGHT OF HEARTS?
WE KNOW THE OUTSIDER WOMAN IS YOUR LOVER.
WE HAVE OUR WAYS OF GATHERING INFORMATION.
EVEN A ROLE-HOLDER VALUES THE LIFE OF HIS LOVER, RIGHT?

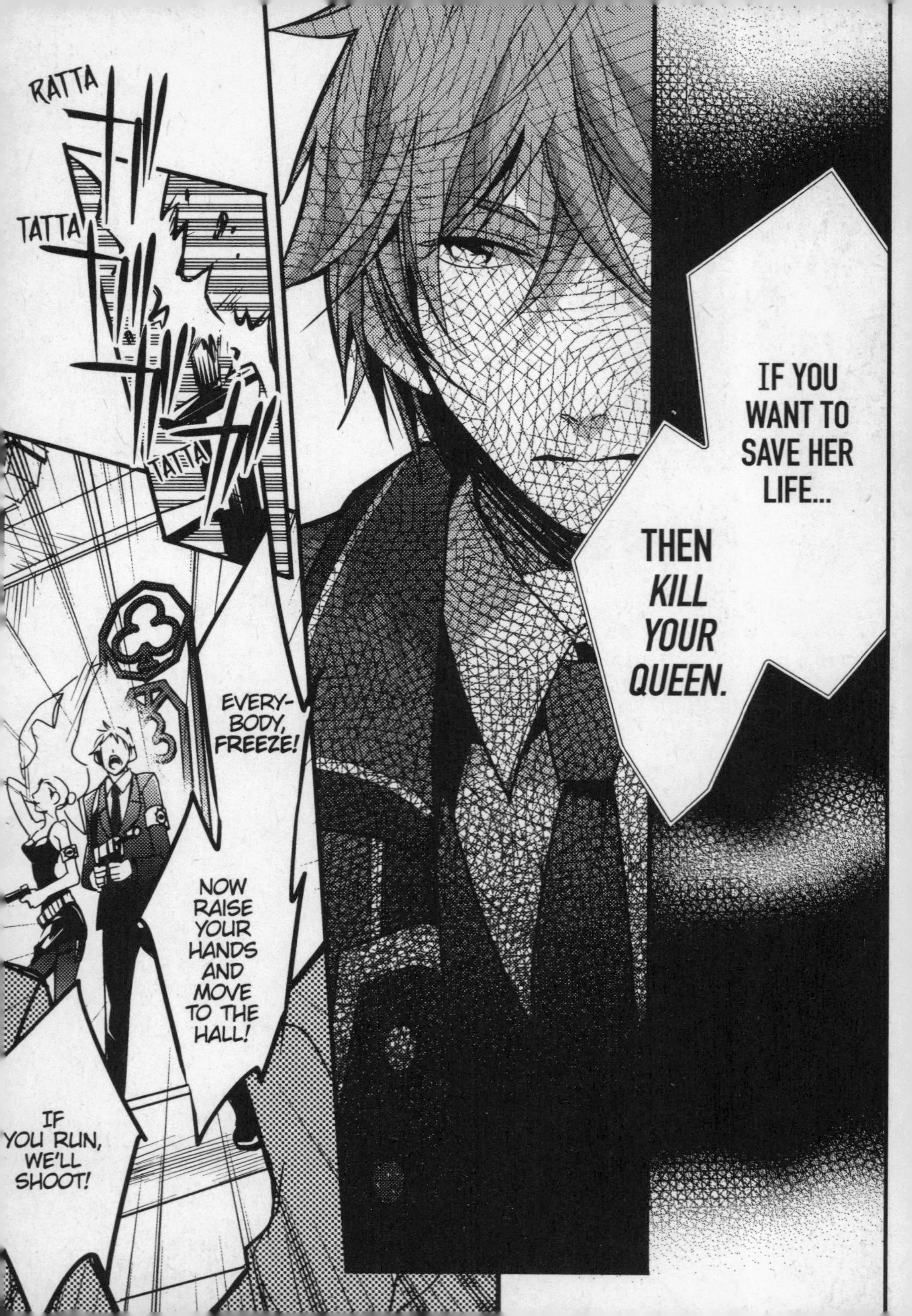
IF YOU WANT TO SAVE HER LIFE...
THEN *KILL YOUR* QUEEN.
RATTA
TATTA
TATTA
EVERY-BODY, FREEZE!
NOW RAISE YOUR HANDS AND MOVE TO THE HALL!
IF YOU RUN, WE'LL SHOOT!

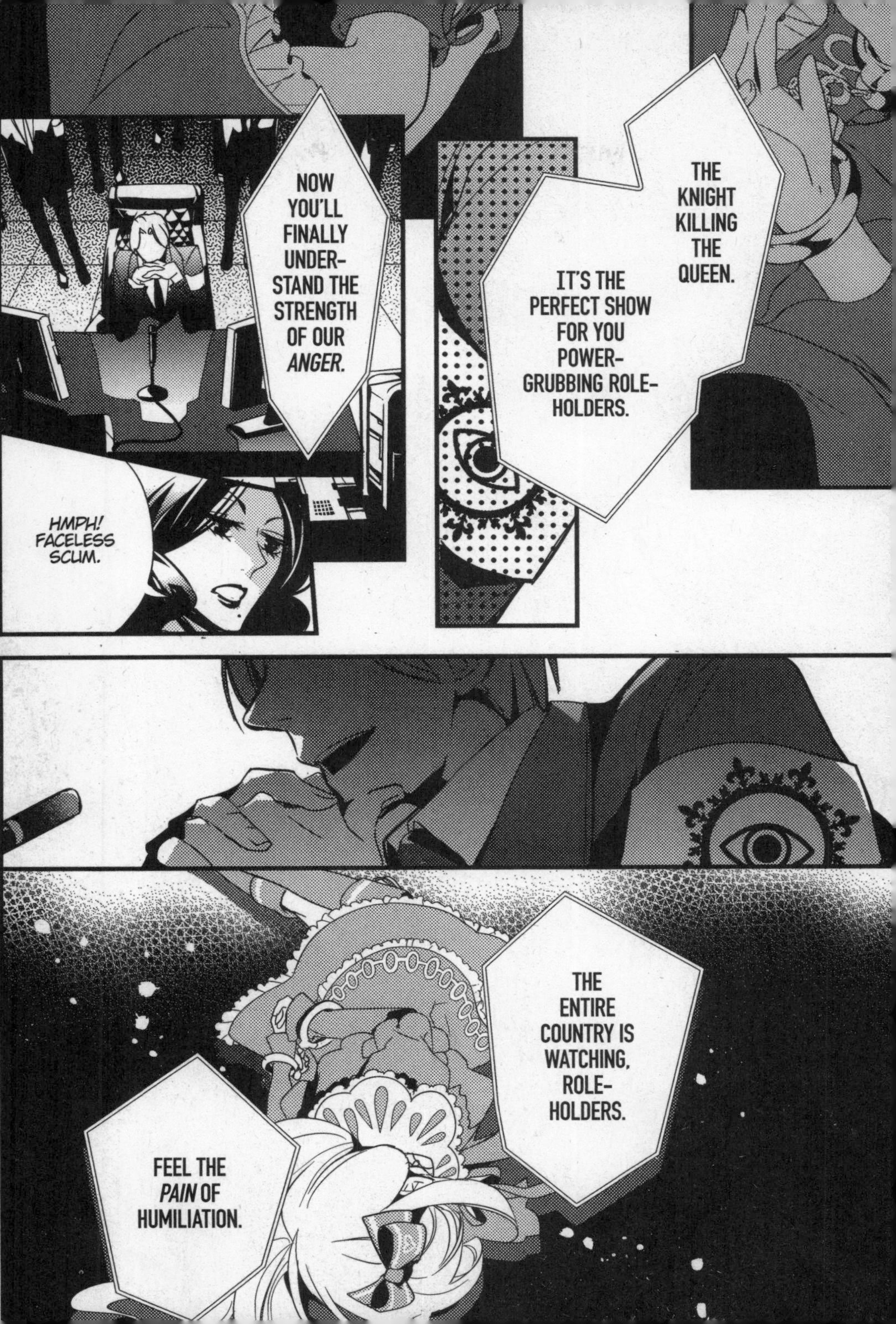
THE KNIGHT KILLING THE QUEEN.
IT'S THE PERFECT SHOW FOR YOU POWER-GRUBBING ROLE-HOLDERS.
NOW YOU'LL FINALLY UNDER-STAND THE STRENGTH OF OUR *ANGER*.
HMPH! FACELESS SCUM.
THE ENTIRE COUNTRY IS WATCHING, ROLE-HOLDERS.
FEEL THE *PAIN* OF HUMILIATION.

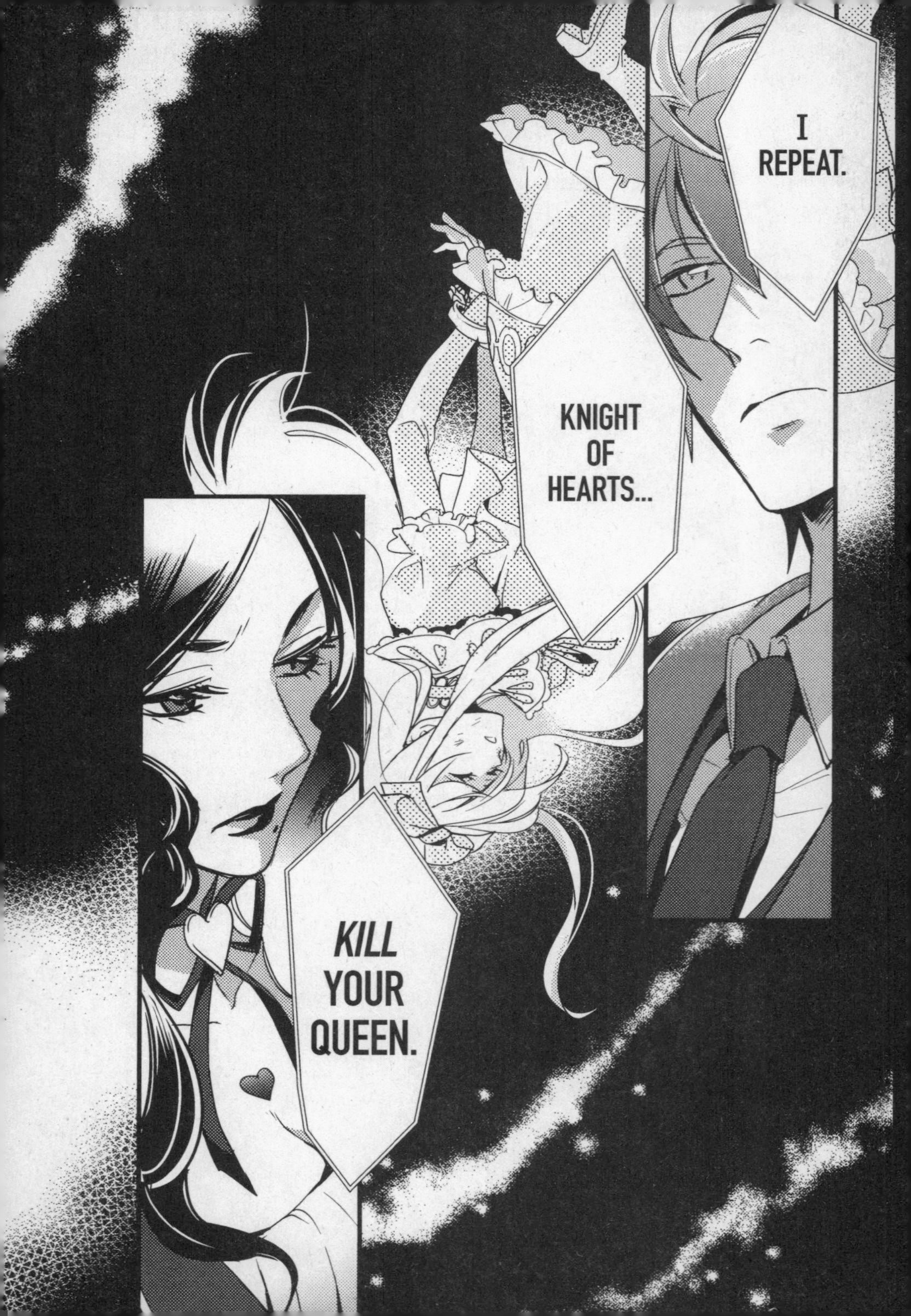
I REPEAT.
KNIGHT OF HEARTS...
*KILL* YOUR QUEEN.

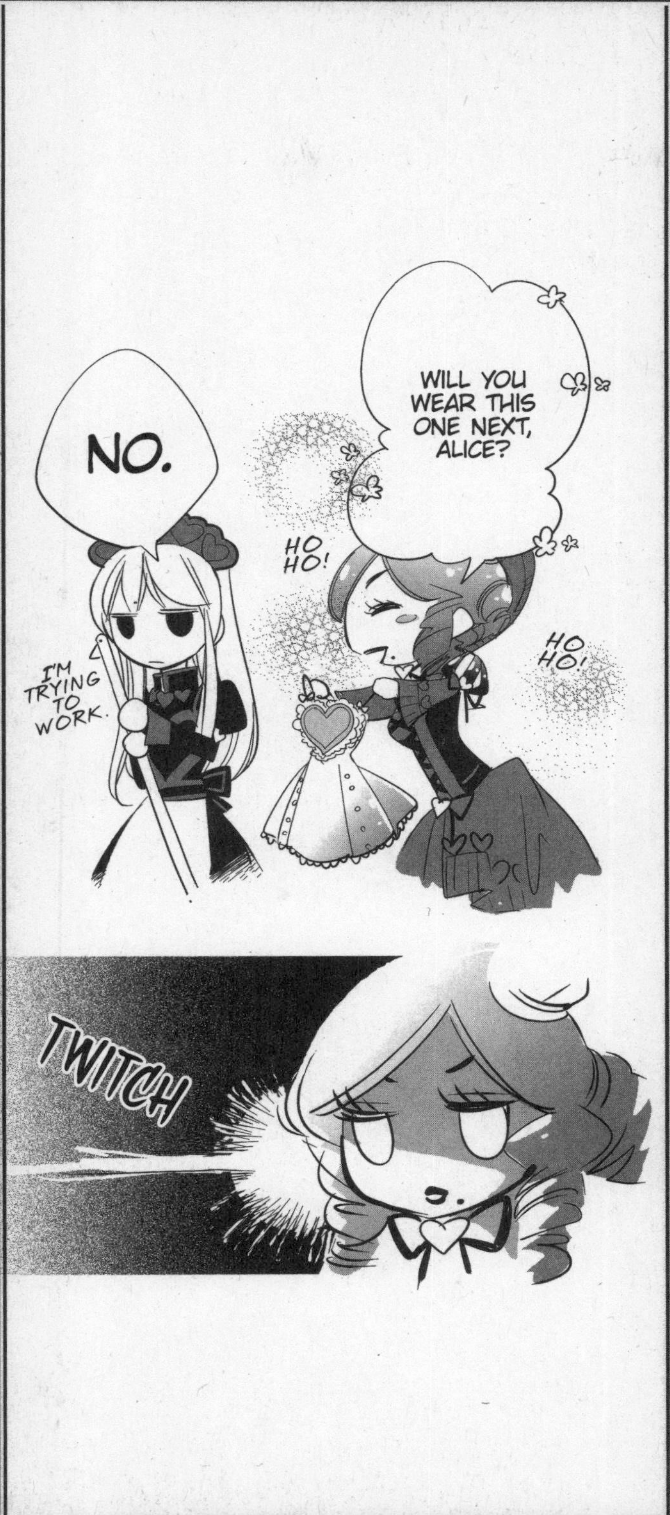

WILL YOU WEAR THIS ONE NEXT, ALICE?
HO HO!
HO HO!
NO.
I'M TRYING TO WORK.
TWITCH

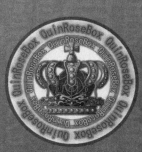

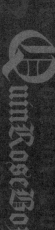

HAVE THE MAID UNIFORMS CHANGED AT ONCE!
IT IS AN ORDER FROM YOUR QUEEN!
UH-OH.
NEW DESIGN
LEAVE THE DESIGNS OF THE NEW ONES TO ME!
I'LL DRESS MY DEAR LOVE...
SO JUBI-LANTLY!

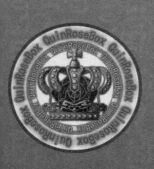

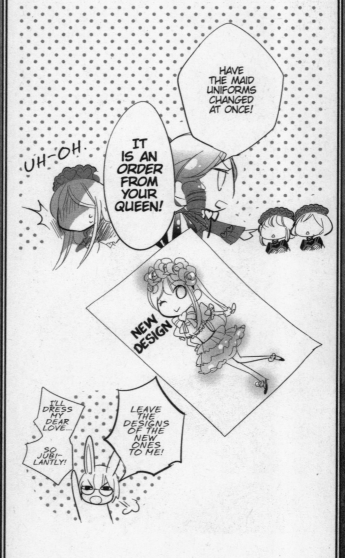

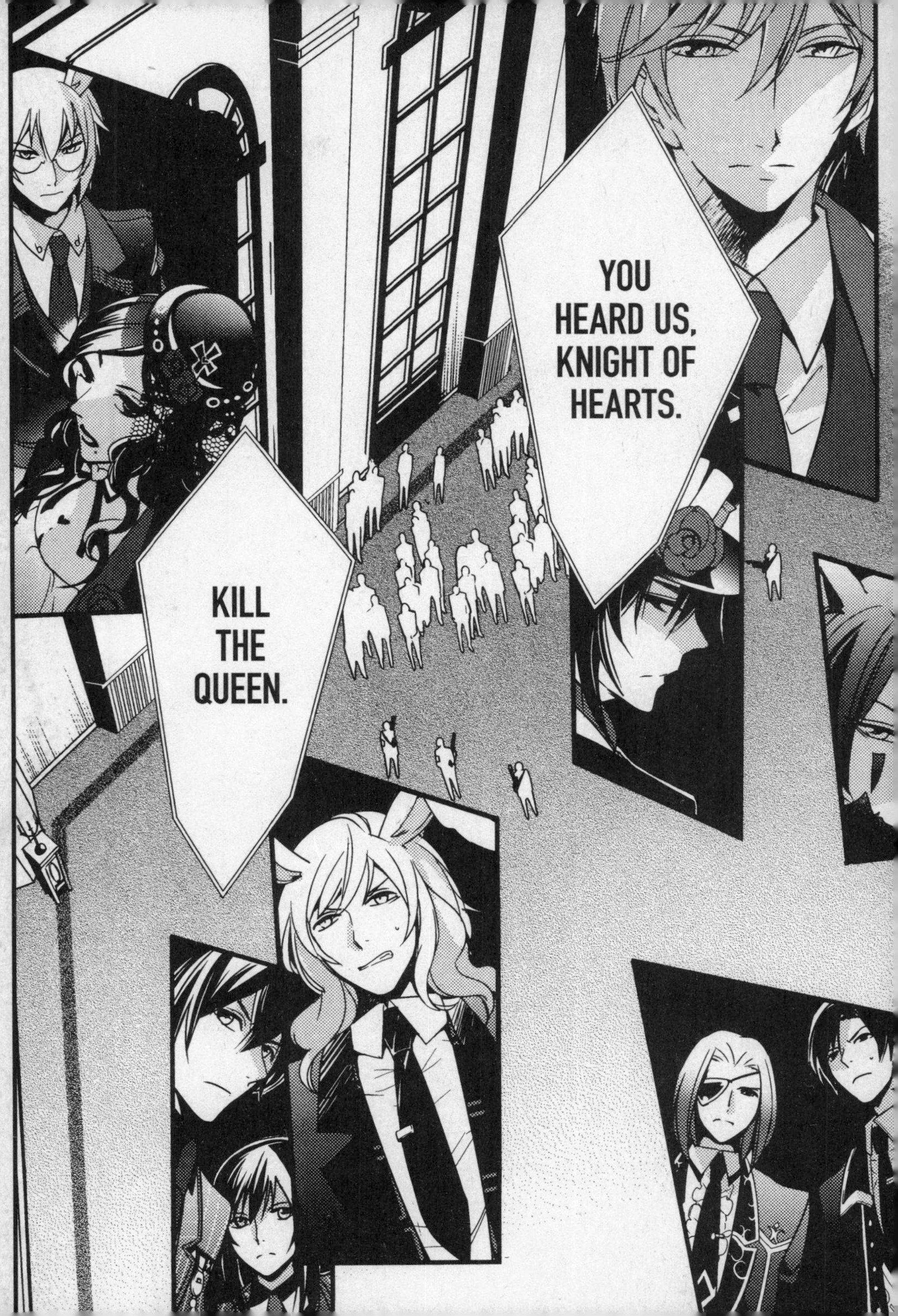
YOU HEARD US, KNIGHT OF HEARTS.
KILL THE QUEEN.

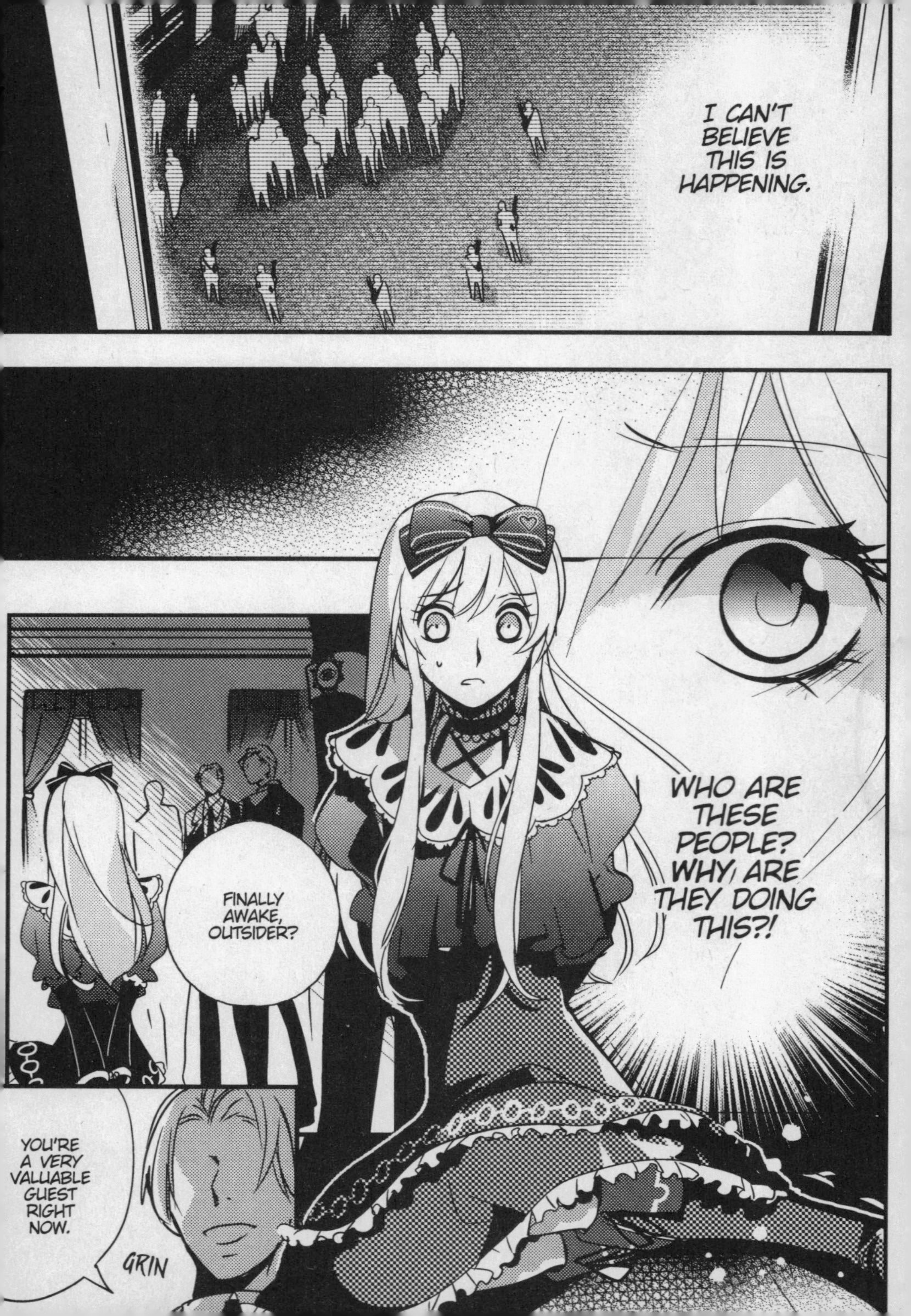
I CAN'T BELIEVE THIS IS HAPPENING.
WHO ARE THESE PEOPLE? WHY ARE THEY DOING THIS?!
FINALLY AWAKE, OUTSIDER?
YOU'RE A VERY VALUABLE GUEST RIGHT NOW.
GRIN

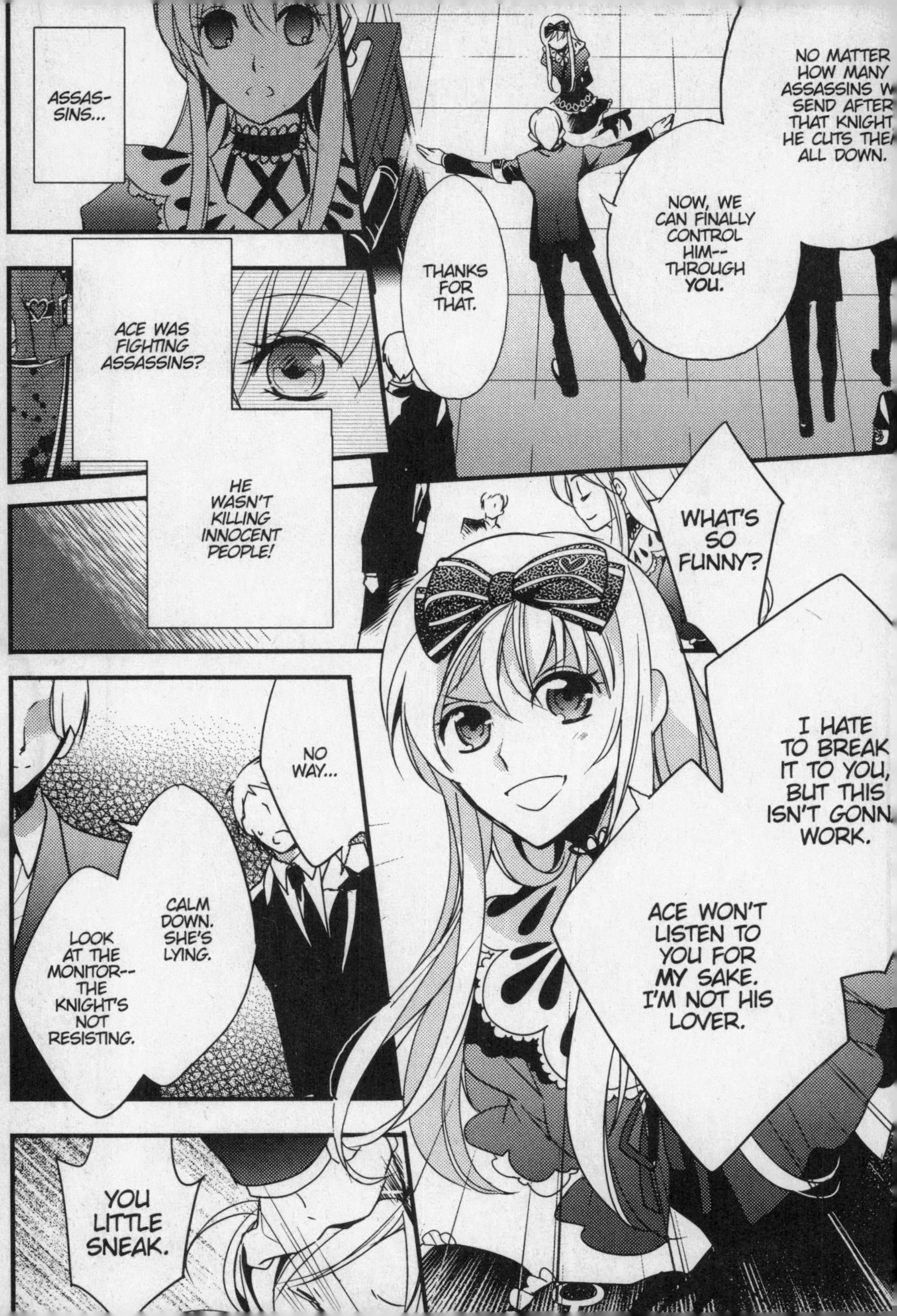
NO MATTER HOW MANY ASSASSINS W SEND AFTER THAT KNIGHT HE CUTS THE ALL DOWN.
NOW, WE CAN FINALLY CONTROL HIM-- THROUGH YOU.
THANKS FOR THAT.
ASSAS-SINS...
ACE WAS FIGHTING ASSASSINS?
HE WASN'T KILLING INNOCENT PEOPLE!
WHAT'S SO FUNNY?
I HATE TO BREAK IT TO YOU, BUT THIS ISN'T GONN WORK.
ACE WON'T LISTEN TO YOU FOR MY SAKE. I'M NOT HIS LOVER.
NO WAY...
CALM DOWN. SHE'S LYING.
LOOK AT THE MONITOR-- THE KNIGHT'S NOT RESISTING.
YOU LITTLE SNEAK.

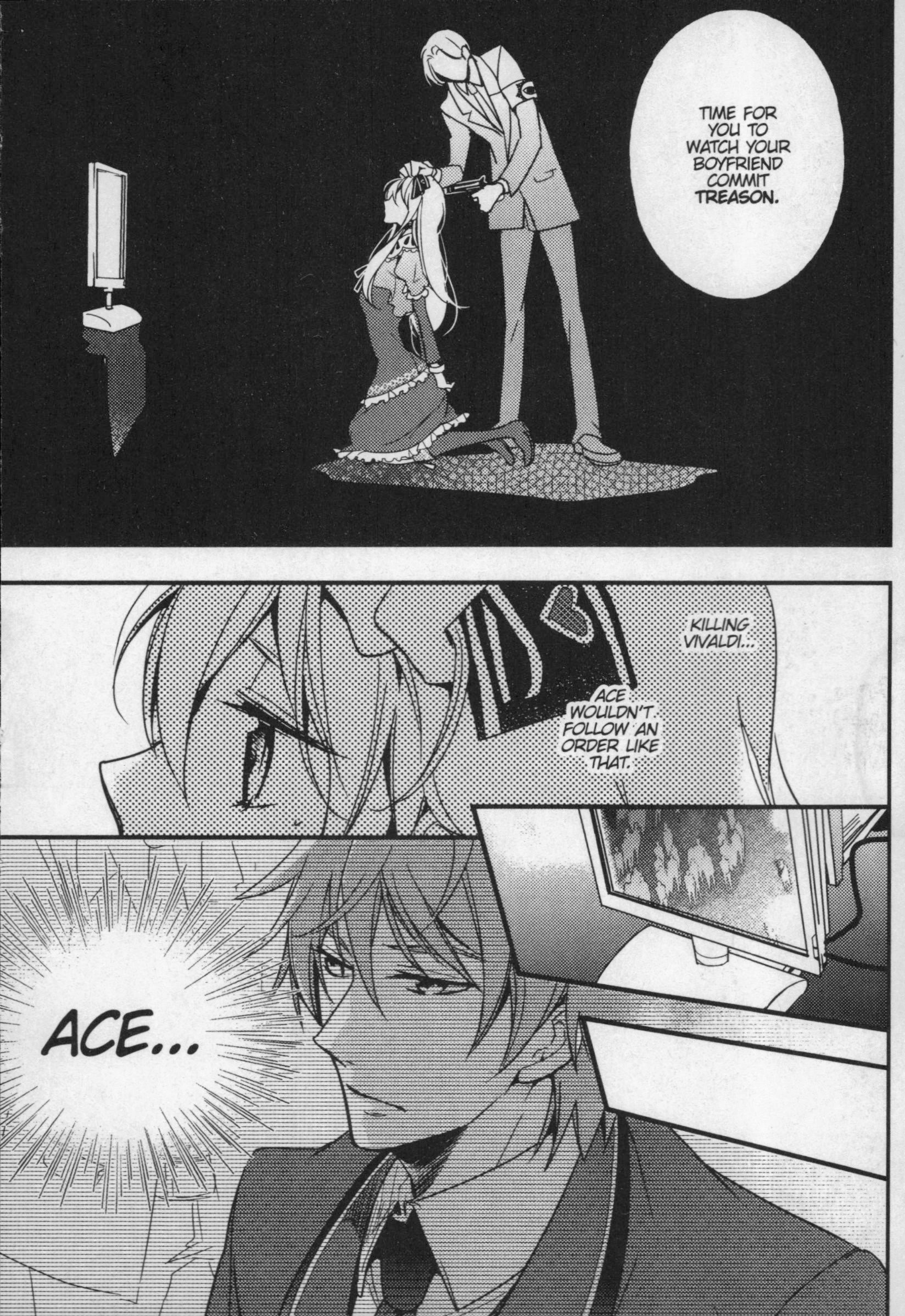
TIME FOR YOU TO WATCH YOUR BOYFRIEND COMMIT TREASON.
KILLING VIVALDI...
ACE WOULDN'T FOLLOW AN ORDER LIKE THAT.
ACE...

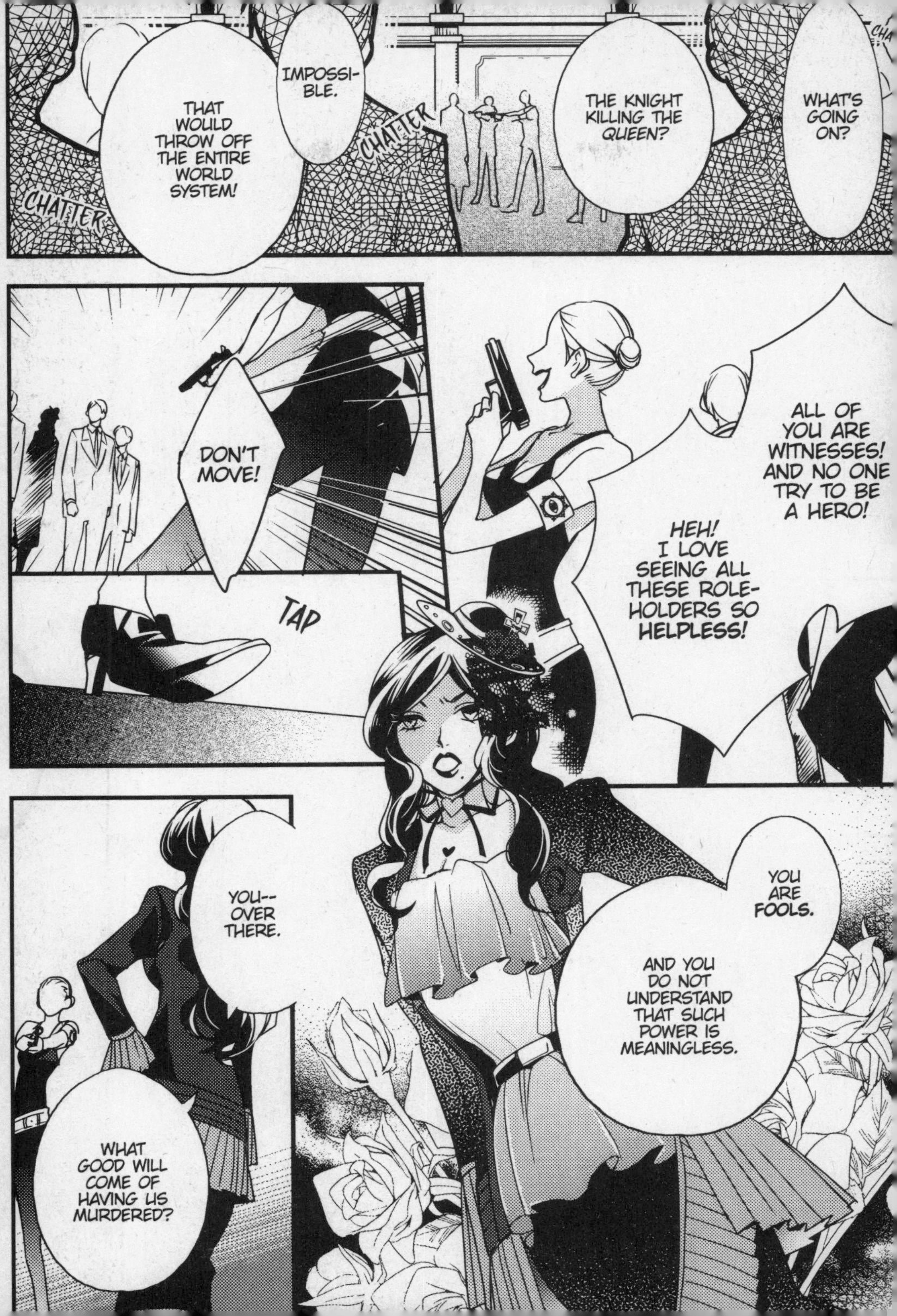
WHAT'S GOING ON?
THE KNIGHT KILLING THE QUEEN?
CHATTER
IMPOSSI-BLE.
THAT WOULD THROW OFF THE ENTIRE WORLD SYSTEM!
CHATTER
ALL OF YOU ARE WITNESSES! AND NO ONE TRY TO BE A HERO!
HEH! I LOVE SEEING ALL THESE ROLE-HOLDERS SO HELPLESS!
DON'T MOVE!
TAP
YOU ARE FOOLS.
AND YOU DO NOT UNDERSTAND THAT SUCH POWER IS MEANINGLESS.
YOU-- OVER THERE.
WHAT GOOD WILL COME OF HAVING US MURDERED?

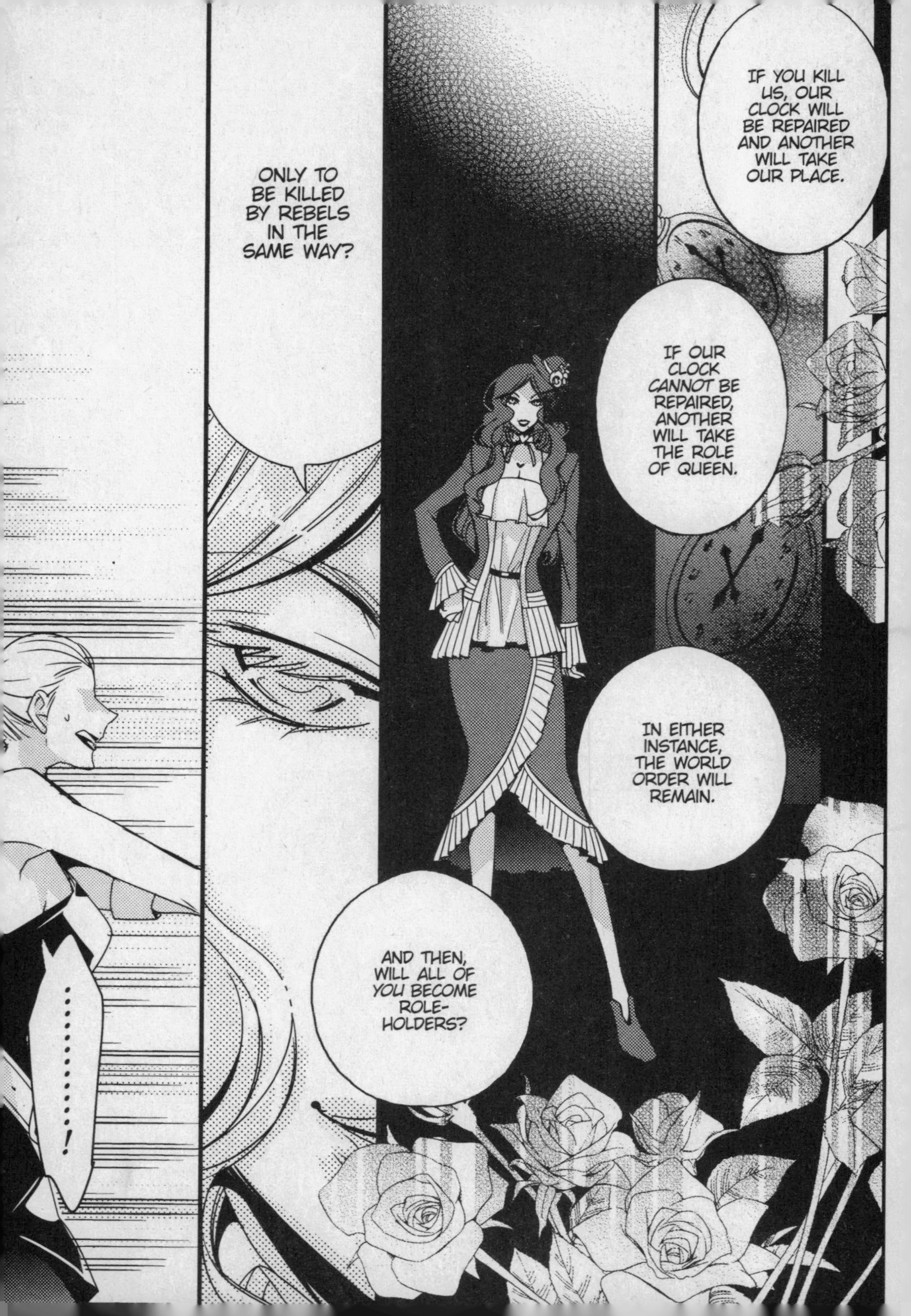
IF YOU KILL US, OUR CLOCK WILL BE REPAIRED AND ANOTHER WILL TAKE OUR PLACE.
IF OUR CLOCK CANNOT BE REPAIRED, ANOTHER WILL TAKE THE ROLE OF QUEEN.
IN EITHER INSTANCE, THE WORLD ORDER WILL REMAIN.
AND THEN, WILL ALL OF YOU BECOME ROLE-HOLDERS?
ONLY TO BE KILLED BY REBELS IN THE SAME WAY?
......!

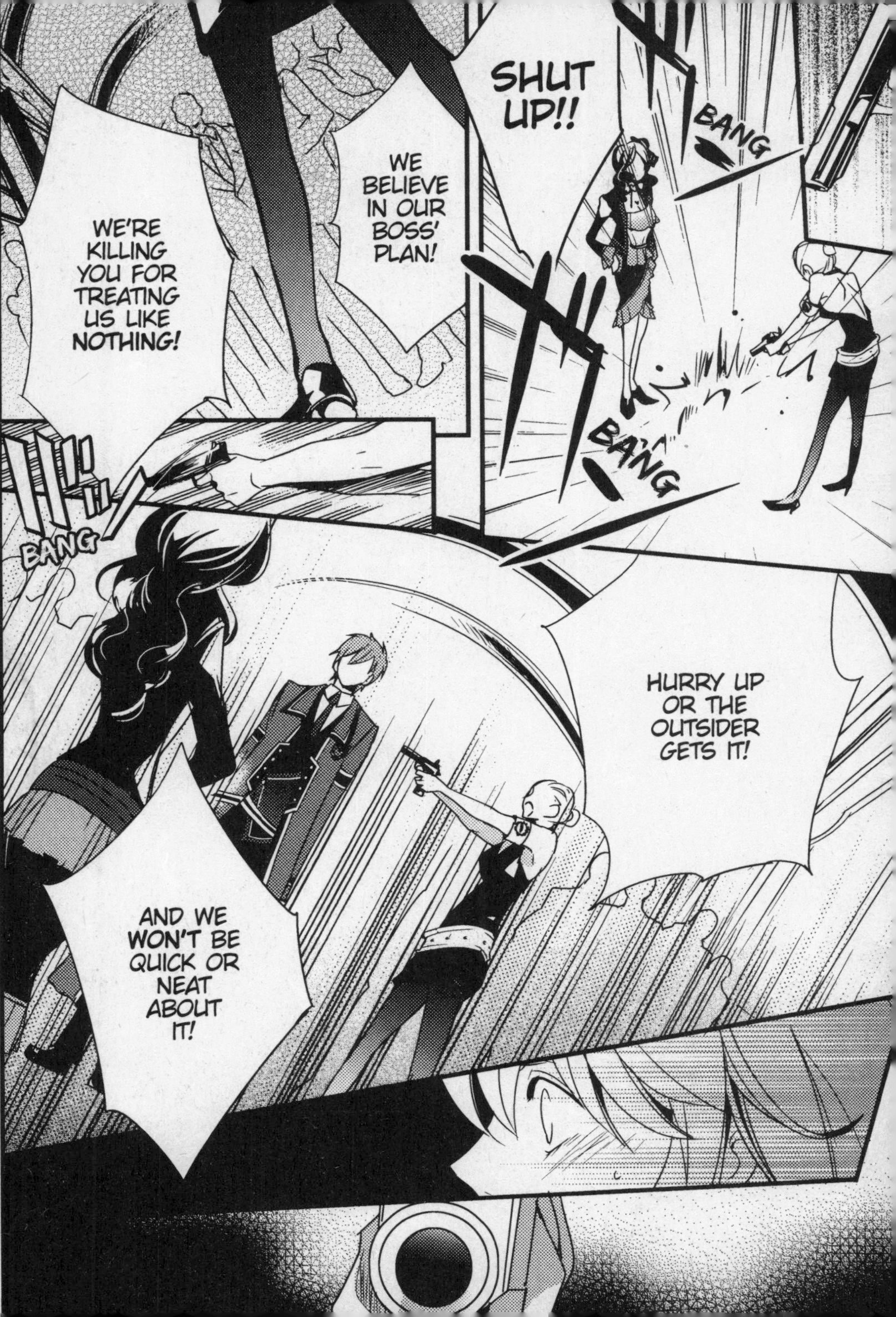
BANG
SHUT UP!!
BANG
WE BELIEVE IN OUR BOSS' PLAN!
WE'RE KILLING YOU FOR TREATING US LIKE NOTHING!
BANG
HURRY UP OR THE OUTSIDER GETS IT!
AND WE WON'T BE QUICK OR NEAT ABOUT IT!

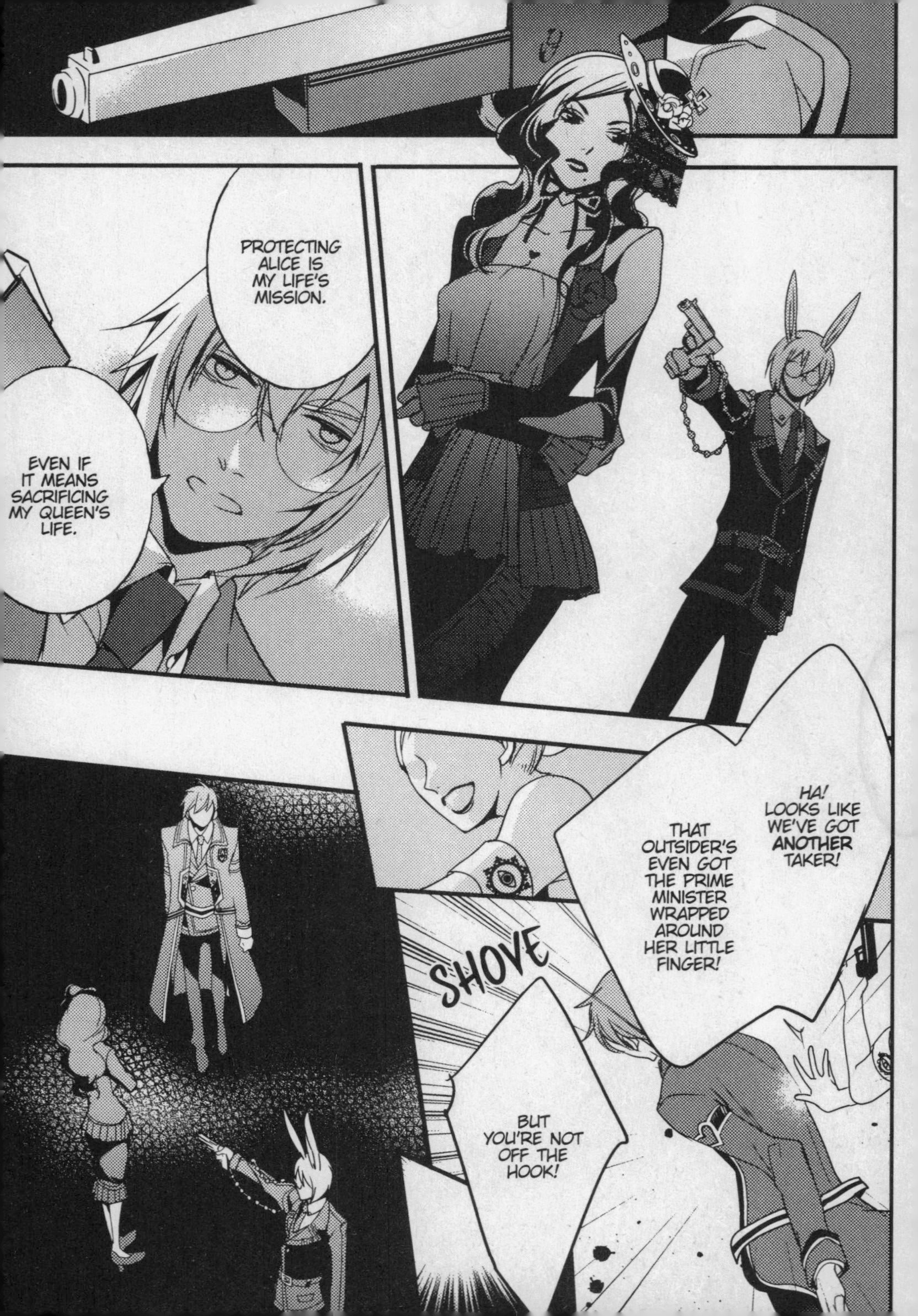
PROTECTING ALICE IS MY LIFE'S MISSION.
EVEN IF IT MEANS SACRIFICING MY QUEEN'S LIFE.
HA! LOOKS LIKE WE'VE GOT **ANOTHER** TAKER!
THAT OUTSIDER'S EVEN GOT THE PRIME MINISTER WRAPPED AROUND HER LITTLE FINGER!
SHOVE
BUT YOU'RE NOT OFF THE HOOK!

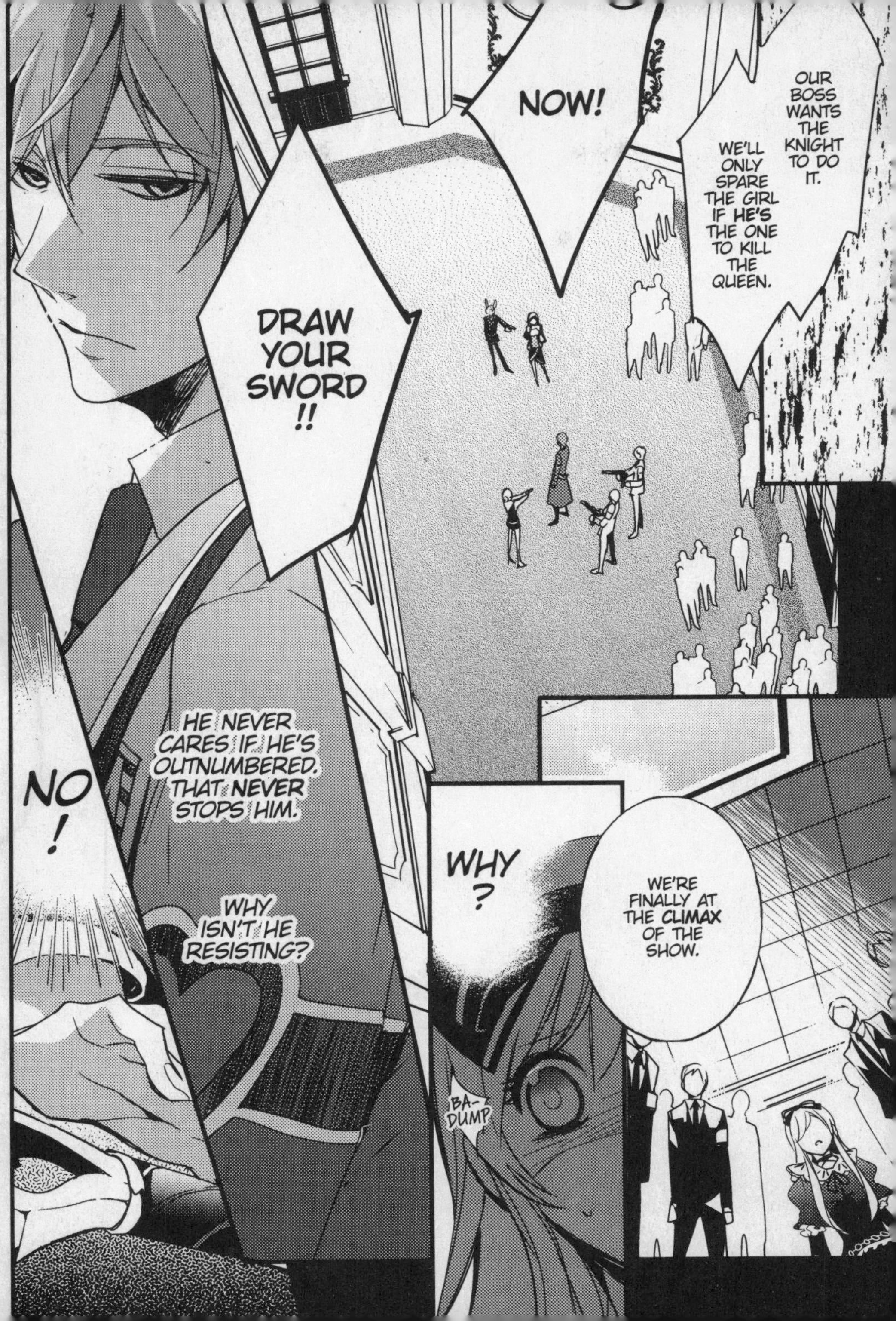
OUR BOSS WANTS THE KNIGHT TO DO IT.
WE'LL ONLY SPARE THE GIRL IF HE'S THE ONE TO KILL THE QUEEN.
NOW!
DRAW YOUR SWORD!!
WE'RE FINALLY AT THE CLIMAX OF THE SHOW.
WHY?
BA-DUMP
HE NEVER CARES IF HE'S OUTNUMBERED. THAT NEVER STOPS HIM.
NO!
WHY ISN'T HE RESISTING?

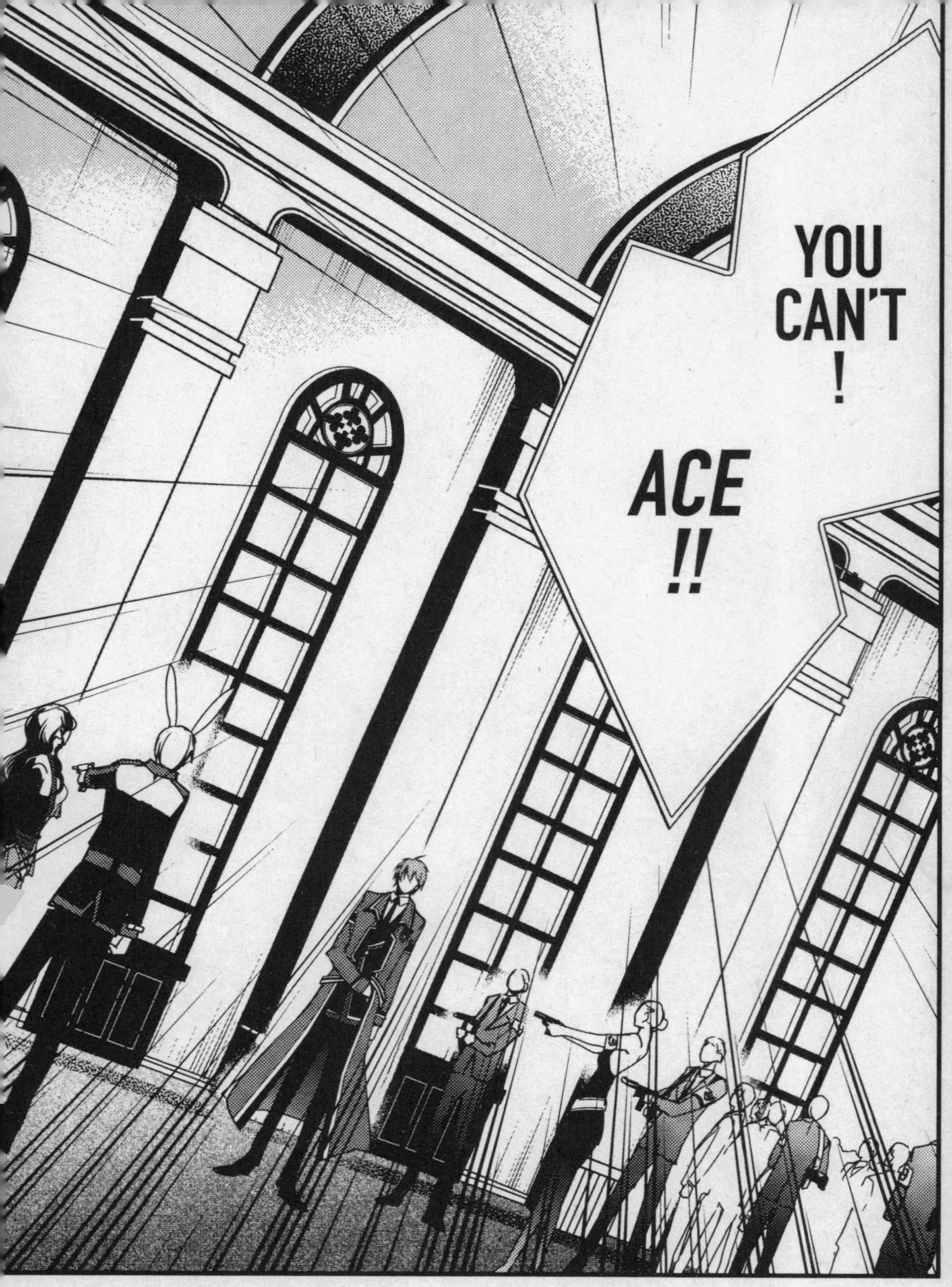
YOU CAN'T! ACE!!

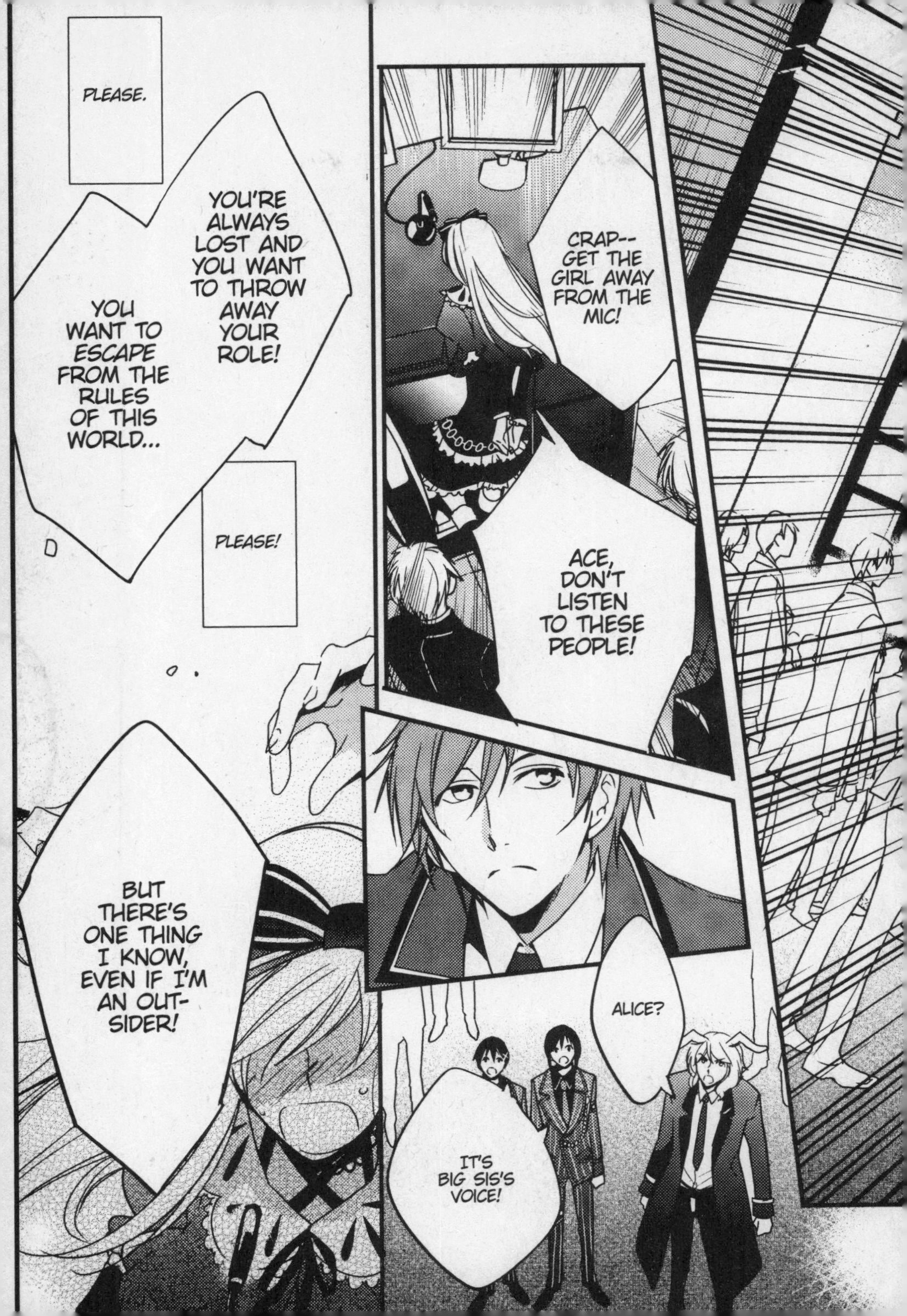
CRAP-- GET THE GIRL AWAY FROM THE MIC!
ACE, DON'T LISTEN TO THESE PEOPLE!
ALICE?
IT'S BIG SIS'S VOICE!
PLEASE.
YOU'RE ALWAYS LOST AND YOU WANT TO THROW AWAY YOUR ROLE!
YOU WANT TO ESCAPE FROM THE RULES OF THIS WORLD...
PLEASE!
BUT THERE'S ONE THING I KNOW, EVEN IF I'M AN OUT-SIDER!

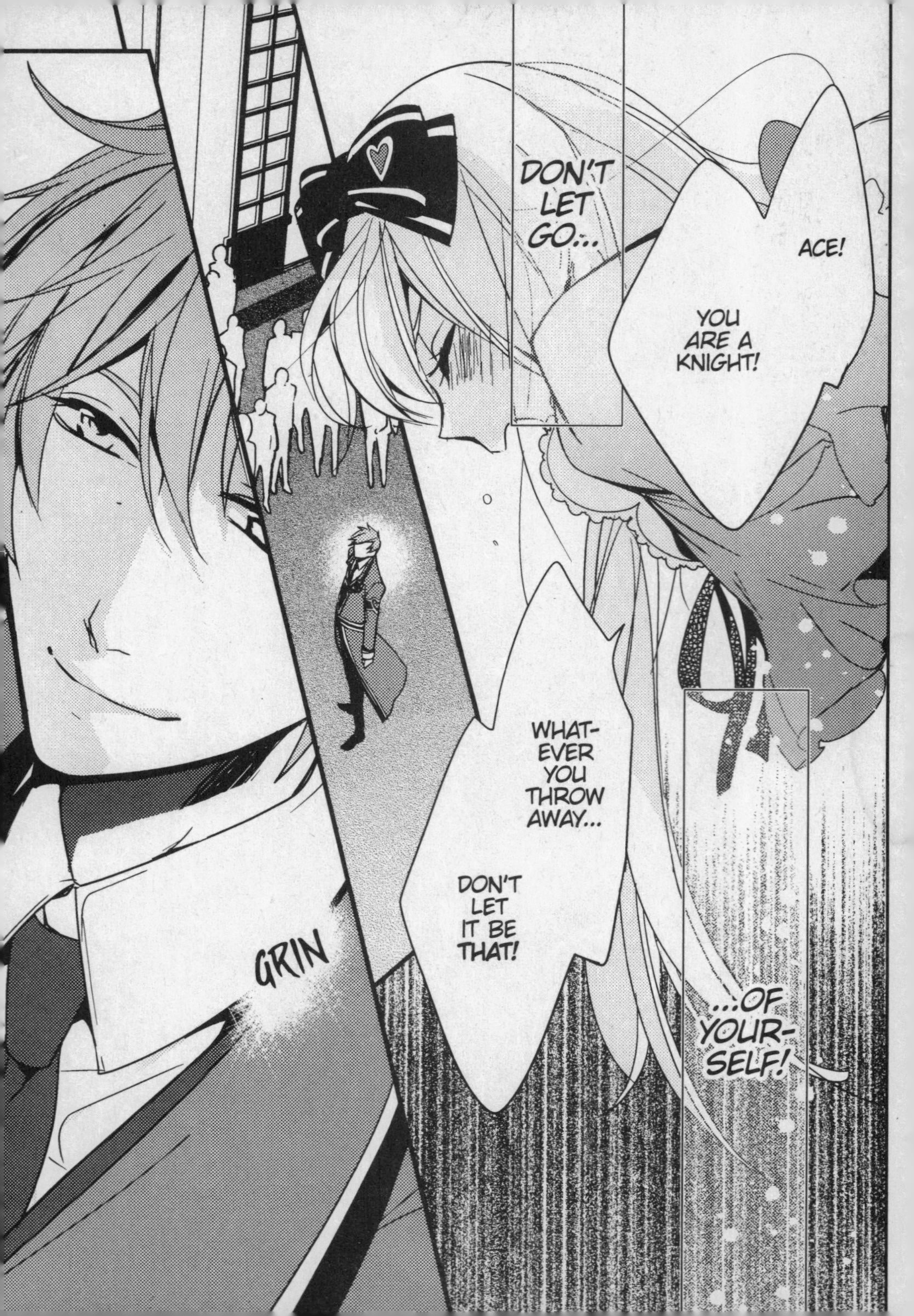
ACE!
YOU ARE A KNIGHT!
WHAT-EVER YOU THROW AWAY...
DON'T LET IT BE THAT!
DON'T LET GO...
...OF YOUR-SELF!
GRIN

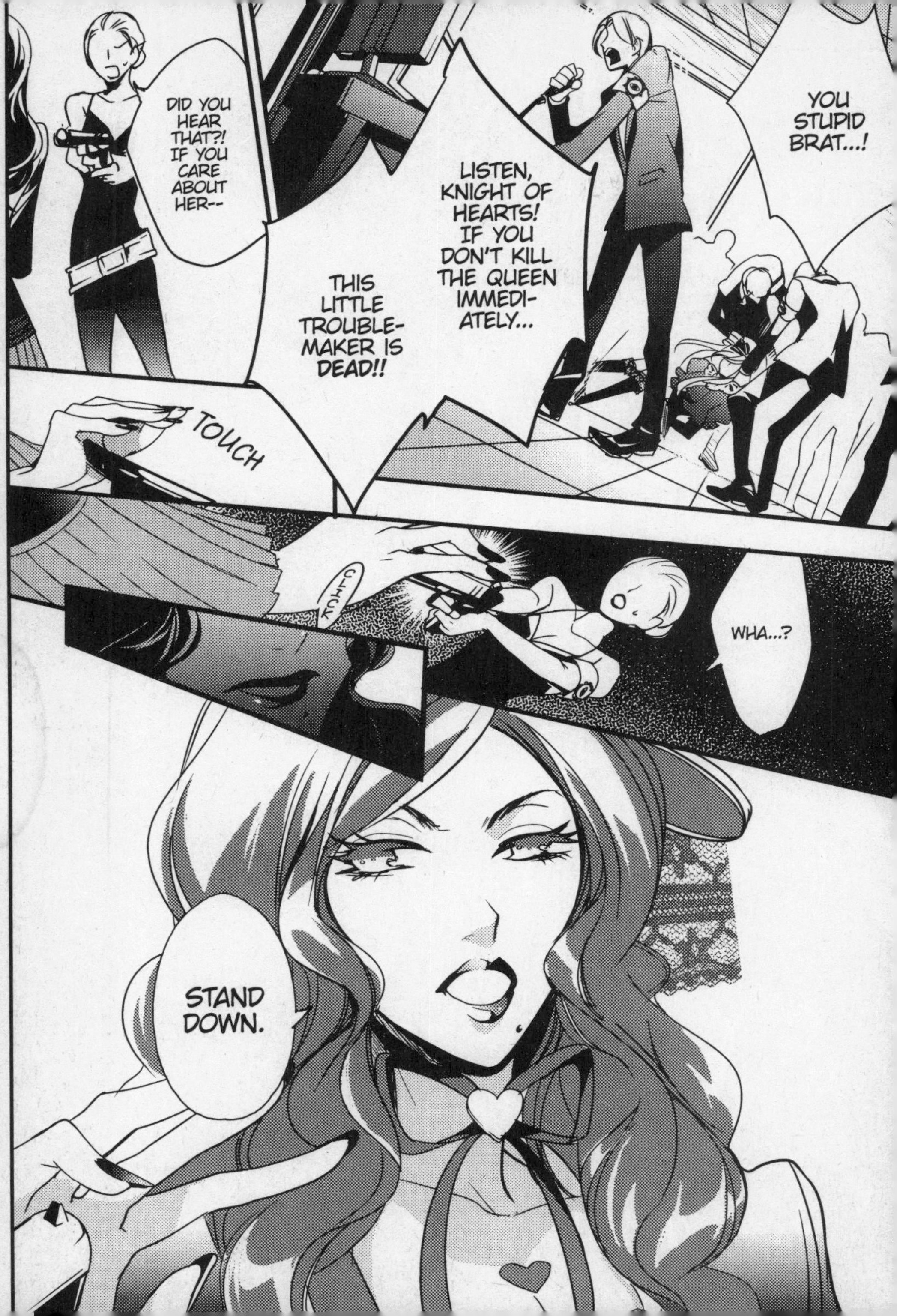
YOU STUPID BRAT...!
LISTEN, KNIGHT OF HEARTS! IF YOU DON'T KILL THE QUEEN IMMEDIATELY...
THIS LITTLE TROUBLEMAKER IS DEAD!!
DID YOU HEAR THAT?! IF YOU CARE ABOUT HER--
TOUCH
WHA...?
CLICK
STAND DOWN.

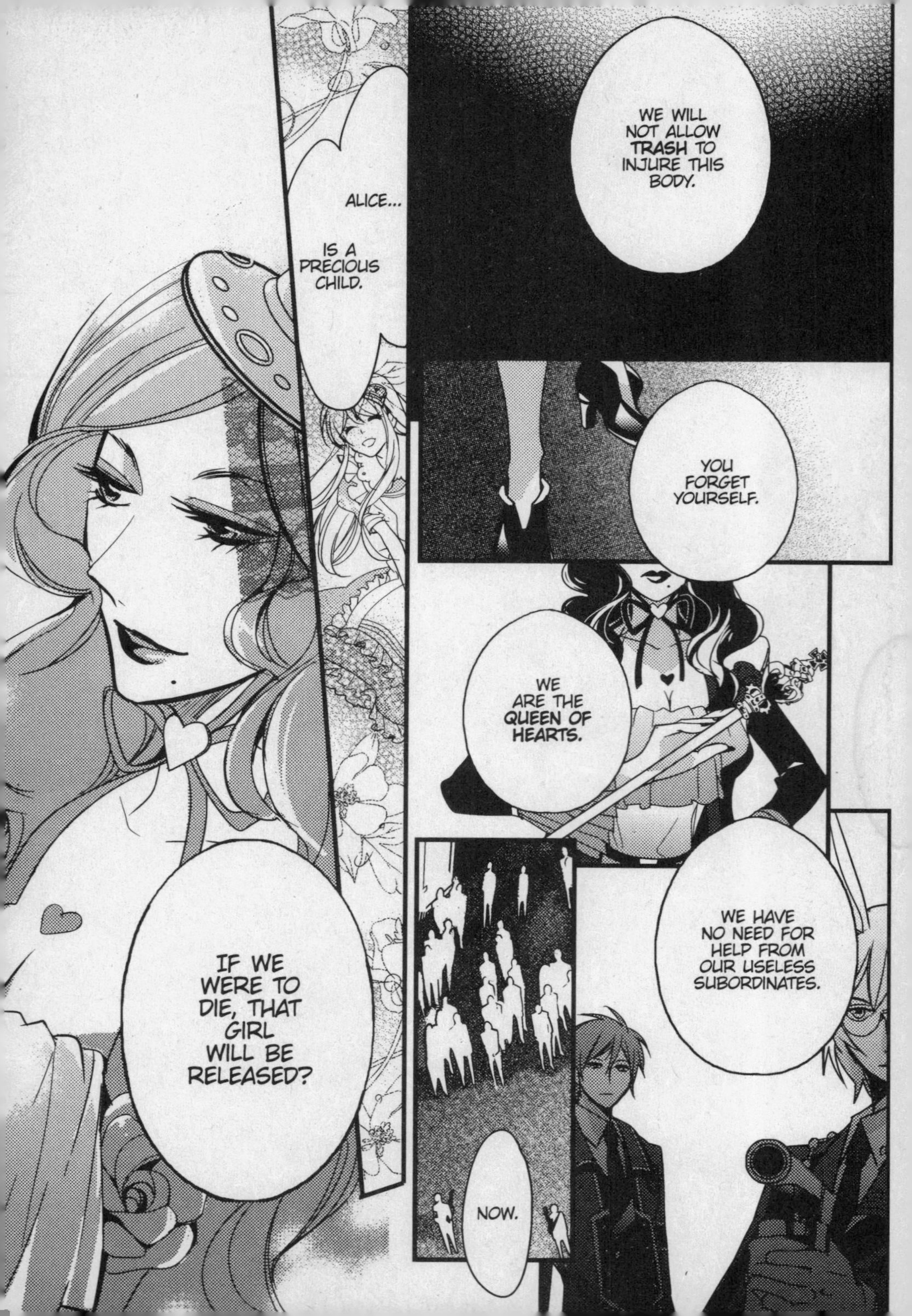
WE WILL NOT ALLOW TRASH TO INJURE THIS BODY.
YOU FORGET YOURSELF.
WE ARE THE QUEEN OF HEARTS.
WE HAVE NO NEED FOR HELP FROM OUR USELESS SUBORDINATES.
NOW.
ALICE...
IS A PRECIOUS CHILD.
IF WE WERE TO DIE, THAT GIRL WILL BE RELEASED?

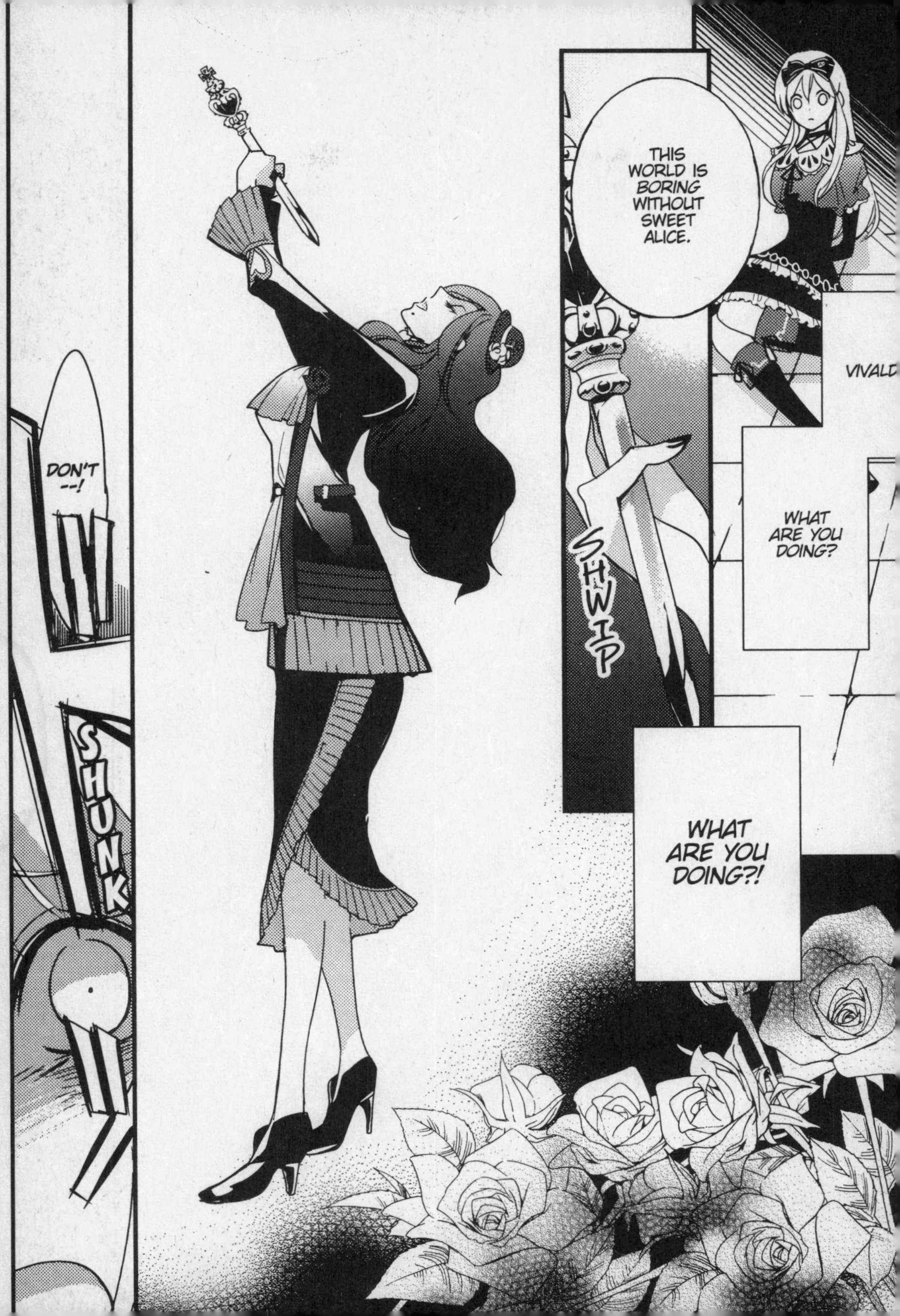
THIS WORLD IS BORING WITHOUT SWEET ALICE.
VIVALD
WHAT ARE YOU DOING?
SHWIP
WHAT ARE YOU DOING?!
DON'T --!
SHUNK

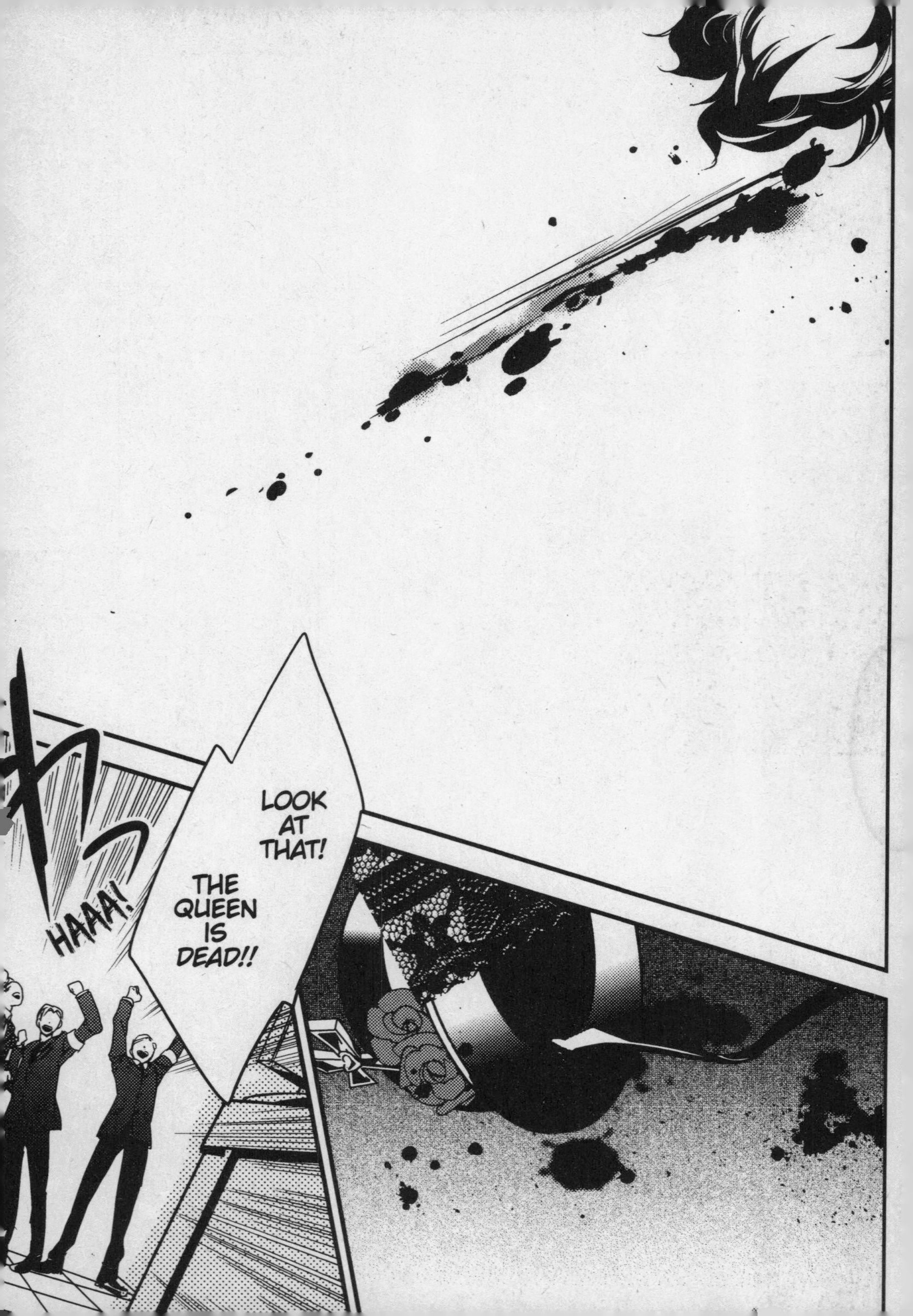
LOOK AT THAT!
THE QUEEN IS DEAD!!
HAAA!

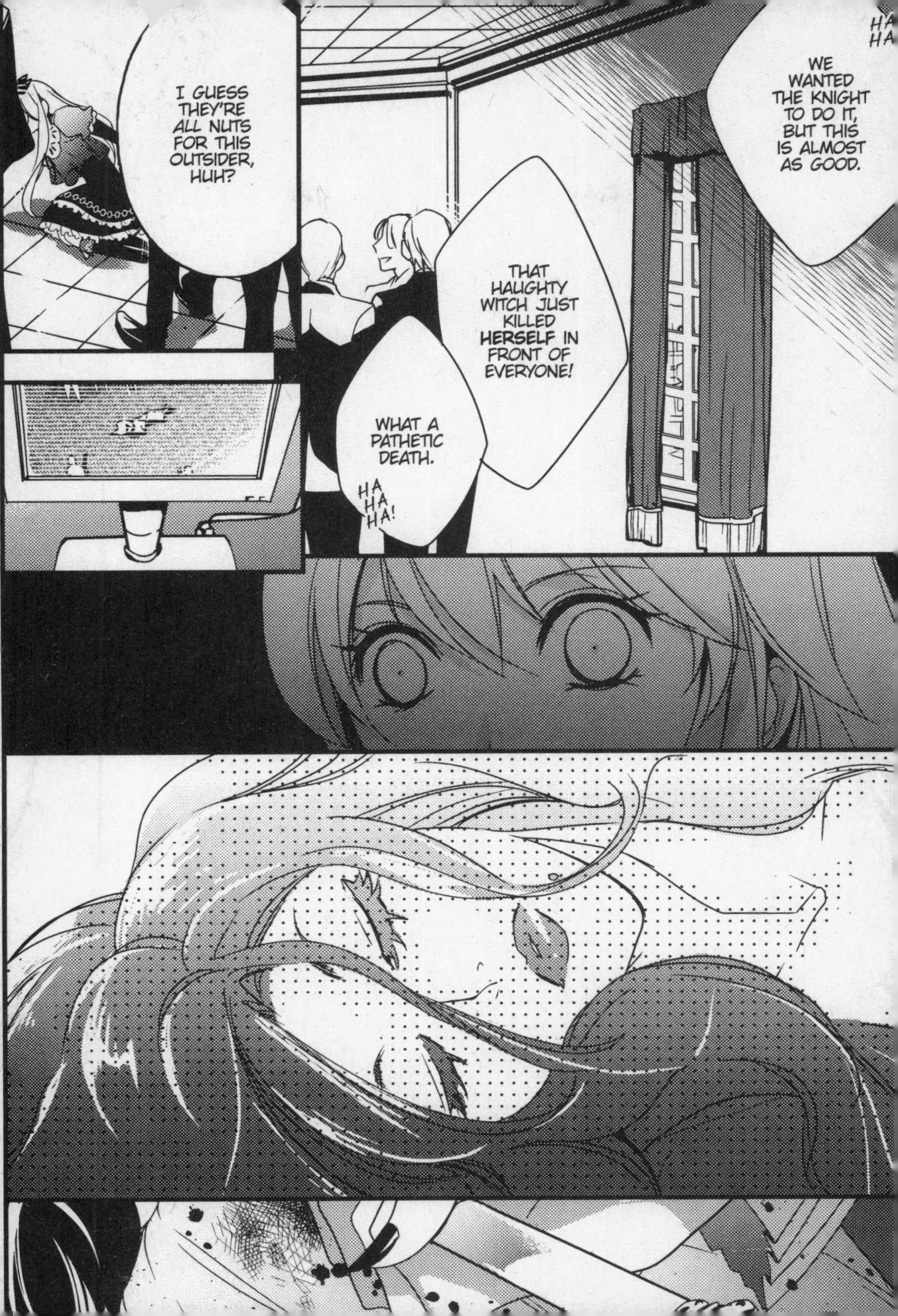
HA HA
WE WANTED THE KNIGHT TO DO IT, BUT THIS IS ALMOST AS GOOD.
THAT HAUGHTY WITCH JUST KILLED **HERSELF** IN FRONT OF EVERYONE!
WHAT A PATHETIC DEATH.
HA HA HA!
I GUESS THEY'RE ALL NUTS FOR THIS OUTSIDER, HUH?

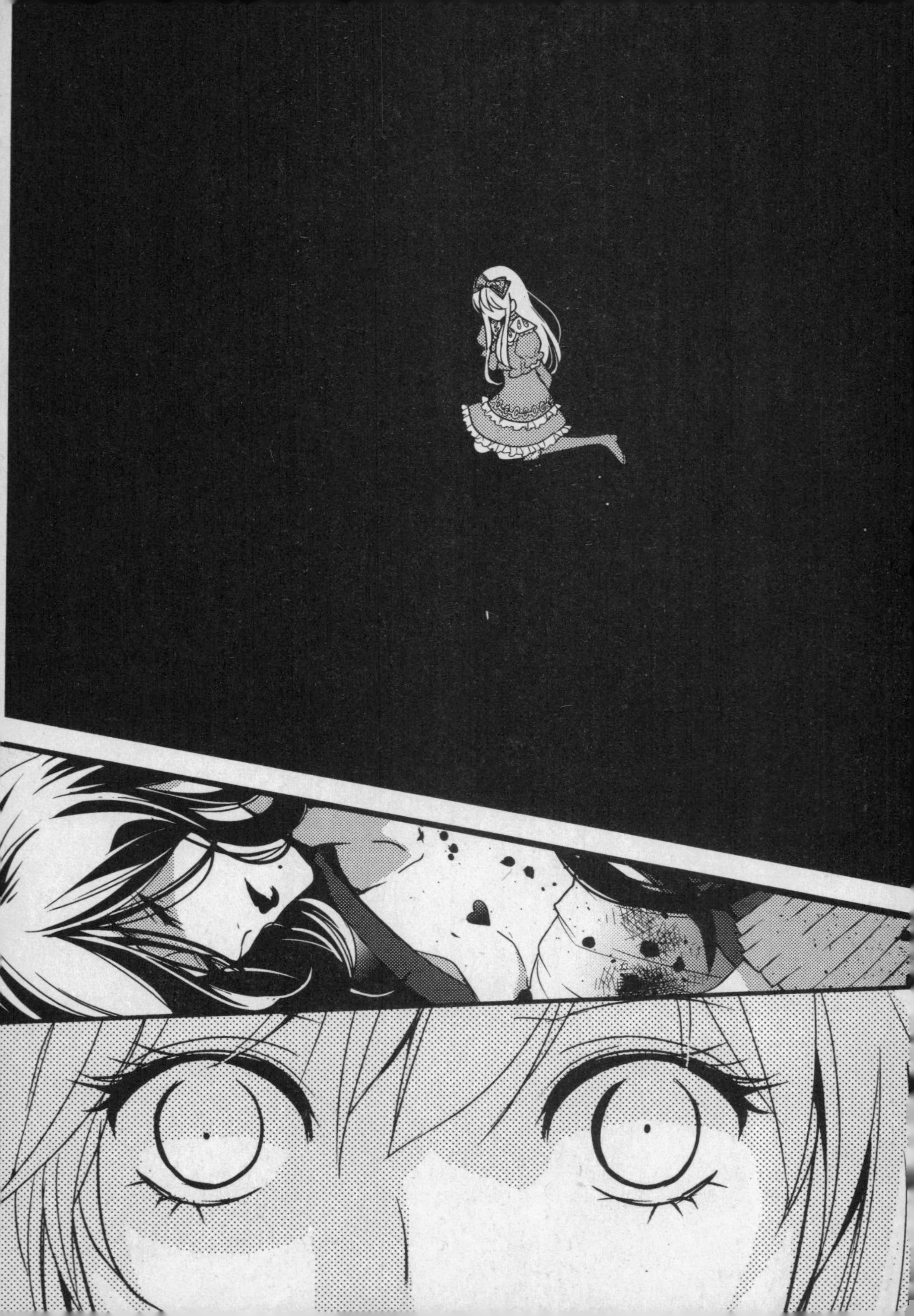

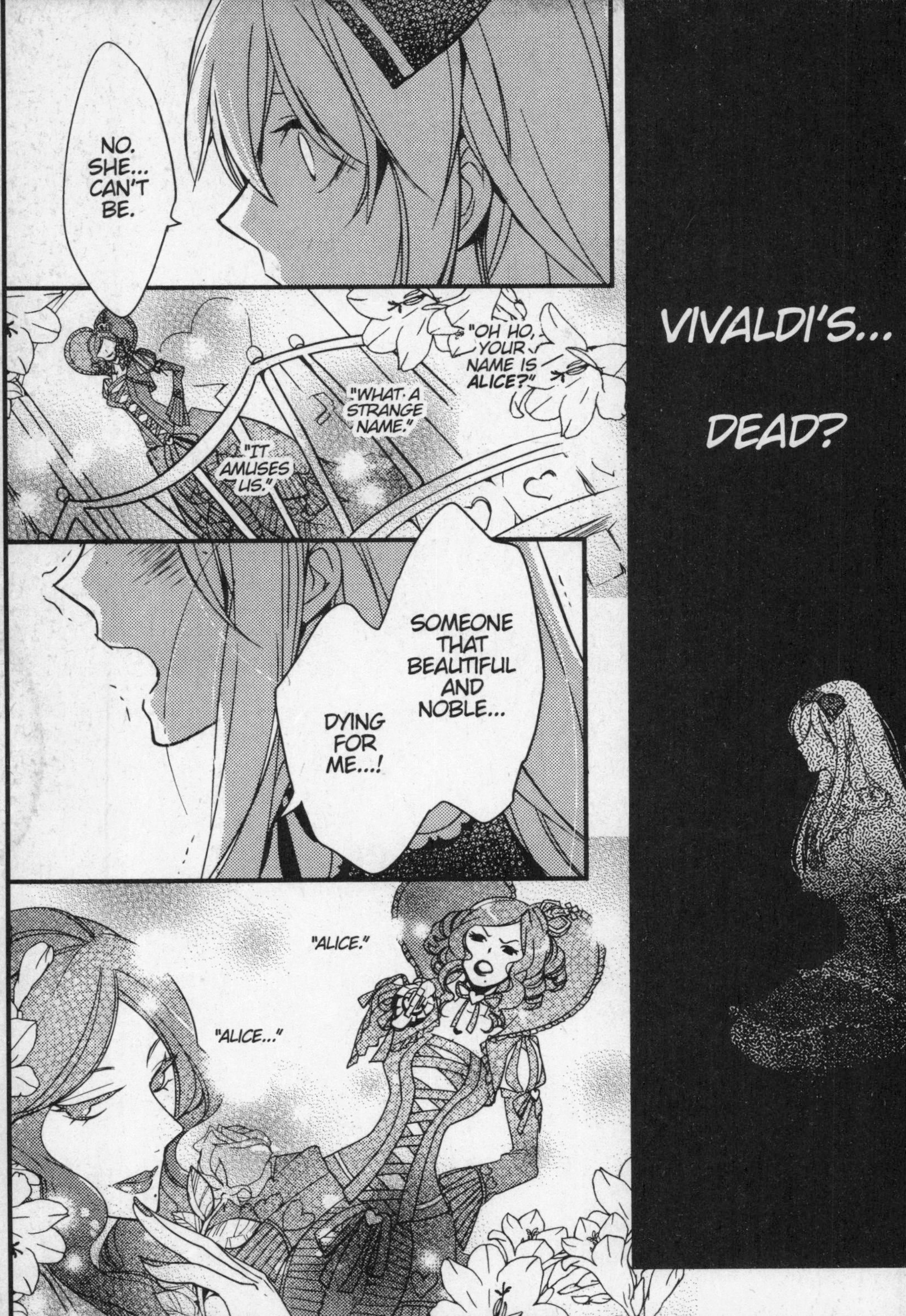
VIVALDI'S...
DEAD?
NO. SHE... CAN'T BE.
"OH HO, YOUR NAME IS ALICE?"
"WHAT A STRANGE NAME."
"IT AMUSES US."
SOMEONE THAT BEAUTIFUL AND NOBLE...
DYING FOR ME...!
"ALICE."
"ALICE..."

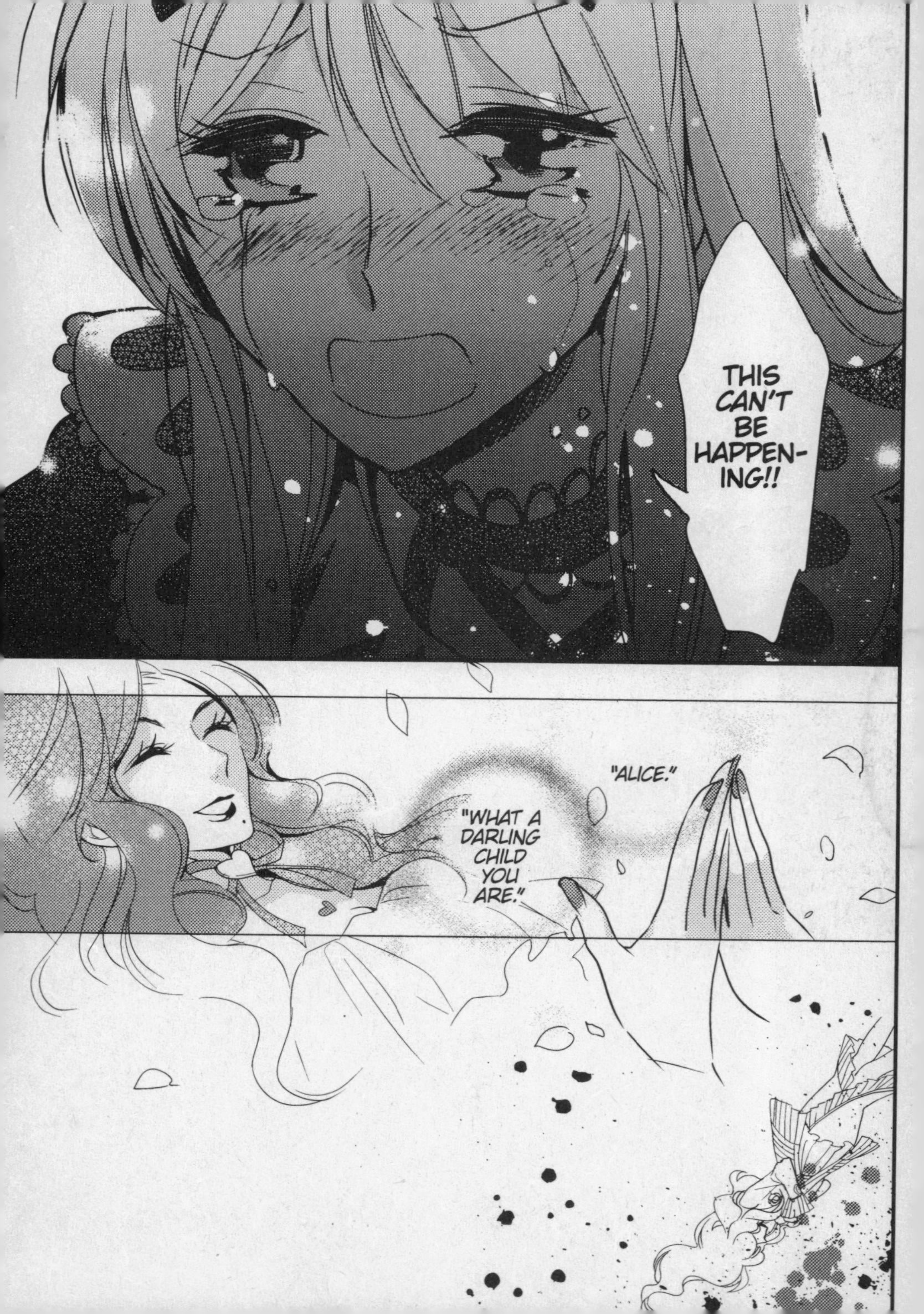
THIS CAN'T BE HAPPENING!!
"ALICE."
"WHAT A DARLING CHILD YOU ARE."

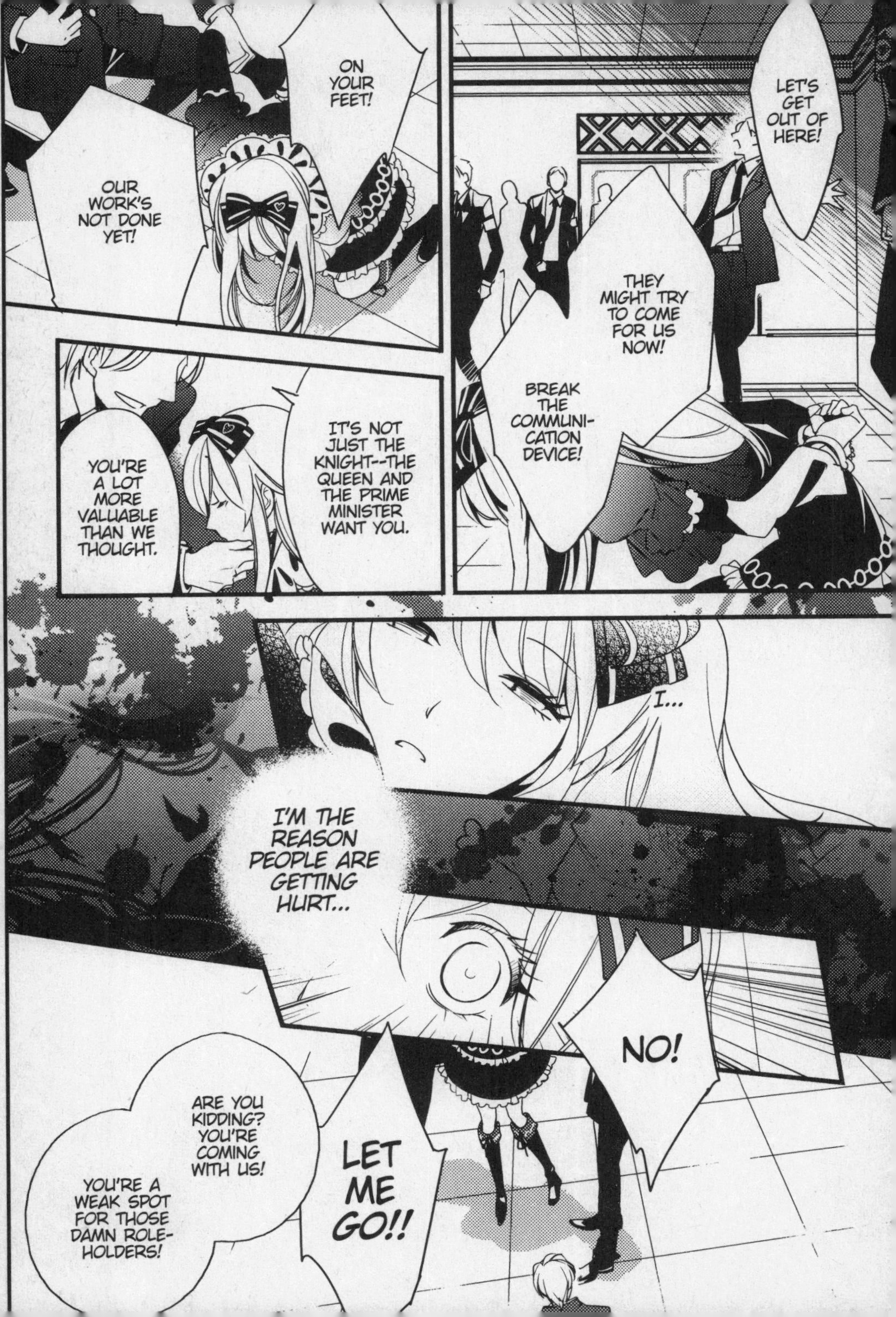
LET'S GET OUT OF HERE!
THEY MIGHT TRY TO COME FOR US NOW!
BREAK THE COMMUNICATION DEVICE!
ON YOUR FEET!
OUR WORK'S NOT DONE YET!
IT'S NOT JUST THE KNIGHT--THE QUEEN AND THE PRIME MINISTER WANT YOU.
YOU'RE A LOT MORE VALUABLE THAN WE THOUGHT.
I...
I'M THE REASON PEOPLE ARE GETTING HURT...
NO!
LET ME GO!!
ARE YOU KIDDING? YOU'RE COMING WITH US!
YOU'RE A WEAK SPOT FOR THOSE DAMN ROLE-HOLDERS!

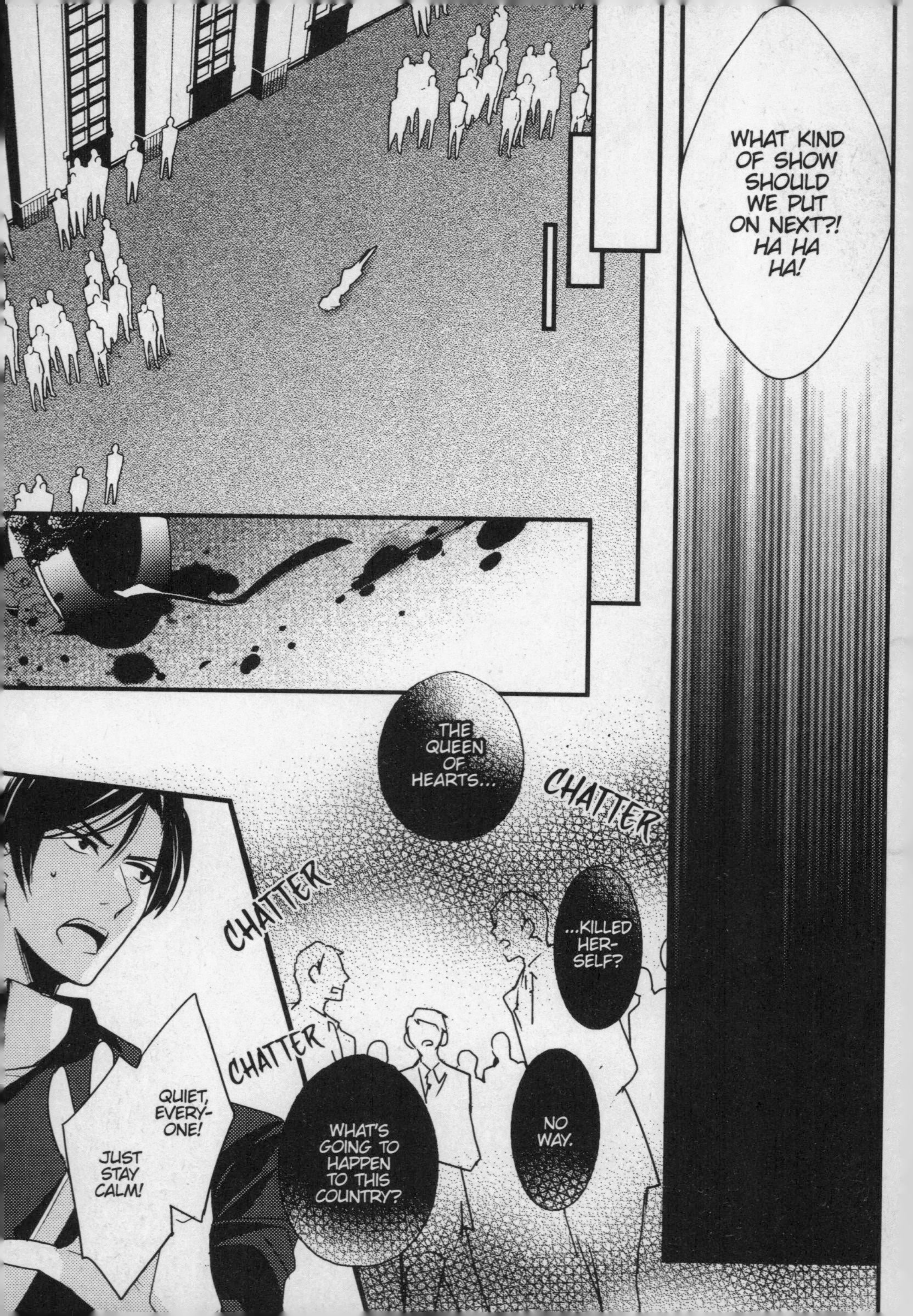
WHAT KIND OF SHOW SHOULD WE PUT ON NEXT?! HA HA HA!
THE QUEEN OF HEARTS...
CHATTER
...KILLED HER-SELF?
CHATTER
NO WAY.
CHATTER
WHAT'S GOING TO HAPPEN TO THIS COUNTRY?
QUIET, EVERY-ONE!
JUST STAY CALM!

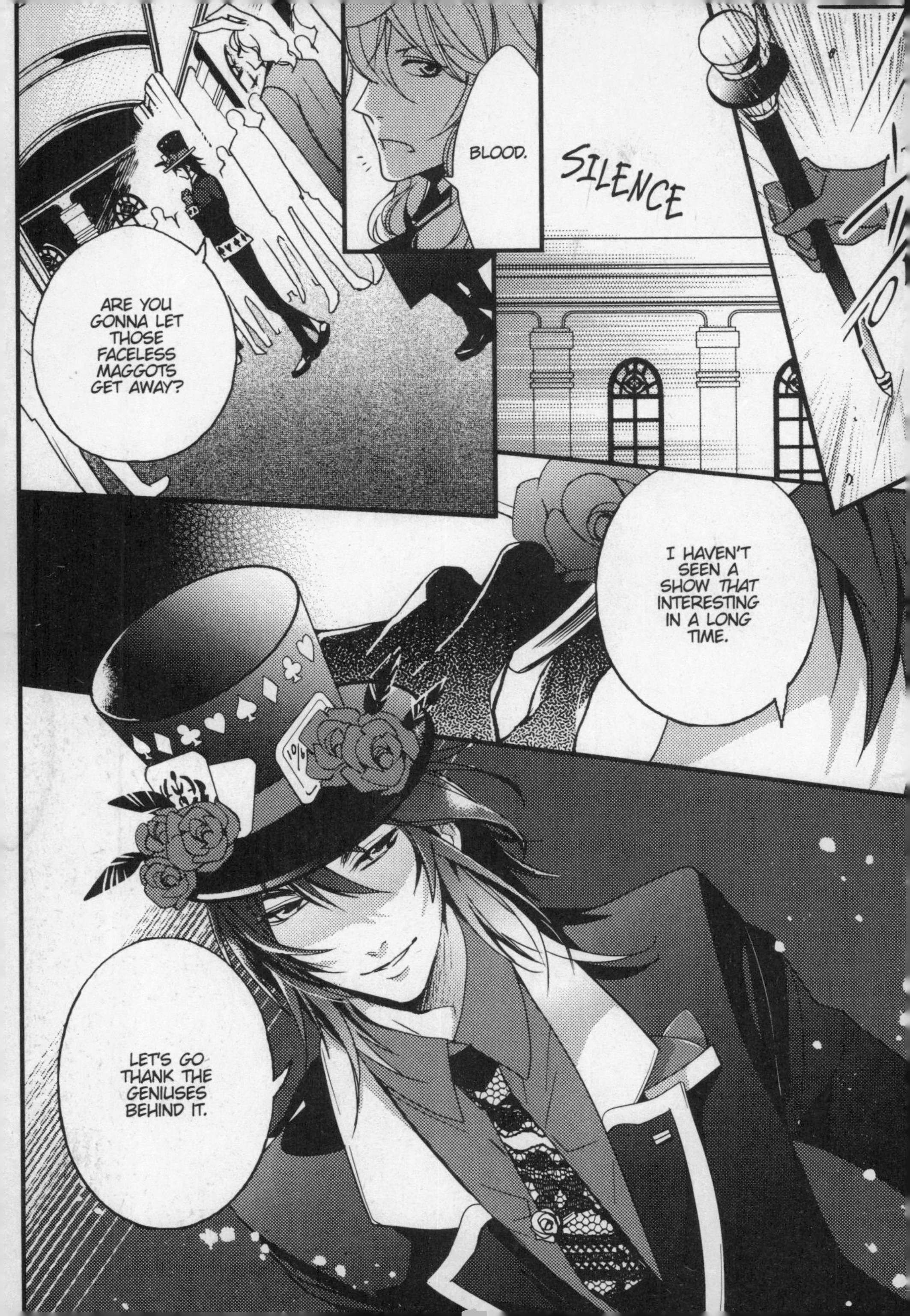
SILENCE
BLOOD.
ARE YOU GONNA LET THOSE FACELESS MAGGOTS GET AWAY?
I HAVEN'T SEEN A SHOW *THAT* INTERESTING IN A LONG TIME.
LET'S GO THANK THE GENIUSES BEHIND IT.

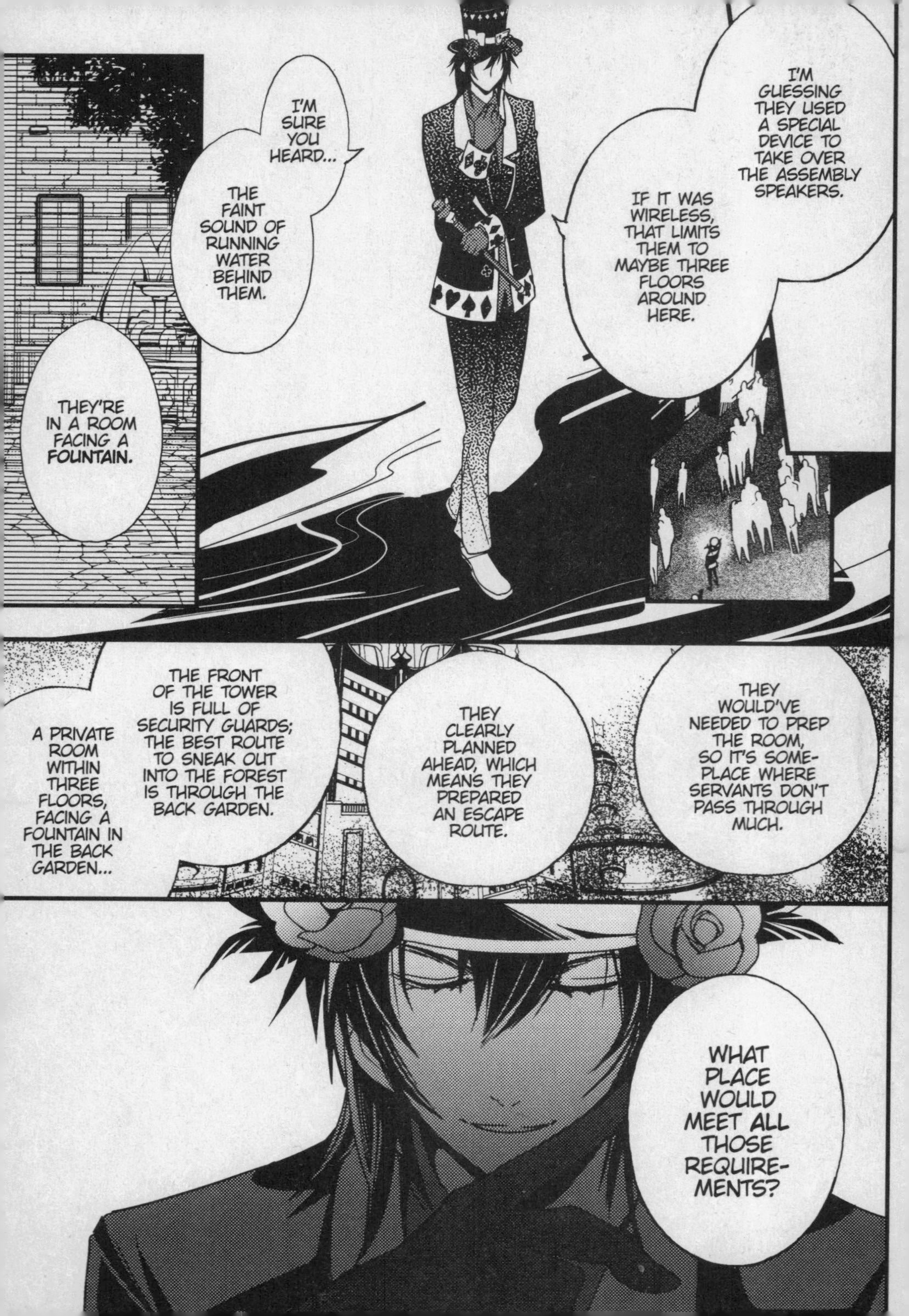
I'M GUESSING THEY USED A SPECIAL DEVICE TO TAKE OVER THE ASSEMBLY SPEAKERS.
IF IT WAS WIRELESS, THAT LIMITS THEM TO MAYBE THREE FLOORS AROUND HERE.
I'M SURE YOU HEARD...
THE FAINT SOUND OF RUNNING WATER BEHIND THEM.
THEY'RE IN A ROOM FACING A **FOUNTAIN.**
THEY WOULD'VE NEEDED TO PREP THE ROOM, SO IT'S SOME-PLACE WHERE SERVANTS DON'T PASS THROUGH MUCH.
THEY CLEARLY PLANNED AHEAD, WHICH MEANS THEY PREPARED AN ESCAPE ROUTE.
THE FRONT OF THE TOWER IS FULL OF SECURITY GUARDS; THE BEST ROUTE TO SNEAK OUT INTO THE FOREST IS THROUGH THE BACK GARDEN.
A PRIVATE ROOM WITHIN THREE FLOORS, FACING A FOUNTAIN IN THE BACK GARDEN...
WHAT PLACE WOULD MEET **ALL** THOSE REQUIRE-MENTS?

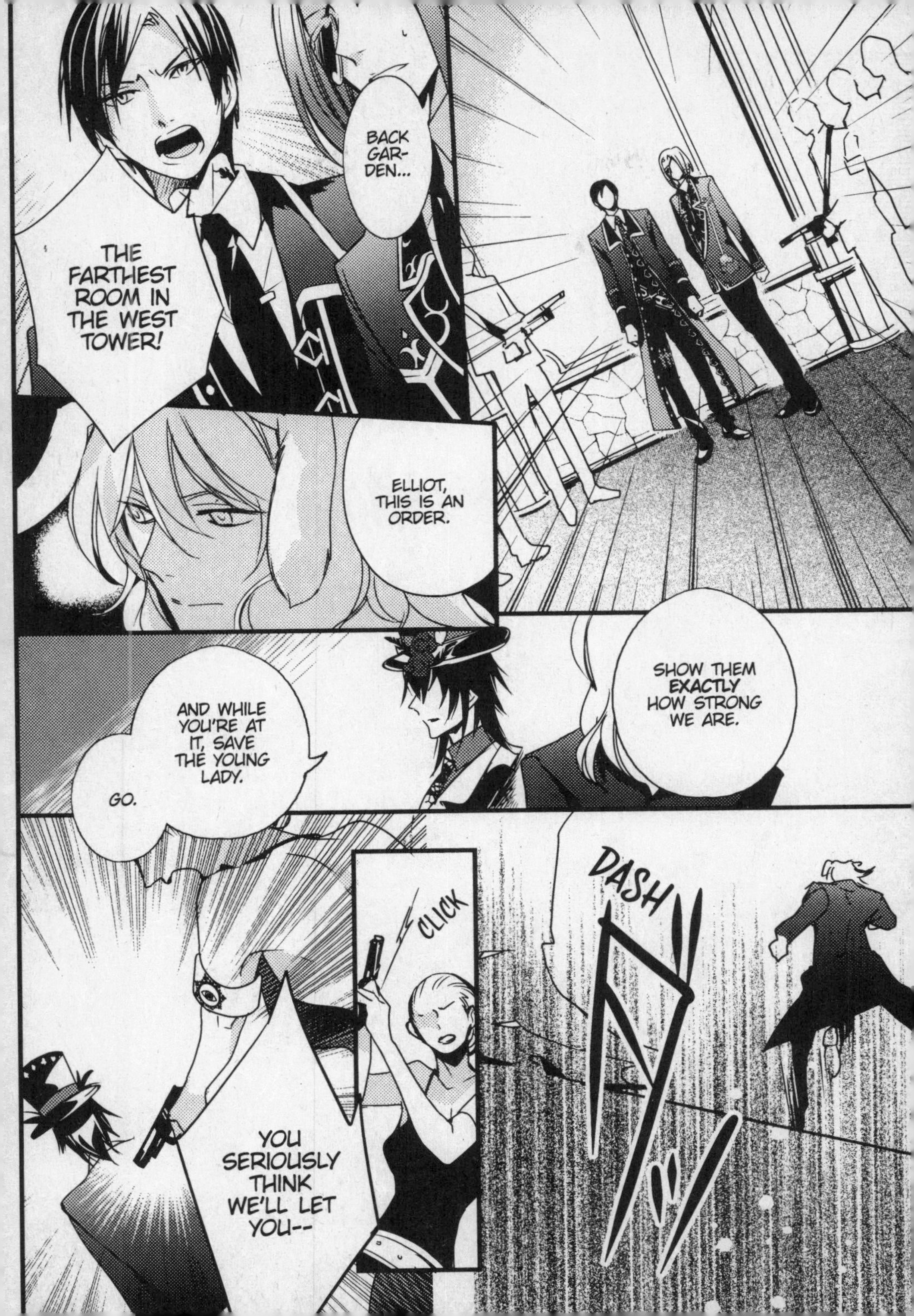
BACK GAR-DEN...
THE FARTHEST ROOM IN THE WEST TOWER!
ELLIOT, THIS IS AN ORDER.
SHOW THEM EXACTLY HOW STRONG WE ARE.
AND WHILE YOU'RE AT IT, SAVE THE YOUNG LADY.
GO.
DASH
CLICK
YOU SERIOUSLY THINK WE'LL LET YOU--

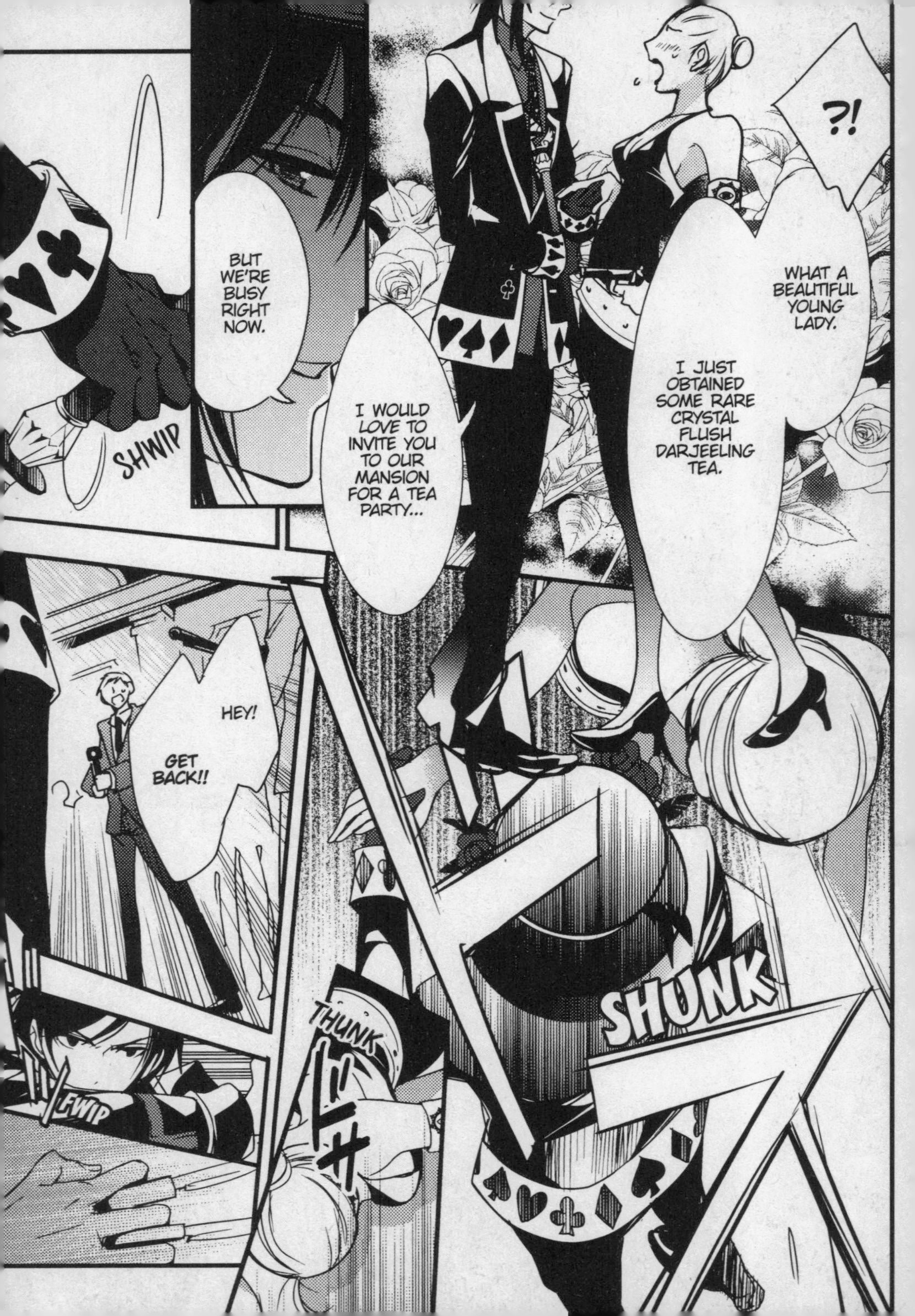
?!
WHAT A BEAUTIFUL YOUNG LADY.
I JUST OBTAINED SOME RARE CRYSTAL FLUSH DARJEELING TEA.
I WOULD LOVE TO INVITE YOU TO OUR MANSION FOR A TEA PARTY...
BUT WE'RE BUSY RIGHT NOW.
SHWIP
SHUNK
THUNK
HEY!
GET BACK!!
FWIP

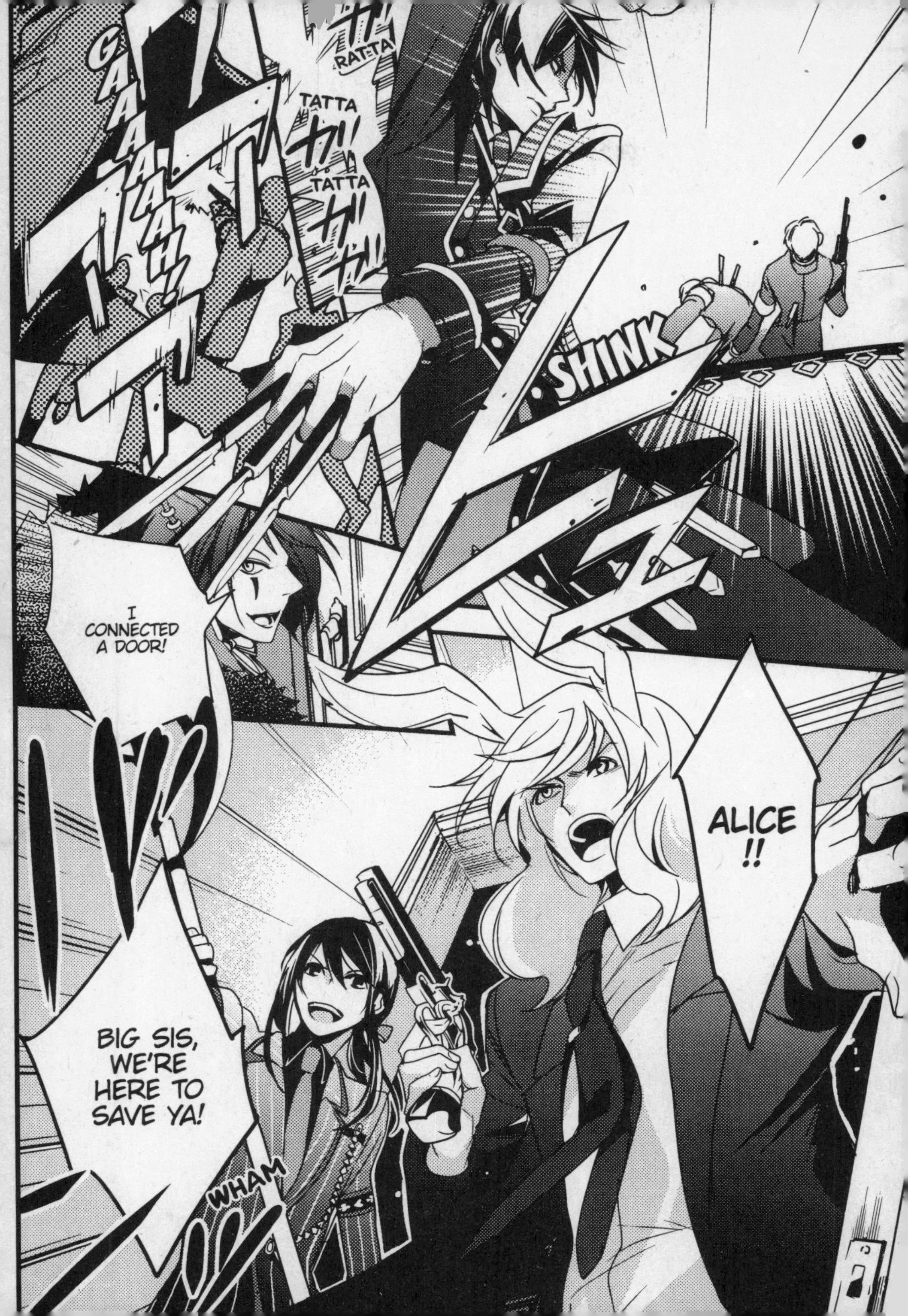

SHINK
RAT-TA
TATTA
TATTA
GAAAAAAH!
I CONNECTED A DOOR!
ALICE!!
BIG SIS, WE'RE HERE TO SAVE YA!
WHAM

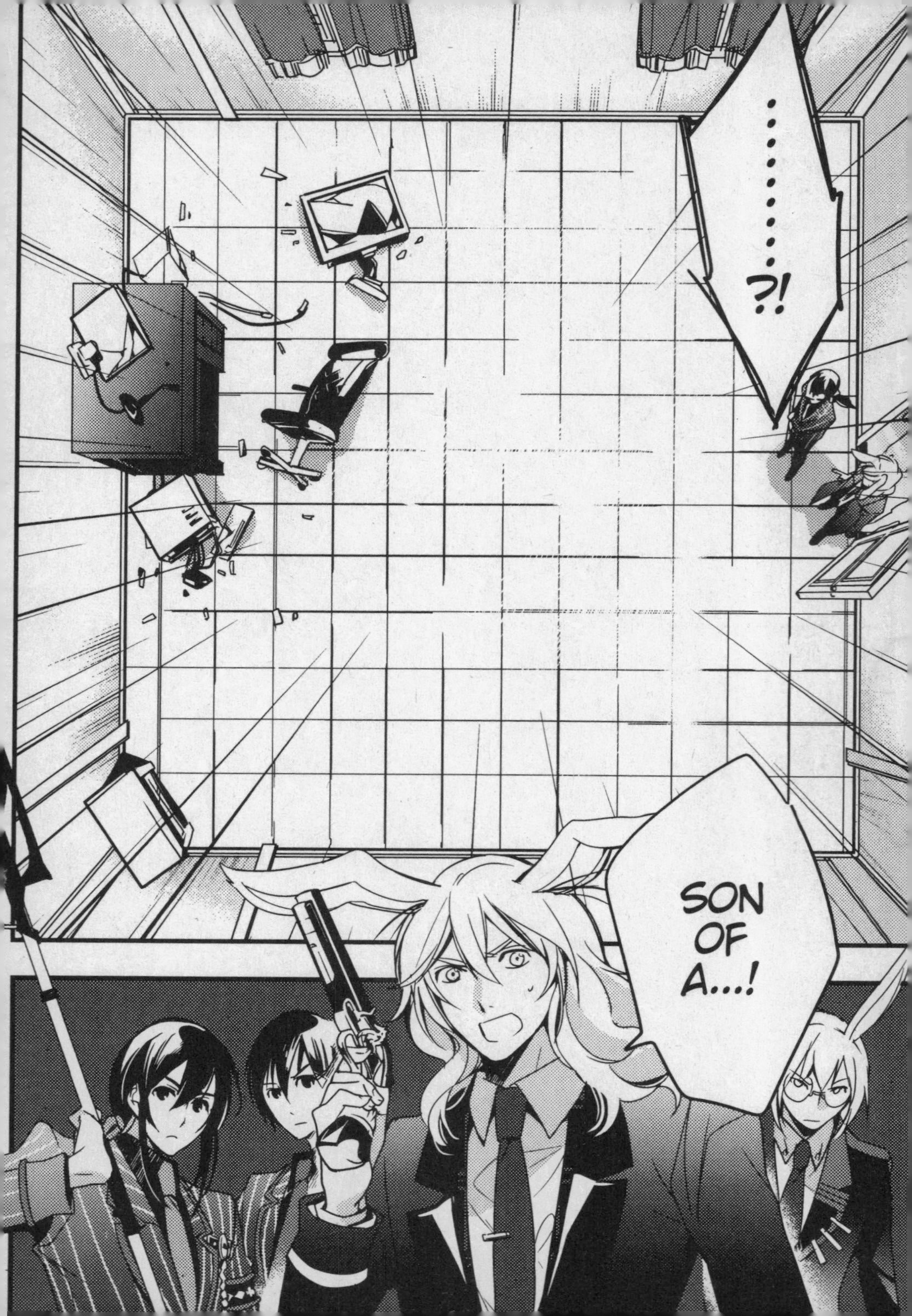

.........?!
SON OF A...!

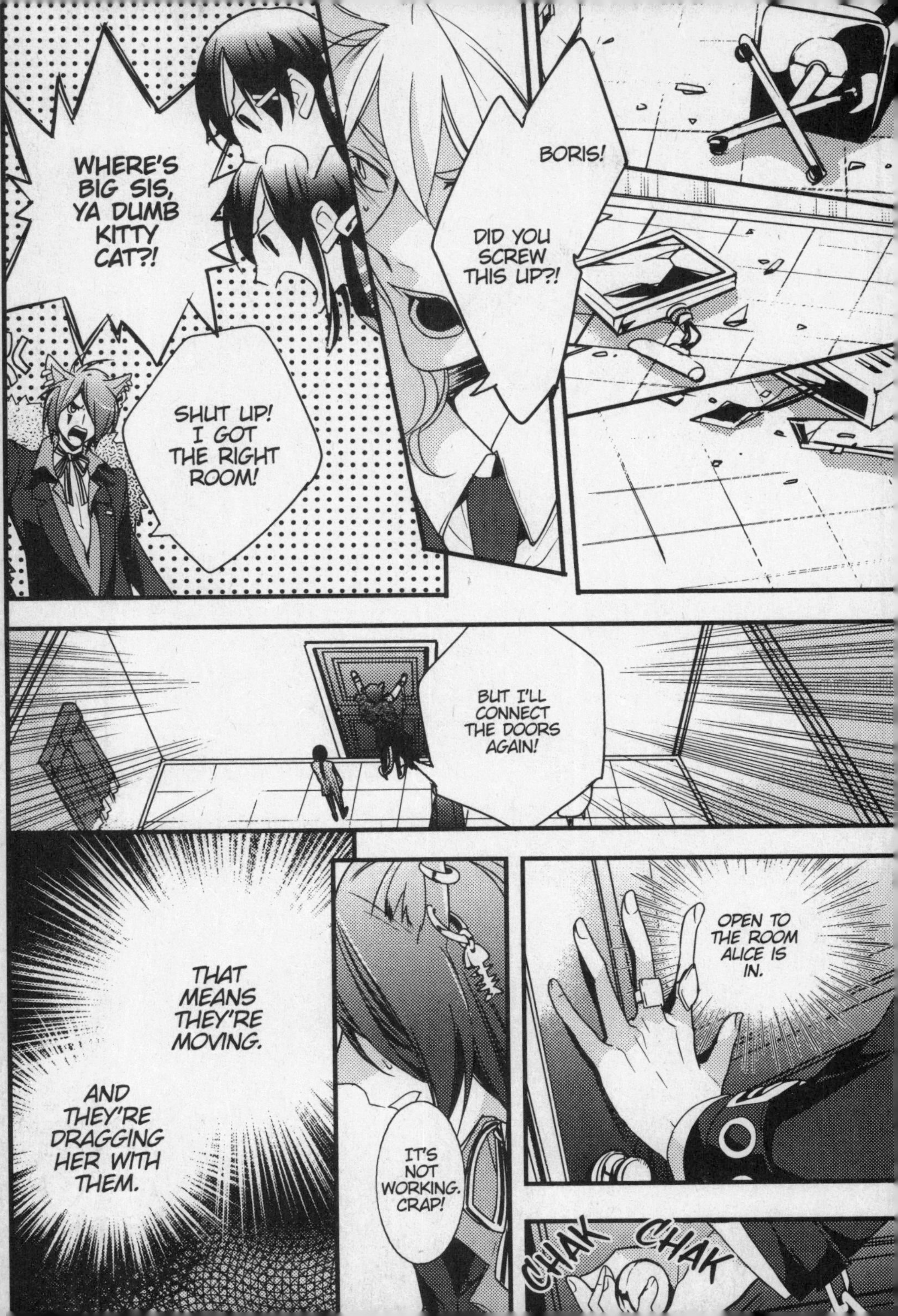
BORIS!
DID YOU SCREW THIS UP?!
WHERE'S BIG SIS, YA DUMB KITTY CAT?!
SHUT UP! I GOT THE RIGHT ROOM!
BUT I'LL CONNECT THE DOORS AGAIN!
OPEN TO THE ROOM ALICE IS IN.
CHAK CHAK
IT'S NOT WORKING. CRAP!
THAT MEANS THEY'RE MOVING.
AND THEY'RE DRAGGING HER WITH THEM.

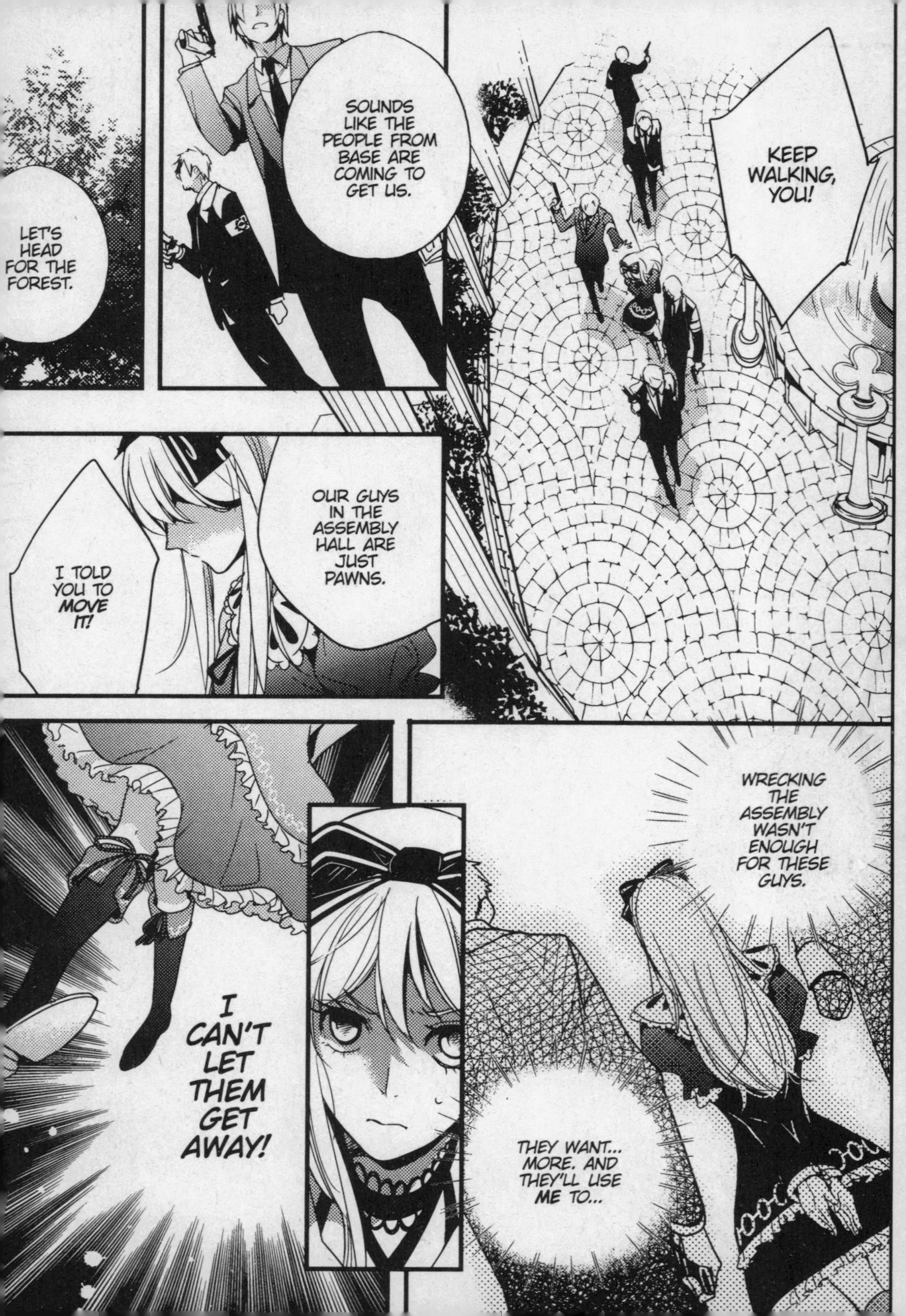
KEEP WALKING, YOU!
SOUNDS LIKE THE PEOPLE FROM BASE ARE COMING TO GET US.
LET'S HEAD FOR THE FOREST.
OUR GUYS IN THE ASSEMBLY HALL ARE JUST PAWNS.
I TOLD YOU TO *MOVE IT!*
WRECKING THE ASSEMBLY WASN'T ENOUGH FOR THESE GUYS.
THEY WANT... MORE. AND THEY'LL USE ME TO...
I CAN'T LET THEM GET AWAY!

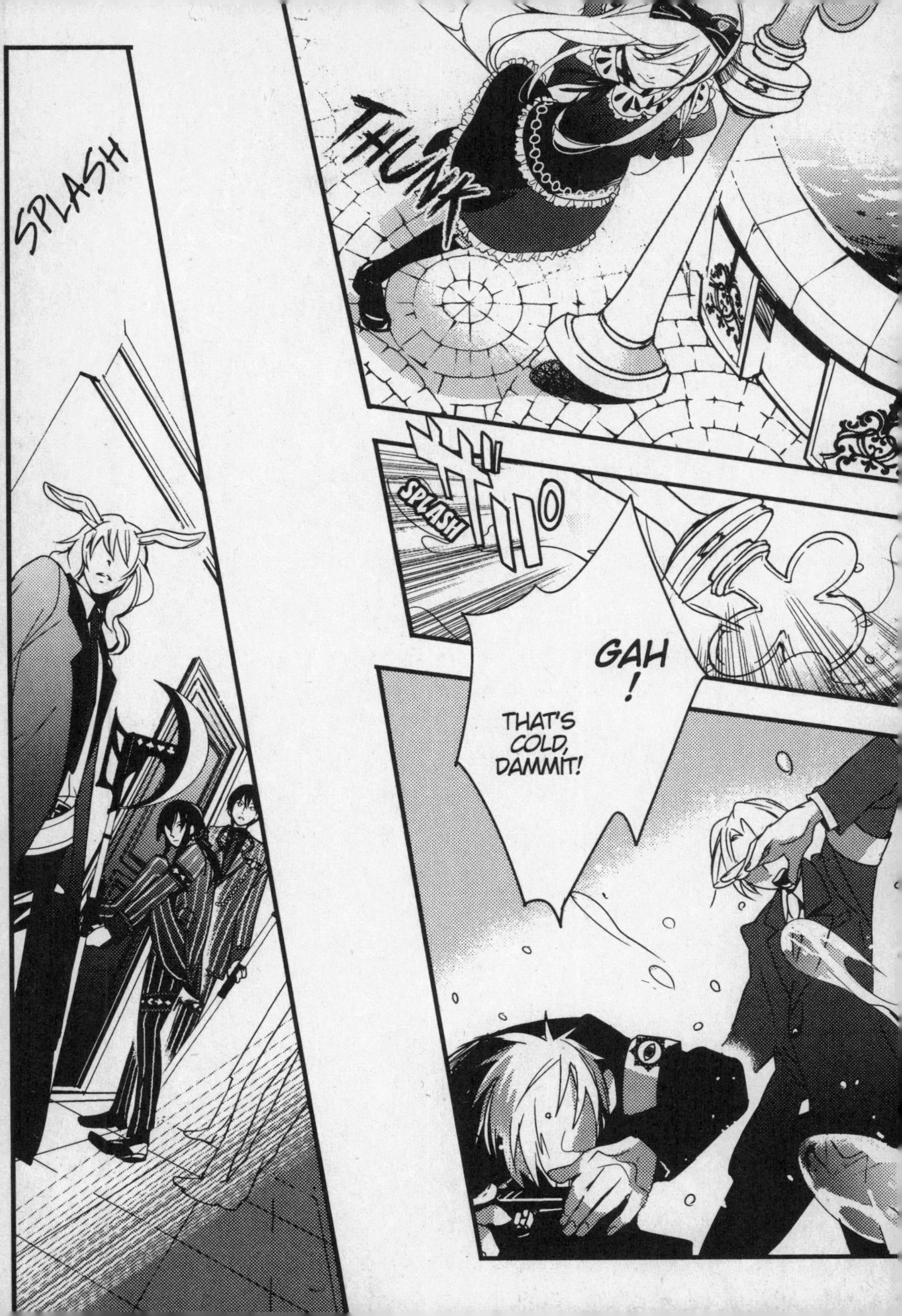
THUNK
SPLASH
GAH!
THAT'S COLD, DAMMIT!
SPLASH

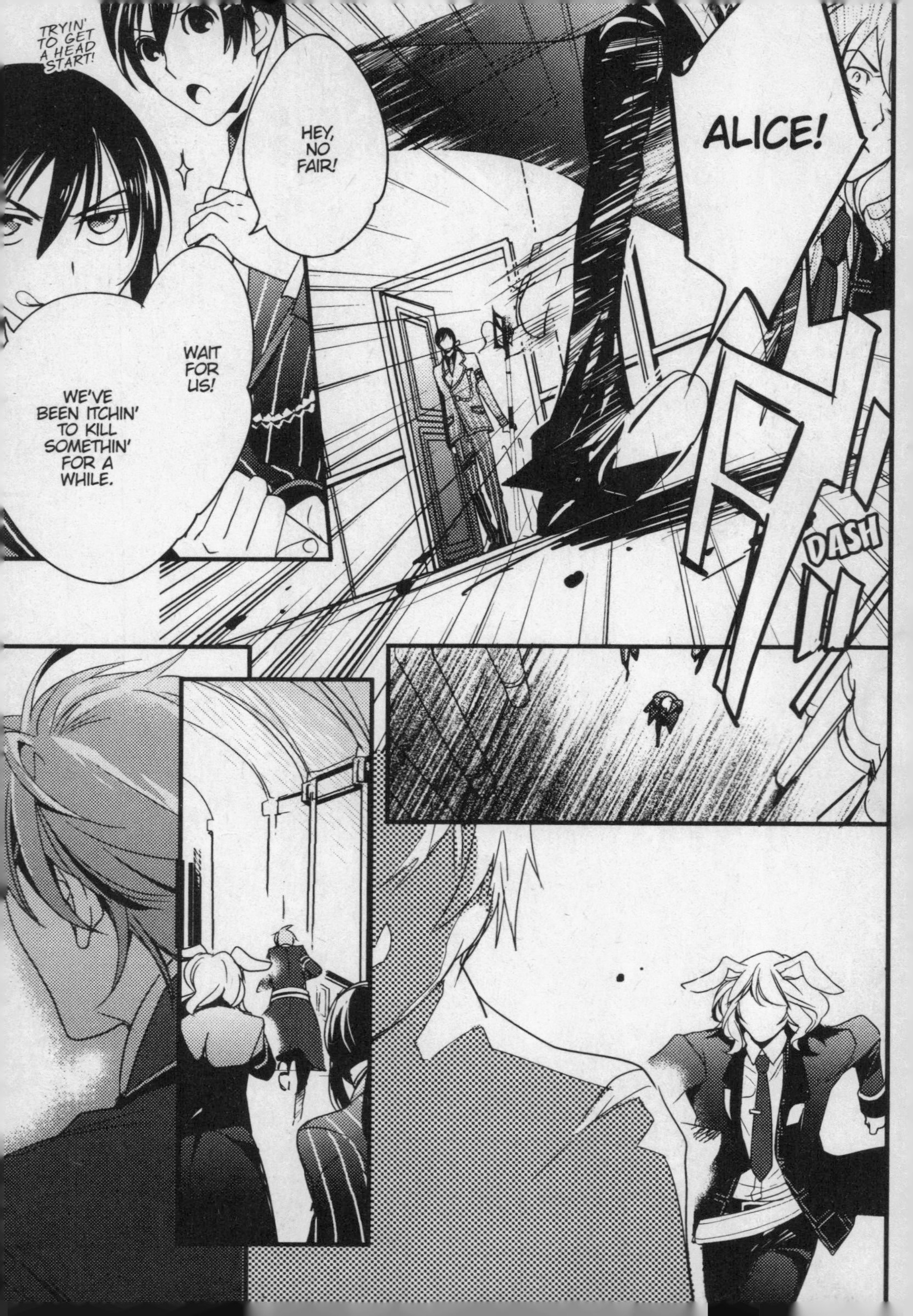
ALICE!
DASH
TRYIN' TO GET A HEAD START!
HEY, NO FAIR!
WAIT FOR US!
WE'VE BEEN ITCHIN' TO KILL SOMETHIN' FOR A WHILE.

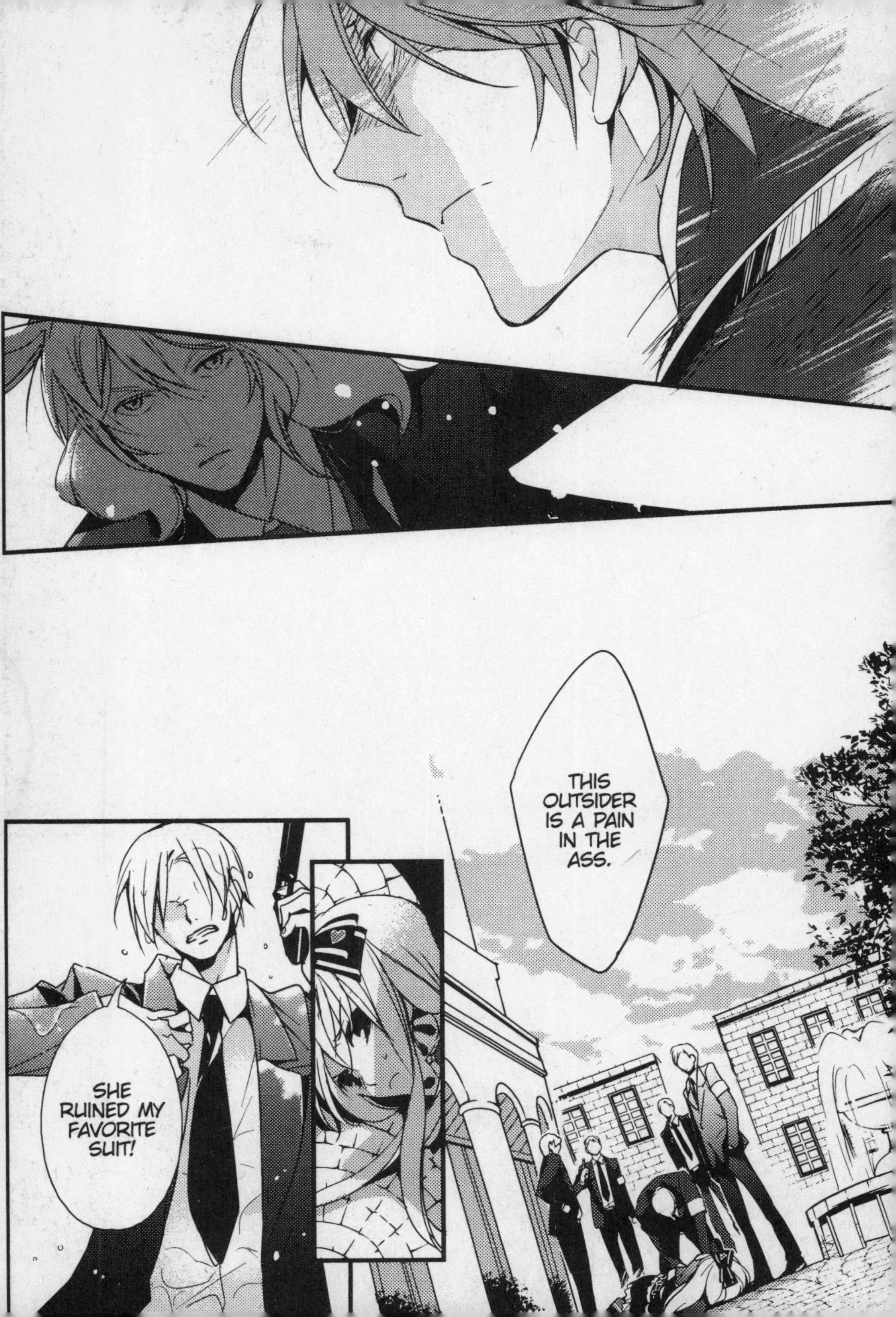
THIS OUTSIDER IS A PAIN IN THE ASS.
SHE RUINED MY FAVORITE SUIT!

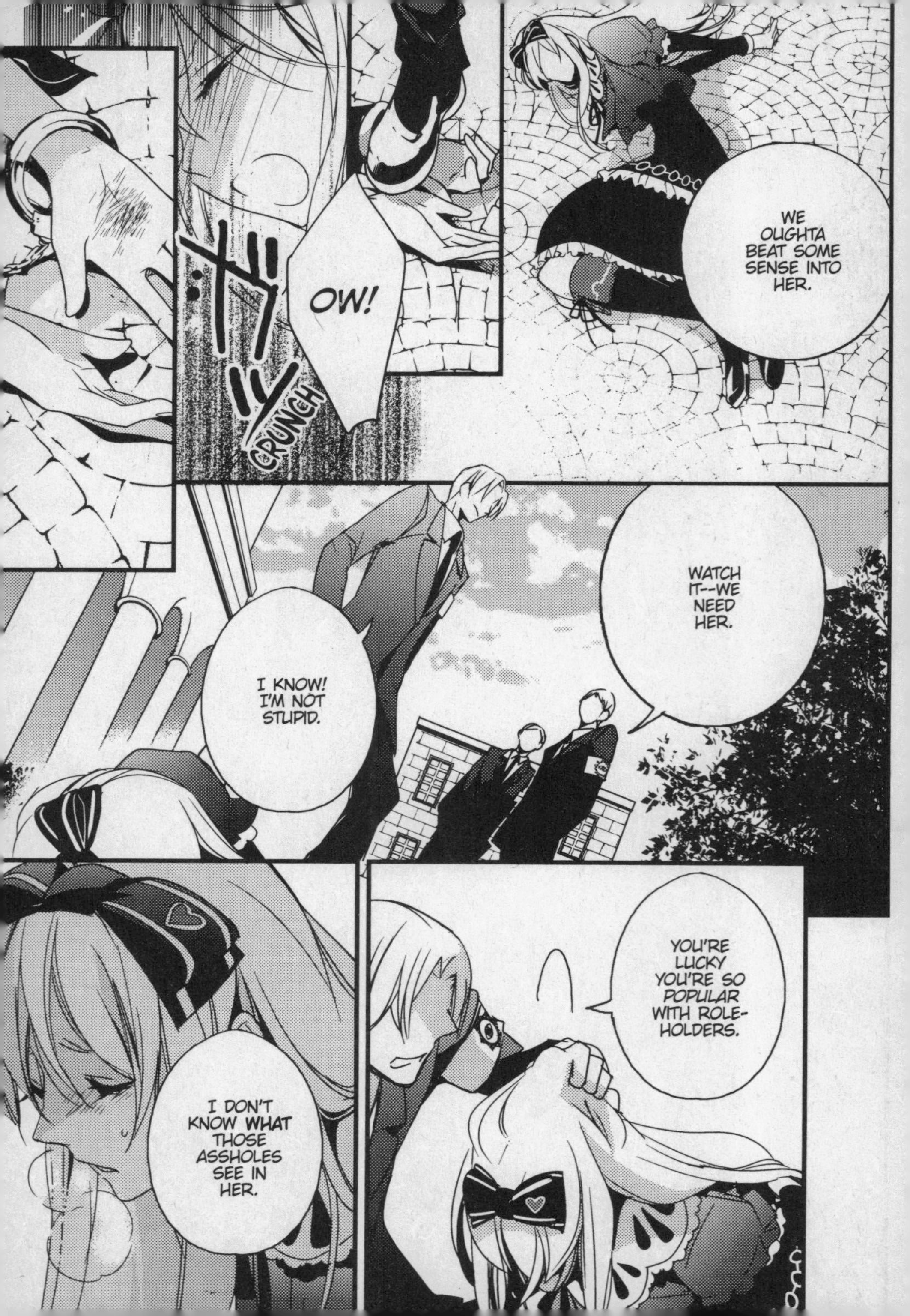
WE OUGHTA BEAT SOME SENSE INTO HER.
OW!
CRUNCH
WATCH IT--WE NEED HER.
I KNOW! I'M NOT STUPID.
YOU'RE LUCKY YOU'RE SO POPULAR WITH ROLE-HOLDERS.
I DON'T KNOW WHAT THOSE ASSHOLES SEE IN HER.

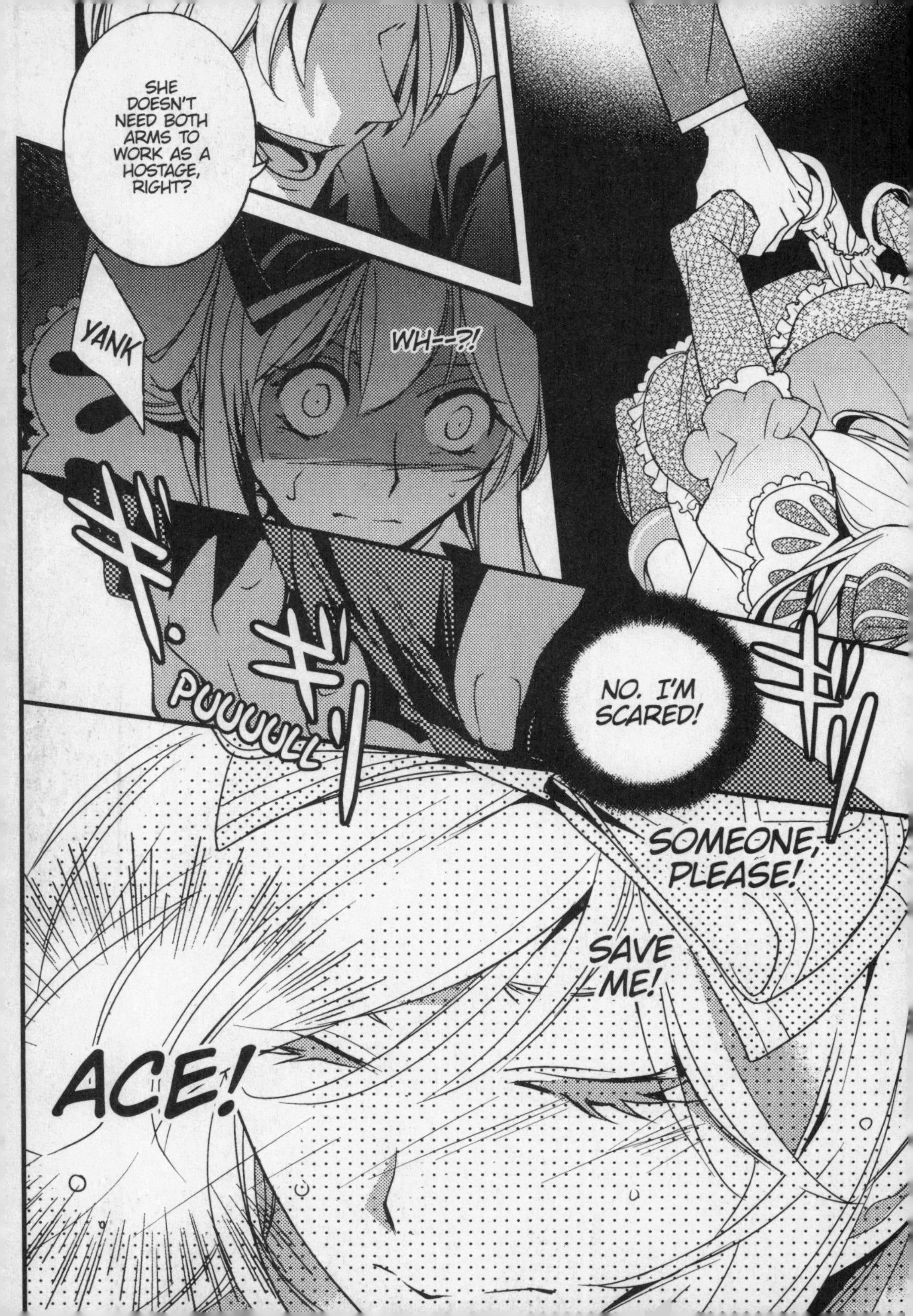
SHE DOESN'T NEED BOTH ARMS TO WORK AS A HOSTAGE, RIGHT?
YANK
WH--?!
PUUUULL
NO. I'M SCARED!
SOMEONE, PLEASE!
SAVE ME!
ACE!

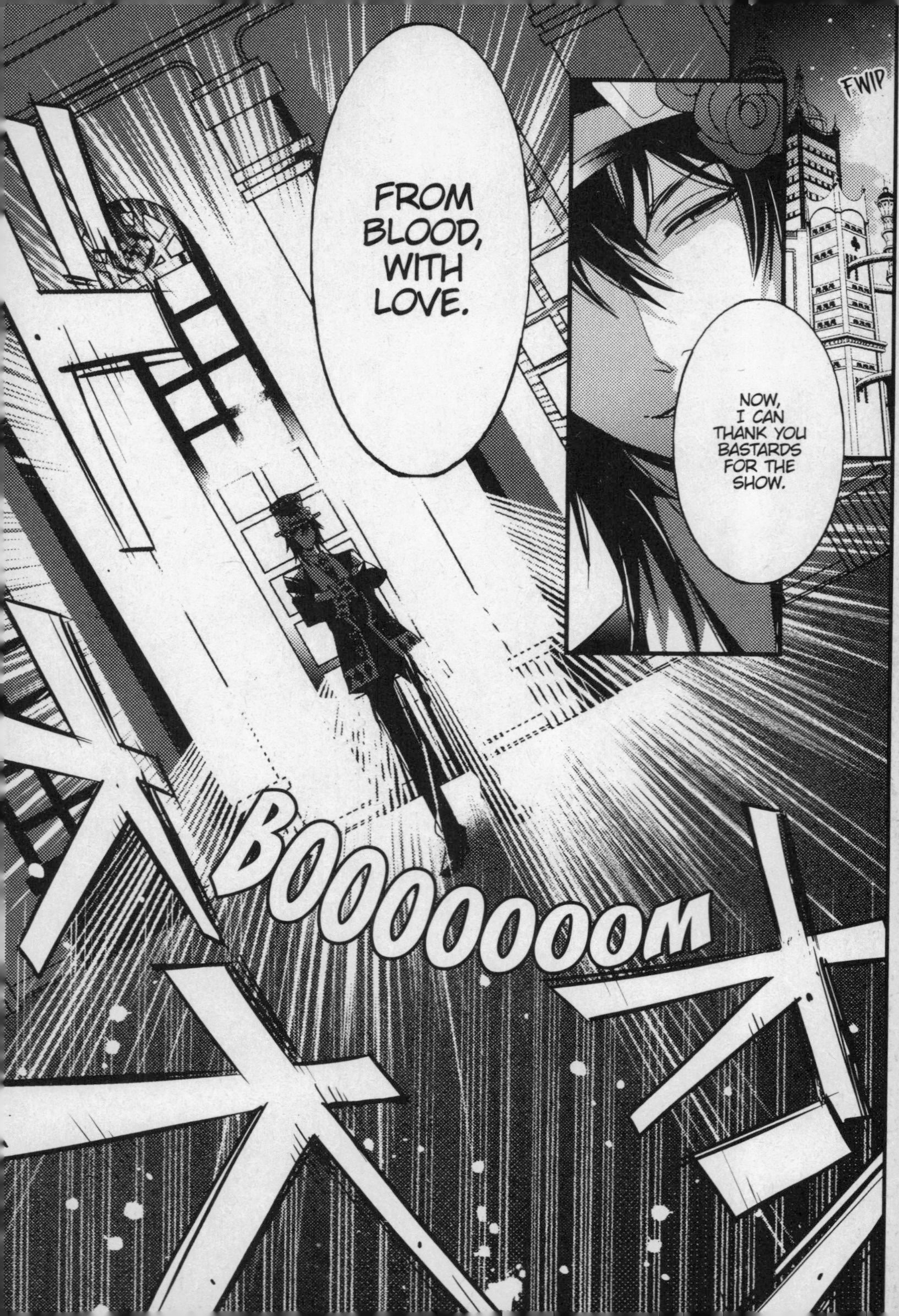
FWIP
NOW, I CAN THANK YOU BASTARDS FOR THE SHOW.
FROM BLOOD, WITH LOVE.
BOOOOOOOM

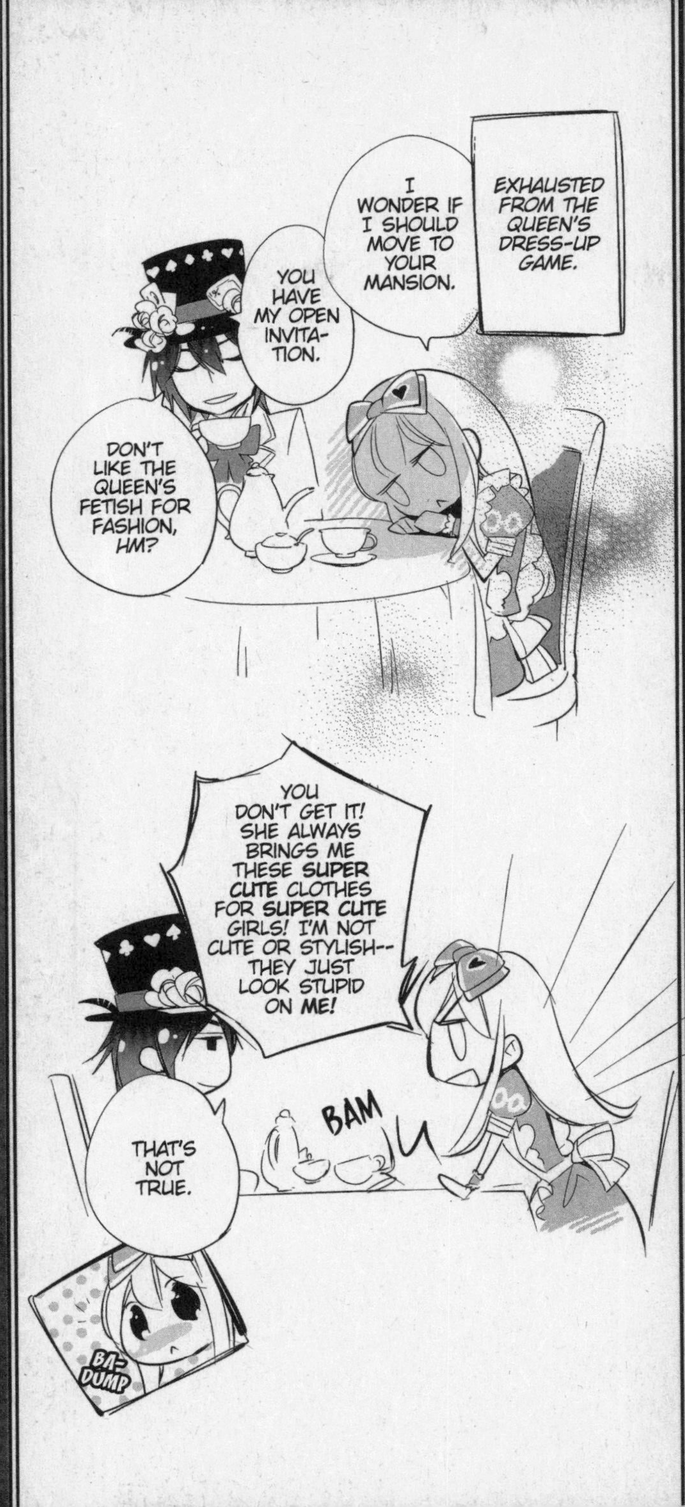
EXHAUSTED FROM THE QUEEN'S DRESS-UP GAME.
I WONDER IF I SHOULD MOVE TO YOUR MANSION.
YOU HAVE MY OPEN INVITATION.
DON'T LIKE THE QUEEN'S FETISH FOR FASHION, HM?
YOU DON'T GET IT! SHE ALWAYS BRINGS ME THESE **SUPER CUTE** CLOTHES FOR **SUPER CUTE** GIRLS! I'M NOT CUTE OR STYLISH-- THEY JUST LOOK STUPID ON **ME!**
BAM
THAT'S NOT TRUE.
BA-DUMP

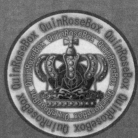

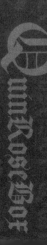

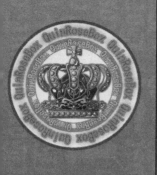

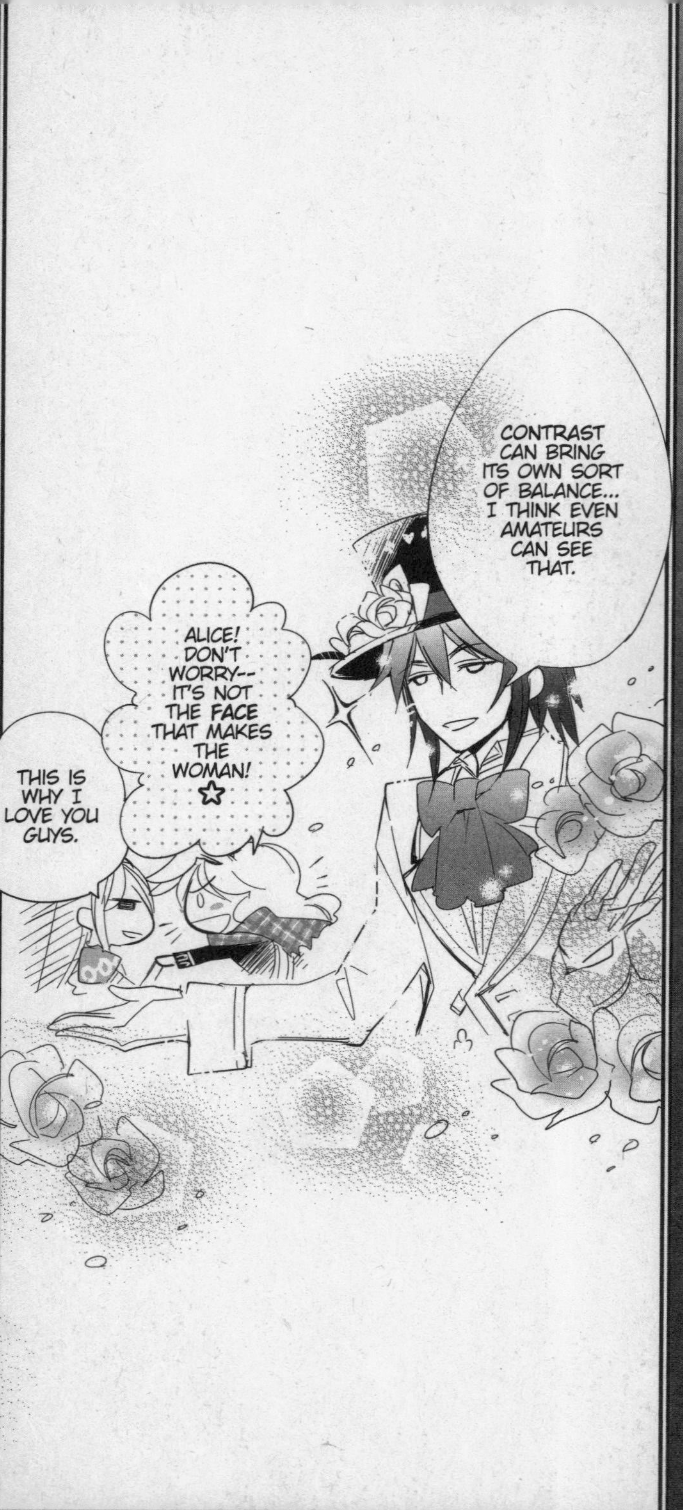
CONTRAST CAN BRING ITS OWN SORT OF BALANCE... I THINK EVEN AMATEURS CAN SEE THAT.
ALICE! DON'T WORRY-- IT'S NOT THE FACE THAT MAKES THE WOMAN! ☆
THIS IS WHY I LOVE YOU GUYS.

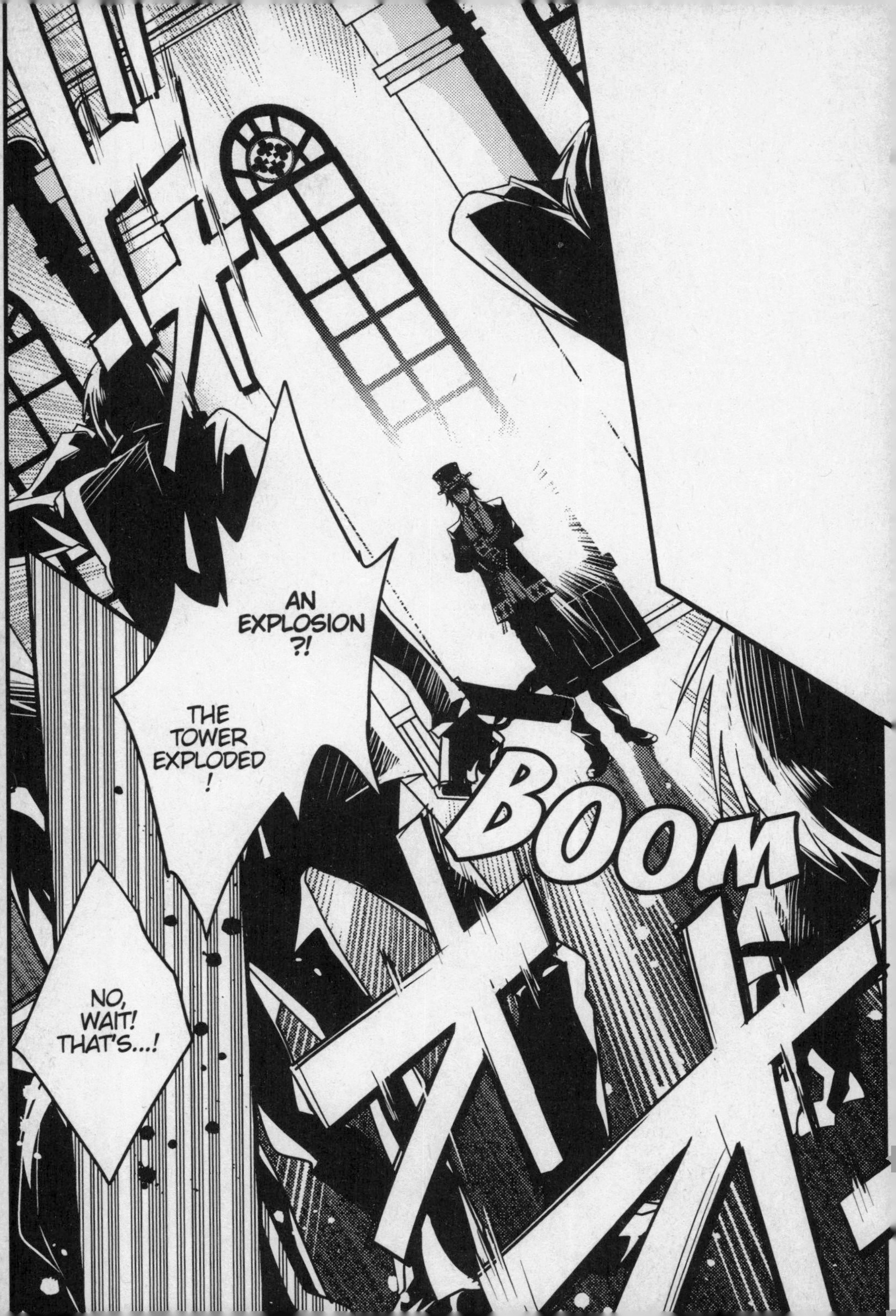
AN EXPLOSION ?!
THE TOWER EXPLODED !
BOOM
NO, WAIT! THAT'S...!

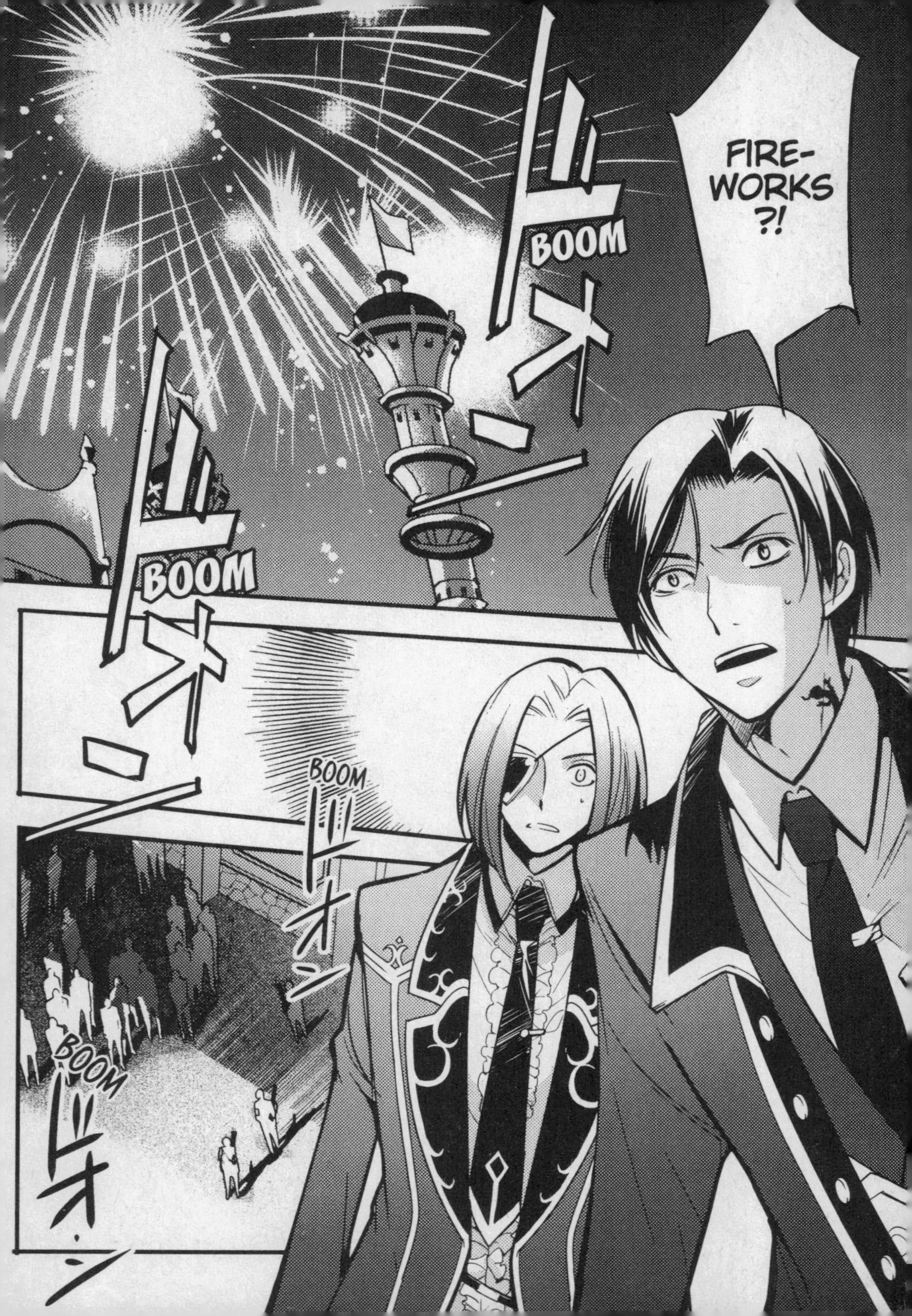
FIRE-WORKS?!
BOOM
BOOM
BOOM
BOOM

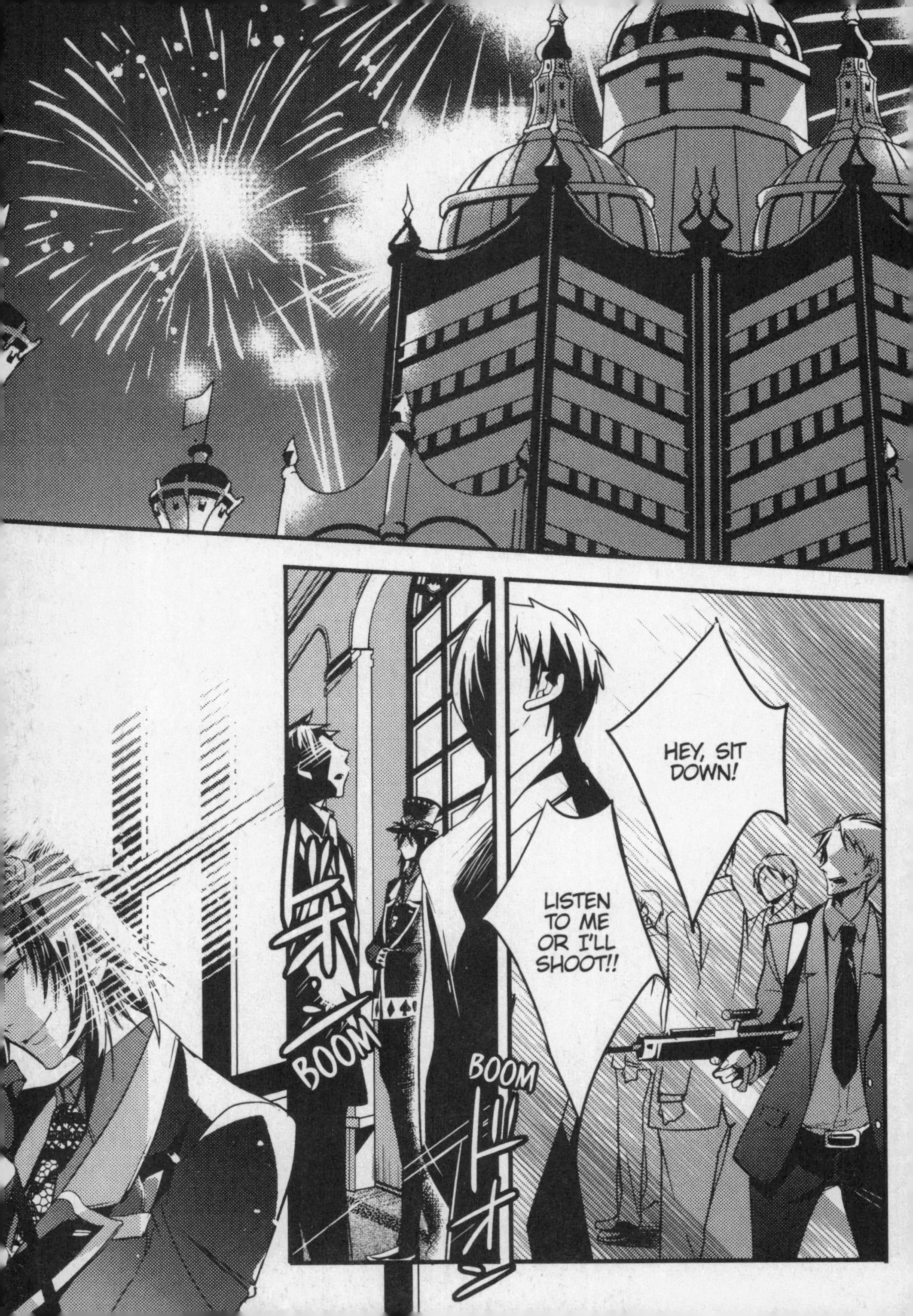
HEY, SIT DOWN!
LISTEN TO ME OR I'LL SHOOT!!
BOOM
BOOM

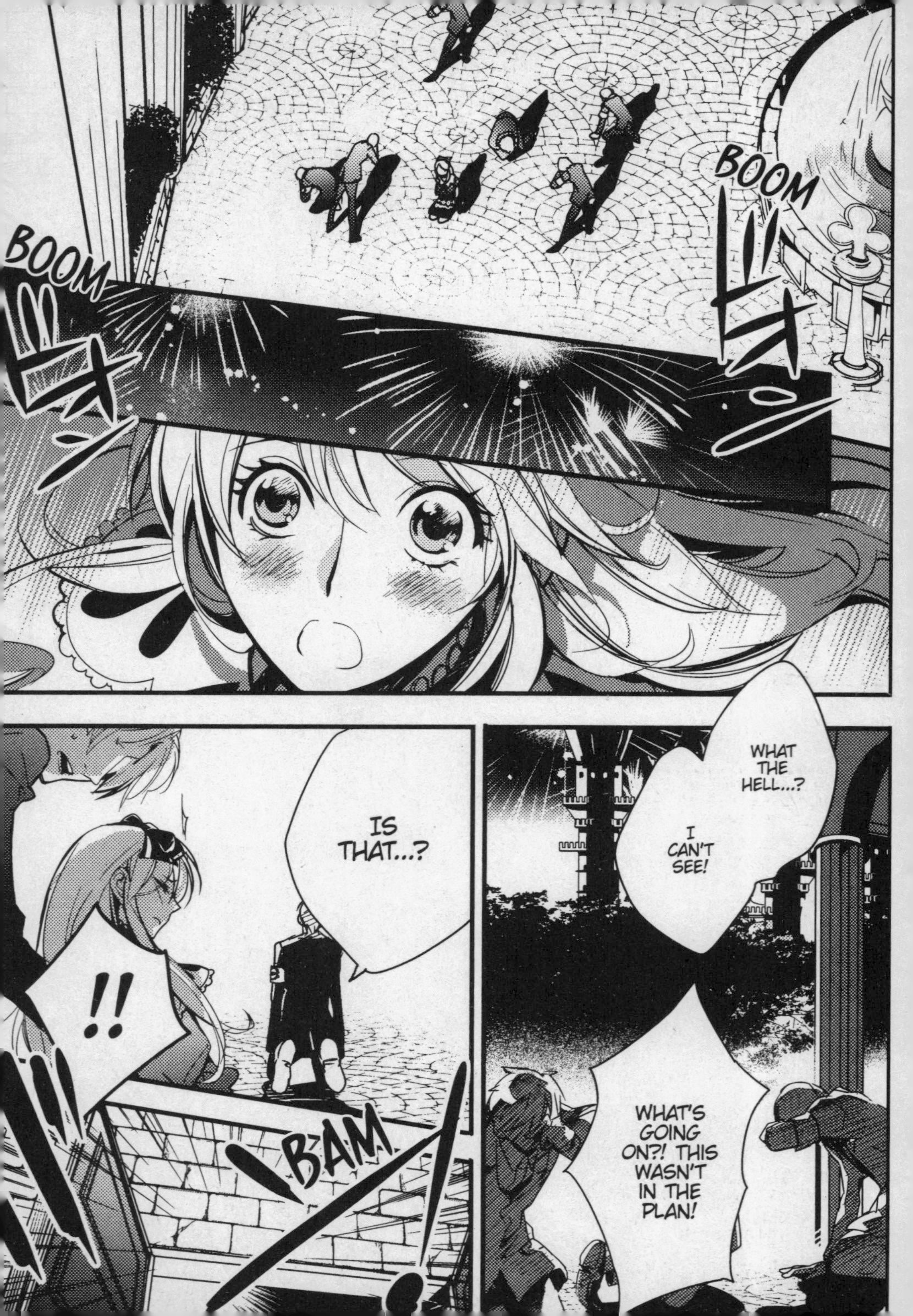
BOOM
BOOM
WHAT THE HELL...?
I CAN'T SEE!
WHAT'S GOING ON?! THIS WASN'T IN THE PLAN!
IS THAT...?
!!
BAM

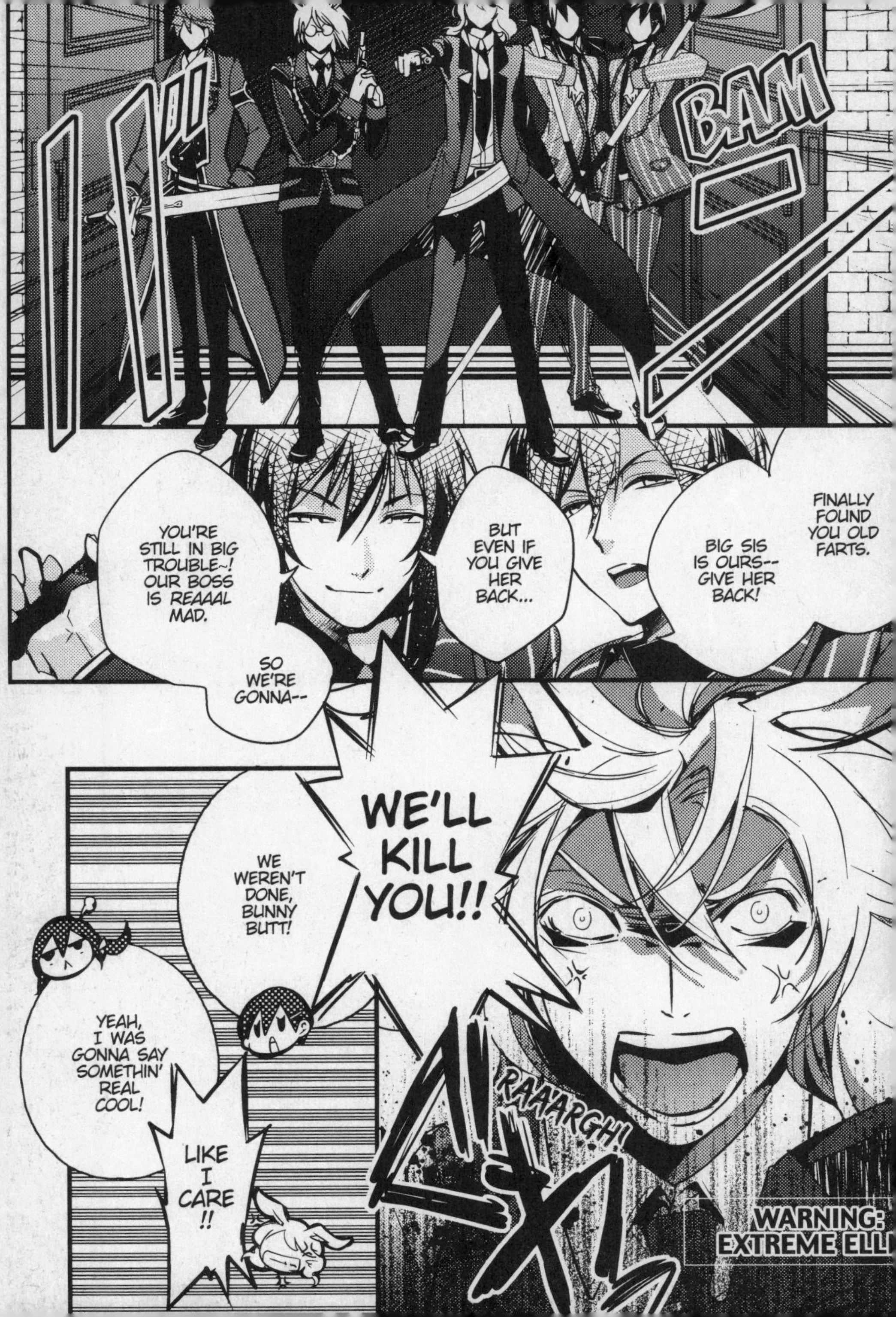
BAM
FINALLY FOUND YOU OLD FARTS.
BIG SIS IS OURS-- GIVE HER BACK!
BUT EVEN IF YOU GIVE HER BACK...
YOU'RE STILL IN BIG TROUBLE~! OUR BOSS IS REAAAL MAD.
SO WE'RE GONNA--
WE'LL KILL YOU!!
RAAAARGH!
WARNING: EXTREME ELL
WE WEREN'T DONE, BUNNY BUTT!
YEAH, I WAS GONNA SAY SOMETHIN' REAL COOL!
LIKE I CARE!!

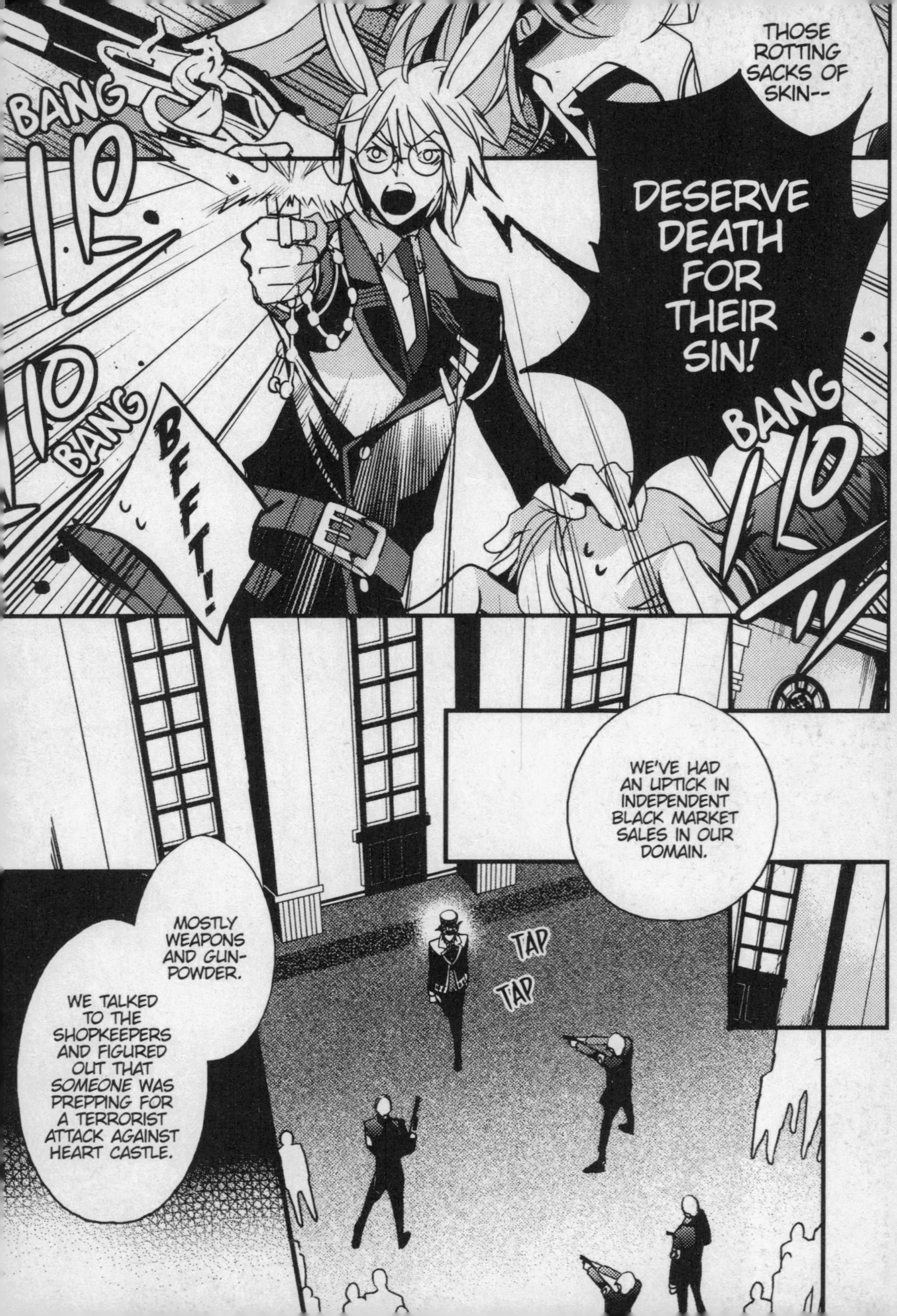
THOSE ROTTING SACKS OF SKIN--
DESERVE DEATH FOR THEIR SIN!
BANG
BANG
BANG
BFFT!!
WE'VE HAD AN UPTICK IN INDEPENDENT BLACK MARKET SALES IN OUR DOMAIN.
TAP
TAP
MOSTLY WEAPONS AND GUN-POWDER.
WE TALKED TO THE SHOPKEEPERS AND FIGURED OUT THAT SOMEONE WAS PREPPING FOR A TERRORIST ATTACK AGAINST HEART CASTLE.

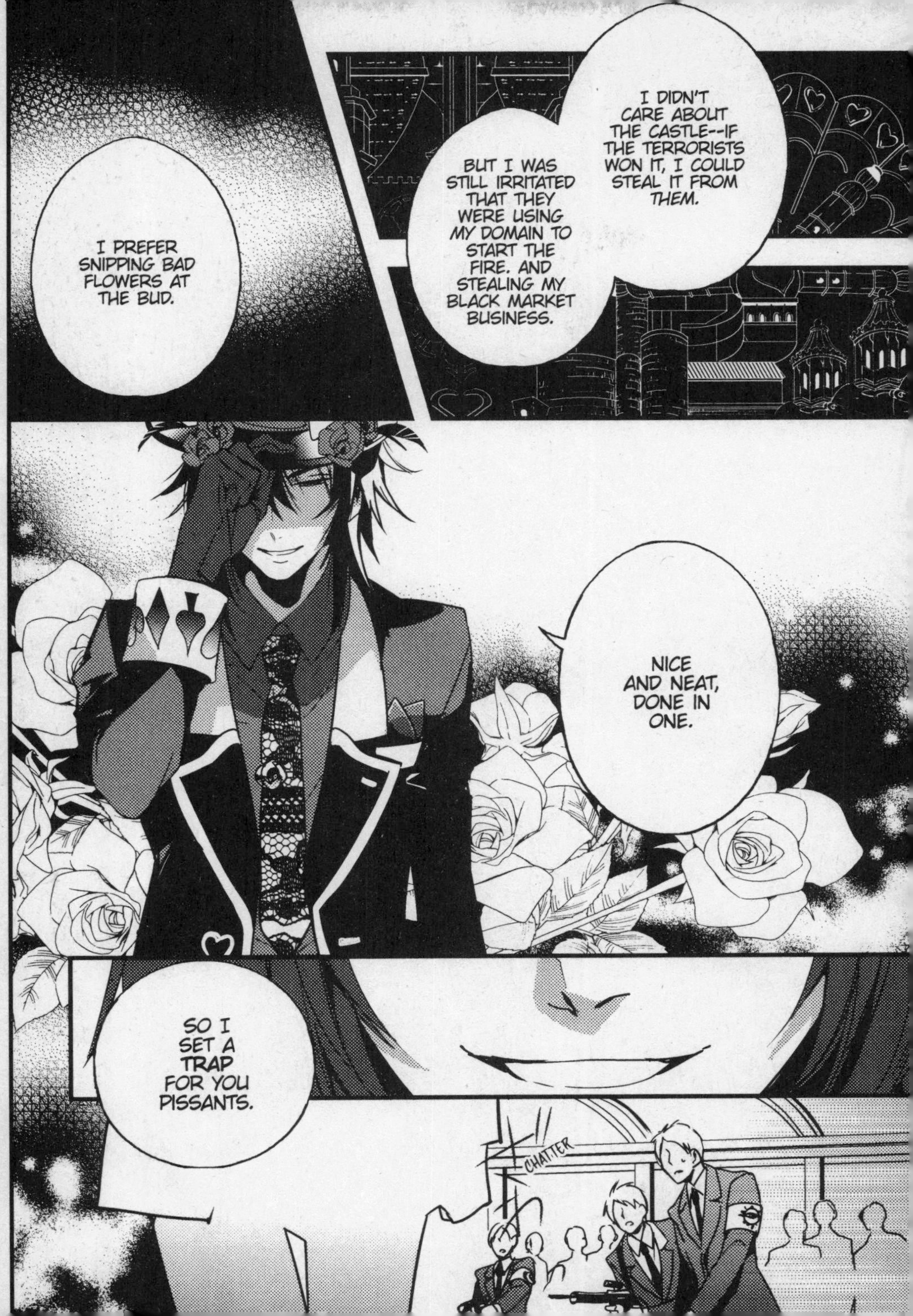
I DIDN'T CARE ABOUT THE CASTLE--IF THE TERRORISTS WON IT, I COULD STEAL IT FROM THEM.
BUT I WAS STILL IRRITATED THAT THEY WERE USING MY DOMAIN TO START THE FIRE. AND STEALING MY BLACK MARKET BUSINESS.
I PREFER SNIPPING BAD FLOWERS AT THE BUD.
NICE AND NEAT, DONE IN ONE.
SO I SET A TRAP FOR YOU PISSANTS.
CHATTER

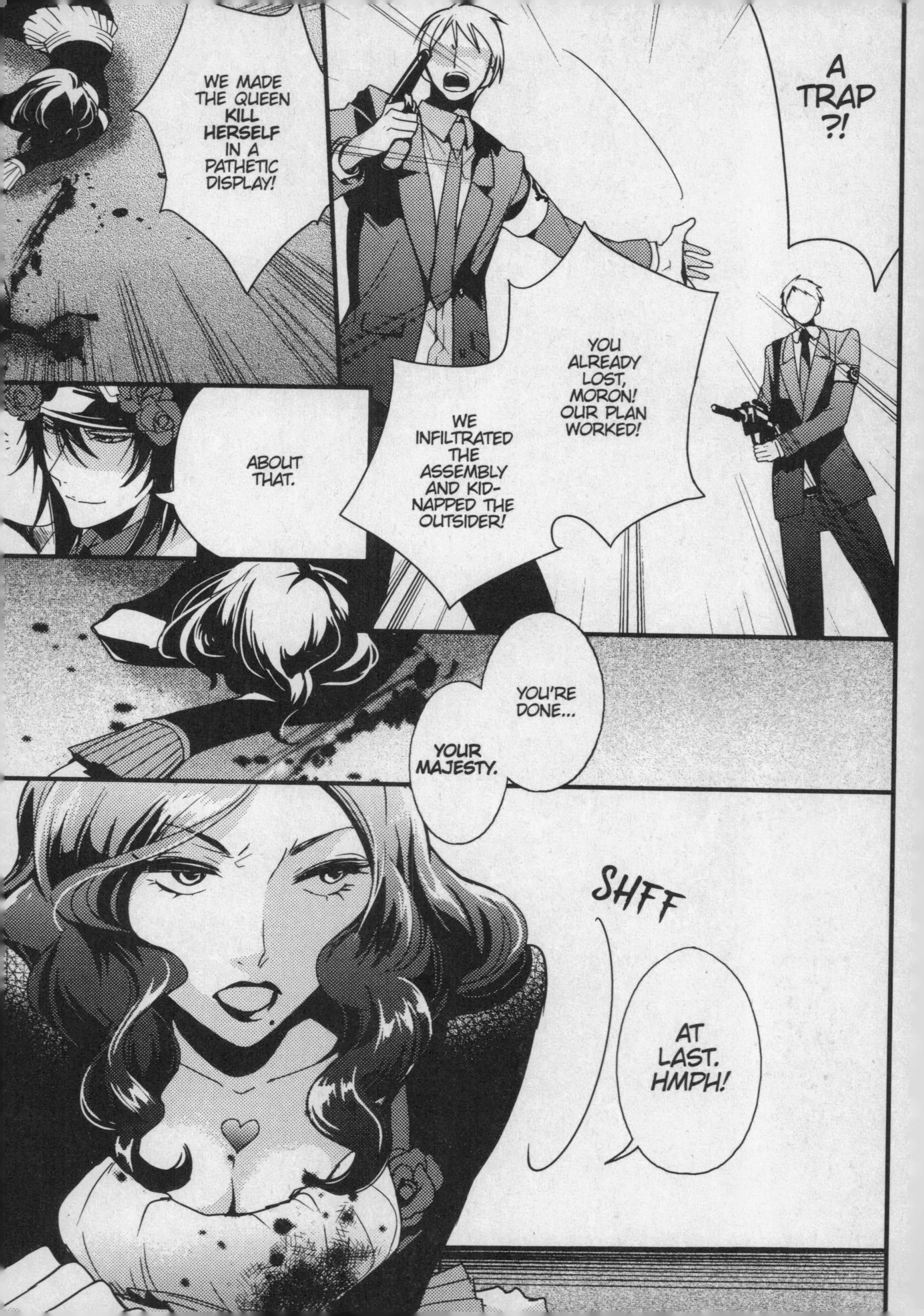
A TRAP ?!
YOU ALREADY LOST, MORON! OUR PLAN WORKED!
WE INFILTRATED THE ASSEMBLY AND KID-NAPPED THE OUTSIDER!
WE MADE THE QUEEN KILL HERSELF IN A PATHETIC DISPLAY!
ABOUT THAT.
YOU'RE DONE...
YOUR MAJESTY.
SHFF
AT LAST. HMPH!

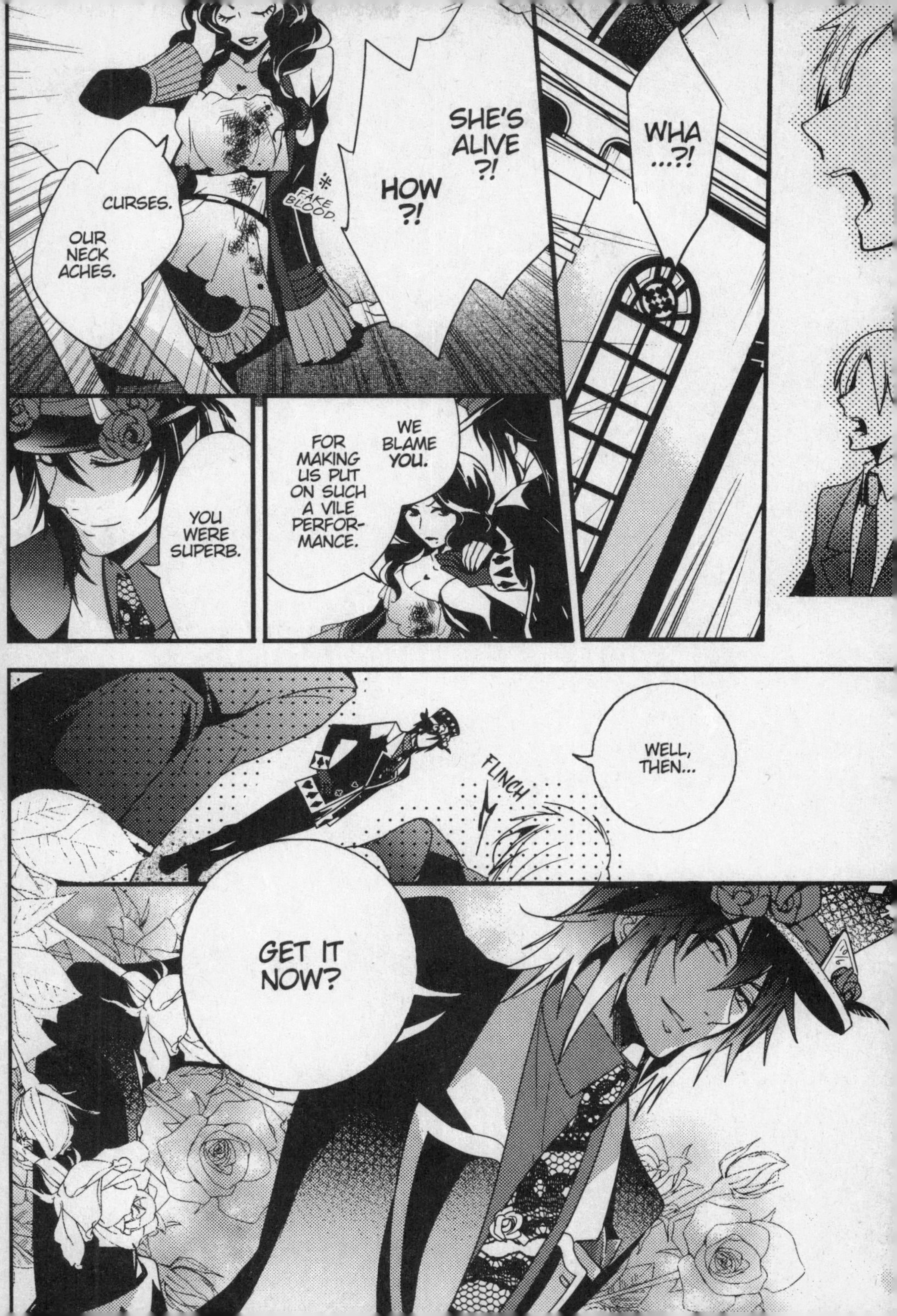
WHA ...?!
SHE'S ALIVE ?!
HOW ?!
※FAKE BLOOD.
CURSES.
OUR NECK ACHES.
WE BLAME YOU.
FOR MAKING US PUT ON SUCH A VILE PERFORMANCE.
YOU WERE SUPERB.
WELL, THEN...
FLINCH
GET IT NOW?

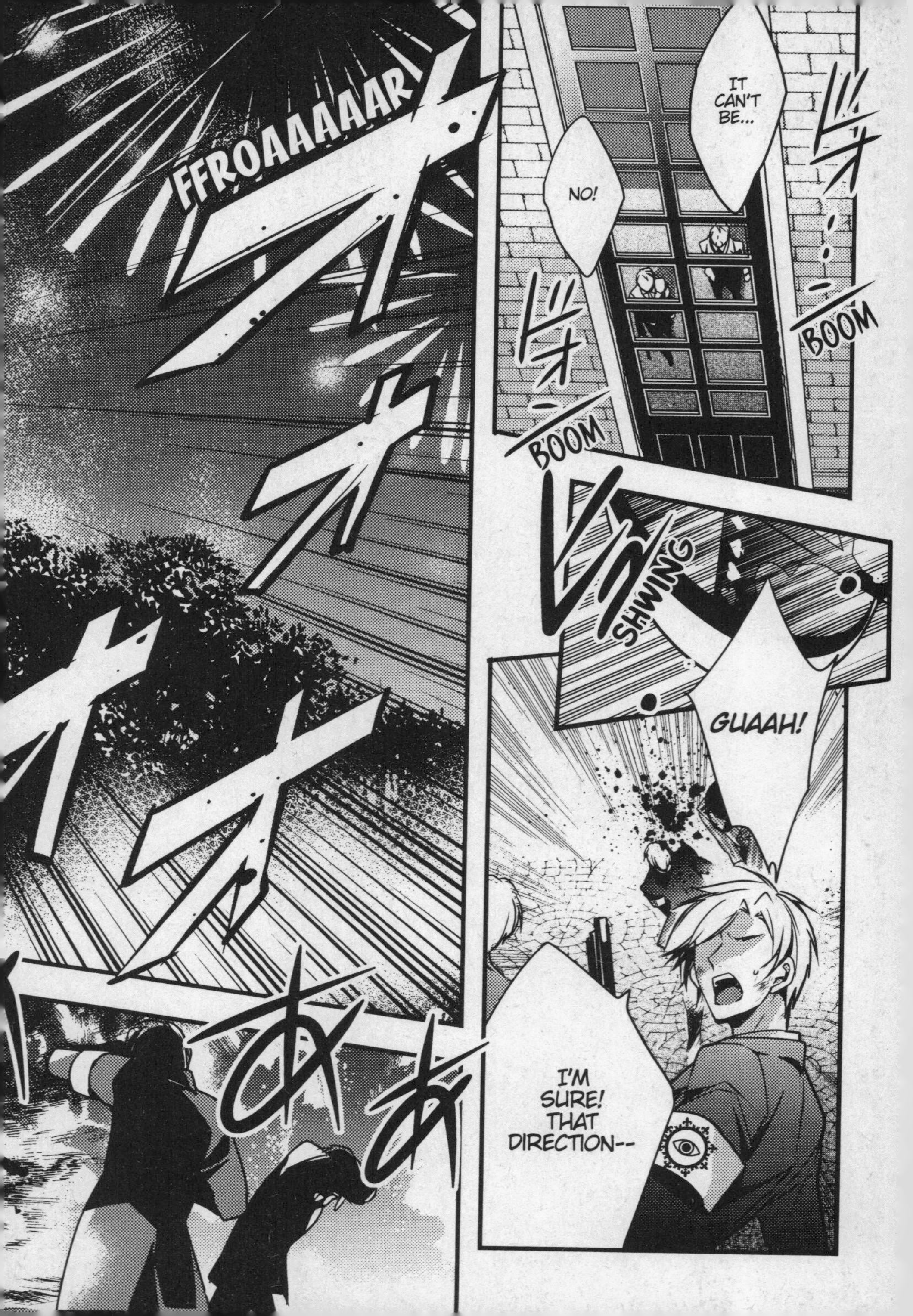
IT CAN'T BE...
NO!
BOOM
BOOM
SHWING
GUAAH!
I'M SURE! THAT DIRECTION--
FFROAAAAAR

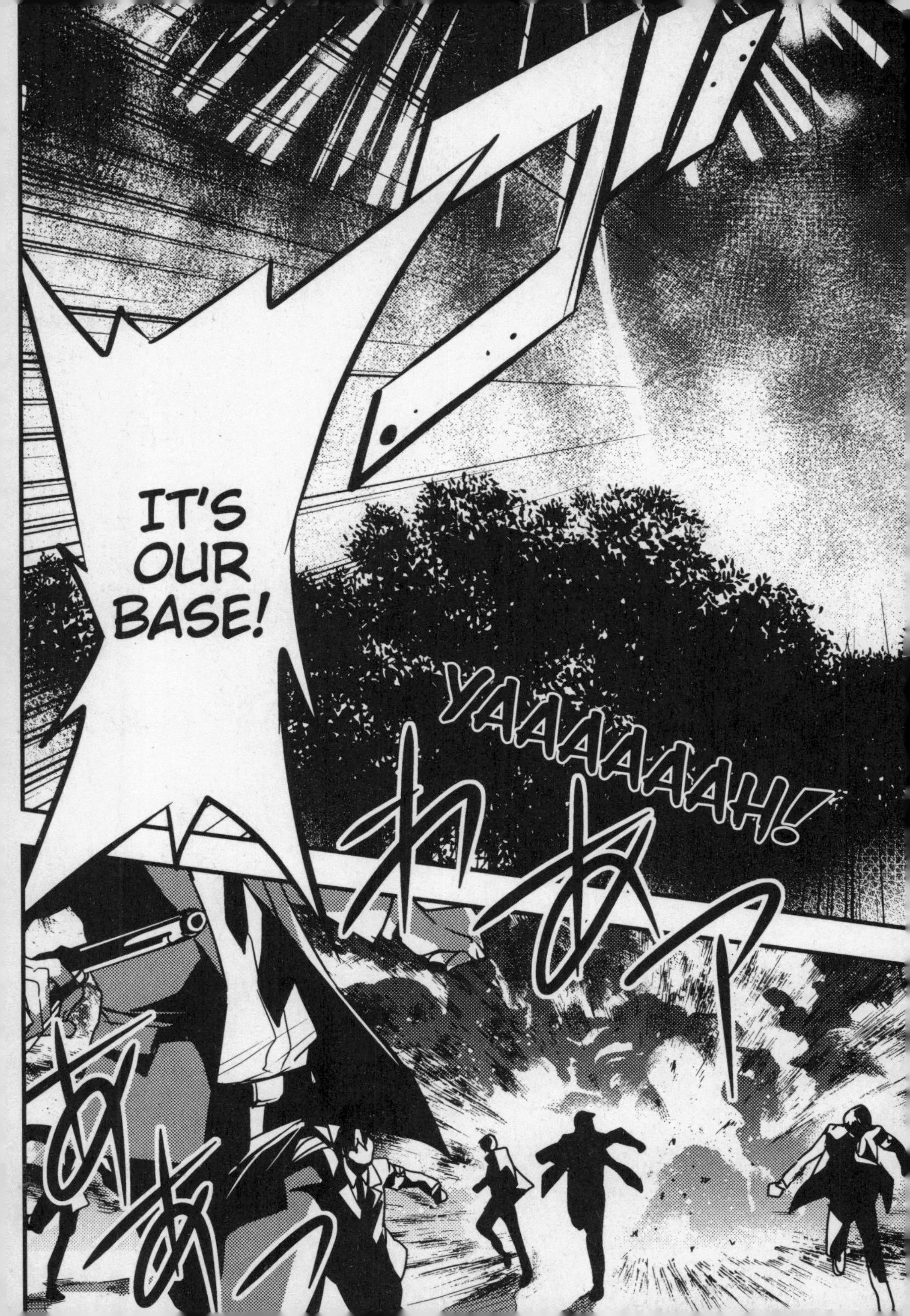
IT'S OUR BASE!
YAAAAAAAAH!

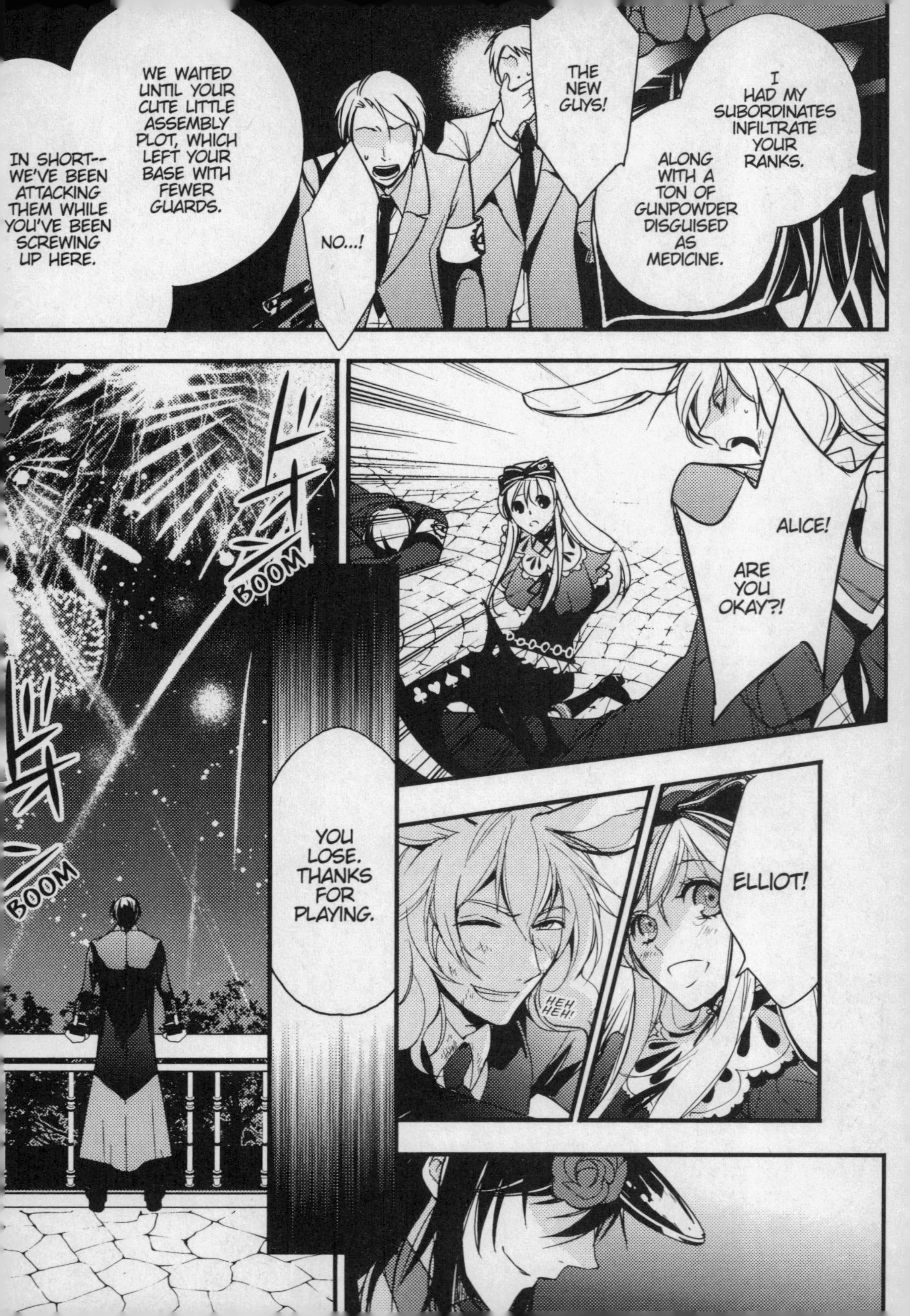
I HAD MY SUBORDINATES INFILTRATE YOUR RANKS.
ALONG WITH A TON OF GUNPOWDER DISGUISED AS MEDICINE.
THE NEW GUYS!
NO...!
WE WAITED UNTIL YOUR CUTE LITTLE ASSEMBLY PLOT, WHICH LEFT YOUR BASE WITH FEWER GUARDS.
IN SHORT-- WE'VE BEEN ATTACKING THEM WHILE YOU'VE BEEN SCREWING UP HERE.
ALICE!
ARE YOU OKAY?!
ELLIOT!
YOU LOSE. THANKS FOR PLAYING.
HEH HEH!
BOOM
BOOM

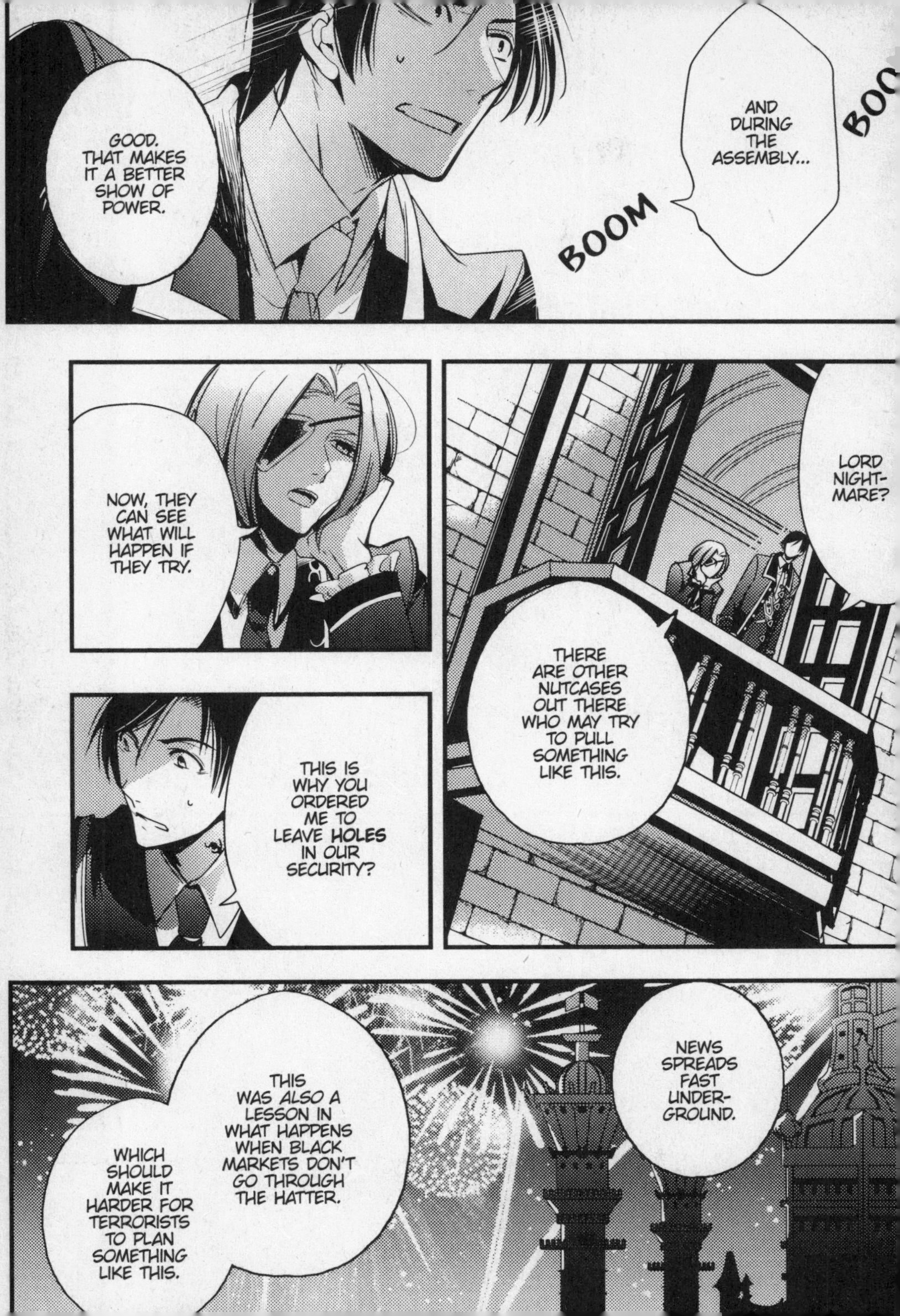
AND DURING THE ASSEMBLY...
BOOM
BOOM
GOOD. THAT MAKES IT A BETTER SHOW OF POWER.
LORD NIGHTMARE?
THERE ARE OTHER NUTCASES OUT THERE WHO MAY TRY TO PULL SOMETHING LIKE THIS.
NOW, THEY CAN SEE WHAT WILL HAPPEN IF THEY TRY.
THIS IS WHY YOU ORDERED ME TO LEAVE HOLES IN OUR SECURITY?
NEWS SPREADS FAST UNDERGROUND.
THIS WAS ALSO A LESSON IN WHAT HAPPENS WHEN BLACK MARKETS DON'T GO THROUGH THE HATTER.
WHICH SHOULD MAKE IT HARDER FOR TERRORISTS TO PLAN SOMETHING LIKE THIS.

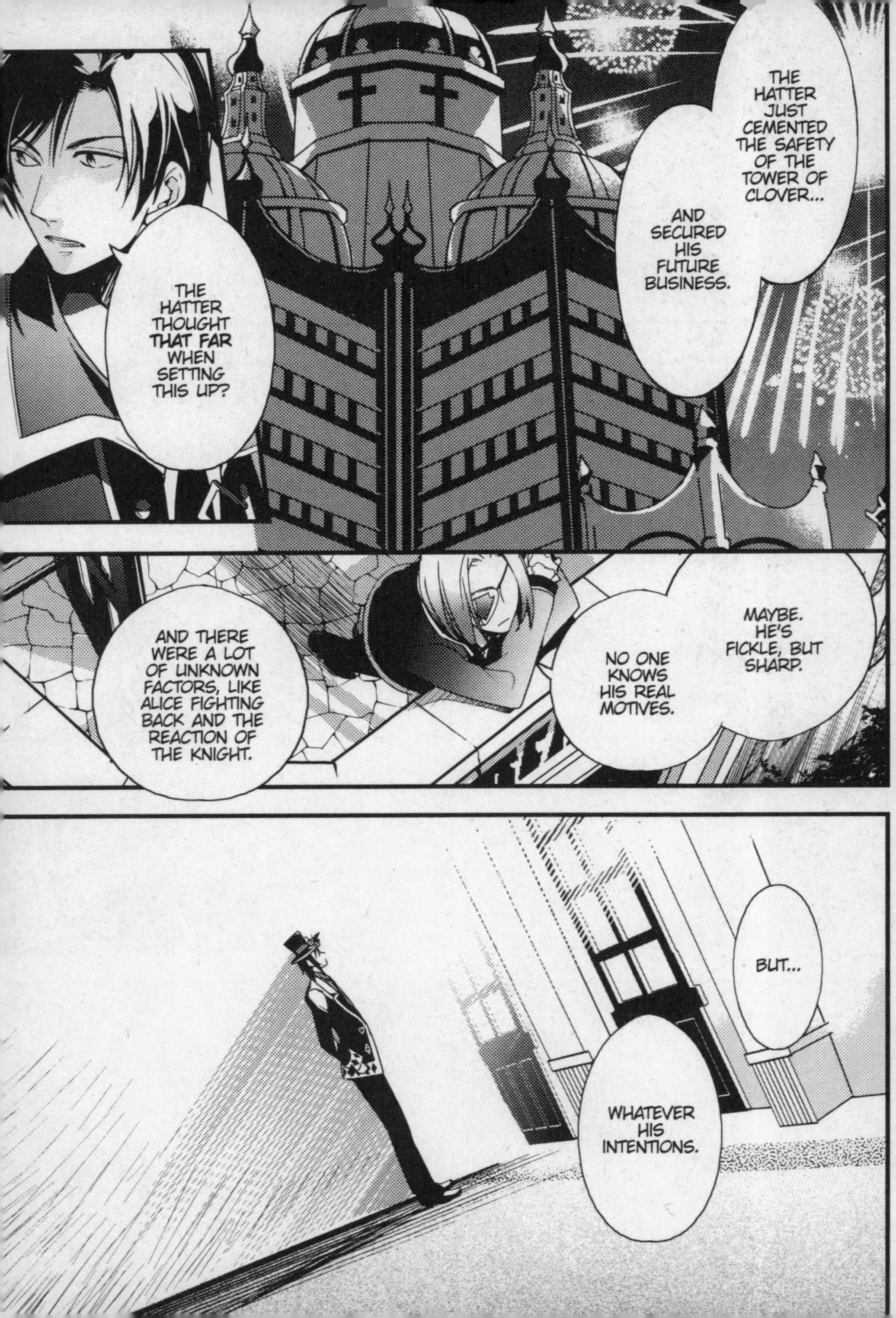
THE HATTER JUST CEMENTED THE SAFETY OF THE TOWER OF CLOVER...
AND SECURED HIS FUTURE BUSINESS.
THE HATTER THOUGHT THAT FAR WHEN SETTING THIS UP?
MAYBE. HE'S FICKLE, BUT SHARP.
NO ONE KNOWS HIS REAL MOTIVES.
AND THERE WERE A LOT OF UNKNOWN FACTORS, LIKE ALICE FIGHTING BACK AND THE REACTION OF THE KNIGHT.
BUT...
WHATEVER HIS INTENTIONS.

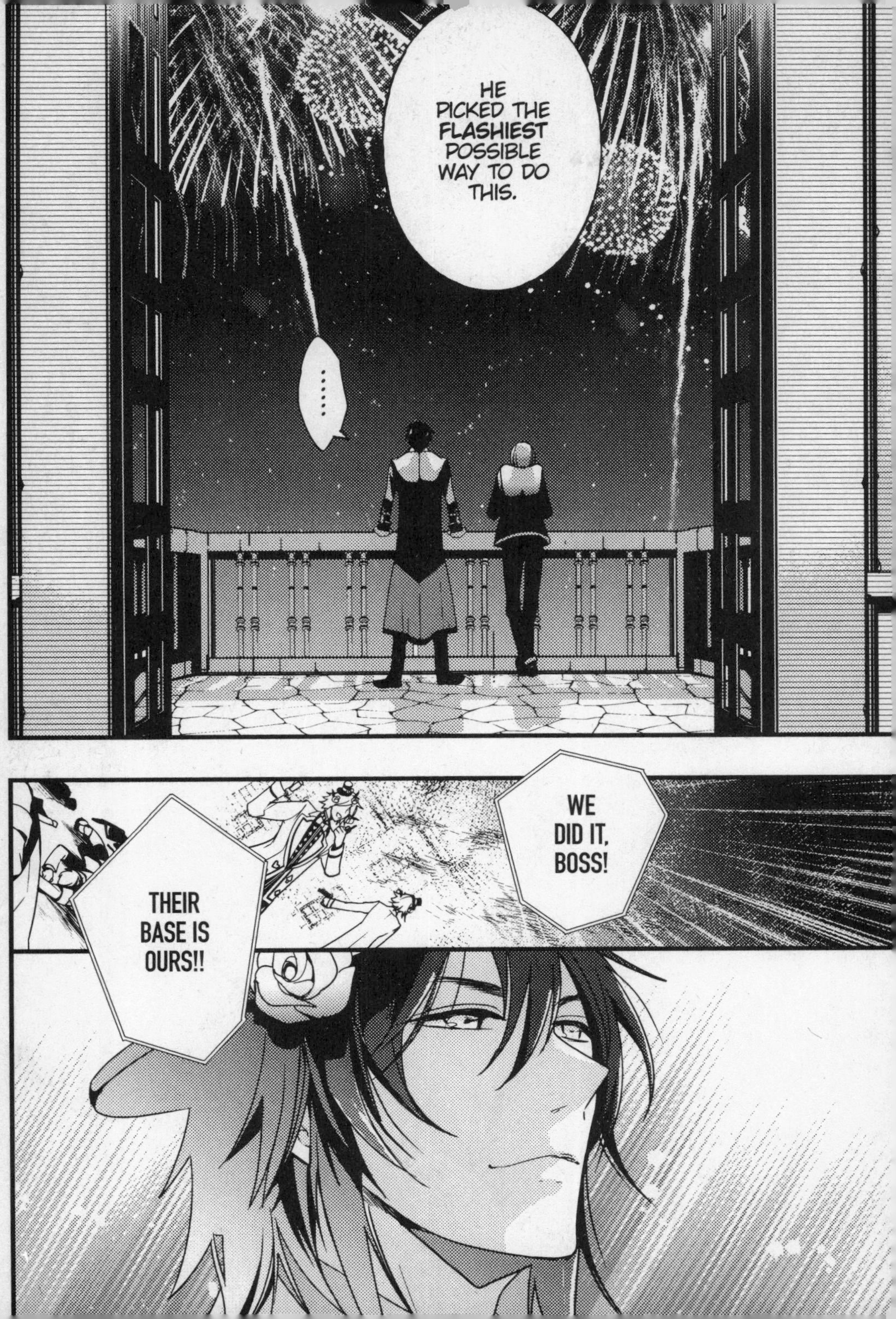
HE PICKED THE FLASHIEST POSSIBLE WAY TO DO THIS.
......
WE DID IT, BOSS!
THEIR BASE IS OURS!!

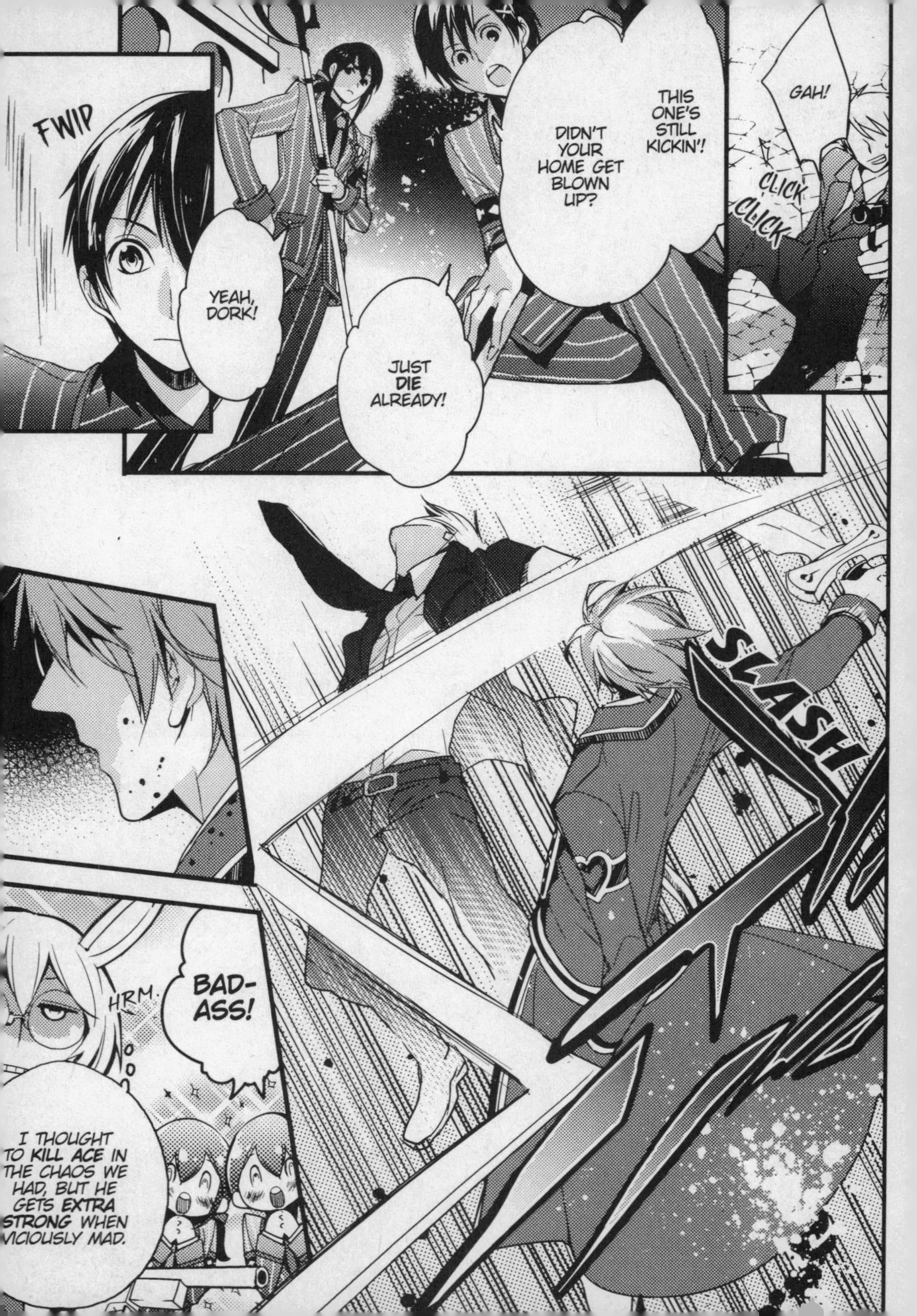
GAH!
CLICK CLICK
THIS ONE'S STILL KICKIN'!
DIDN'T YOUR HOME GET BLOWN UP?
JUST DIE ALREADY!
YEAH, DORK!
FWIP
SLASH
BAD-ASS!
HRM.
I THOUGHT TO KILL ACE IN THE CHAOS WE HAD, BUT HE GETS EXTRA STRONG WHEN VICIOUSLY MAD.

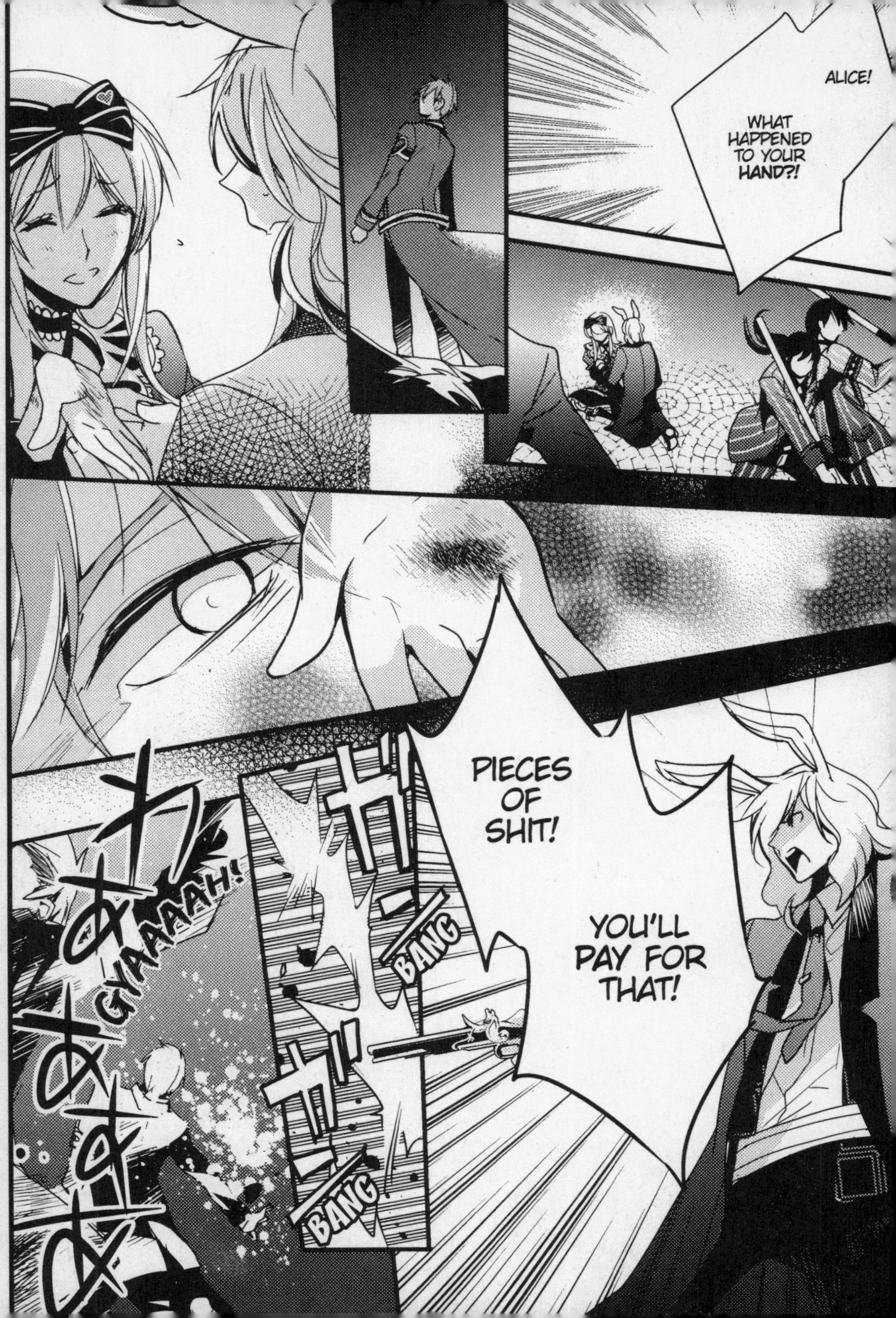
ALICE!
WHAT HAPPENED TO YOUR HAND?!
PIECES OF SHIT!
YOU'LL PAY FOR THAT!
BANG
BANG
GYAAAAH!

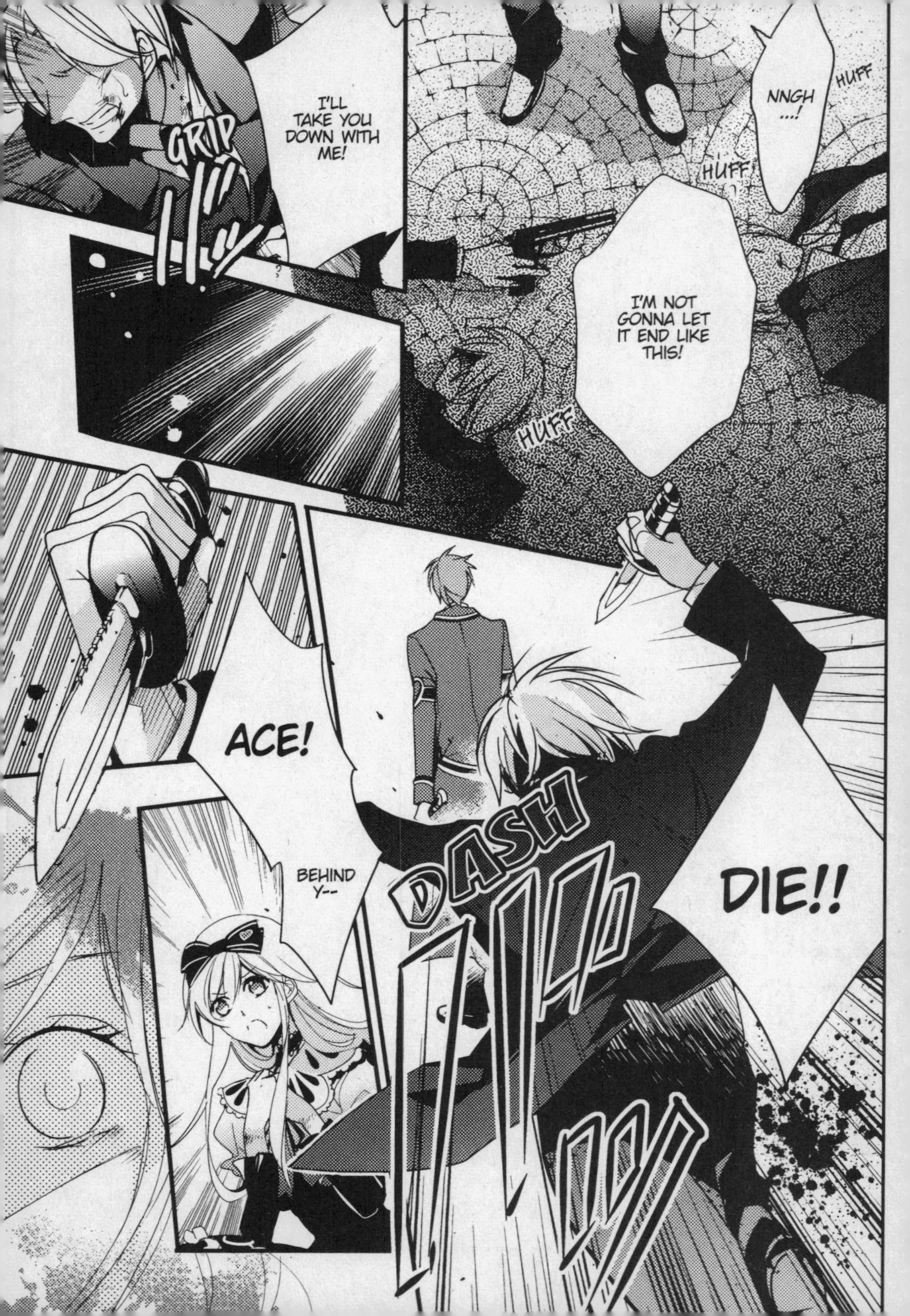
NNGH ...!
HUFF
HUFF
I'M NOT GONNA LET IT END LIKE THIS!
HUFF
I'LL TAKE YOU DOWN WITH ME!
GRIP
DIE!!
DASH
ACE!
BEHIND Y--

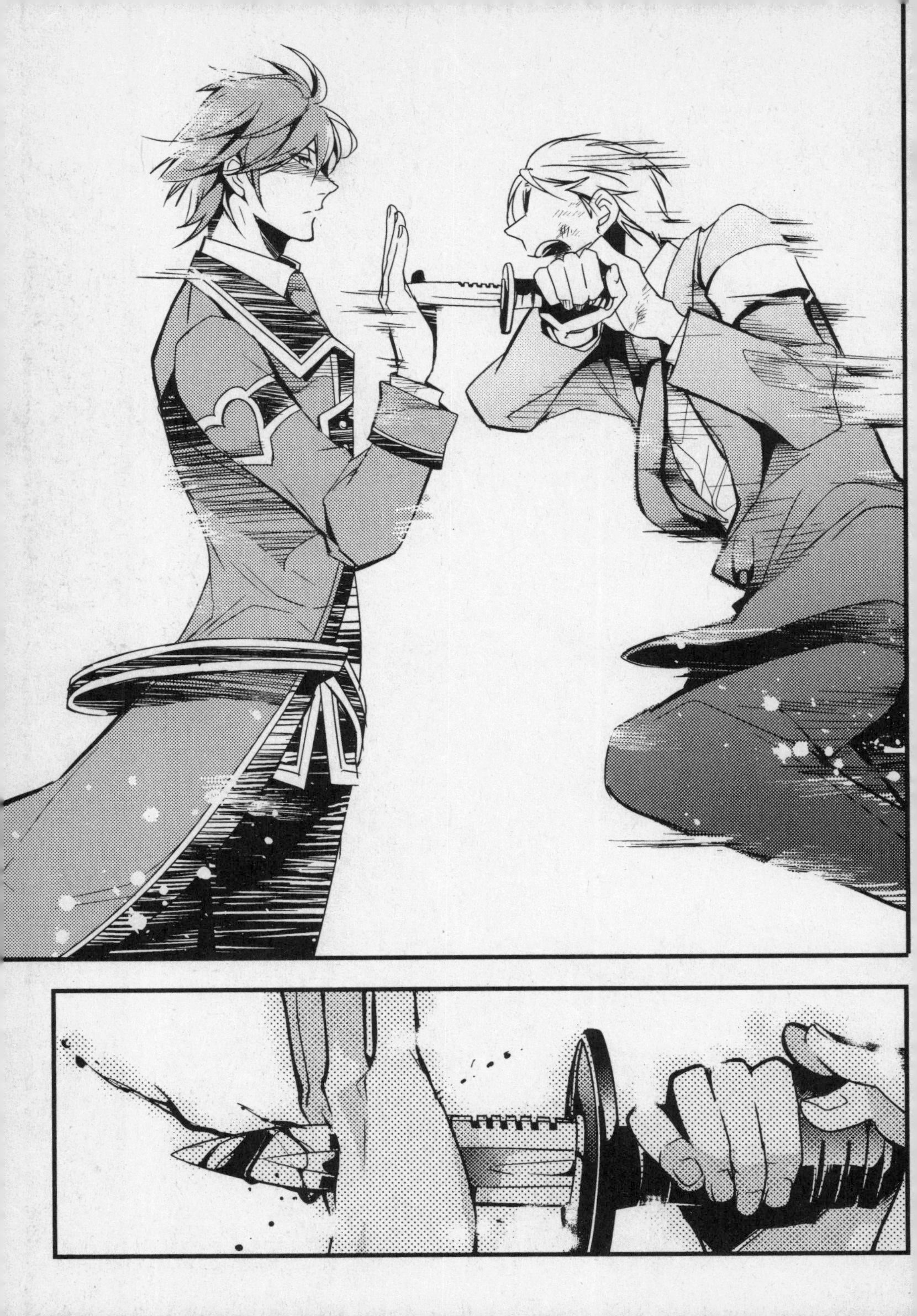

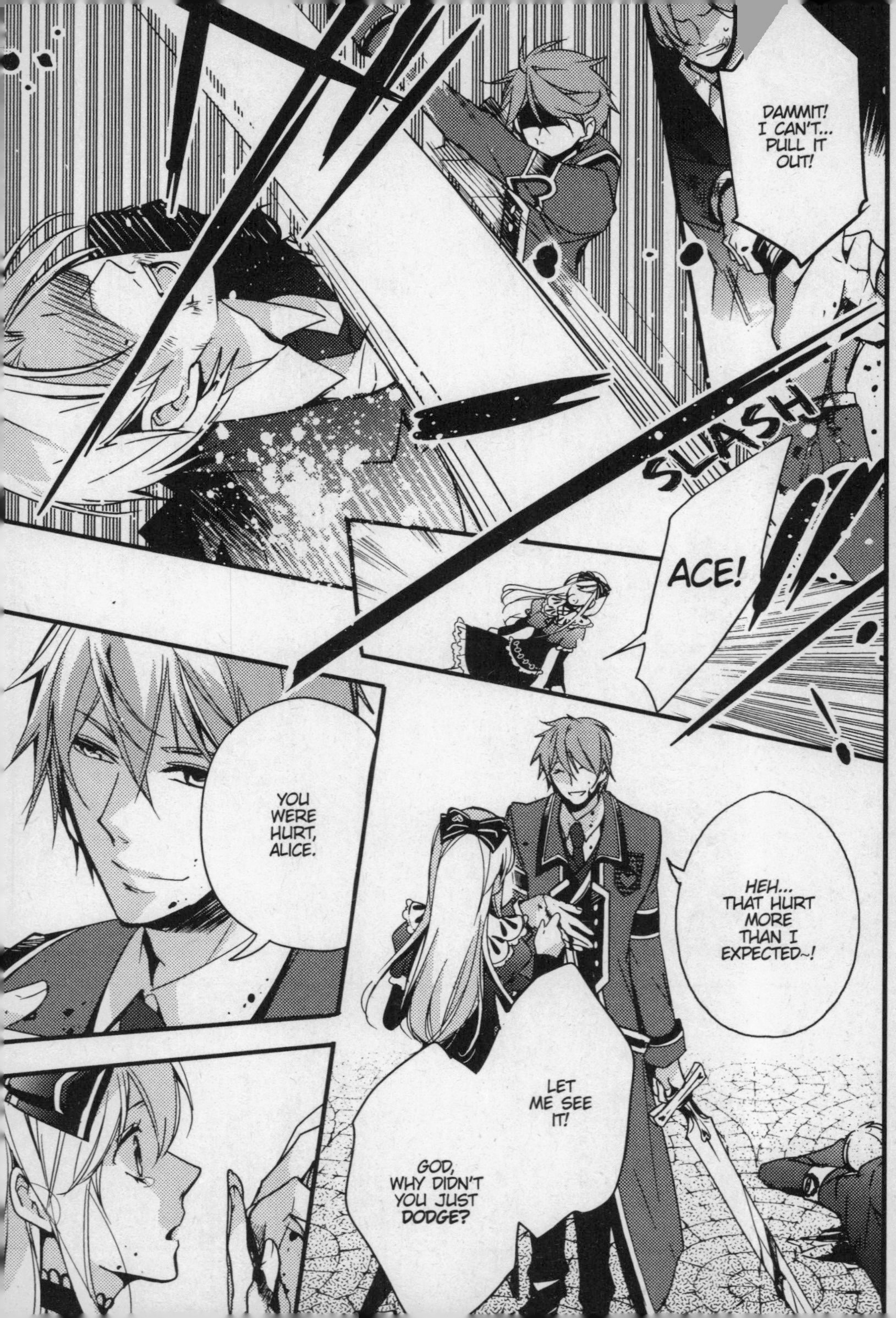
DAMMIT! I CAN'T... PULL IT OUT!
SLASH
ACE!
!
HEH... THAT HURT MORE THAN I EXPECTED~!
LET ME SEE IT!
GOD, WHY DIDN'T YOU JUST DODGE?
YOU WERE HURT, ALICE.

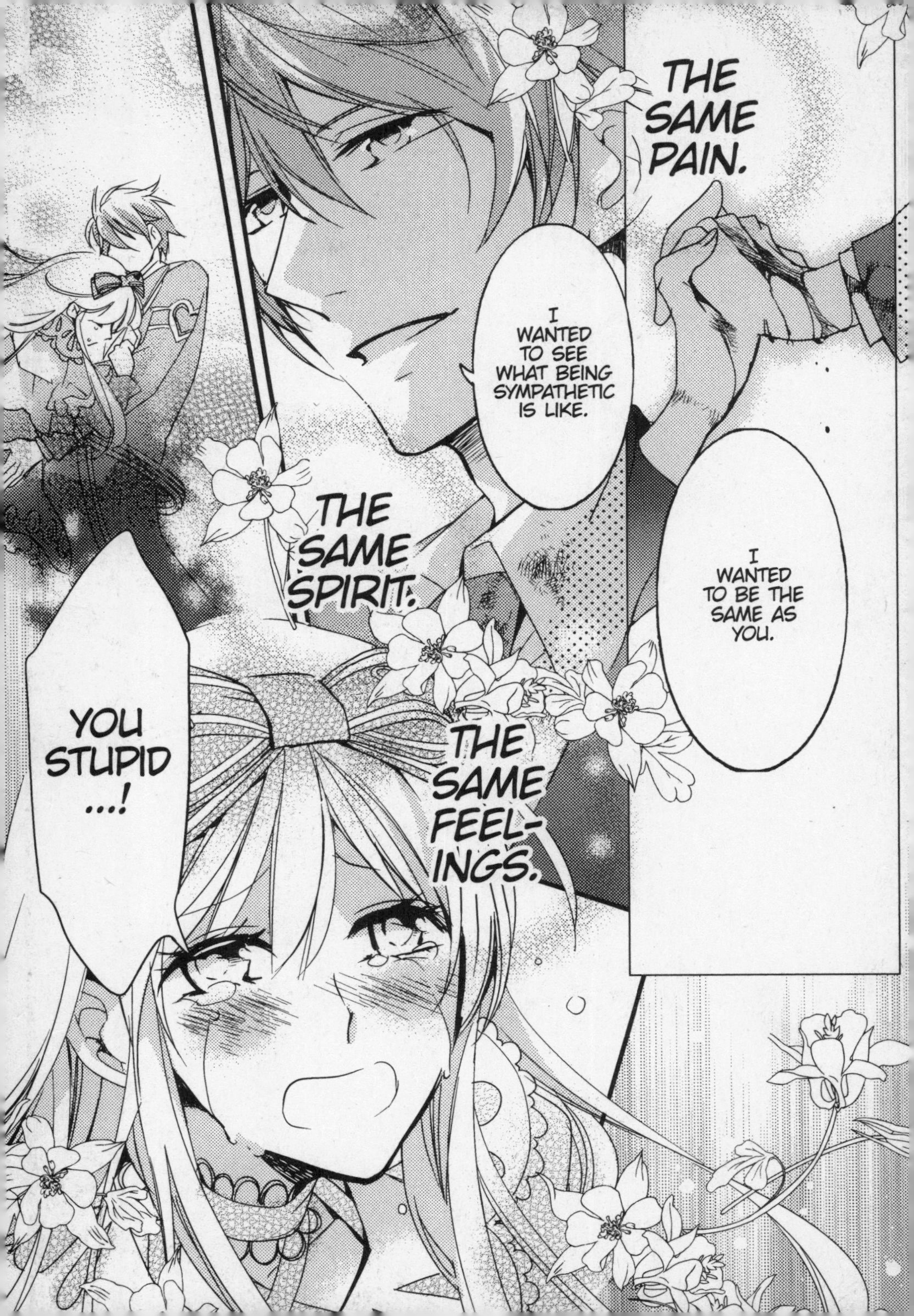
THE SAME PAIN.
I WANTED TO SEE WHAT BEING SYMPATHETIC IS LIKE.
I WANTED TO BE THE SAME AS YOU.
THE SAME SPIRIT.
THE SAME FEEL-INGS.
YOU STUPID ...!

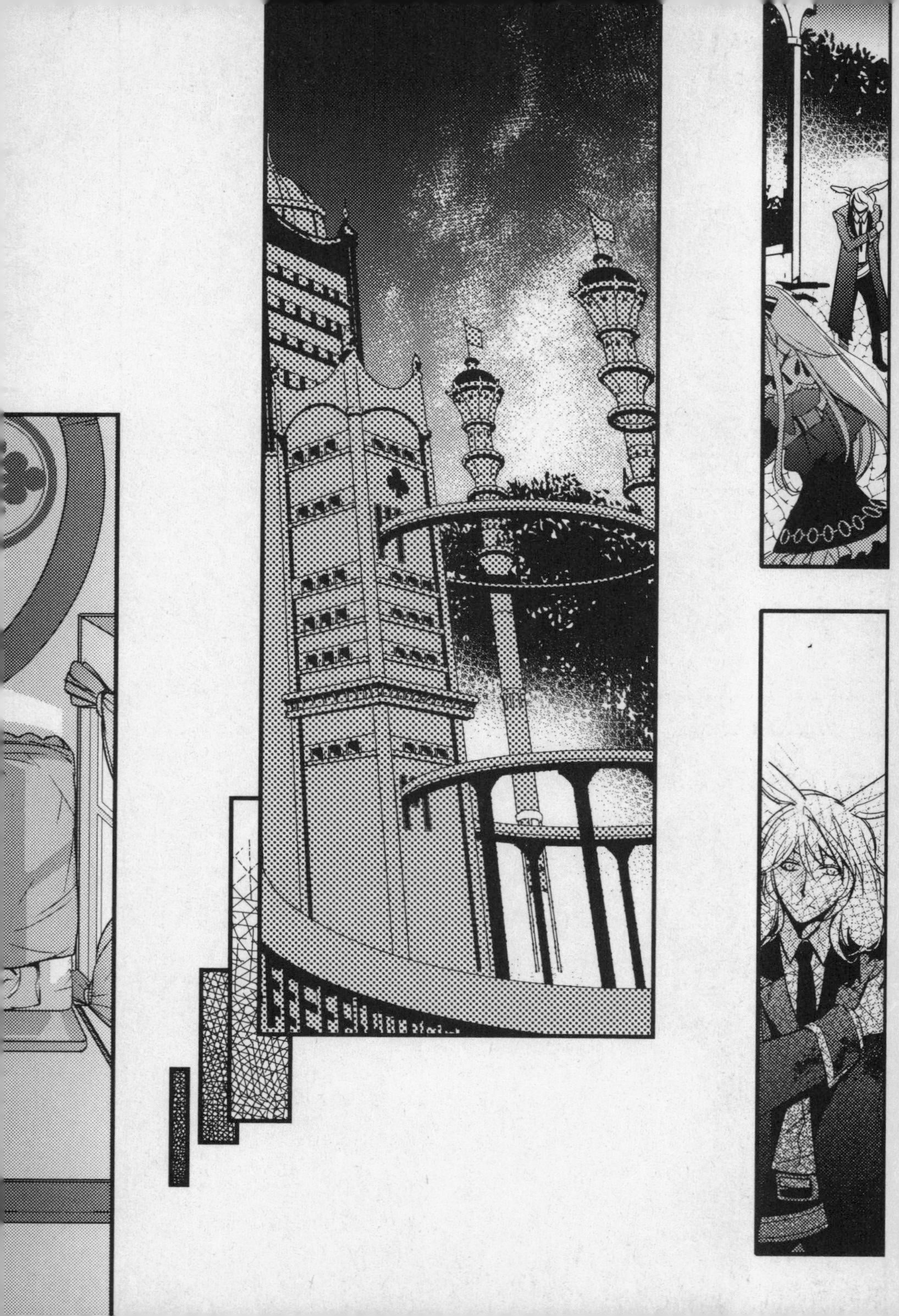

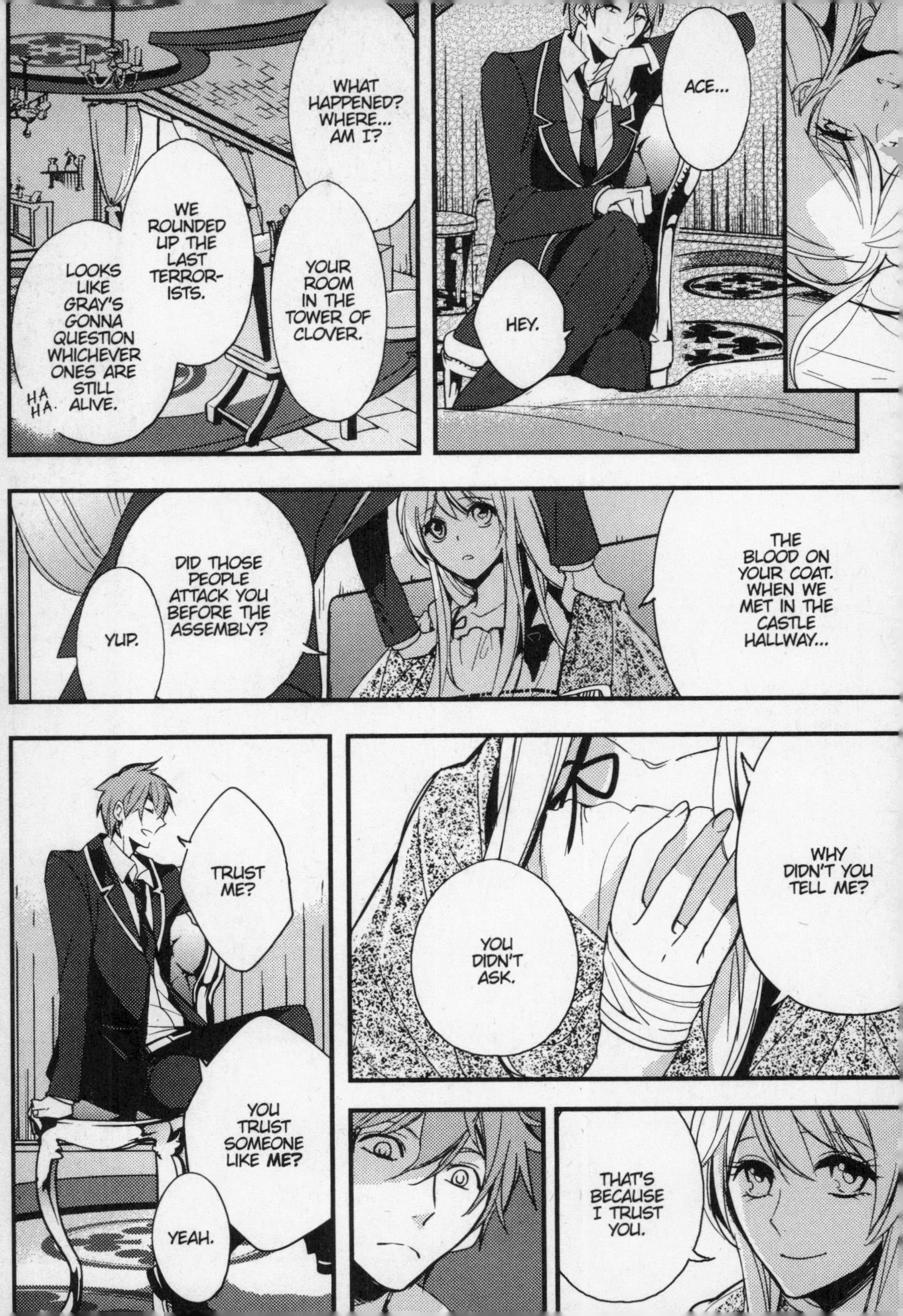
ACE...
HEY.
WHAT HAPPENED? WHERE... AM I?
YOUR ROOM IN THE TOWER OF CLOVER.
WE ROUNDED UP THE LAST TERRORISTS.
LOOKS LIKE GRAY'S GONNA QUESTION WHICHEVER ONES ARE STILL ALIVE.
HA HA.
THE BLOOD ON YOUR COAT. WHEN WE MET IN THE CASTLE HALLWAY...
DID THOSE PEOPLE ATTACK YOU BEFORE THE ASSEMBLY?
YUP.
WHY DIDN'T YOU TELL ME?
YOU DIDN'T ASK.
THAT'S BECAUSE I TRUST YOU.
TRUST ME?
YOU TRUST SOMEONE LIKE ME?
YEAH.

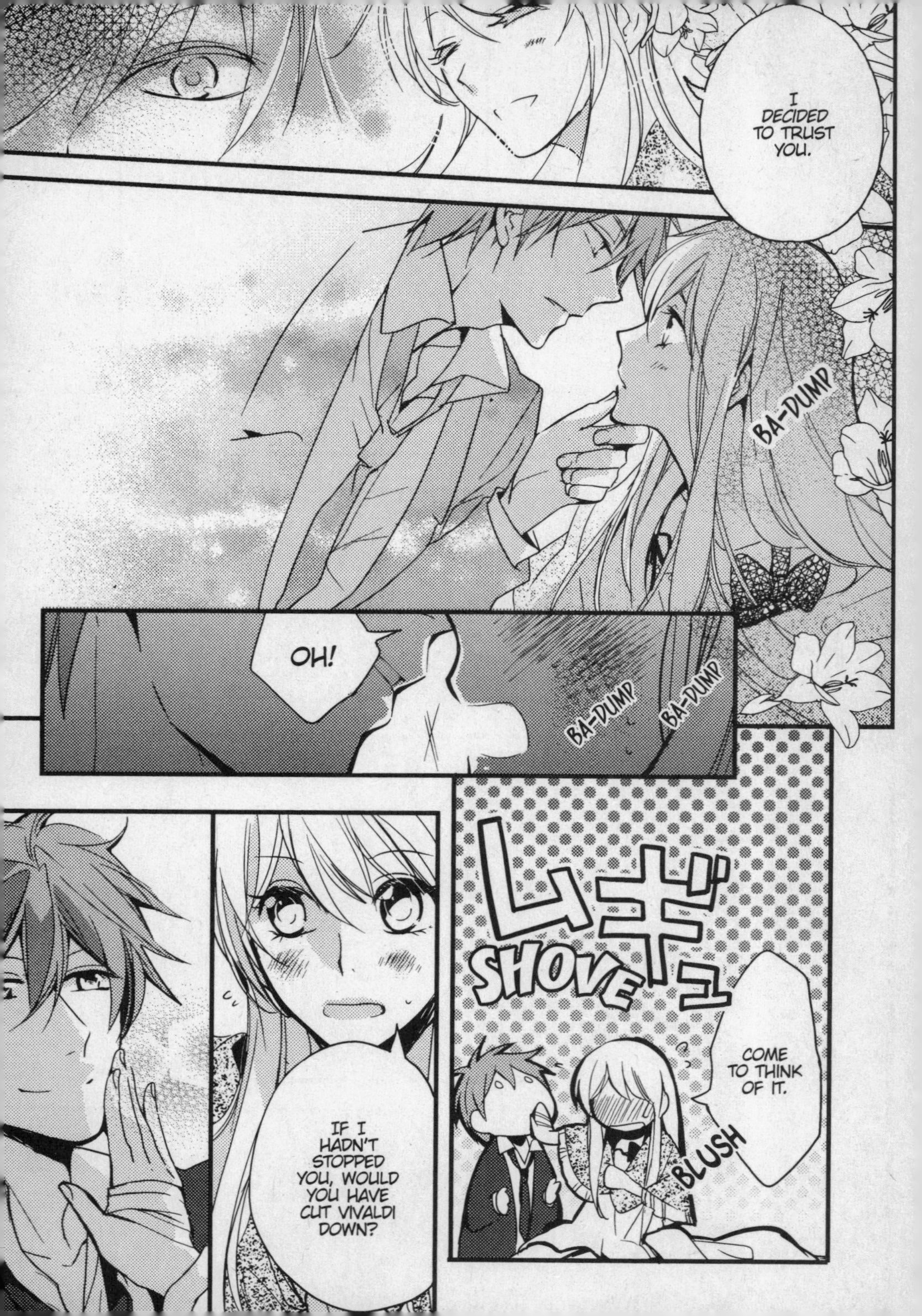
I DECIDED TO TRUST YOU.
BA-DUMP
OH!
BA-DUMP
BA-DUMP
ムギュ
SHOVE
COME TO THINK OF IT.
BLUSH
IF I HADN'T STOPPED YOU, WOULD YOU HAVE CUT VIVALDI DOWN?

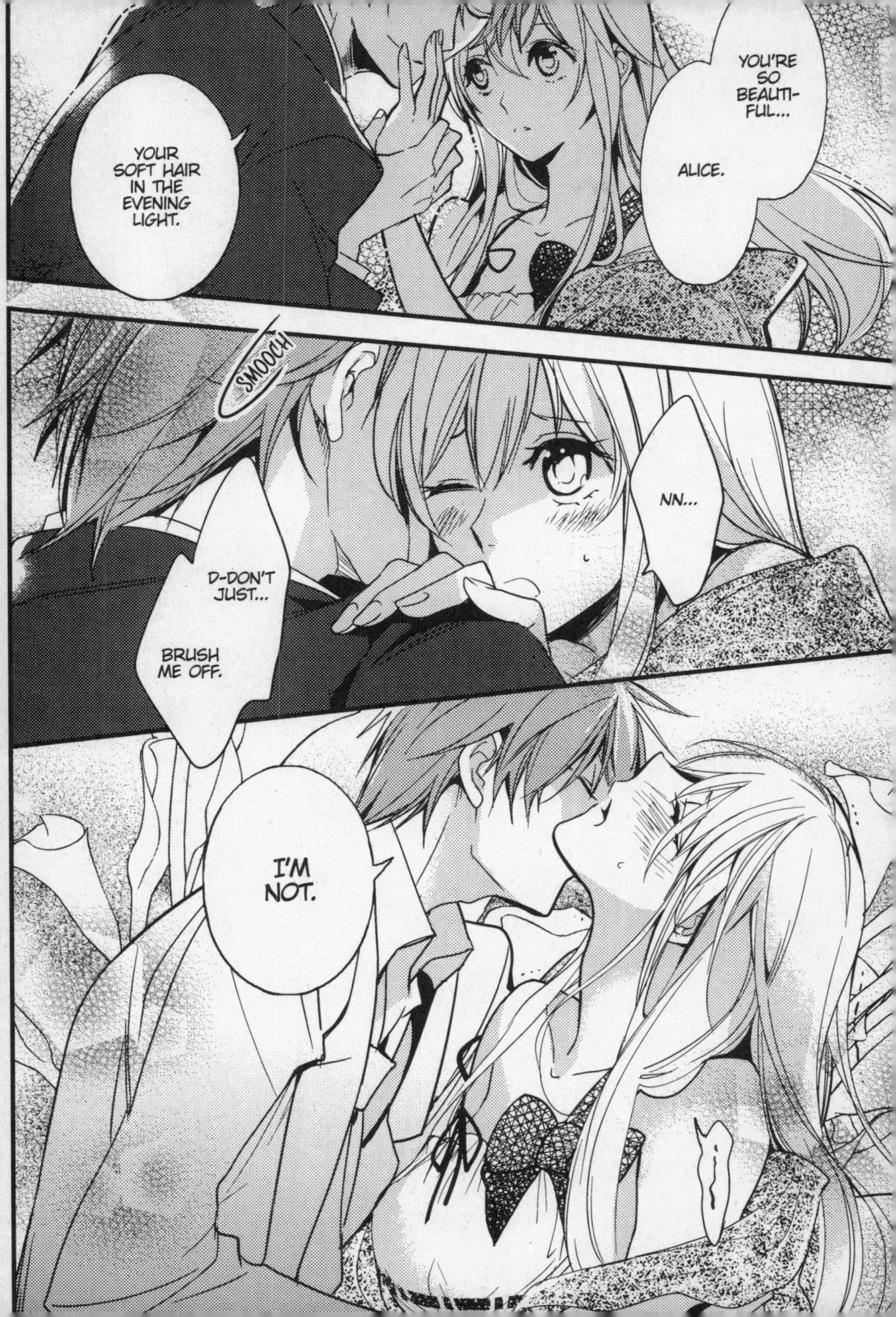
YOU'RE SO BEAUTIFUL...
ALICE.
YOUR SOFT HAIR IN THE EVENING LIGHT.
NN...
SMOOCH
D-DON'T JUST...
BRUSH ME OFF.
I'M NOT.

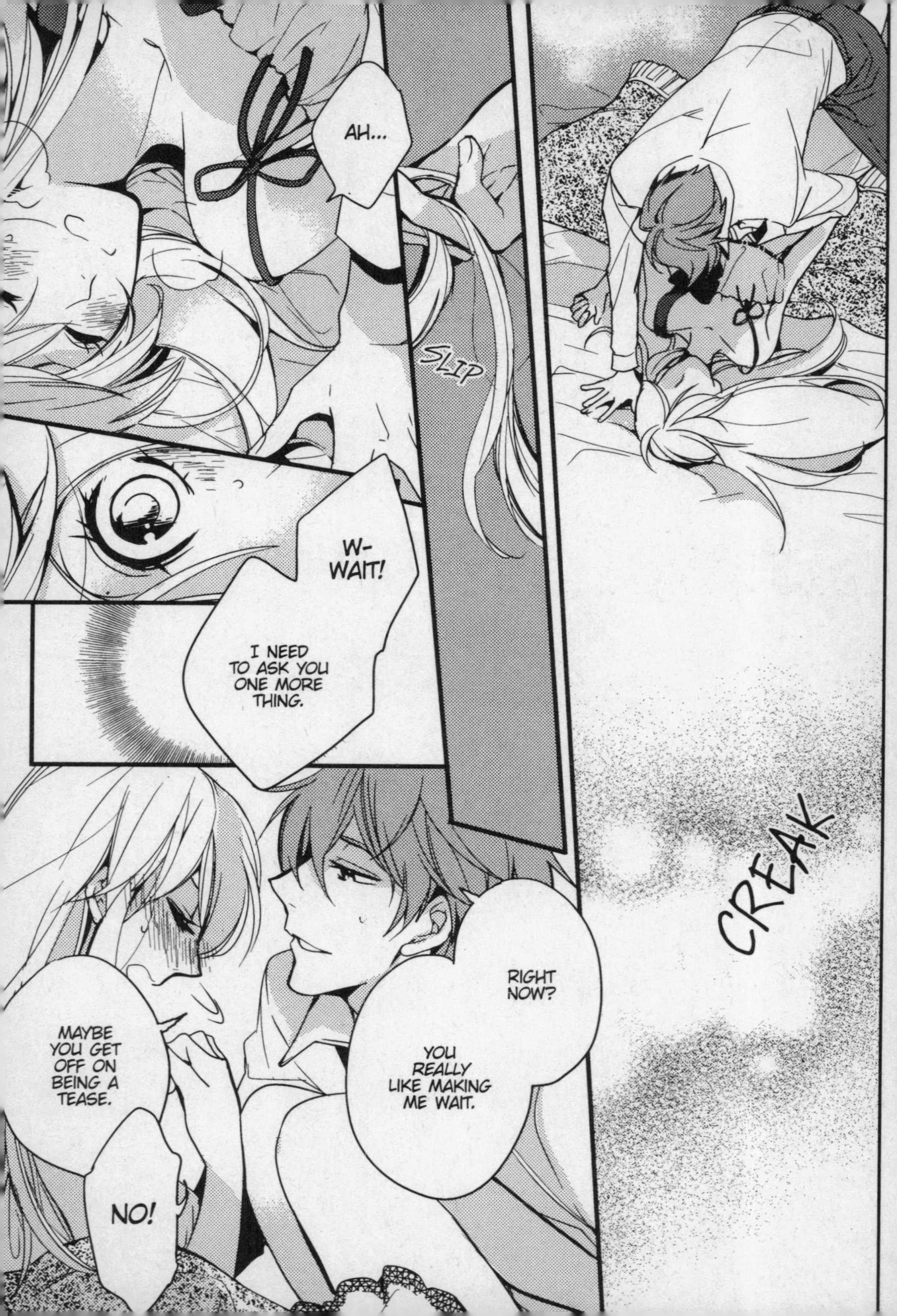
CREAK
AH...
SLIP
W-WAIT!
I NEED TO ASK YOU ONE MORE THING.
RIGHT NOW?
YOU REALLY LIKE MAKING ME WAIT.
MAYBE YOU GET OFF ON BEING A TEASE.
NO!

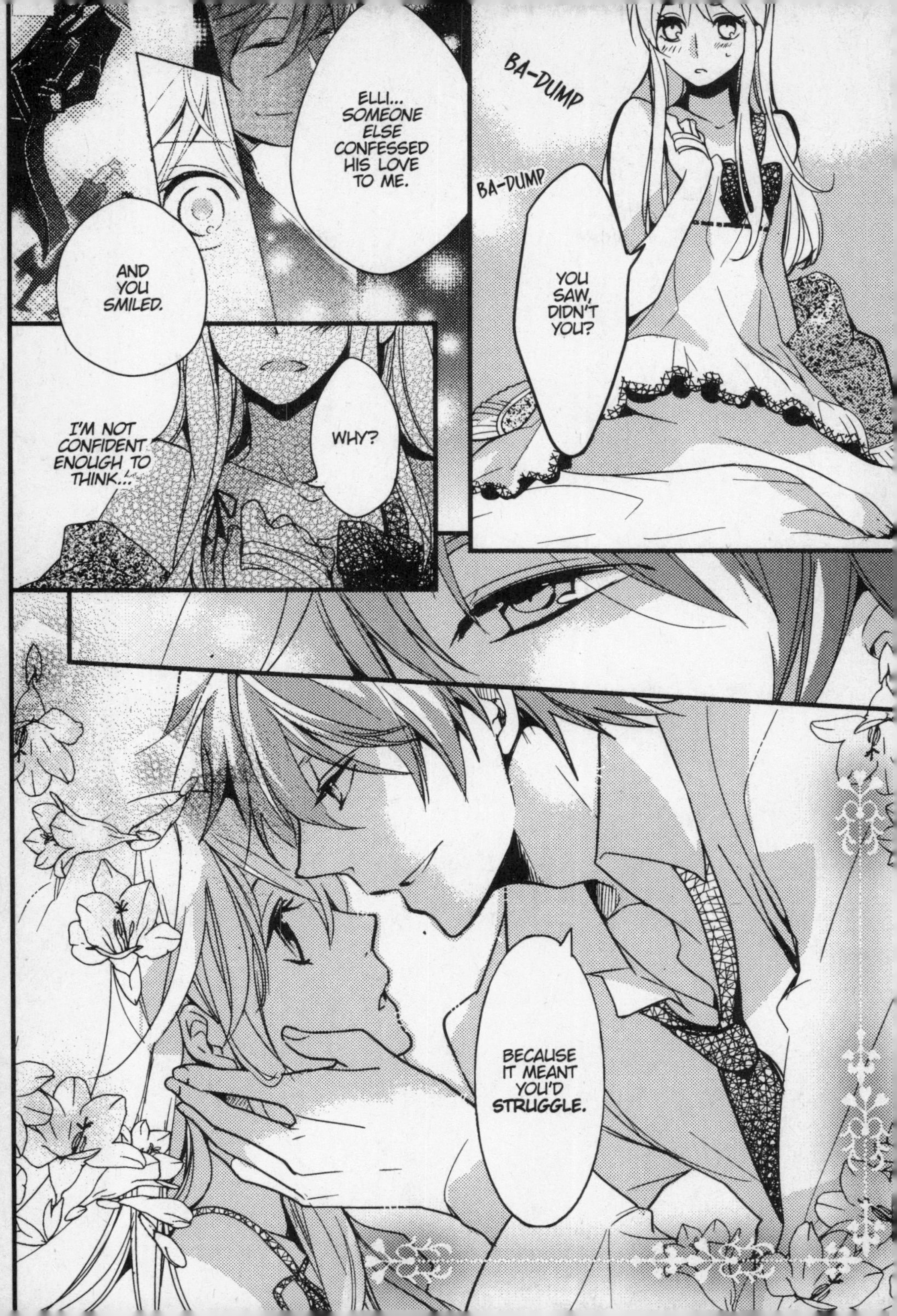
BA-DUMP
BA-DUMP
YOU SAW, DIDN'T YOU?
ELLI... SOMEONE ELSE CONFESSED HIS LOVE TO ME.
AND YOU SMILED.
WHY?
I'M NOT CONFIDENT ENOUGH TO THINK...
BECAUSE IT MEANT YOU'D STRUGGLE.

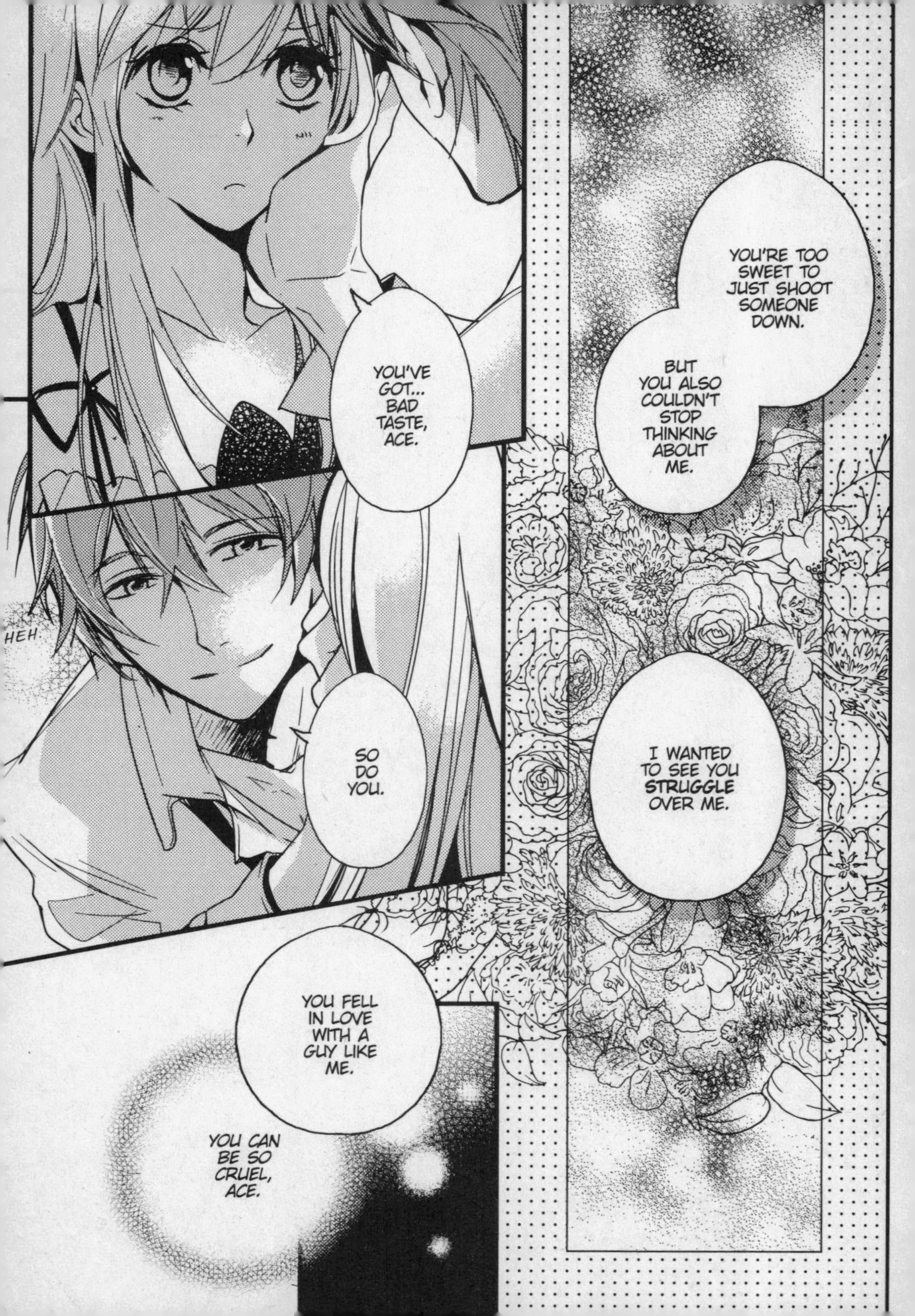
YOU'RE TOO SWEET TO JUST SHOOT SOMEONE DOWN.
BUT YOU ALSO COULDN'T STOP THINKING ABOUT ME.
I WANTED TO SEE YOU STRUGGLE OVER ME.
YOU'VE GOT... BAD TASTE, ACE.
HEH
SO DO YOU.
YOU FELL IN LOVE WITH A GUY LIKE ME.
YOU CAN BE SO CRUEL, ACE.

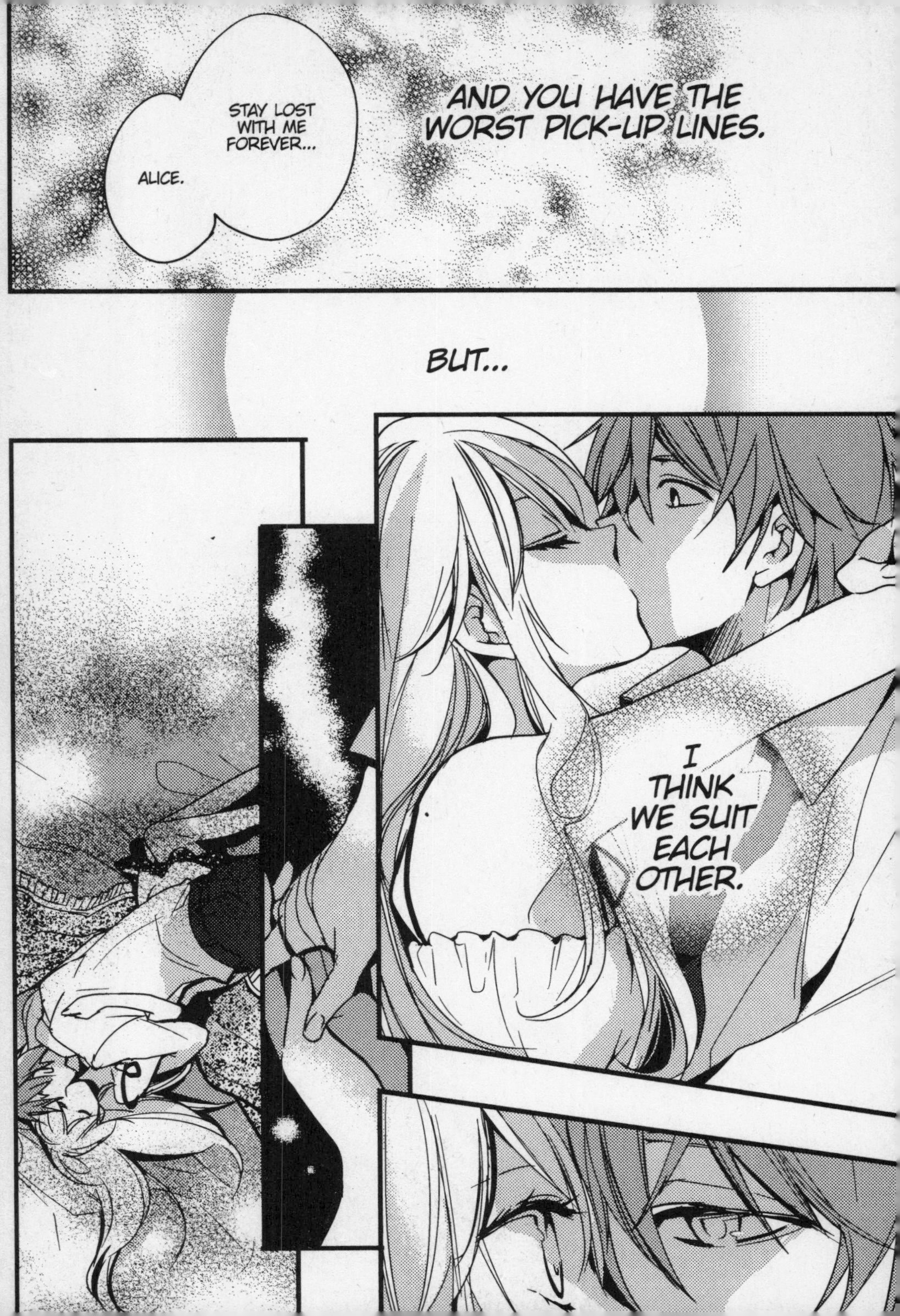
AND YOU HAVE THE WORST PICK-UP LINES.
STAY LOST WITH ME FOREVER...
ALICE.
BUT...
I THINK WE SUIT EACH OTHER.

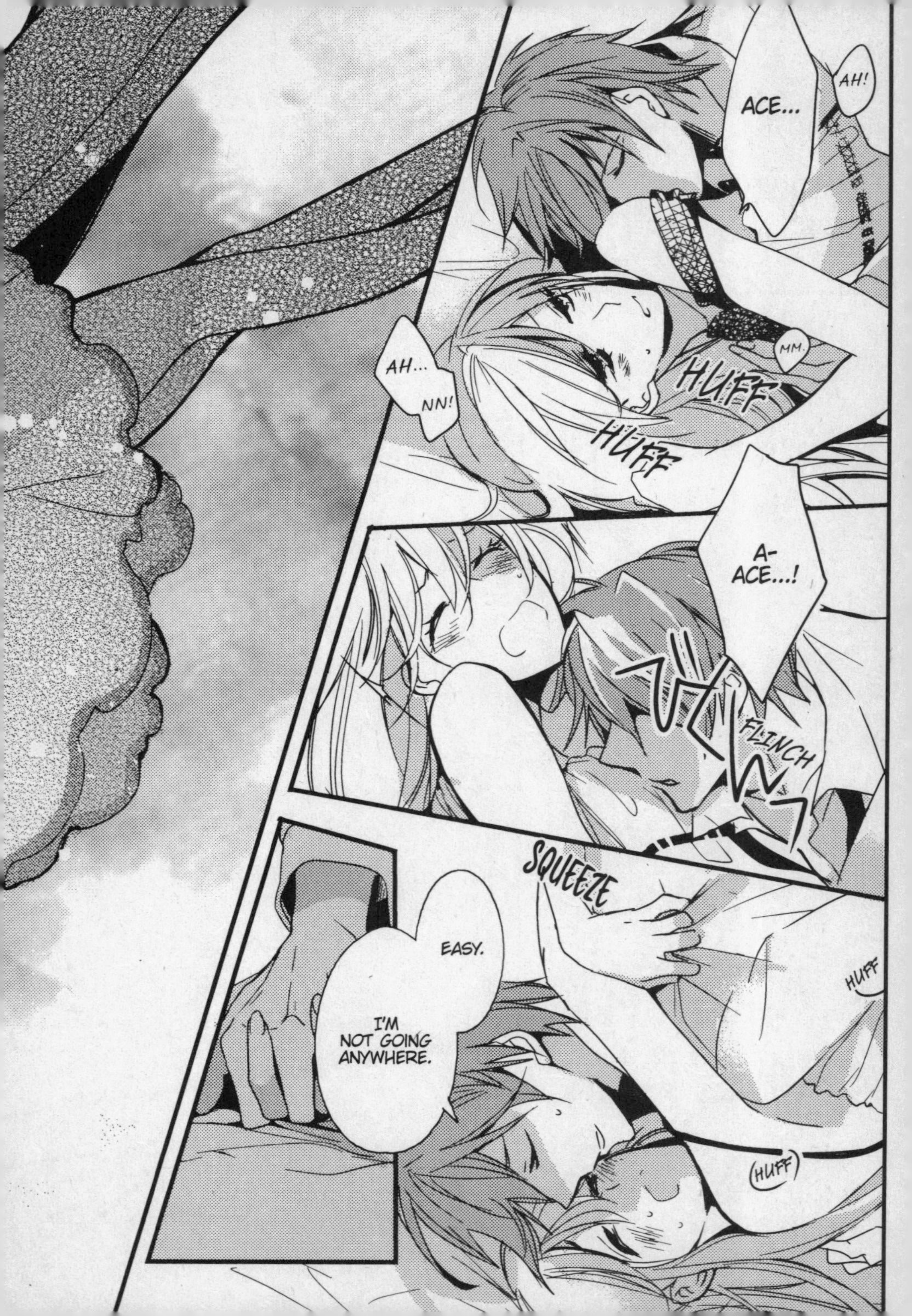
AH!
ACE...
MM.
HUFF
HUFF
AH... NN!
A- ACE...!
FLINCH
SQUEEZE
HUFF
EASY.
I'M NOT GOING ANYWHERE.
(HUFF)

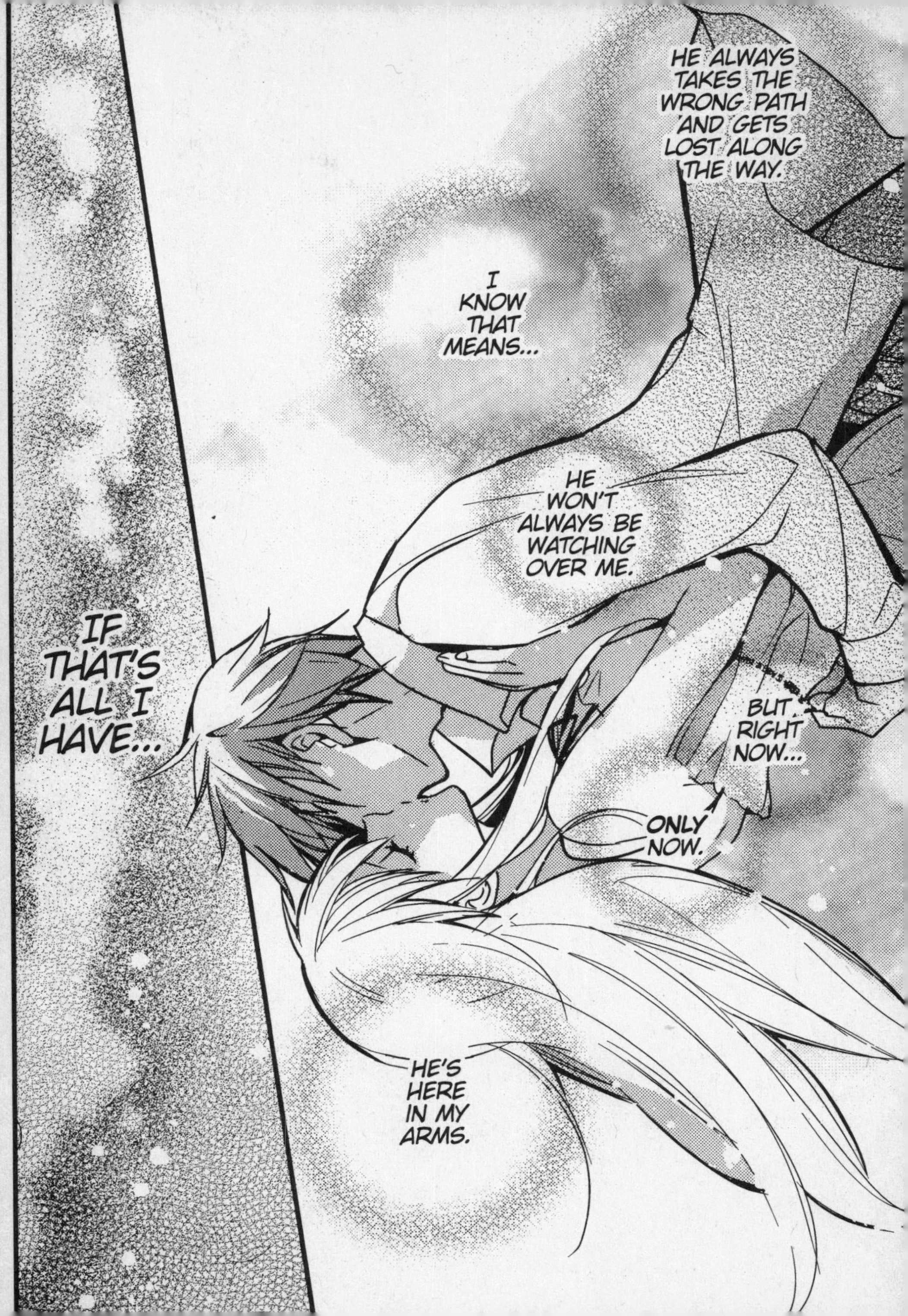
HE ALWAYS TAKES THE WRONG PATH AND GETS LOST ALONG THE WAY.
I KNOW THAT MEANS...
HE WON'T ALWAYS BE WATCHING OVER ME.
BUT RIGHT NOW...
ONLY NOW.
HE'S HERE IN MY ARMS.
IF THAT'S ALL I HAVE...

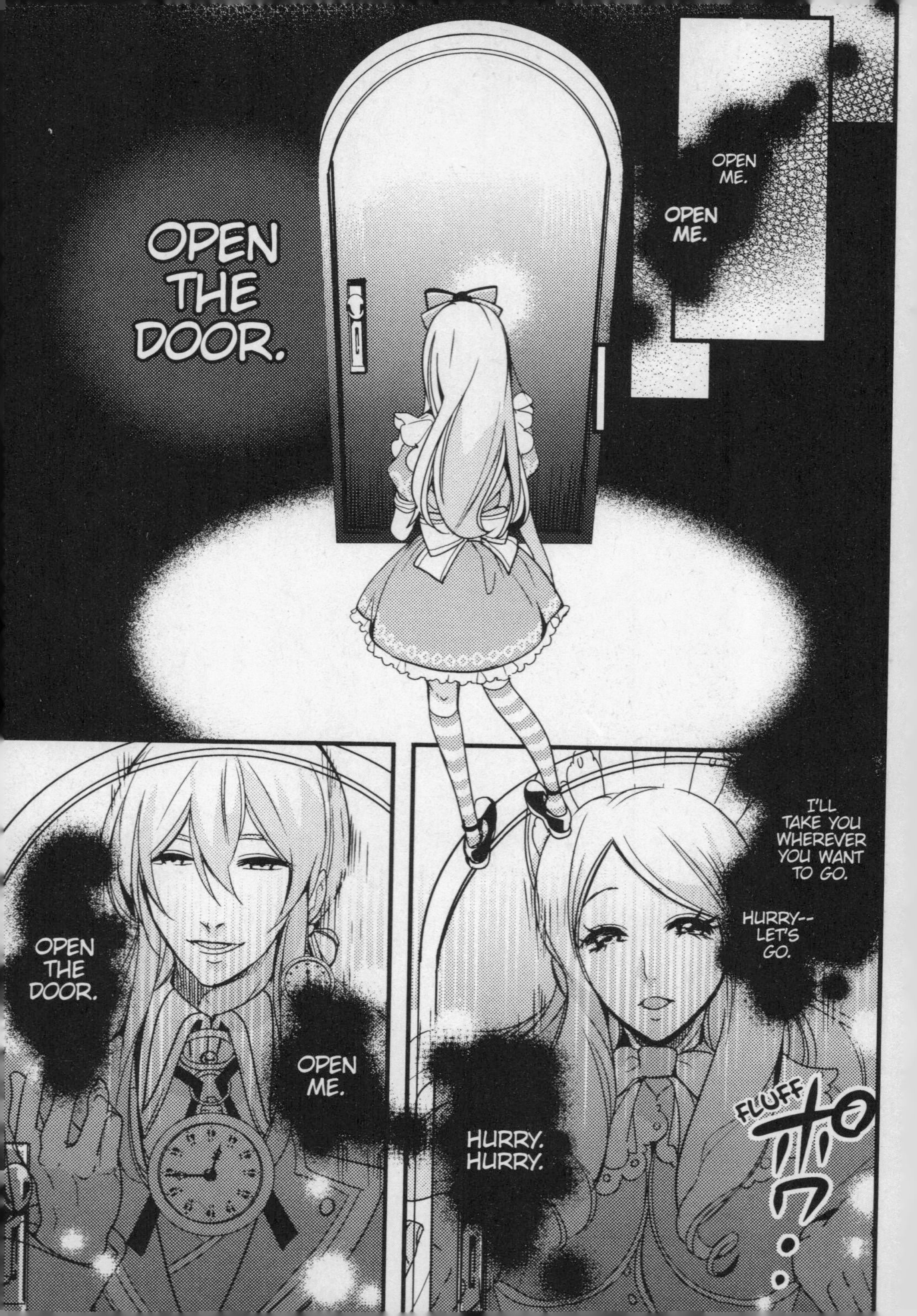
OPEN ME.
OPEN ME.
OPEN THE DOOR.
I'LL TAKE YOU WHEREVER YOU WANT TO GO.
HURRY-- LET'S GO.
FLUFF
HURRY. HURRY.
OPEN ME.
OPEN THE DOOR.

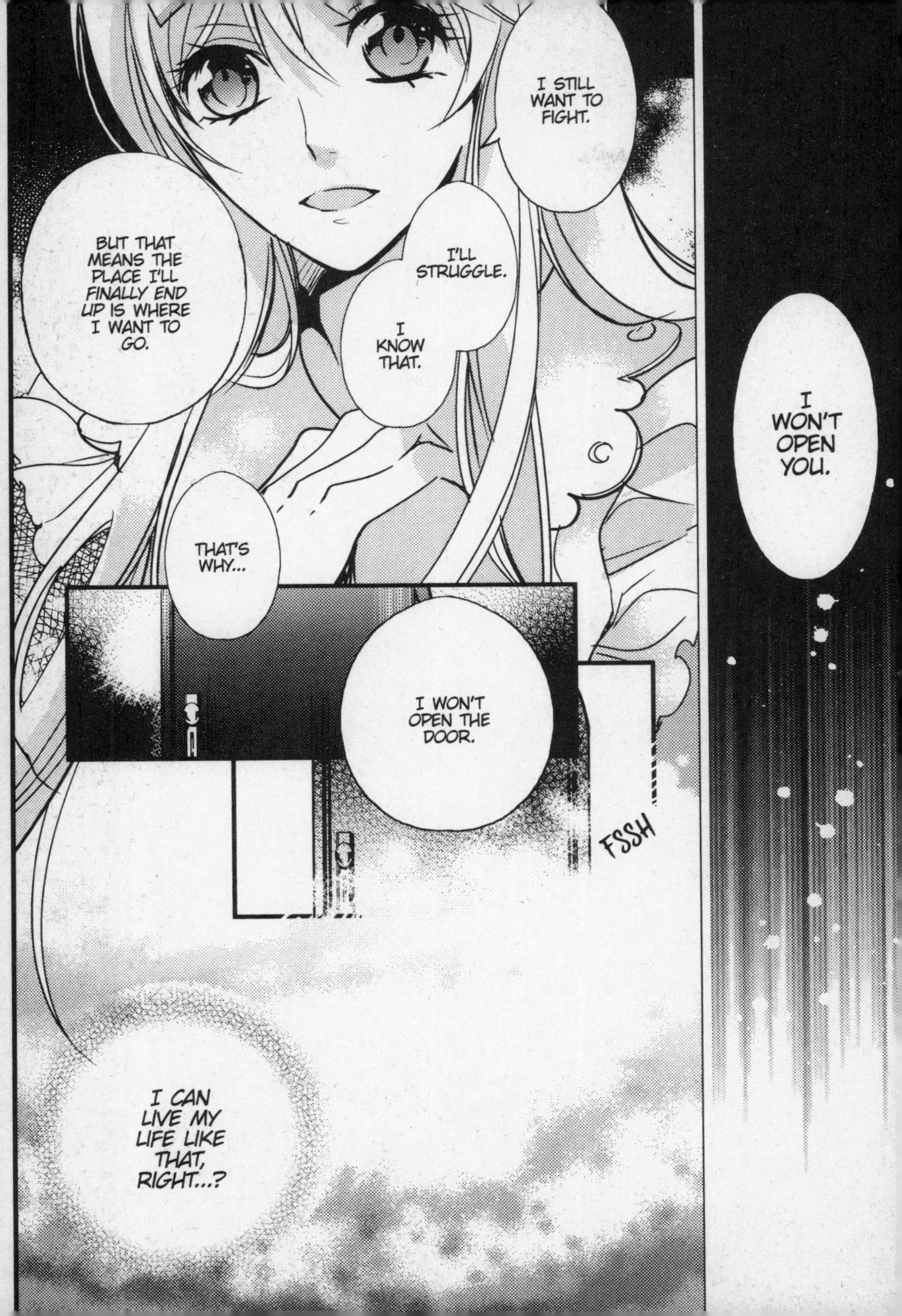
I WON'T OPEN YOU.
I STILL WANT TO FIGHT.
I'LL STRUGGLE.
BUT THAT MEANS THE PLACE I'LL FINALLY END UP IS WHERE I WANT TO GO.
I KNOW THAT.
THAT'S WHY...
I WON'T OPEN THE DOOR.
FSSH
I CAN LIVE MY LIFE LIKE THAT, RIGHT...?

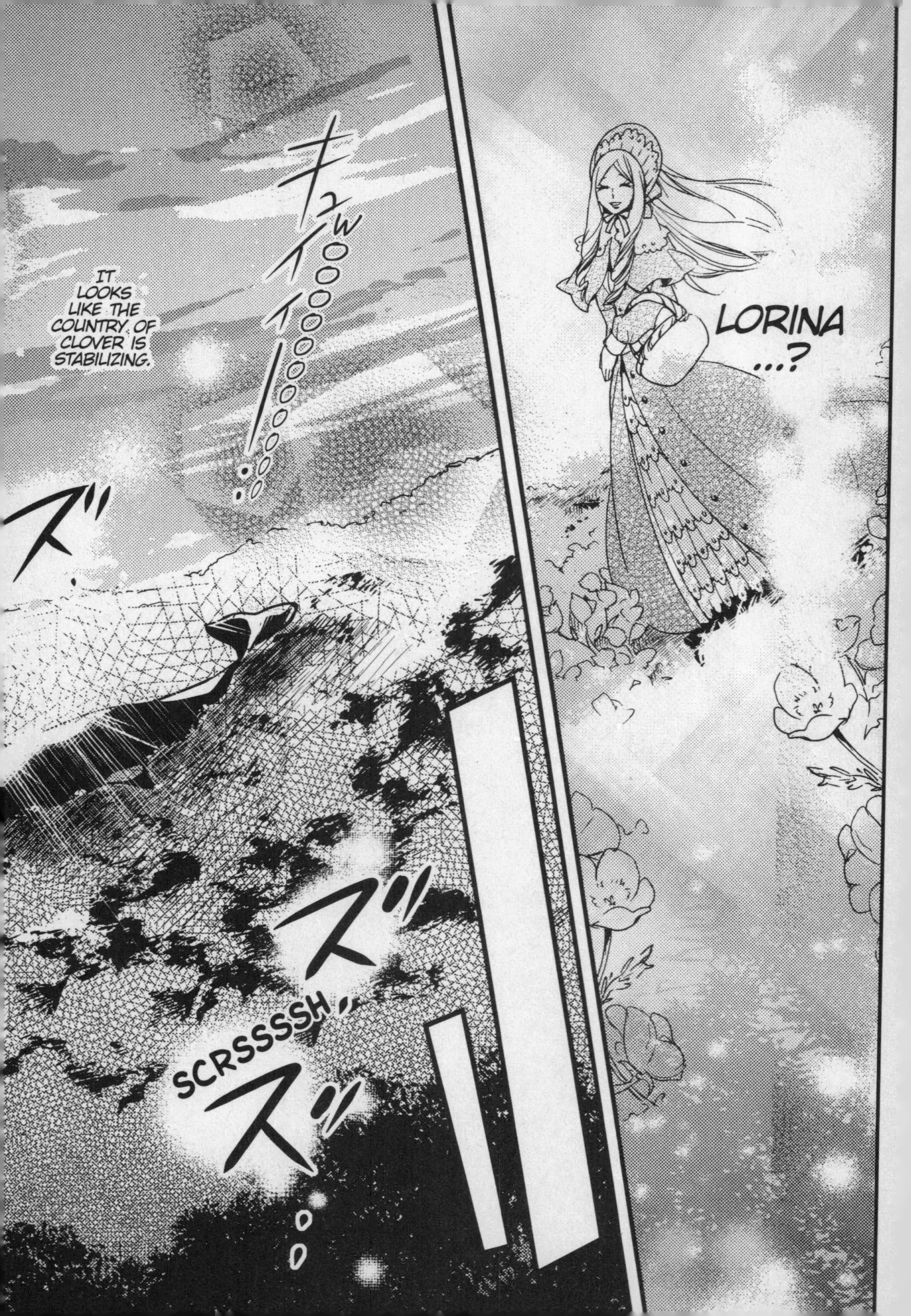
LORINA ...?
IT LOOKS LIKE THE COUNTRY OF CLOVER IS STABILIZING.
SCRSSSSH

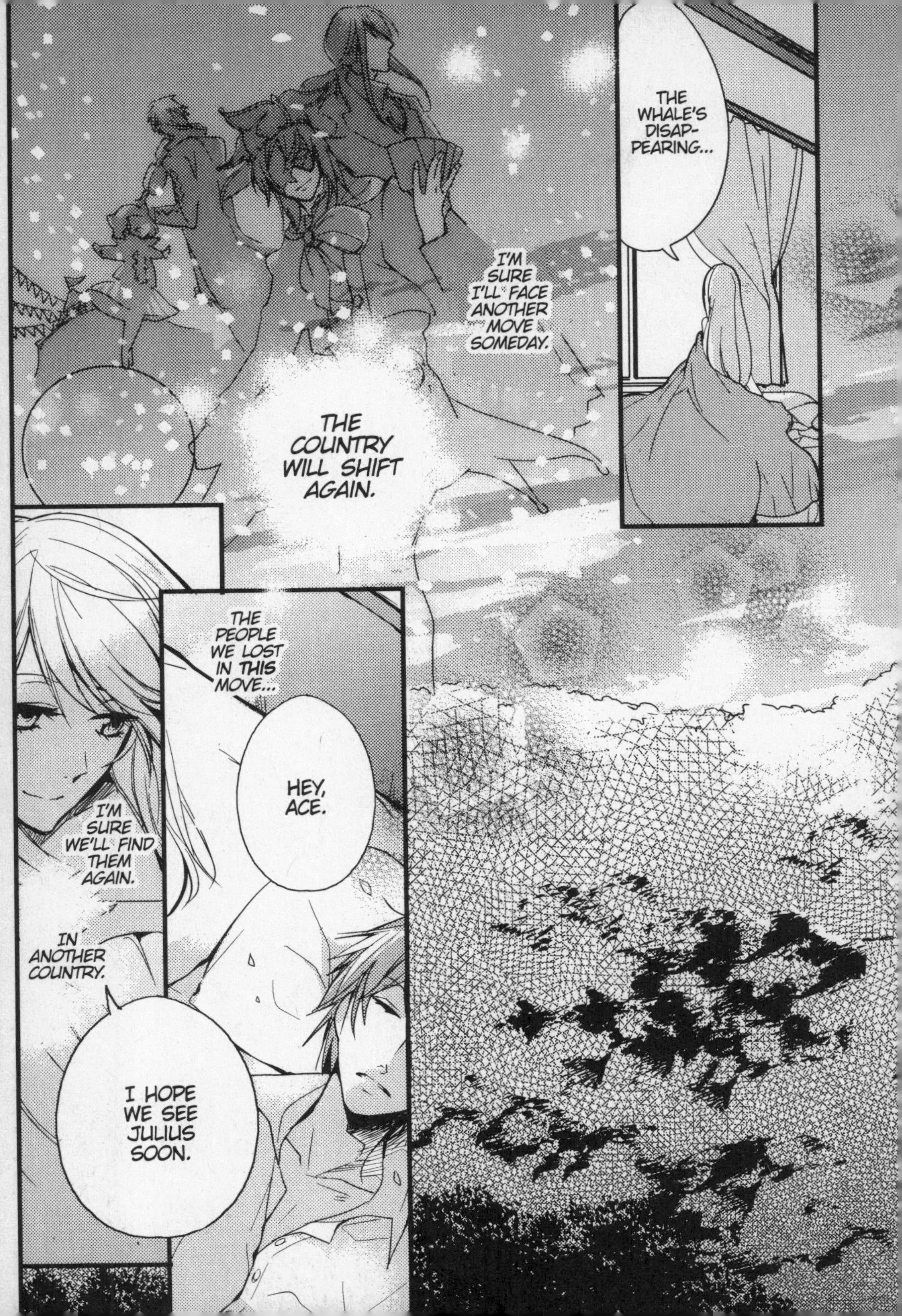
THE WHALE'S DISAPPEARING...
I'M SURE I'LL FACE ANOTHER MOVE SOMEDAY.
THE COUNTRY WILL SHIFT AGAIN.
THE PEOPLE WE LOST IN THIS MOVE...
HEY, ACE.
I HOPE WE SEE JULIUS SOON.
I'M SURE WE'LL FIND THEM AGAIN.
IN ANOTHER COUNTRY.

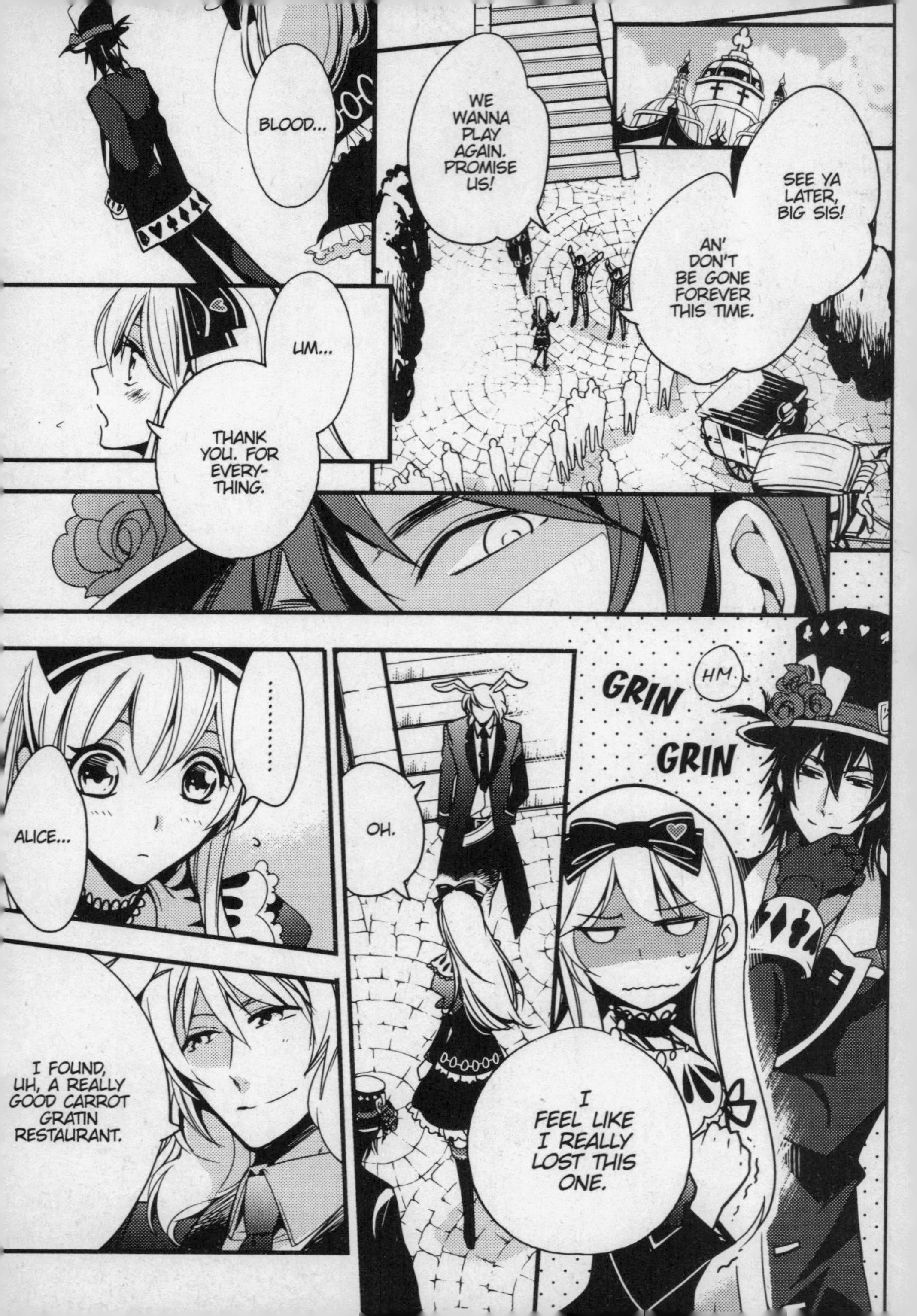
SEE YA LATER, BIG SIS!
AN' DON'T BE GONE FOREVER THIS TIME.
WE WANNA PLAY AGAIN. PROMISE US!
BLOOD...
UM...
THANK YOU. FOR EVERYTHING.
HM.
GRIN
GRIN
I FEEL LIKE I REALLY LOST THIS ONE.
OH.
......
ALICE...
I FOUND, UH, A REALLY GOOD CARROT GRATIN RESTAURANT.

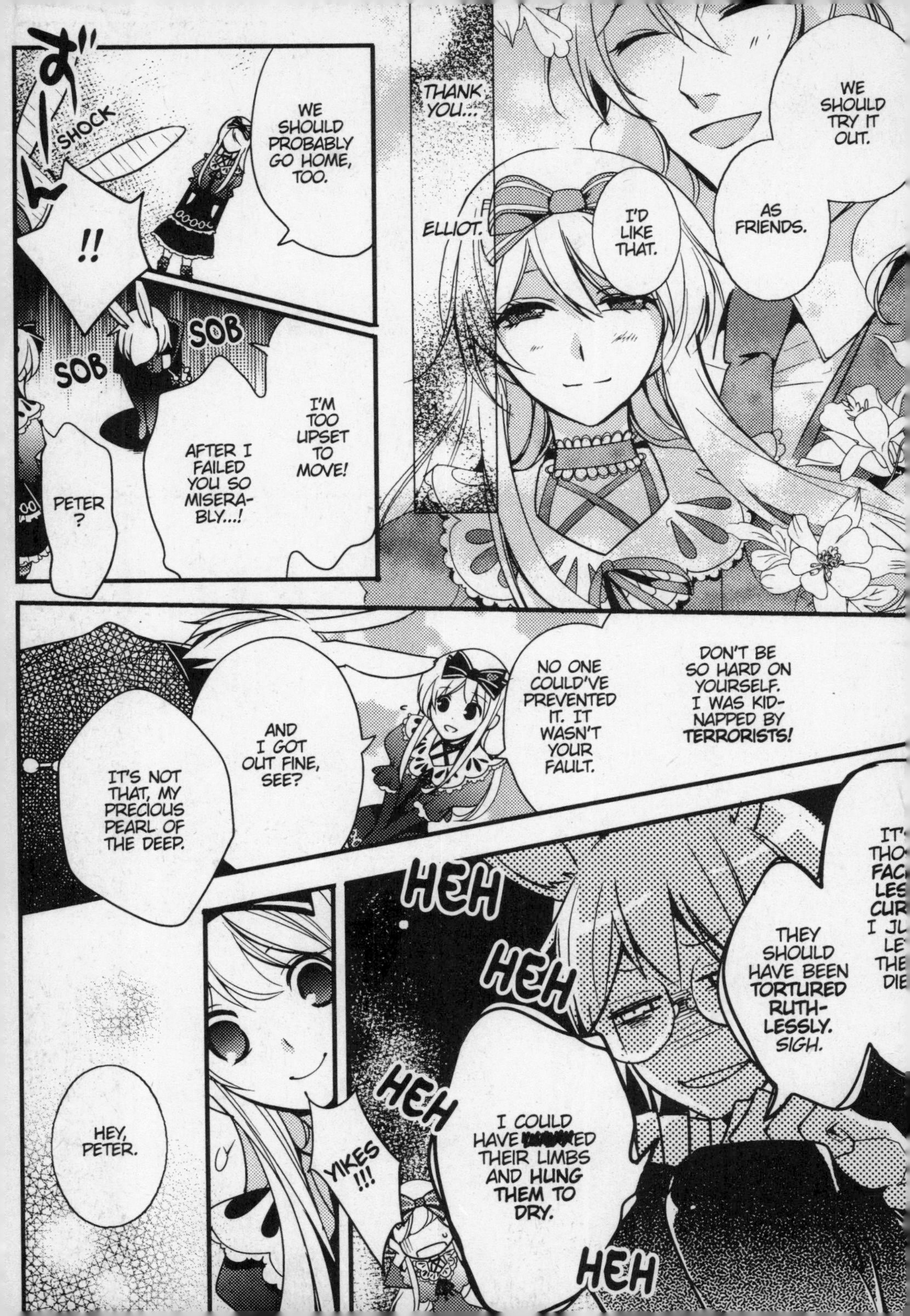
WE SHOULD TRY IT OUT.
AS FRIENDS.
I'D LIKE THAT.
THANK YOU...
ELLIOT.
WE SHOULD PROBABLY GO HOME, TOO.
SHOCK
!!
SOB
SOB
I'M TOO UPSET TO MOVE!
AFTER I FAILED YOU SO MISERA-BLY...!
PETER ?
DON'T BE SO HARD ON YOURSELF. I WAS KID-NAPPED BY TERRORISTS!
NO ONE COULD'VE PREVENTED IT. IT WASN'T YOUR FAULT.
AND I GOT OUT FINE, SEE?
IT'S NOT THAT, MY PRECIOUS PEARL OF THE DEEP.
THEY SHOULD HAVE BEEN TORTURED RUTH-LESSLY. SIGH.
HEH
HEH
I COULD HAVE [redacted]ED THEIR LIMBS AND HUNG THEM TO DRY.
HEH
HEH
YIKES !!!
HEY, PETER.

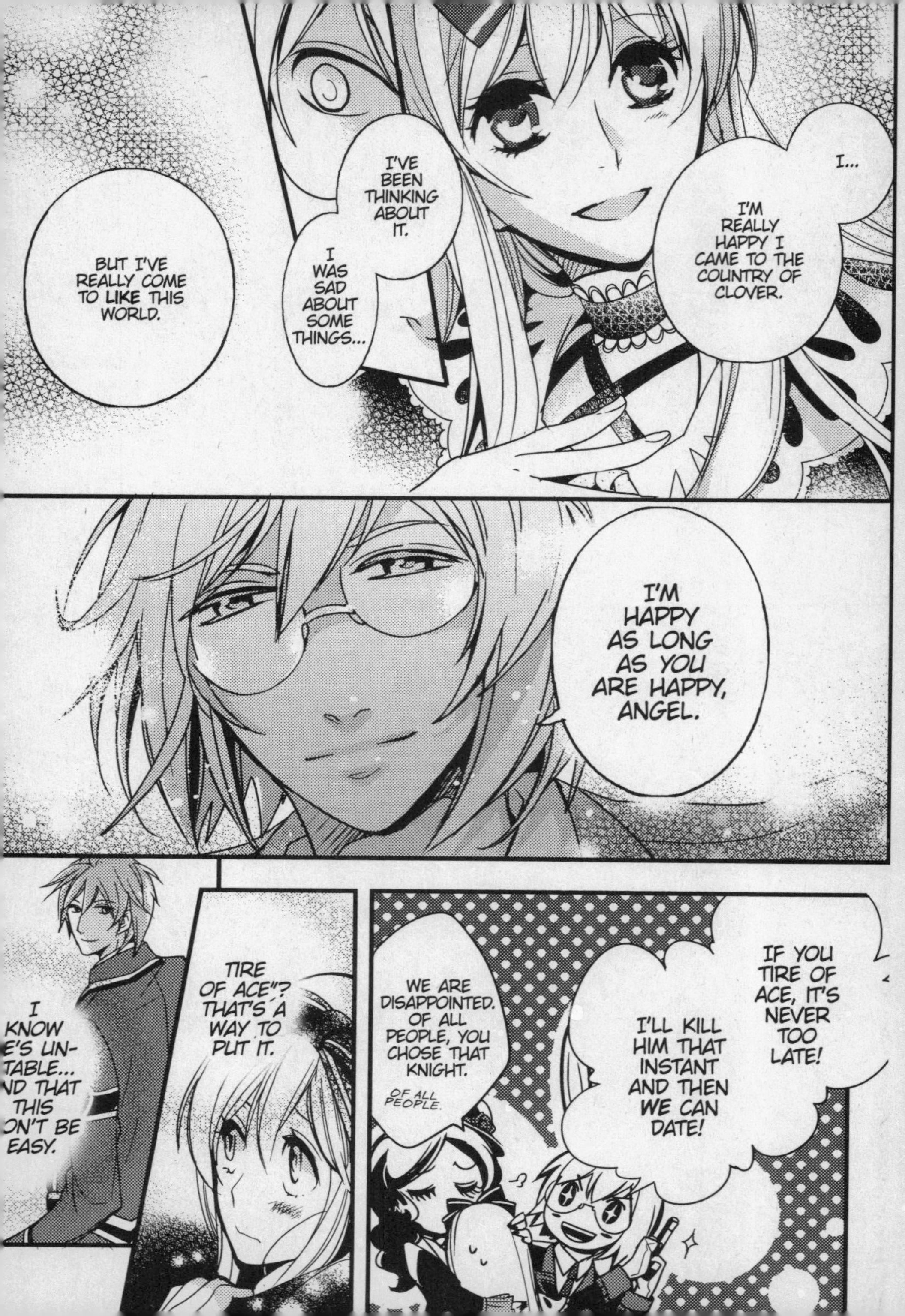
I...
I'M REALLY HAPPY I CAME TO THE COUNTRY OF CLOVER.
I'VE BEEN THINKING ABOUT IT.
I WAS SAD ABOUT SOME THINGS...
BUT I'VE REALLY COME TO LIKE THIS WORLD.
I'M HAPPY AS LONG AS YOU ARE HAPPY, ANGEL.
IF YOU TIRE OF ACE, IT'S NEVER TOO LATE!
I'LL KILL HIM THAT INSTANT AND THEN WE CAN DATE!
WE ARE DISAPPOINTED. OF ALL PEOPLE, YOU CHOSE THAT KNIGHT.
OF ALL PEOPLE.
TIRE OF ACE"? THAT'S A WAY TO PUT IT.
I KNOW E'S UN-TABLE... ND THAT THIS ON'T BE EASY.

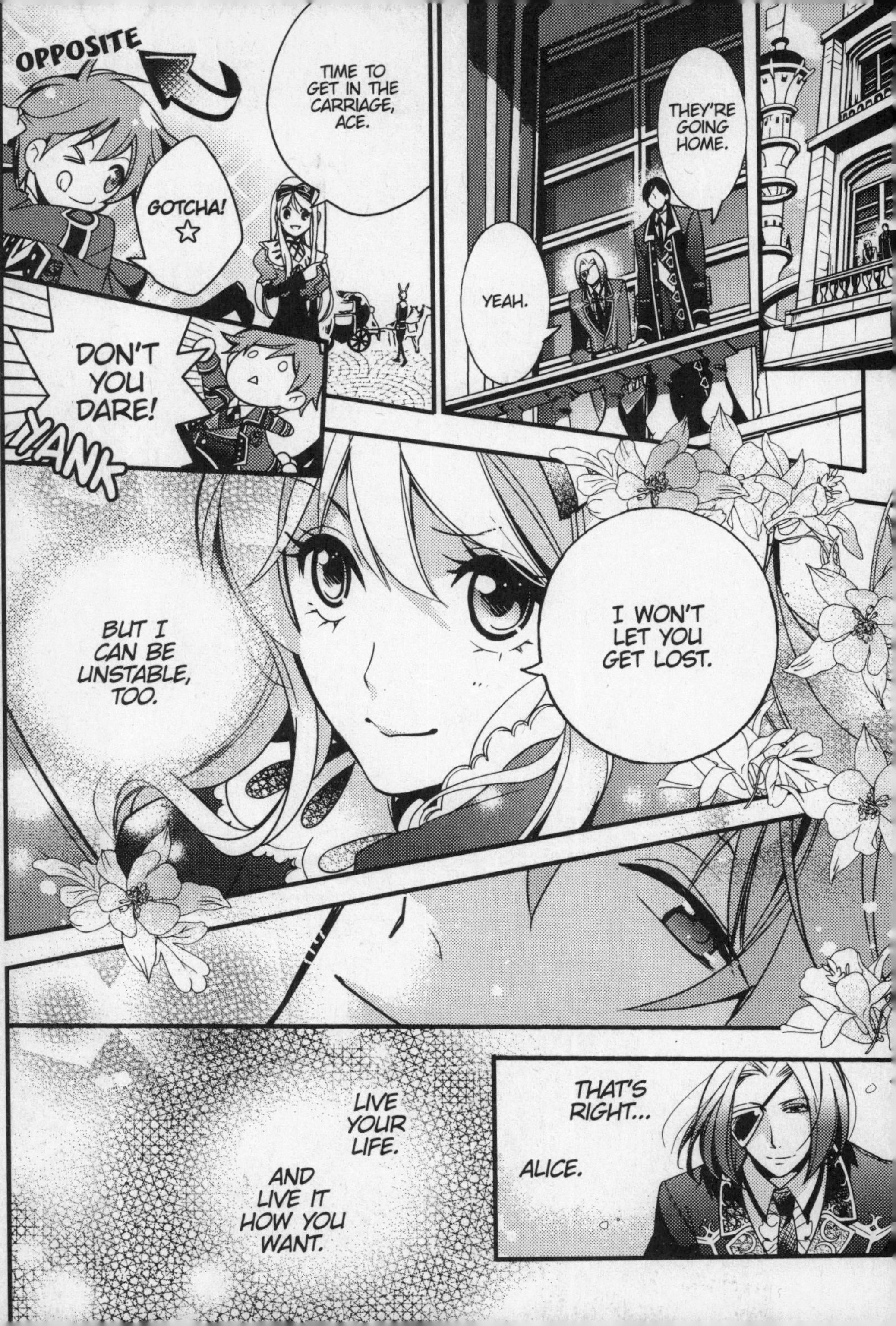
THEY'RE GOING HOME.
YEAH.
TIME TO GET IN THE CARRIAGE, ACE.
OPPOSITE
GOTCHA! ☆
DON'T YOU DARE!
YANK
I WON'T LET YOU GET LOST.
BUT I CAN BE UNSTABLE, TOO.
THAT'S RIGHT...
ALICE.
LIVE YOUR LIFE.
AND LIVE IT HOW YOU WANT.

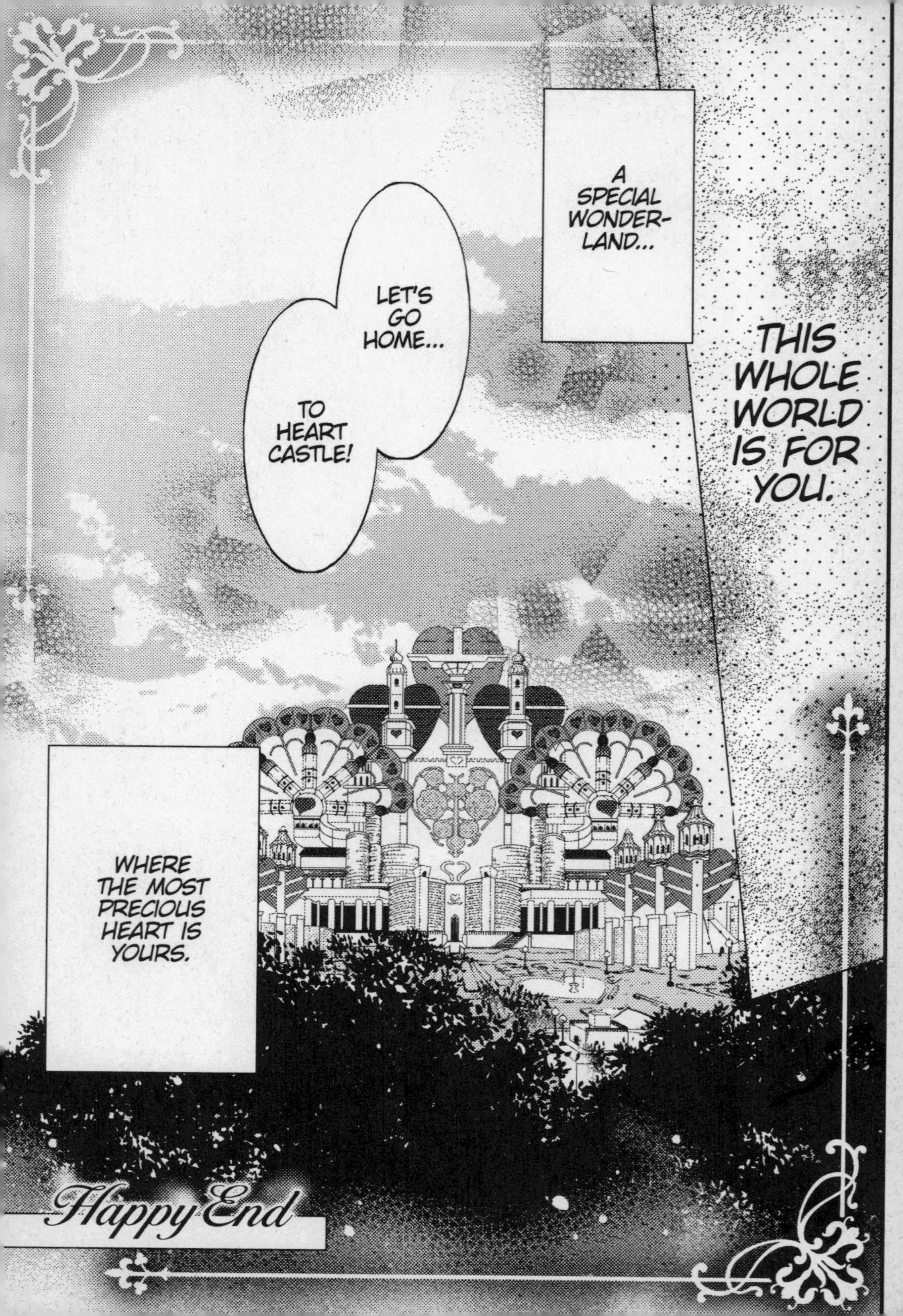
A SPECIAL WONDER-LAND...
THIS WHOLE WORLD IS FOR YOU.
LET'S GO HOME...
TO HEART CASTLE!
WHERE THE MOST PRECIOUS HEART IS YOURS.
Happy End

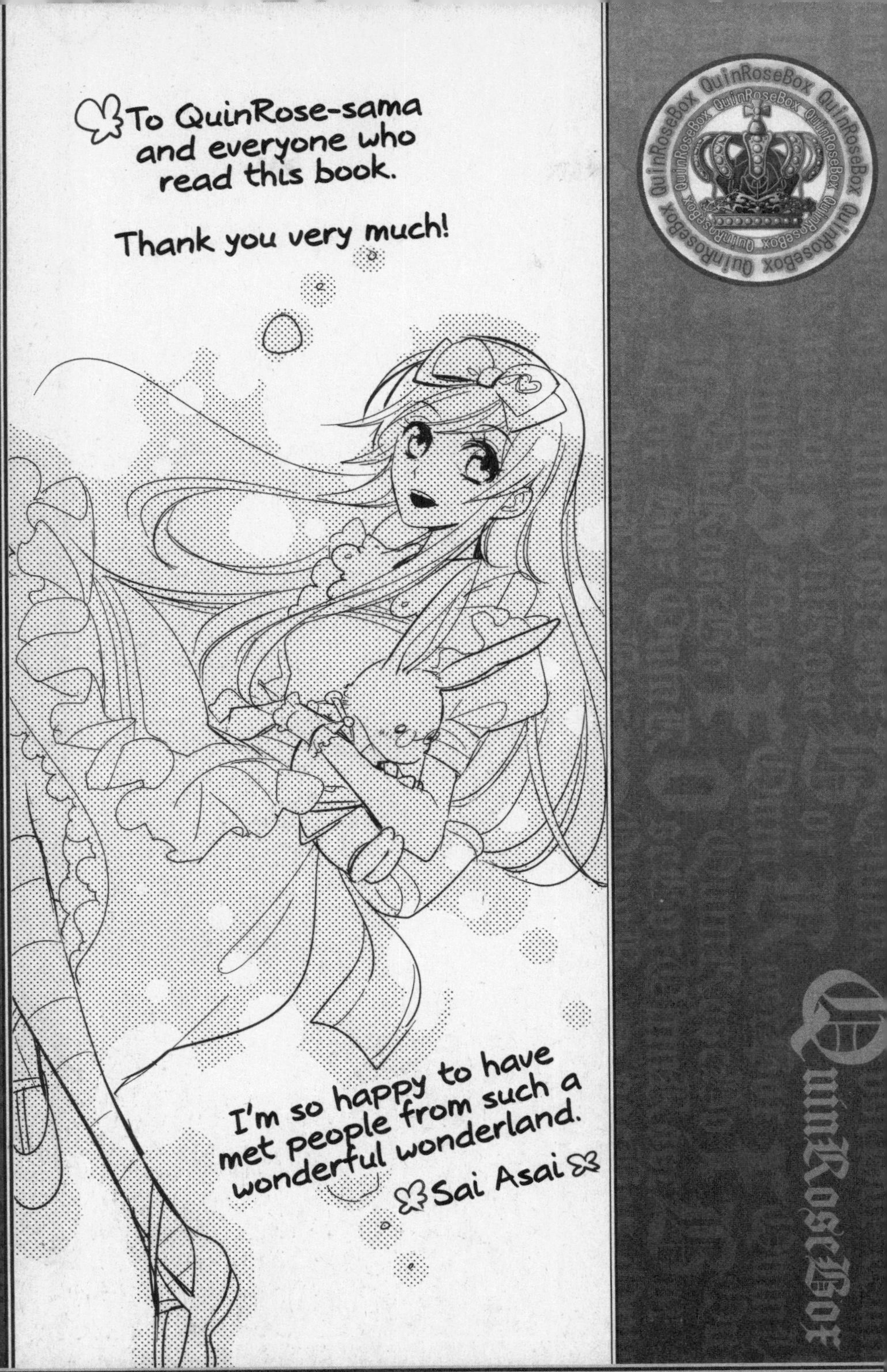
To QuinRose-sama and everyone who read this book.
Thank you very much!
I'm so happy to have met people from such a wonderful wonderland.
Sai Asai

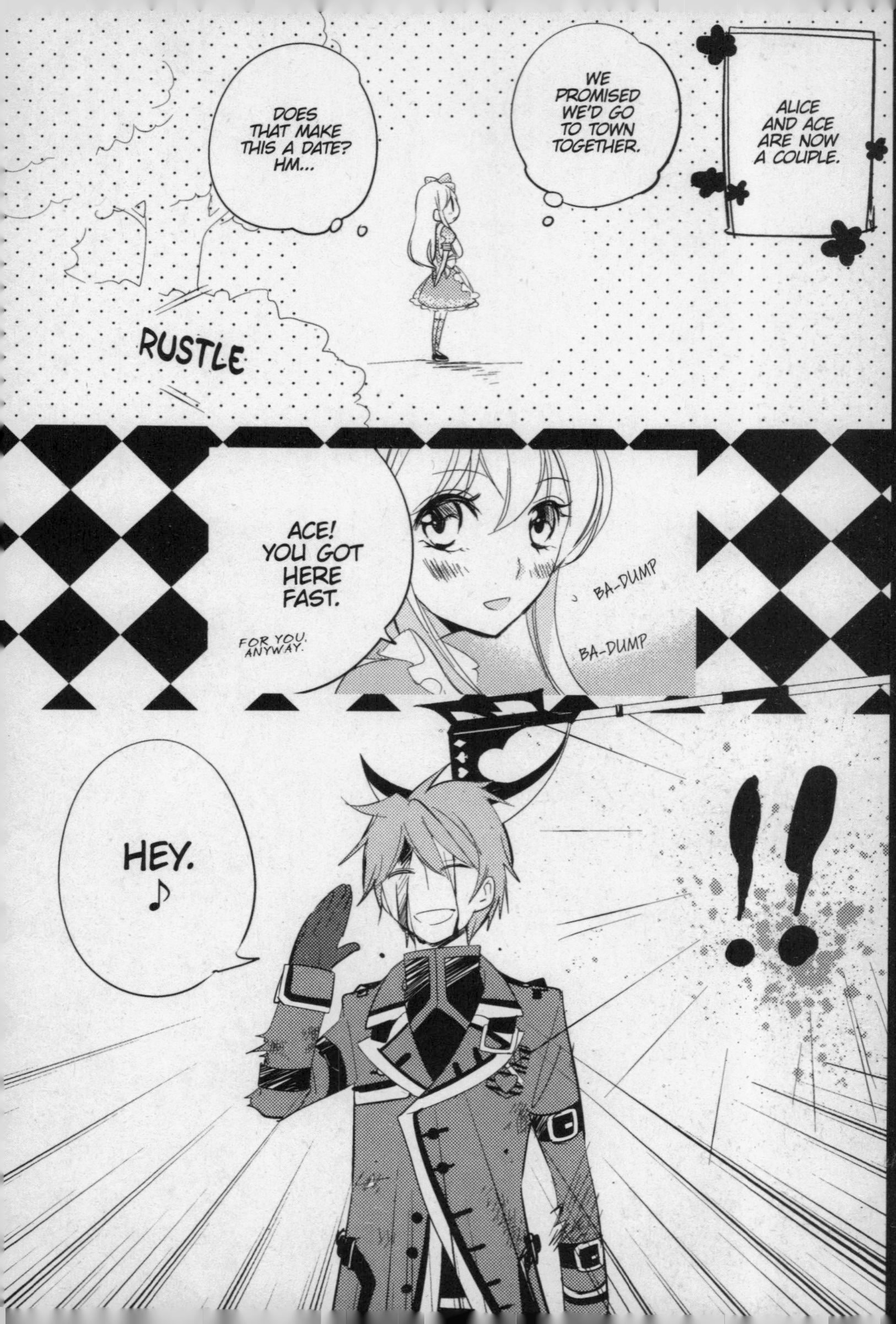
ALICE AND ACE ARE NOW A COUPLE.
WE PROMISED WE'D GO TO TOWN TOGETHER.
DOES THAT MAKE THIS A DATE? HM...
RUSTLE
BA-DUMP
BA-DUMP
ACE! YOU GOT HERE FAST.
FOR YOU, ANYWAY.
!!
HEY. ♪

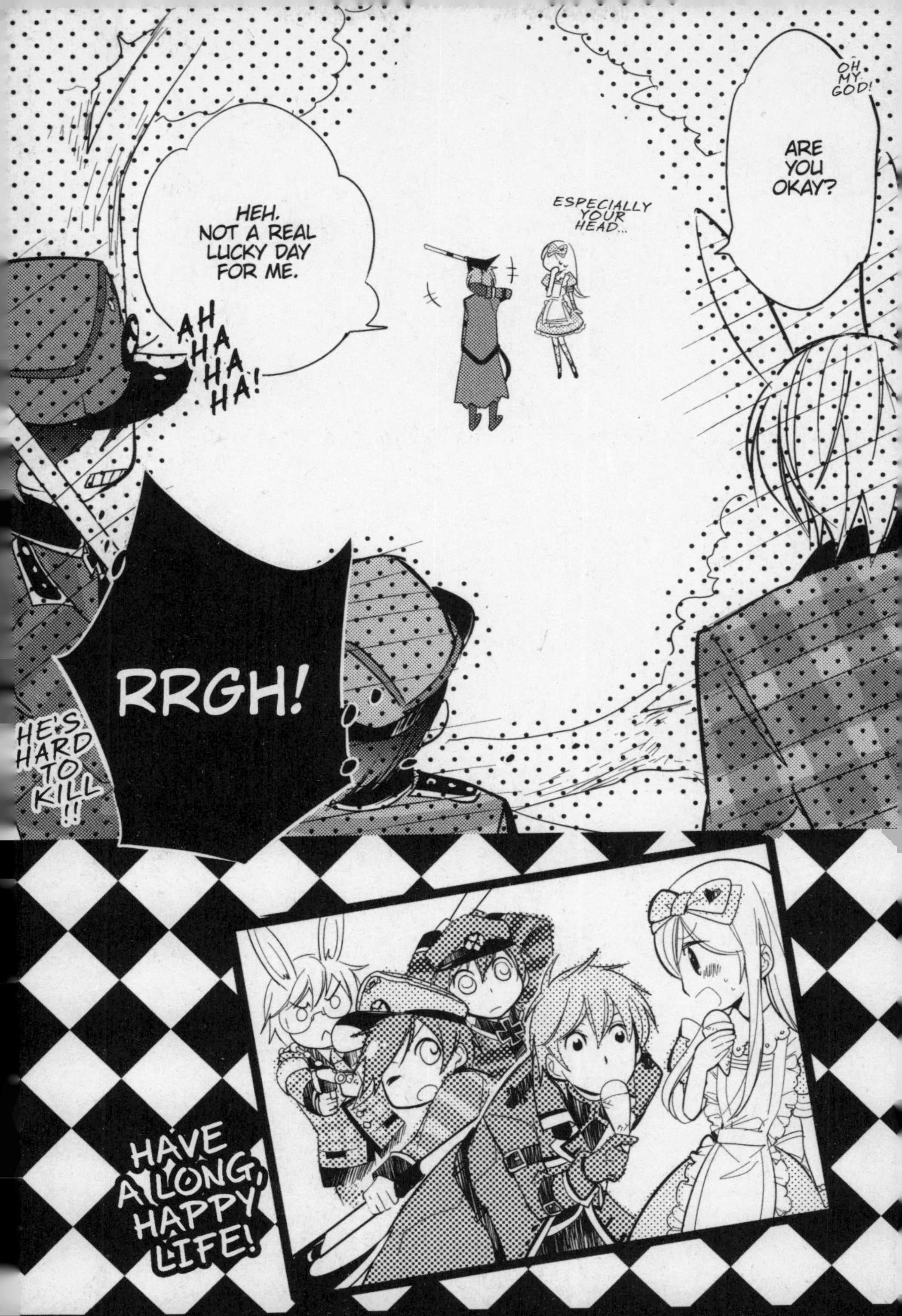
OH MY GOD!
ARE YOU OKAY?
ESPECIALLY YOUR HEAD...
HEH. NOT A REAL LUCKY DAY FOR ME.
AH HA HA HA HA!
RRGH!
HE'S HARD TO KILL!!
HAVE A LONG, HAPPY LIFE!

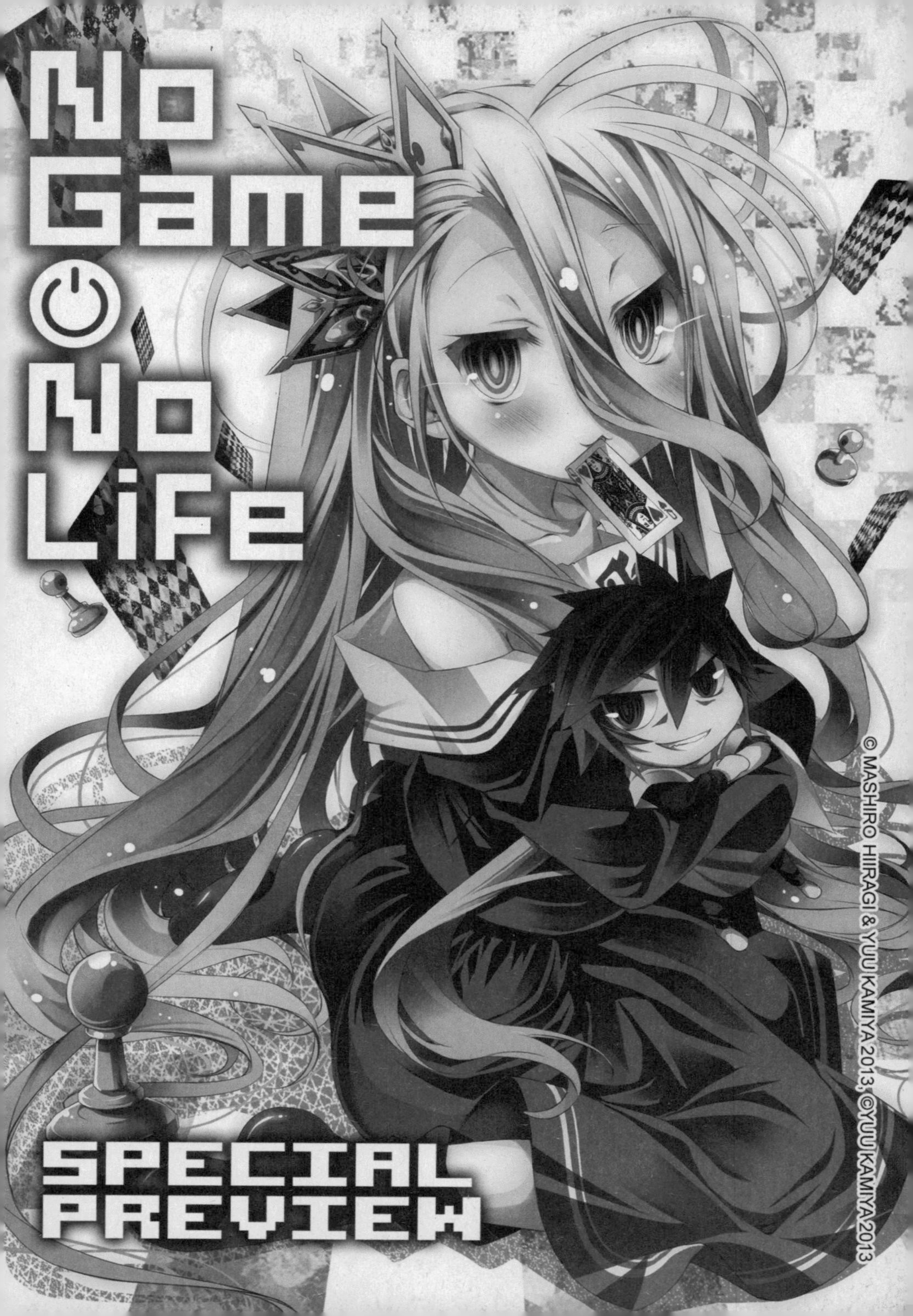
No Game No Life
SPECIAL PREVIEW
© MASHIRO HIIRAGI & YUU KAMIYA2013, ©YUU KAMIYA2013

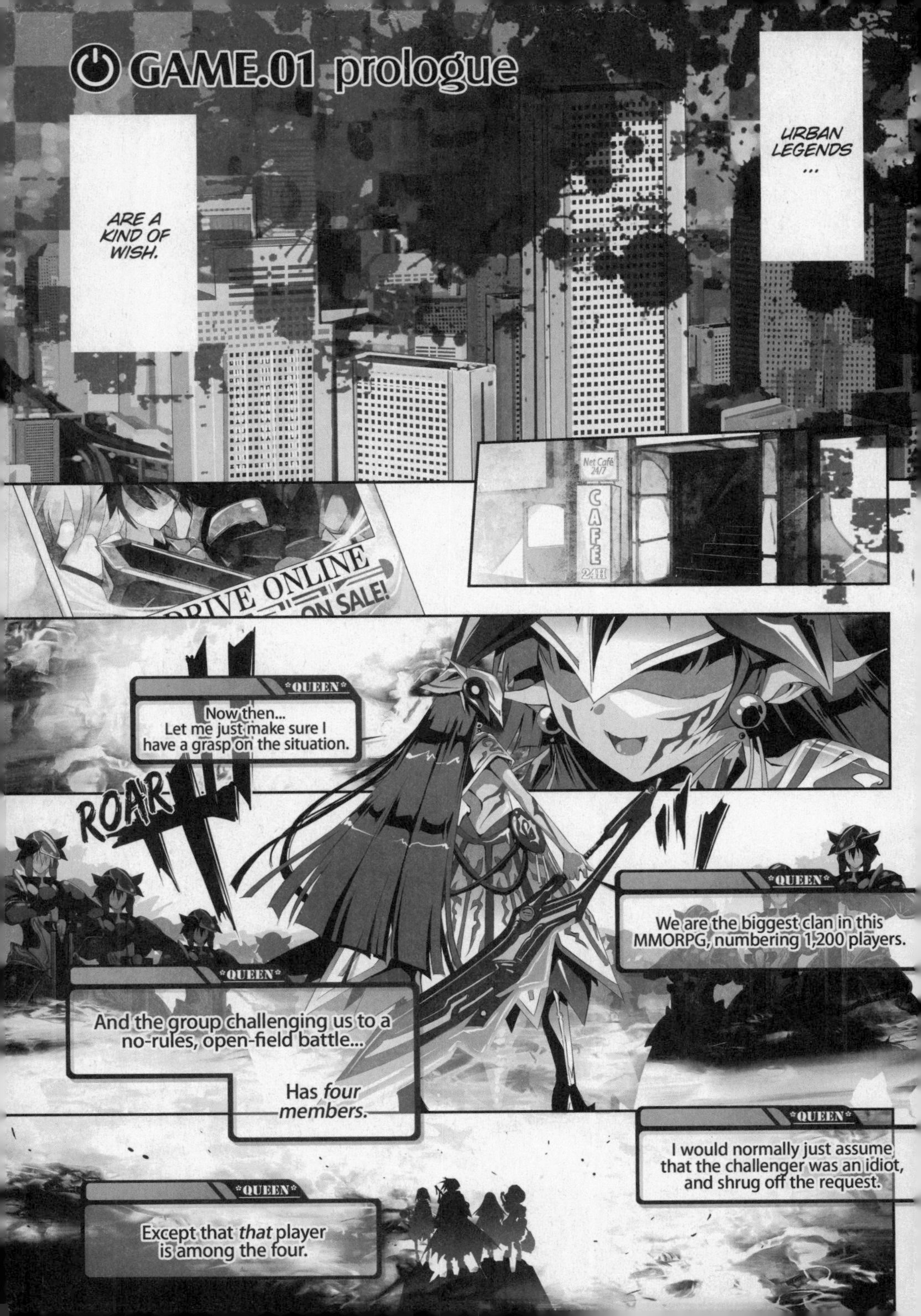
GAME.01 prologue
URBAN LEGENDS ...
ARE A KIND OF WISH.
Net Café 24/7
CAFÉ 24H
DRIVE ONLINE
ON SALE!
*QUEEN*
Now then... Let me just make sure I have a grasp on the situation.
ROAR
*QUEEN*
We are the biggest clan in this MMORPG, numbering 1,200 players.
*QUEEN*
And the group challenging us to a no-rules, open-field battle...
Has *four members.*
*QUEEN*
I would normally just assume that the challenger was an idiot, and shrug off the request.
*QUEEN*
Except that *that* player is among the four.

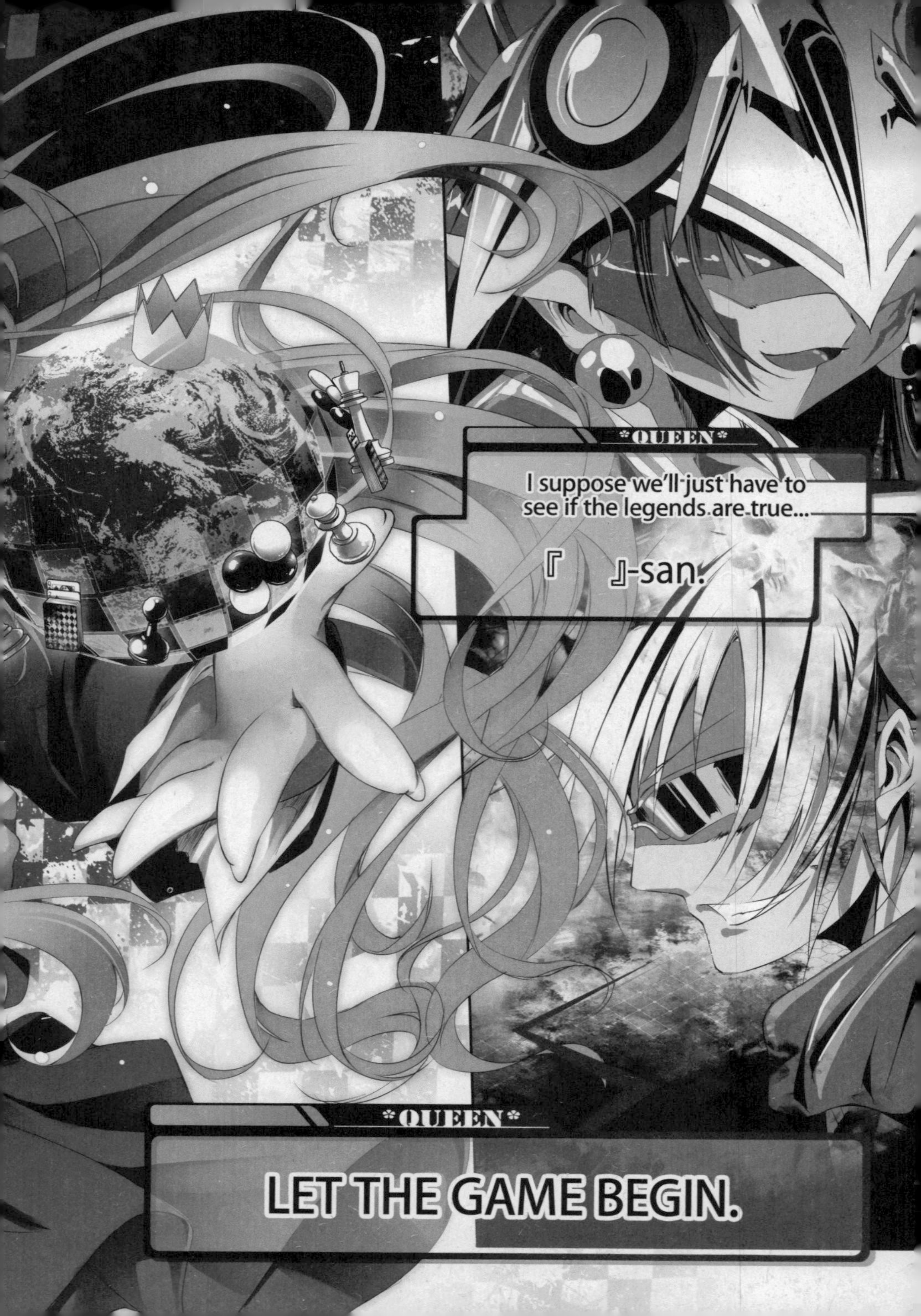
*QUEEN*
I suppose we'll just have to see if the legends are true...
『　』-san.
*QUEEN*
LET THE GAME BEGIN.

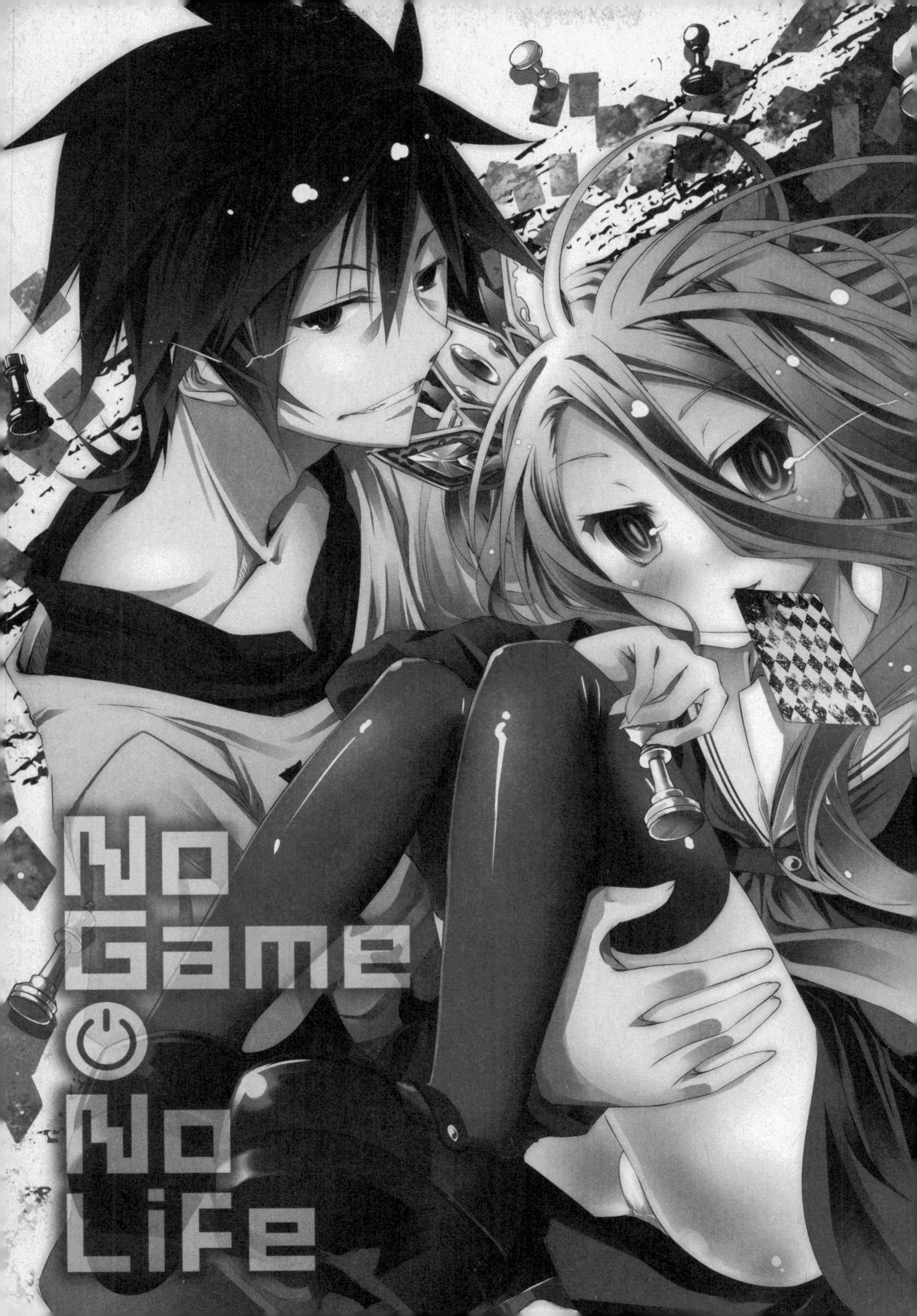
No Game No Life

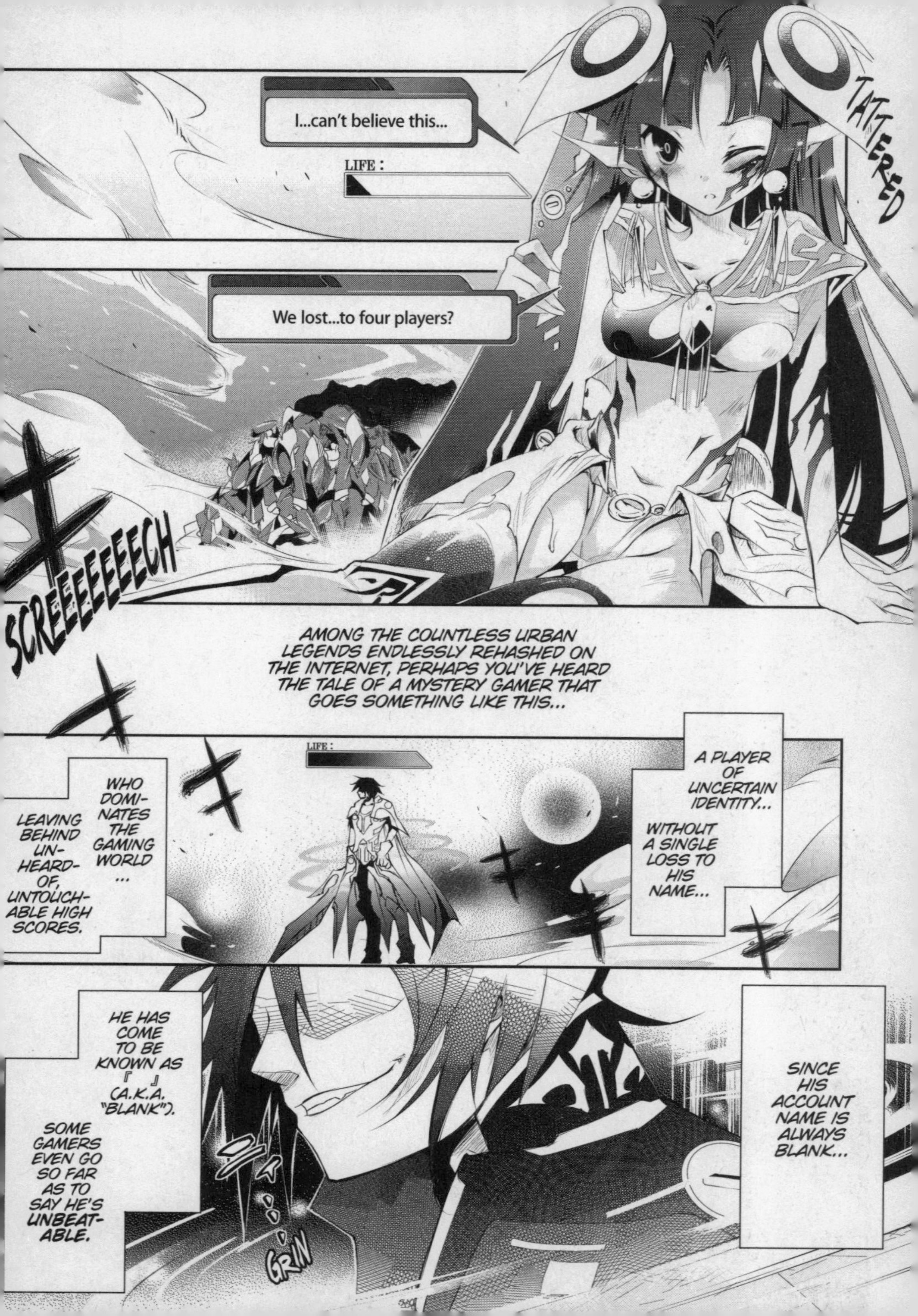
TATTERED
I...can't believe this...
LIFE :
We lost...to four players?
SCREEEEEEEECH
AMONG THE COUNTLESS URBAN LEGENDS ENDLESSLY REHASHED ON THE INTERNET, PERHAPS YOU'VE HEARD THE TALE OF A MYSTERY GAMER THAT GOES SOMETHING LIKE THIS...
A PLAYER OF UNCERTAIN IDENTITY...
WITHOUT A SINGLE LOSS TO HIS NAME...
LIFE :
WHO DOMINATES THE GAMING WORLD...
LEAVING BEHIND UNHEARD-OF, UNTOUCHABLE HIGH SCORES.
SINCE HIS ACCOUNT NAME IS ALWAYS BLANK...
HE HAS COME TO BE KNOWN AS 『 』 (A.K.A. "BLANK").
SOME GAMERS EVEN GO SO FAR AS TO SAY HE'S UNBEATABLE.
GRIN

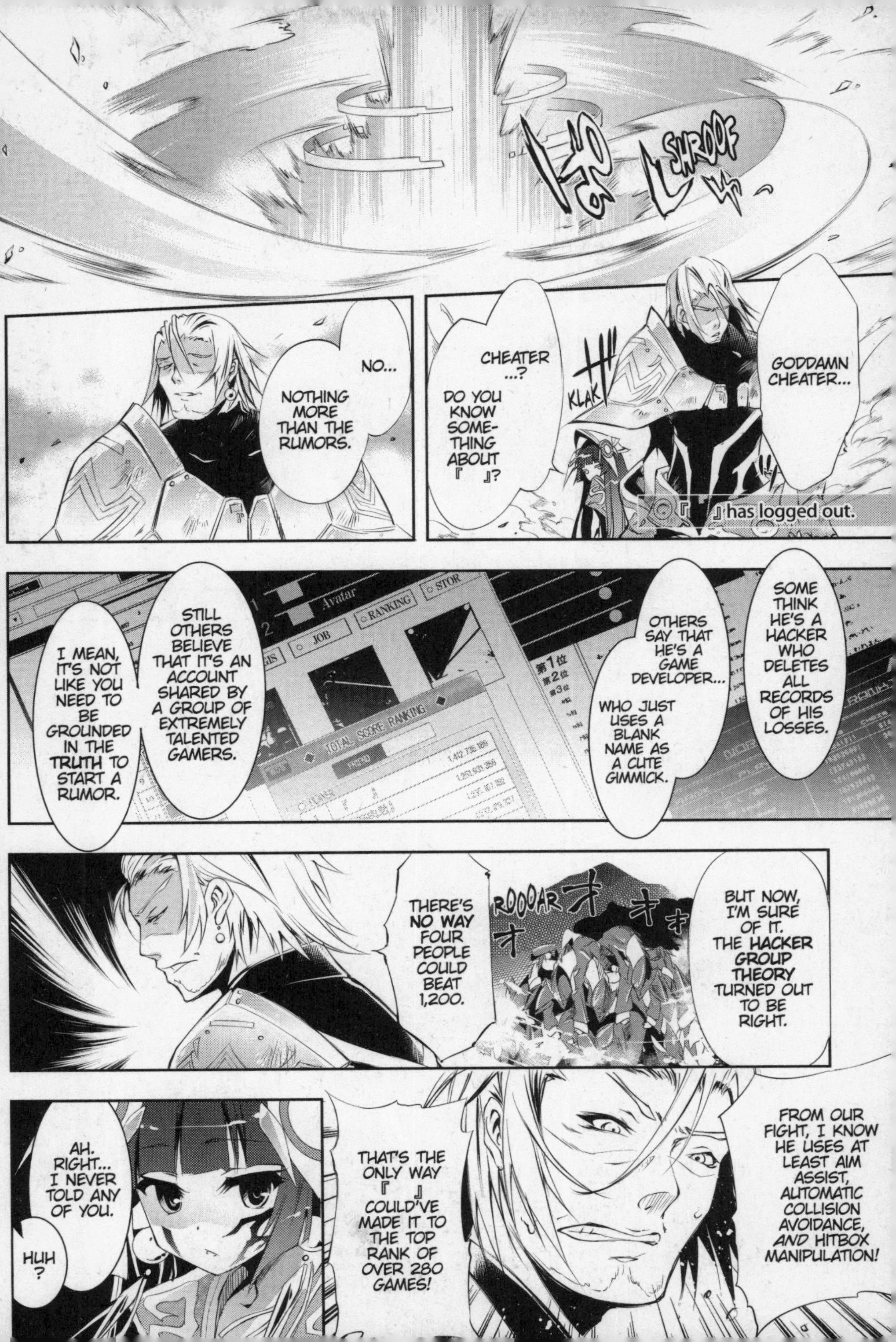

SHROOF
GODDAMN CHEATER...
KLAK
『 』has logged out.
CHEATER ...? DO YOU KNOW SOMETHING ABOUT『 』?
NO... NOTHING MORE THAN THE RUMORS.
SOME THINK HE'S A HACKER WHO DELETES ALL RECORDS OF HIS LOSSES.
OTHERS SAY THAT HE'S A GAME DEVELOPER... WHO JUST USES A BLANK NAME AS A CUTE GIMMICK.
Avatar
STOR
RANKING
JOB
TOTAL SCORE RANKING
FRIEND
STILL OTHERS BELIEVE THAT IT'S AN ACCOUNT SHARED BY A GROUP OF EXTREMELY TALENTED GAMERS.
I MEAN, IT'S NOT LIKE YOU NEED TO BE GROUNDED IN THE TRUTH TO START A RUMOR.
BUT NOW, I'M SURE OF IT. THE HACKER GROUP THEORY TURNED OUT TO BE RIGHT.
ROOOAR
THERE'S NO WAY FOUR PEOPLE COULD BEAT 1,200.
FROM OUR FIGHT, I KNOW HE USES AT LEAST AIM ASSIST, AUTOMATIC COLLISION AVOIDANCE, AND HITBOX MANIPULATION!
THAT'S THE ONLY WAY『 』COULD'VE MADE IT TO THE TOP RANK OF OVER 280 GAMES!
AH. RIGHT... I NEVER TOLD ANY OF YOU.
HUH?

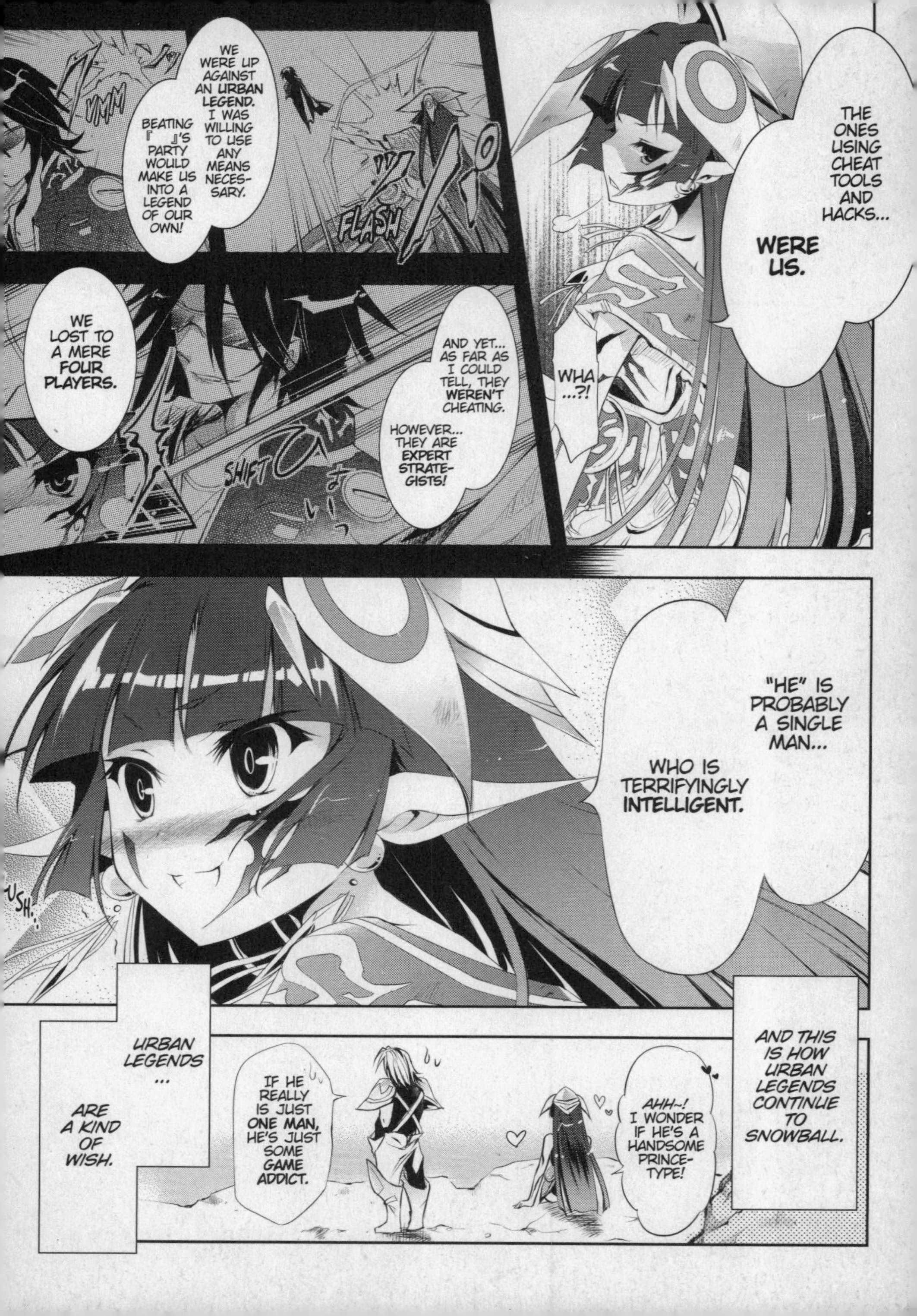
THE ONES USING CHEAT TOOLS AND HACKS...
WERE US.
WHA ...?!
WE WERE UP AGAINST AN URBAN LEGEND. I WAS WILLING TO USE ANY MEANS NECES-SARY.
BEATING 『 』'S PARTY WOULD MAKE US INTO A LEGEND OF OUR OWN!
VMM
FLASH
AND YET... AS FAR AS I COULD TELL, THEY WEREN'T CHEATING.
HOWEVER... THEY ARE EXPERT STRATE-GISTS!
WE LOST TO A MERE FOUR PLAYERS.
SHIFT
"HE" IS PROBABLY A SINGLE MAN...
WHO IS TERRIFYINGLY INTELLIGENT.
AND THIS IS HOW URBAN LEGENDS CONTINUE TO SNOWBALL.
AHH~! I WONDER IF HE'S A HANDSOME PRINCE-TYPE!
IF HE REALLY IS JUST ONE MAN, HE'S JUST SOME GAME ADDICT.
URBAN LEGENDS ...
ARE A KIND OF WISH.

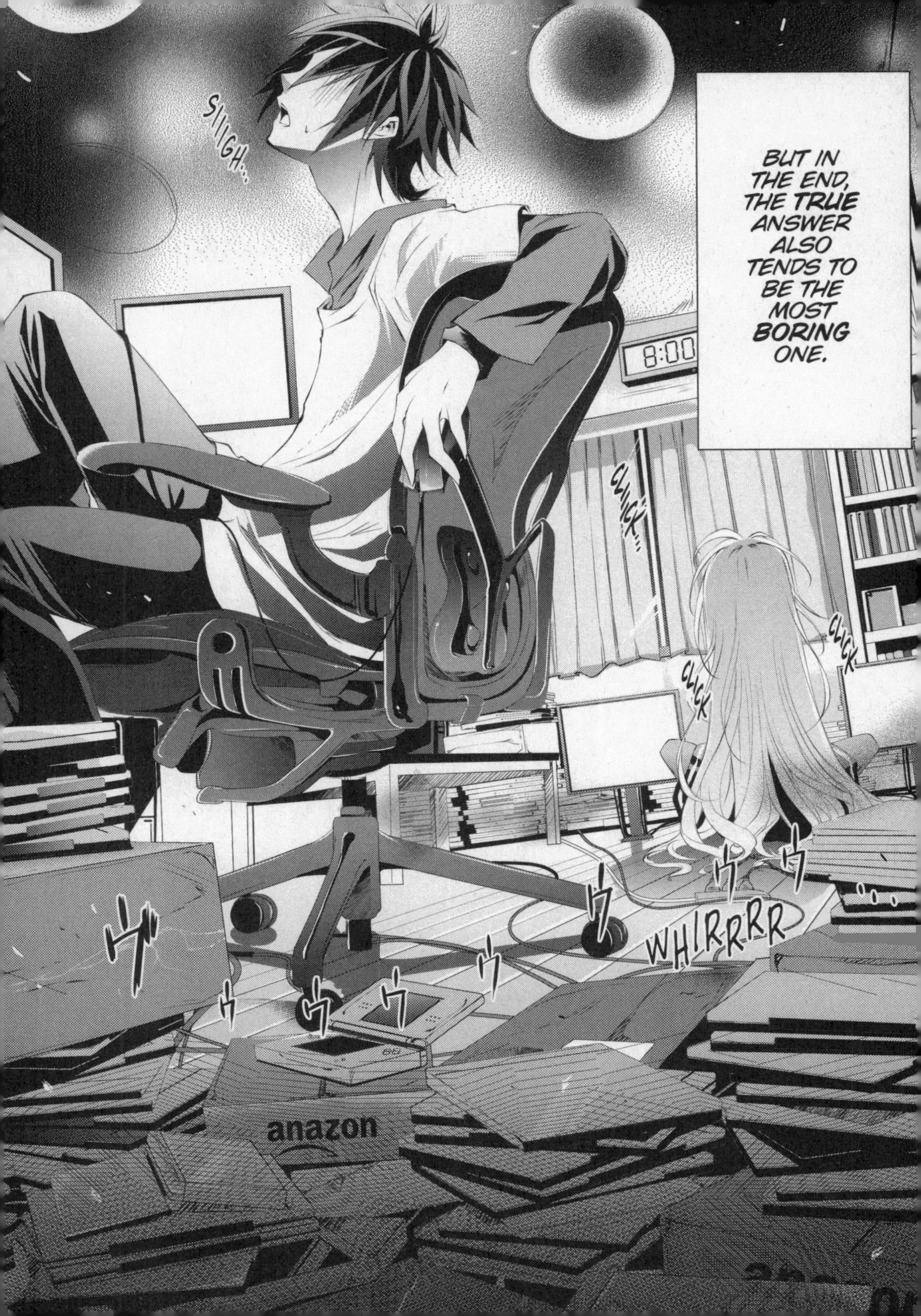
BUT IN THE END, THE TRUE ANSWER ALSO TENDS TO BE THE MOST BORING ONE.
SIIIGH...
CLICK...
CLICK
CLICK
8:00
WHIRRRR
anazon

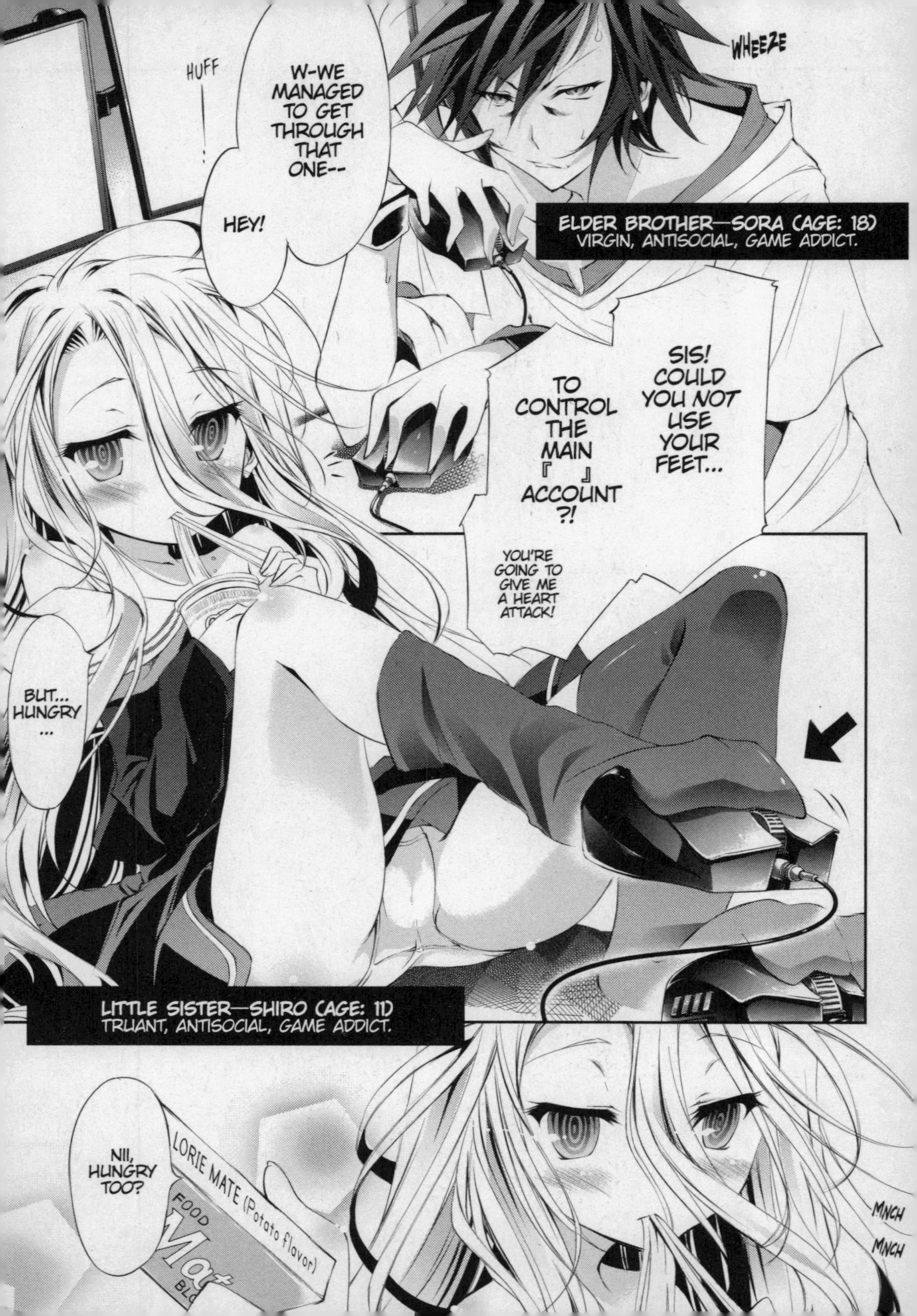
WHEEZE
HUFF
W-WE MANAGED TO GET THROUGH THAT ONE--
HEY!
ELDER BROTHER—SORA (AGE: 18)
VIRGIN, ANTISOCIAL, GAME ADDICT.
SIS! COULD YOU NOT USE YOUR FEET...
TO CONTROL THE MAIN 『 』 ACCOUNT ?!
YOU'RE GOING TO GIVE ME A HEART ATTACK!
BUT... HUNGRY ...
LITTLE SISTER—SHIRO (AGE: 11)
TRUANT, ANTISOCIAL, GAME ADDICT.
MNCH
MNCH
NII, HUNGRY TOO?
LORIE MATE (Potato flavor)

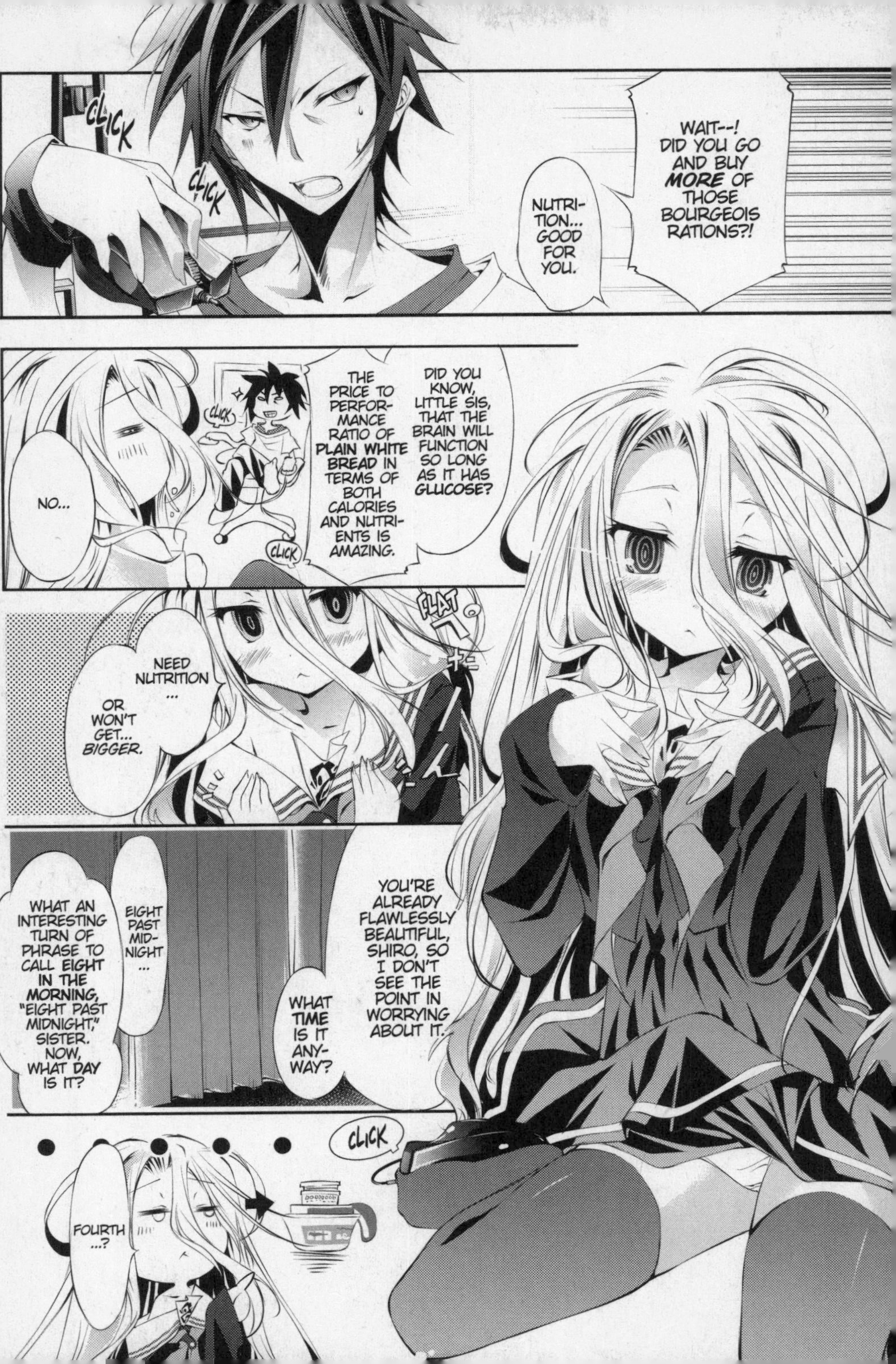
CLICK
CLICK
WAIT--! DID YOU GO AND BUY MORE OF THOSE BOURGEOIS RATIONS?!
NUTRITION... GOOD FOR YOU.
CLICK
DID YOU KNOW, LITTLE SIS, THAT THE BRAIN WILL FUNCTION SO LONG AS IT HAS GLUCOSE?
THE PRICE TO PERFORMANCE RATIO OF PLAIN WHITE BREAD IN TERMS OF BOTH CALORIES AND NUTRIENTS IS AMAZING.
CLICK
CLICK
NO...
FLAT
NEED NUTRITION ... OR WON'T GET... BIGGER.
YOU'RE ALREADY FLAWLESSLY BEAUTIFUL, SHIRO, SO I DON'T SEE THE POINT IN WORRYING ABOUT IT.
WHAT TIME IS IT ANYWAY?
EIGHT PAST MIDNIGHT ...
WHAT AN INTERESTING TURN OF PHRASE TO CALL EIGHT IN THE MORNING, "EIGHT PAST MIDNIGHT," SISTER. NOW, WHAT DAY IS IT?
FOURTH ...?

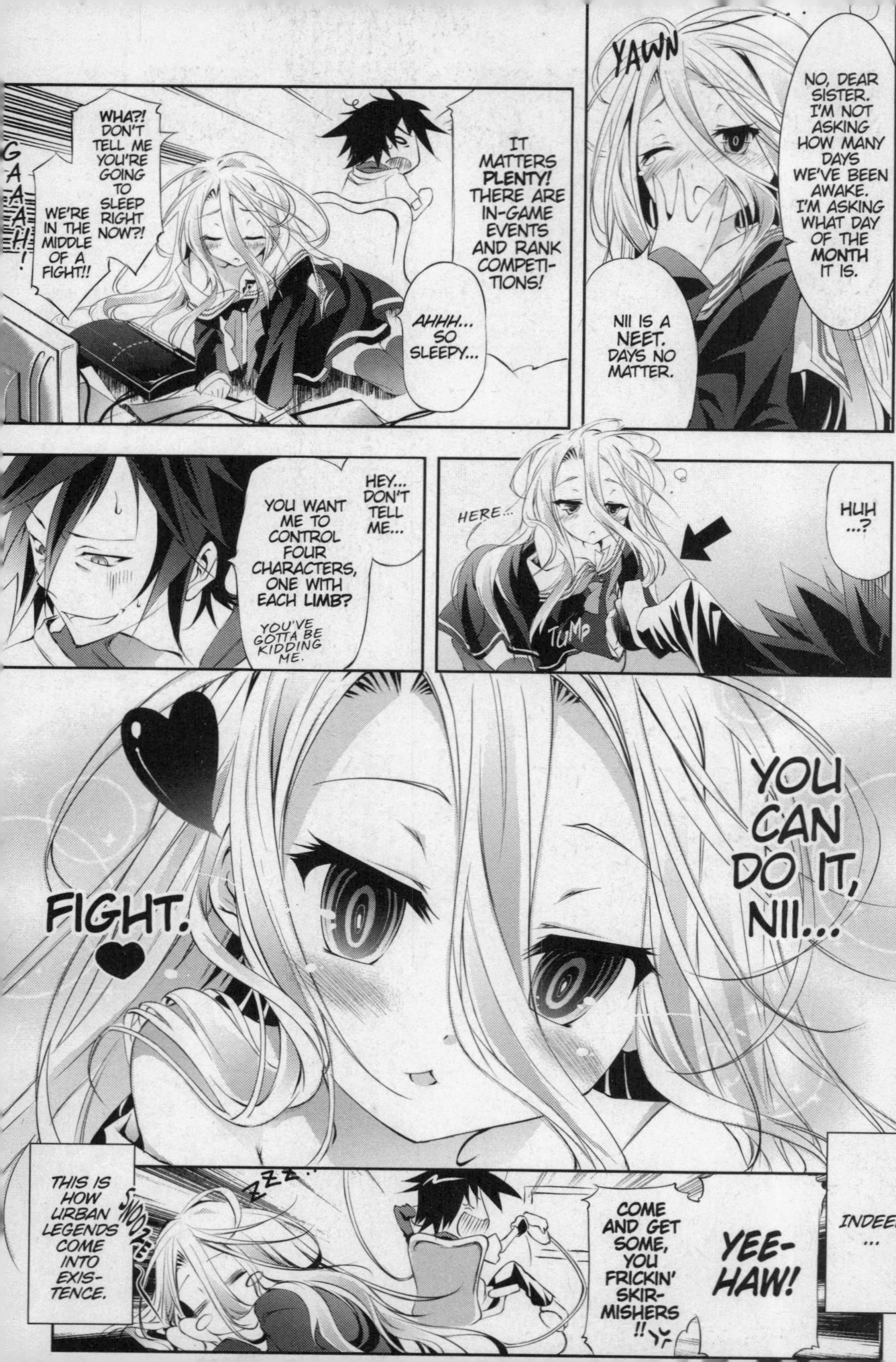
...
YAWN
NO, DEAR SISTER. I'M NOT ASKING HOW MANY DAYS WE'VE BEEN AWAKE. I'M ASKING WHAT DAY OF THE MONTH IT IS.
NII IS A NEET. DAYS NO MATTER.
IT MATTERS PLENTY! THERE ARE IN-GAME EVENTS AND RANK COMPETITIONS!
AHHH... SO SLEEPY...
WHA?! DON'T TELL ME YOU'RE GOING TO SLEEP RIGHT NOW?!
WE'RE IN THE MIDDLE OF A FIGHT!!
GAAAH!
HUH ...?
HERE...
TUMP
HEY... DON'T TELL ME...
YOU WANT ME TO CONTROL FOUR CHARACTERS, ONE WITH EACH LIMB?
YOU'VE GOTTA BE KIDDING ME.
YOU CAN DO IT, NII...
FIGHT. ♥
INDEED ...
YEE-HAW!
COME AND GET SOME, YOU FRICKIN' SKIRMISHERS!!
ZZZ...
SNOOZE
THIS IS HOW URBAN LEGENDS COME INTO EXISTENCE.

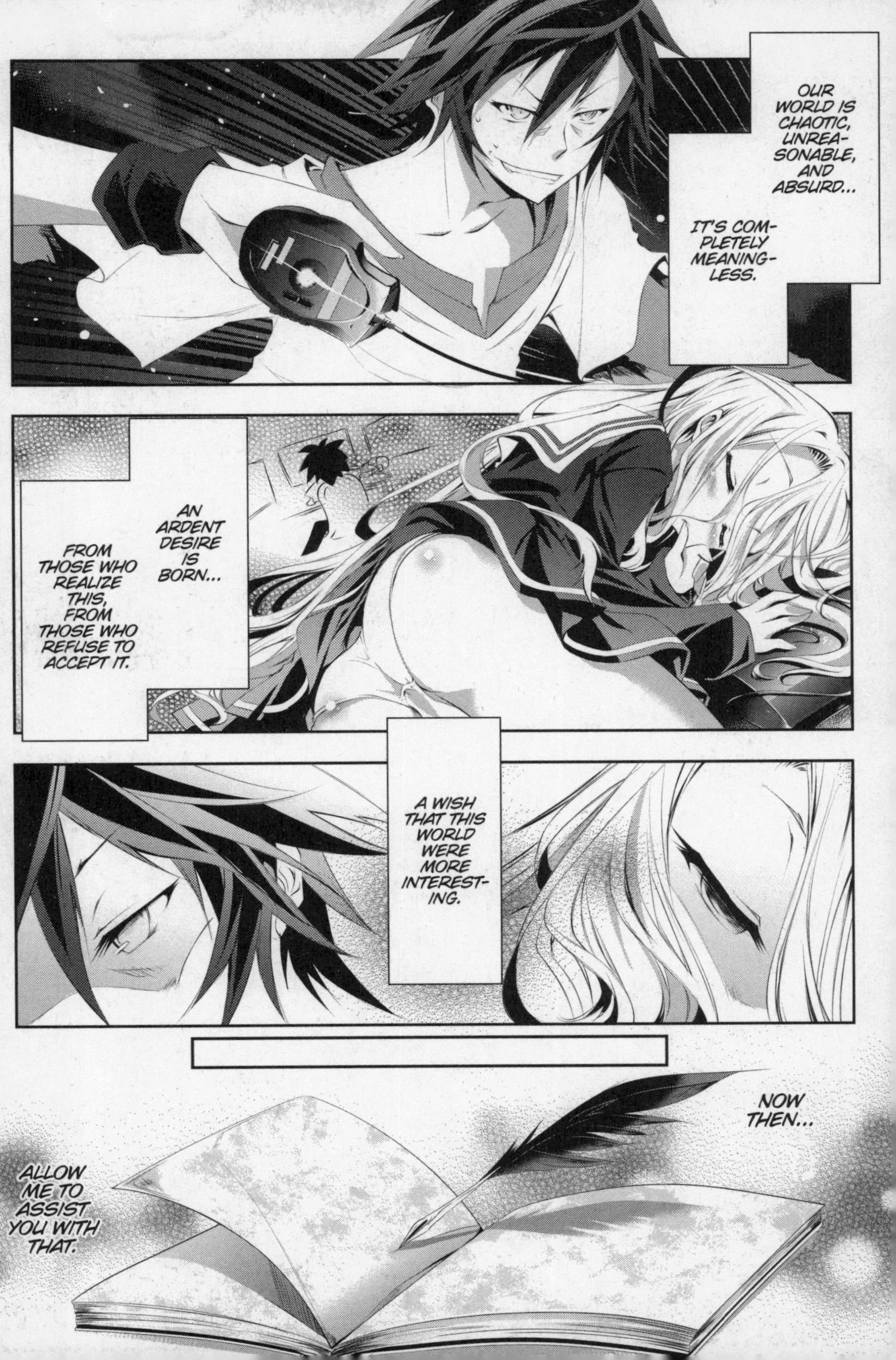
OUR WORLD IS CHAOTIC, UNREA-SONABLE, AND ABSURD...
IT'S COM-PLETELY MEANING-LESS.
AN ARDENT DESIRE IS BORN...
FROM THOSE WHO REALIZE THIS, FROM THOSE WHO REFUSE TO ACCEPT IT.
A WISH THAT THIS WORLD WERE MORE INTEREST-ING.
NOW THEN...
ALLOW ME TO ASSIST YOU WITH THAT.

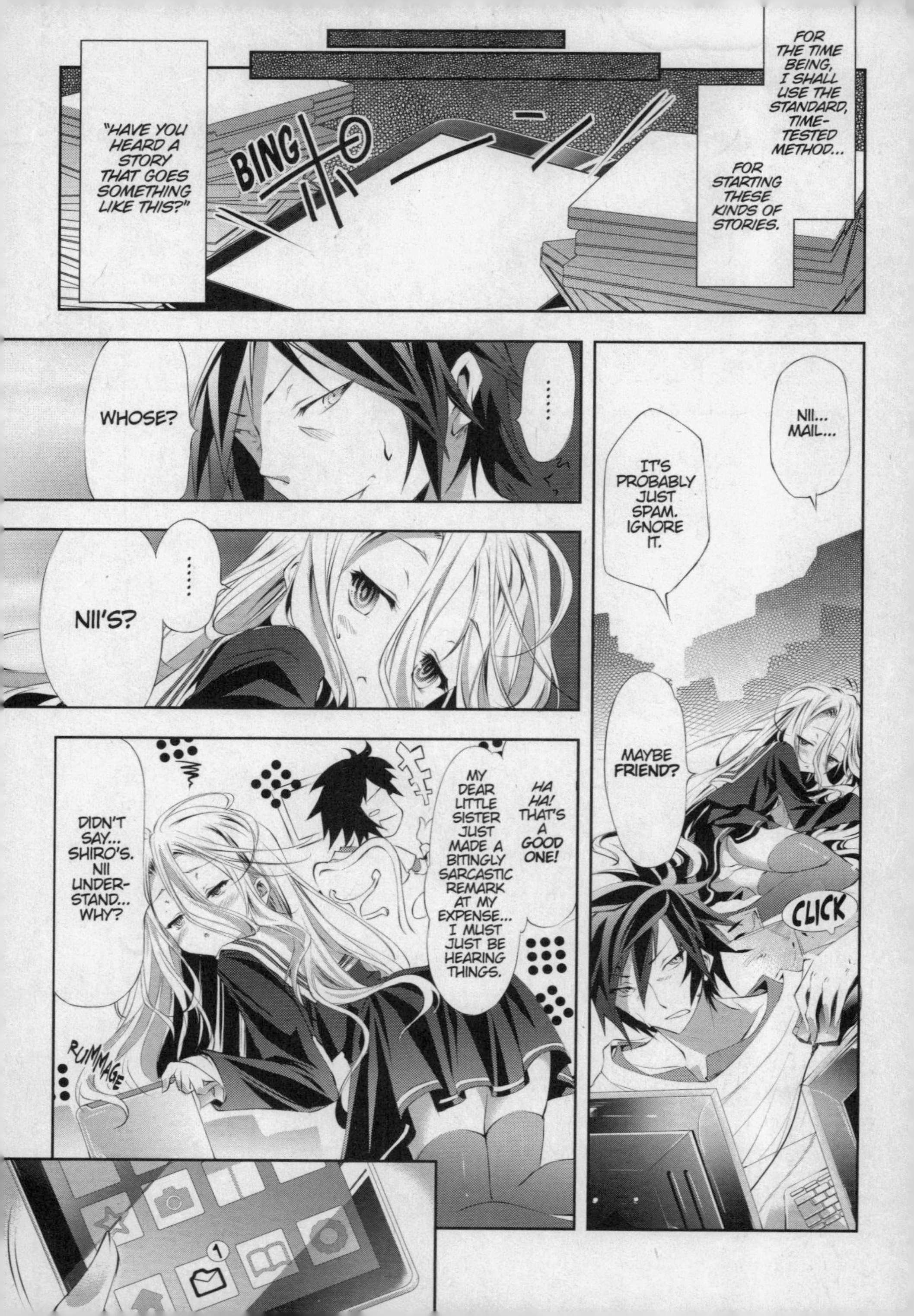
FOR THE TIME BEING, I SHALL USE THE STANDARD, TIME-TESTED METHOD...
FOR STARTING THESE KINDS OF STORIES.
BING
"HAVE YOU HEARD A STORY THAT GOES SOMETHING LIKE THIS?"
NII... MAIL...
IT'S PROBABLY JUST SPAM. IGNORE IT.
MAYBE FRIEND?
CLICK
......
WHOSE?
......
NII'S?
HA HA! THAT'S A GOOD ONE!
MY DEAR LITTLE SISTER JUST MADE A BITINGLY SARCASTIC REMARK AT MY EXPENSE... I MUST JUST BE HEARING THINGS.
DIDN'T SAY... SHIRO'S. NII UNDER-STAND... WHY?
RUMMAGE
1

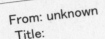

CLICK CLICK

HM?
SURE.

NII... E-MAIL.

LOOK ON PC.

From: unknown
Title:

Have you two siblings ever felt like you were born into the wrong world?
http://www.unknowntheworld/nextpage/20×

WHAT THE...?

AND...

HOW DID HE KNOW THAT 『 』 IS TWO SIBLINGS?

Have you two siblings to the wrong wo

WE'VE RECEIVED CHALLENGES, INTERVIEW REQUESTS, THREATS, AND LIBEL ON MANY OCCASIONS...

BUT THIS IS A FIRST.

THERE'S NO WAY SOMEONE COULD KNOW...

WHO WE ARE...

Continued in *NO GAME NO LIFE Vol. 1!*

# COMING SOON

### DECEMBER 2014
Alice in the Country of Joker:
The Nightmare Trilogy Vol. 2

### JANUARY 2015
Alice in the Country of Clover:
The Lizard Aide

### FEBRUARY 2015
Alice in the Country of Joker:
Circus and Liar's Game Vol. 7

### MARCH 2015
Alice in the Country of Joker:
The Nightmare Trilogy Vol. 3